Heliocentric Astrology

or
Essentials of Astronomy and Solar Mentality with Tables of Ephemeris to 1913

By

Holmes Whittier Merton

writing as

Yarmo Vedra

Copyright © 2013 Read Books Ltd.
This book is copyright and may not be
reproduced or copied in any way without
the express permission of the publisher in writing

British Library Cataloguing-in-Publication Data
A catalogue record for this book is available from the
British Library

A Brief History of Astronomy

Astronomy is the oldest of the natural sciences, dating back to antiquity, with its origins in the religious, mythological and astrological practices of pre-history. Early cultures identified celestial objects with gods and spirits – and related these objects (and their movements) to worldly phenomena. Rains, droughts, seasons and tides were all explained via the heavenly realm. It is generally believed that the first 'professional' astronomers were priests and that their understanding of the skies was seen as 'divine', hence astronomy's ancient connection to what is now called 'astrology'. This area of knowledge, a complex mix of belief and science, has been developed all over the world – from cultures and countries as diverse as China, India, the ancient Egyptians, Mesopotamia, Mesoamerica, the medieval Islamic and the western world. It is, of course, still evolving today.

In the last couple of decades, our understanding of prehistoric European astronomy in particular has radically changed. This occurred with the discoveries of ancient astronomical artefacts such as the world's oldest observatory, the 'Goseck circle.' Located in Germany, the site proves that Bronze Age Central Europeans had a much more sophisticated grasp of mathematics and astronomy than was previously assumed. According to Berlin archaeologist Klaus Goldmann, 'European civilization goes further back than most of us ever believed.' The enclosure is one of hundreds of similar wooden circular Henges built throughout Austria, Germany, and the Czech Republic during a 200-year period around 4,900 BC. While the sites vary in size (the one at Goseck is around 220 feet in diameter) they all have the same features: A narrow ditch surrounding a circular wooden wall, with a few large gates equally spaced around the outer edge. These gaps were used to observe the sun in the course of the calendar year and at the winter solstice, observers at the centre would have seen the sun rise and set through the south east and southwest gates.

The Ancient Greeks further developed astronomy, which they treated as a branch of mathematics, to a highly sophisticated level. The first geometrical, three-dimensional models to explain the apparent motion of the planets were developed in the fourth century BC by Eudoxus of Cnidus and Callippus of Cyzicus. Their models were based on nested homocentric spheres centred upon the Earth. A different approach to celestial phenomena was taken by natural philosophers such as Plato and Aristotle. They were less concerned with developing mathematical predictive models than with developing an explanation of the *reasons* for the motions of the Cosmos. In his *Timaeus* Plato described the universe as a spherical body divided into circles carrying the planets and governed according to harmonic intervals by a world soul. Aristotle, drawing on the mathematical model of Eudoxus, proposed that the universe was made of a complex system of concentric spheres, whose circular motions combined to carry the planets around the earth. This basic cosmological model prevailed, in various forms, until the sixteenth century AD.

Depending on the historian's viewpoint, the acme or corruption of physical Greek astronomy is seen with Ptolemy of Alexandria, who wrote the classic comprehensive presentation of geocentric astronomy, the *Megale Syntaxis* (Great Synthesis). Better known by its Arabic title *Almagest*, it had a lasting effect on astronomy up to the Renaissance. In this work, Ptolemy ventured into the realm of cosmology, developing a physical model of his geometric system, in a universe many times smaller than earlier (more realistic) conceptions It was not until the scholarly endeavours of Nicolaus Copernicus that astronomy developed much beyond this point. Copernicus was the first astronomer to propose a heliocentric system, in which the planets moved around the sun *not* the earth. His *De revolutionibus* provided a full mathematical discussion of his system, using the geometrical techniques that had been traditional in astronomy since before the time of Ptolemy. Copernicus's work was later defended, expanded upon and modified by Galileo Galilei and Johannes Kepler.

Galileo is considered the father of observational astronomy. He was among the first to use a telescope to observe the sky, and after constructing a 20x refractor telescope he discovered the four largest moons of Jupiter in 1610. This was the first observation of satellites orbiting another planet. He also found that our Moon had craters and observed (and correctly explained) sunspots. Galileo argued that these observations supported the Copernican system and were, to some extent, incompatible with the model of the Earth at the centre of the universe. Kepler built on this work, and was one of the first scholars to unite physics and astronomy. Kepler was the first to attempt to derive mathematical predictions of celestial motions from assumed physical causes. Combining his physical insights with the unprecedentedly accurate naked-eye observations made by Tycho Brahe, Kepler discovered the three laws of planetary motion that now carry his name.

Isaac Newton further developed these ties, through his law of 'universal gravitation.' Realising that the same force that attracted objects to the surface of the Earth held the moon in orbit around the Earth, Newton was able to explain – in one theoretical framework – all known gravitational phenomena. In his *Philosophiae Naturalis Principia Mathematica*, he derived Kepler's laws from first principles. Much of modern physics (and indeed modern astronomy, as the two are now very closely linked) builds on these very discoveries. Outside of England however, Newton's theory took a long time to become established; Descartes' theory of vortices held sway in France, and Huygens, Leibnitz and Cassini accepted only parts of Newton's system, preferring their own philosophies. It wasn't until Voltaire published a popular account in 1738 that the tide changed. In America, it was not until the mid-seventeenth century that astronomical thought began to move away from the much respected Aristotelian philosophy.

Today, astronomy is a vast and incredibly complex field of research, studied by scientists all over the globe. Although in previous centuries noted astronomers were exclusively male, at the turn of the twentieth century women began to play a role in the great discoveries. It was during this most recent century that most of our current knowledge was gained. With the help of the use of photography, fainter objects were observed. Our sun was found to be part of a galaxy made up of more than 10^{10} stars (ten billion stars). The existence of other galaxies, one of the matters of *the great debate*, was settled by Edwin Hubble, who identified the Andromeda nebula as a different galaxy, and many others at large distances and receding, moving away from our galaxy. Physical cosmology, a discipline that has a large intersection with astronomy, also made huge advances during the twentieth century; the *hot big bang* model was heavily supported by evidence such as the redshifts of very distant galaxies and radio sources, the cosmic microwave background radiation, Hubble's law and cosmological abundances of elements.

As is evident from this incredibly short introduction to astronomy, it is a branch of knowledge that has changed massively from its early beginnings. Having said this, the study of the stars, skies and heavenly realms has continued to be an enduring source of human fascination. The work of scholars such as Newton, Kepler, Galileo, Ptolemy and Aristotle has had a massive impact on the way we understand the world around us. This collection celebrates the work of these early astronomers. There is still so much to discover, so many assumptions to be questioned - and the scientists of today are heavily indebted to the pioneers of the past, who did just this. We hope the current reader enjoys this book.

PREFACE.

Heliocentric Astrology is a new system of personally determining the primary fund of Mental and Physical forces and their results in mental aptitudes that dominate the nature of the individual as based upon

THE DATE OF BIRTH.

This system is a key to the intellectual, social and industrial course of personal destiny ; to the harmonies of thought, marriage and home life.

It also contains the Harmonies, Chords and Contrasts of the Vital forces of the Solar System, the essentials of Astronomy, and those elements of Mythology that relate to the Astrological Arts.

A DIURNAL EPHEMERIS OF THE MOON AND PLANETS FROM THE YEAR 1830 TO 1913.

TABLE OF CONTENTS.

	PAGE
ARGUMENT AND INTENTION, ...	9
Argument and Intention of Heliocentric Astrology, . . .	9
Earlier Geocentric System, ...	11
METHOD OF MAKING DELINEATIONS, ...	14
ASTRONOMY, ...	18
Astronomy; Basis of Astrology, ...	18
Celestial Sphere, ...	19
Latitude; Mundane and Celestial, ...	20
Longitude and Right Ascension, ...	20
Northern Celestial Hemisphere. Ecliptic, ...	22
Inclination of the Poles and Plane of Ecliptic, ...	23
The Constellations from 45° N. to 45° South, . . , . .	24
Path of the Planets through the Zodiac, ...	25
ASTROLOGICAL LAWS, ...	28
Law of the Ellipse, ...	29
Intuition of the Ancients, ...	32
THREE GRAND DIVISIONS, ...	34
THE TWELVE GREAT FUNCTIONS, ...	37

	PAGE		PAGE		PAGE
Aries, . . .	38	Leo, . . .	39	Sagittarius, . .	39
Taurus, . .	38	Virgo, . .	39	Capricorn, . .	40
Gemini, . .	38	Libra, . .	39	Aquarius, . .	40
Cancer, . .	38	Scorpio, . .	39	Pisces, . .	40

	PAGE
LAWS AND EQUATIONS OF POWER, ...	42

	PAGE		PAGE		PAGE
Chords, . .	42	Discords, . .	42	Conservation, .	43
Responses, . .	42	Heredity, . .	43	Mobility, . .	43
Solar Poles, . .	42	Ascent, . .	43	Marriage, . .	43
Mental Chords, .	42	Restraint, . .	43	Formality, . .	43

	PAGE
CHORDS, RESPONSES AND COLORS, ...	44

TABLE OF CONTENTS.

	PAGE		PAGE		PAGE
Pisces,	44	Cancer,	46	Scorpio,	47
Aries,	45	Leo,	46	Sagittarius,	48
Taurus,	45	Virgo,	47	Capricorn,	48
Gemini,	46	Libra,	47	Aquarius,	49

THE TWELVE SIGNS OF THE ZODIAC, ... 50
   (Including the influence of the Moon in all twelve signs.)

ARIES (♈), ... 51

	PAGE		PAGE		PAGE
♈, ☽ in ♈,	52	♈, ☽ in ♌,	53	♈, ☽ in ♐,	55
♈, ☽ in ♉,	53	♈, ☽ in ♍,	54	♈, ☽ in ♑,	56
♈, ☽ in ♊,	53	♈, ☽ in ♎,	54	♈, ☽ in ♒,	56
♈, ☽ in ♋,	53	♈, ☽ in ♏,	55	♈, ☽ in ♓,	56

TAURUS (♉), ... 58

	PAGE		PAGE		PAGE
♉, ☽ in ♈,	59	♉, ☽ in ♌,	61	♉, ☽ in ♐,	62
♉, ☽ in ♉,	59	♉, ☽ in ♍,	61	♉, ☽ in ♑,	63
♉, ☽ in ♊,	60	♉, ☽ in ♎,	61	♉, ☽ in ♒,	63
♉, ☽ in ♋,	60	♉, ☽ in ♏,	62	♉, ☽ in ♓,	64

GEMINI (♊), ... 65

	PAGE		PAGE		PAGE
♊, ☽ in ♈,	66	♊, ☽ in ♌,	67	♊, ☽ in ♐,	69
♊, ☽ in ♉,	66	♊, ☽ in ♍,	68	♊, ☽ in ♑,	69
♊, ☽ in ♊,	66	♊, ☽ in ♎,	68	♊, ☽ in ♒,	70
♊, ☽ in ♋,	67	♊, ☽ in ♏,	69	♊, ☽ in ♓,	70

CANCER (♋), ... 71

	PAGE		PAGE		PAGE
♋, ☽ in ♈,	72	♋, ☽ in ♌,	73	♋, ☽ in ♐,	74
♋, ☽ in ♉,	72	♋, ☽ in ♍,	73	♋, ☽ in ♑,	75
♋, ☽ in ♊,	73	♋, ☽ in ♎,	74	♋, ☽ in ♒,	75
♋, ☽ in ♋,	73	♋, ☽ in ♏,	74	♋, ☽ in ♓,	75

LEO (♌), ... 77

	PAGE		PAGE		PAGE
♌, ☽ in ♈,	78	♌, ☽ in ♌,	79	♌, ☽ in ♐,	81
♌, ☽ in ♉,	78	♌, ☽ in ♍,	80	♌, ☽ in ♑,	81
♌, ☽ in ♊,	78	♌, ☽ in ♎,	80	♌, ☽ in ♒,	81
♌, ☽ in ♋,	79	♌, ☽ in ♏,	80	♌, ☽ in ♓,	82

VIRGO (♍), ... 83

TABLE OF CONTENTS.

	PAGE		PAGE		PAGE
♍, ☽ in ♈,	84	♍, ☽ in ♌,	85	♍, ☽ in ♐,	87
♍, ☽ in ♉,	84	♍, ☽ in ♍,	85	♍, ☽ in ♑,	87
♍, ☽ in ♊,	84	♍, ☽ in ♎,	86	♍, ☽ in ♒,	88
♍, ☽ in ♋,	85	♍, ☽ in ♏,	86	♍, ☽ in ♓,	88

LIBRA (♎), ... 89

	PAGE		PAGE		PAGE
♎, ☽ in ♈,	90	♎, ☽ in ♌,	91	♎, ☽ in ♐,	93
♎, ☽ in ♉,	90	♎, ☽ in ♍,	92	♎, ☽ in ♑,	93
♎, ☽ in ♊,	91	♎, ☽ in ♎,	92	♎, ☽ in ♒,	94
♎, ☽ in ♋,	91	♎, ☽ in ♏,	93	♎, ☽ in ♓,	94

SCORPIO (♏), ... 95

	PAGE		PAGE		PAGE
♏, ☽ in ♈,	96	♏, ☽ in ♌,	98	♏, ☽ in ♐,	99
♏, ☽ in ♉,	97	♏, ☽ in ♍,	98	♏, ☽ in ♑,	99
♏, ☽ in ♊,	97	♏, ☽ in ♎,	98	♏, ☽ in ♒,	100
♏, ☽ in ♋,	97	♏, ☽ in ♏,	99	♏, ☽ in ♓,	100

SAGITTARIUS (♐), ... 101

	PAGE		PAGE		PAGE
♐, ☽ in ♈,	102	♐, ☽ in ♌,	104	♐, ☽ in ♐,	105
♐, ☽ in ♉,	102	♐, ☽ in ♍,	104	♐, ☽ in ♑,	105
♐, ☽ in ♊,	103	♐, ☽ in ♎,	104	♐, ☽ in ♒,	106
♐, ☽ in ♋,	103	♐, ☽ in ♏,	104	♐, ☽ in ♓,	106

CAPRICORN (♑), ... 107

	PAGE		PAGE		PAGE
♑, ☽ in ♈,	108	♑, ☽ in ♌,	109	♑, ☽ in ♐,	111
♑, ☽ in ♉,	108	♑, ☽ in ♍,	110	♑, ☽ in ♑,	111
♑, ☽ in ♊,	109	♑, ☽ in ♎,	110	♑, ☽ in ♒,	111
♑, ☽ in ♋,	109	♑, ☽ in ♏,	110	♑, ☽ in ♓,	112

AQUARIUS (♒), ... 113

	PAGE		PAGE		PAGE
♒, ☽ in ♈,	114	♒, ☽ in ♌,	115	♒, ☽ in ♐,	116
♒, ☽ in ♉,	114	♒, ☽ in ♍,	115	♒, ☽ in ♑,	117
♒, ☽ in ♊,	115	♒, ☽ in ♎,	116	♒, ☽ in ♒,	117
♒, ☽ in ♋,	115	♒, ☽ in ♏,	116	♒, ☽ in ♓,	118

PISCES (♓), ... 119

	PAGE		PAGE		PAGE
♓, ☽ in ♈,	120	♓, ☽ in ♌,	121	♓, ☽ in ♐,	122
♓, ☽ in ♉,	120	♓, ☽ in ♍,	121	♓, ☽ in ♑,	123
♓, ☽ in ♊,	120	♓, ☽ in ♎,	122	♓, ☽ in ♒,	123
♓, ☽ in ♋,	121	♓, ☽ in ♏,	122	♓, ☽ in ♓,	123

TABLE OF CONTENTS.

Helios, or Sol, ... 127
The Moon, of Pisces Region, ... 128
Selene, . . page 128 | Artemus, . page 128 | Diana, . . page 128
The Asteroids, of Scorpio's Region, ... 130
Pluto or Aïdes, . p. 130 | Ceres, . . page 130 | Realm of Pluton, p. 131
Neptune, of Aries Region, ... 131

	PAGE		PAGE		PAGE
♆ in ♈,	132	♆ in ♌,	135	♆ in ♐,	137
♆ in ♉,	132	♆ in ♍,	136	♆ in ♑,	138
♆ in ♊,	135	♆ in ♎,	136	♆ in ♒,	138
♆ in ♋,	135	♆ in ♏,	137	♆ in ♓,	138

Uranus, of Virgo Region, ... 139

	PAGE		PAGE		PAGE
♅ in ♈,	139	♅ in ♌,	140	♅ in ♐,	142
♅ in ♉,	139	♅ in ♍,	141	♅ in ♑,	142
♅ in ♊,	140	♅ in ♎,	141	♅ in ♒,	143
♅ in ♋,	140	♅ in ♏,	142	♅ in ♓,	143

Saturn, of Capricorn Region, ... 144

	PAGE		PAGE		PAGE
♄ in ♈,	145	♄ in ♌,	147	♄ in ♐,	149
♄ in ♉,	146	♄ in ♍,	148	♄ in ♑,	149
♄ in ♊,	146	♄ in ♎,	148	♄ in ♒,	150
♄ in ♋,	147	♄ in ♏,	148	♄ in ♓,	150

Jupiter, of Libra Region, ... 151

	PAGE		PAGE		PAGE
♃ in ♈,	153	♃ in ♌,	155	♃ in ♐,	157
♃ in ♉,	154	♃ in ♍,	155	♃ in ♑,	157
♃ in ♊,	154	♃ in ♎,	156	♃ in ♒,	158
♃ in ♋,	154	♃ in ♏,	156	♃ in ♓,	158

Mars, of Sagittarius Region, ... 159

	PAGE		PAGE		PAGE
♂ in ♈,	159	♂ in ♌,	162	♂ in ♐,	164
♂ in ♉,	160	♂ in ♍,	162	♂ in ♑,	164
♂ in ♊,	161	♂ in ♎,	163	♂ in ♒,	164
♂ in ♋,	161	♂ in ♏,	163	♂ in ♓,	165

TABLE OF CONTENTS.

VENUS, OF CANCER, ... 166

	PAGE		PAGE		PAGE
♀ in ♈,	166	♀ in ♌,	168	♀ in ♐,	170
♀ in ♉,	167	♀ in ♍,	169	♀ in ♑,	170
♀ in ♊,	167	♀ in ♎,	169	♀ in ♒,	171
♀ in ♋,	168	♀ in ♏,	169	♀ in ♓,	171

MERCURY, OF GEMINI, ... 171

	PAGE		PAGE		PAGE
☿ in ♈,	173	☿ in ♌,	175	☿ in ♐,	176
☿ in ♉,	174	☿ in ♍,	175	☿ in ♑,	177
☿ in ♊,	174	☿ in ♎,	175	☿ in ♒,	177
☿ in ♋,	174	☿ in ♏,	176	☿ in ♓,	177

APPENDIX, ... 179

EPHEMERIS, ... 181

ILLUSTRATIONS.

Frontispiece.

FIG.		PAGE
2.	Early Geocentric Astrology,	11
3.	Ephemeris Table of Signs and Moon,	14
4.	Ephemeris Table of Planets,	16
6.	Celestial Sphere,	19
7–8.	Latitude,	20
9–10.	Longitude,	21
11.	Northern Celestial Hemisphere,	22
12.	Inclination of the Pole toward Capricorn,	23
13.	Inclination of the Pole toward Cancer,	23
14.	Plane of the Zodiac,	24
15.	Constellations, 45° N. to 45° S., the 18th to 5th H. R. A.,	25
16.	Constellations, 45° N. to 45° S., the 6th to 17th H. R. A.,	27
17.	Solar System,	28
18.	Law of Ellipse,	29
19.	Three Grand Divisions,	34
20.	Three Grand Divisions (continued),	35
21.	Twelve Grand Functions,	35
22.	Products of the Twelve Functions,	37
23.	Chords, Responses and Colors,	44
24.	Aries; Astronomy and Symbolism,	57
25.	Taurus; Astronomy and Symbolism,	58
26.	Gemini; Astronomy and Symbolism,	65
27.	Cancer; Astronomy and Symbolism,	71
28.	Leo; Astronomy and Symbolism,	77
29.	Virgo; Astronomy and Symbolism,	83
30.	Libra; Astronomy and Symbolism,	89
31.	Scorpio; Astronomy and Symbolism,	95
32.	Sagittarius; Astronomy and Symbolism,	101
33.	Capricorn; Astronomy and Symbolism,	107
34.	Aquarius; Astronomy and Symbolism,	113
35.	Pisces; Astronomy and Symbolism,	119
36.	Apollo,	125
37.	Apollo and the Muses, G. Romano (**Florence**),	127
38.	Monday, Luna (Raphael),	128
39.	Artemis (Vatican, Rome),	129

FIG.		PAGE
40.	Ceres (Vatican, Rome),	130
41.	Neptune, of Aries Region,	133
42.	Saturday, Saturn (Raphael),	144
43.	Cronus,	145
44.	Thursday, Jupiter (Raphael),	151
45.	Jupiter Verospi (Vatican, Rome),	152
46.	Tuesday, Mars (Raphael),	159
47.	Ares, or Mars (Villa Ludovisi, Rome),	160
48.	Friday, Venus (Raphael),	166
49.	Venus (Capitol, Rome),	167
50.	Wednesday, Mercury (Raphael),	172
51.	Hermes, or Mercury,	173

ARGUMENT AND INTENTION.

It is not our purpose to here consider elaborately the substances which compose, and the laws that govern, the Universe.

Of those actions, which, succeeding each other in regular order, we designate as laws, a few must be mentioned in the astronomical part before we proceed to describe the regions of vital forces that seem to determine, in part, the quantity of characteristics of both mental and so-called physical life of those born when the Earth and other planets are in certain angles from the Sun; that is, in certain signs of the Zodiac.

Why the nature of a person is specifically influenced in one direction more than in another may seem strange. However, if one considers for a moment the grand contention of forces that are struggling for supremacy in the Solar region where he is born, and the fact that, even from a material standpoint, the volume, direction and effect of these forces are forever varying; surging; overcoming; and again equalizing each other, it should be easily realized that they may and do influence mentality, destiny and results. It would undoubtedly change a tentative art into a science, if the laws that underlie these effects could be discovered.

It does not disprove the system, nor place it subject to ridicule, because many of the laws at work are not yet known; else must many arts and sciences suffer the same criticism.

We know by experience that the effect of positions, in a measure the distance relations, and the distinctive forces from each body of the Solar system does influence the mental and physical nature of man; and, in fact, all life.

The intuitions of the ancients were as true in this art as in the equally unmeasured phases of ethics; morality; religion, and in some other branches of knowledge.

Their philosophies did not have the scientific and demonstrable basis given the race, since, in its centuries of experience, but the general truths and experienced parts of this art were well considered by them.

The older system of astrology (then the only astronomy) had as its foundation the supposition that the Earth was the center of the Cosmos, and that the mighty bodies of the fixed stars, no less than those of the system now known as the Solar system, moved around the Earth as though it were their stationary and governing center.

It is very evident that, under this conception, every phase of action, rule, and law, concerning the motions and effects of the whole, must of necessity be geocentric. Those imaginary lines of division and the streams of force (so-called power) radiating, as was *thought*, toward the shell, began their course at the center of the Earth, or perhaps at points of its surface, and reached outward toward the regions of the heavens. These regions in turn responded. From them there returned powers of various kinds, capable of determining the nature and destiny of every individual, in harmony with the nature of the bodies and places under which the person was born. Or perhaps some representative god bore the special command or executed the action.

The attitude and relation of the planets and the set configuration of the heavens—once the result of their relations could be determined—would then interpret the nature of every person, born at any place or time.

That the constellations could be hardly more than symbolic was beyond the range of the development of astrology. They made the dial-plate a part of the cause, rather than an aid to interpretation.

The apparent geocyclic paths of the moving planets, sun and other stars, as well as of our satellite, were taken to be their real paths, and the imaginary lines which marked for the astrologer the divisions of the asterisms were thought to be fixed and essential.

Certainly the stars which form the constellations (when seen without the telescope) seem to us, as they did to them, to vary but little in the course of either thirty or sixty centuries.

With the planets and the Sun it was different. As the central body of the whole the Earth was made an accredited claimant of place and power that did not belong to it. Its Sun, and Moon, and some of its stars, appeared to cut excentric paths through the heavens, declining toward the north or south according to the season or the observer's place upon the Earth.

That the Earth appeared flat did not aid the problem. It made it not only more complex, but impossible of solution.

Fig. 2.

Hence we see a vast system, constructed through centuries of observation and experience, yet filled with misconceptions at every vital point of its astronomy.

The effects of astrological positions were marked enough upon the nature of living objects to be noted and classified. As these results were known from an apparent cause, the results were in many ways none the less true than they would have been had the true cause been known.

In fact, human life seemed to be modified and influenced in harmony with the aspects of the Sun, Moon, and planets. And if certain known aspects, or, we may say, astronomical relations, *did* determine much of the nature of a person born under that relation, what difference did it make to the result whether or not the astronomical truth was known?

Astrology, in its early use, was for the few. The many could not understand or practice its forms.

"And did not the whole world exert its energies, create products, suffer and kill; and in varying scenes of grief, passion, intemperance, starvation or plenty, exist merely that the few might, by their power, reap the benefit and receive not alone human homage and human adoration, but the very willing obedience of the stars of heaven—those suns that burn in undying splendor, lamps of the night, yielders of destiny?"—[HOLMES W. MERTON, Lectures.]

From time to time the observed errors of planetary effects were corrected in, or eliminated from, the old astrology, new characters were added to the various positions and attitudes, and practitioners of the older system retained its phraseology, but readjusted its philosophy to conform to the advancing stages of astronomy.

The very advancement of astrology forced a division into two branches; the old vein of knowledge and experiment remained still a tentative Art; the new was formulated into the Science, Astronomy.

Even yet the calculations and delineations of Astrology are determined by the Geocentric aspects and apparent positions of the Sun, planets, and our Moon.

That the geocentric system should require a great many exceptions to what would otherwise be natural and hence invariable rules, is certain. That grave errors are and were probable, their avoidance impossible, seems evident. That no sufficiently scientific, or philosophic, or even intuitive system of laws has been given as an explanation of the cause of planetary influence upon human destiny does not seem strange. This, principally, because the fundamental law, at once the cause and the explanation, was not, so far as we have been able to learn, known in its relation to this subject. This fundamental law will be treated in the chapter on Astrological Law.

HELIOCENTRIC ASTROLOGY.

The greatest difficulty in understanding Astrology has been due to our having a true conception of the motions of the Solar system, through modern astronomy, while compelled to adjust the old formulas to it. There is also a disposition among astrologers to try to find a substantial and recognized cause for every trifling habit, ailment and incident that may befall the person whose nature is under consideration.

If the Art of Astrology were blended into the known laws of mental life, and given its equations of power and activity in due proportion to the magnitudes of the solutions desired, the art would be cleared of much of its obscurity and its less essential conflicts. That would leave to be mastered those greater contests of fate against law; destiny against will; and the relations of organic forces to those of inorganic elements.

From the standpoint of Astrology, casting the horoscope for either destiny, nativity or horary questions, the geocentric (earth centered) system is not, as is supposed, absolutely necessary; nor would the constant or momentary casting of the horoscope, based upon the heliocentric (Sun-centered; literally from the center of the Sun) system require a great amount of calculation largely independent of the work of astronomers.

However we may consider the matter, it is evident that the Sun, a mass 314,760 times, a volume 1,245,126 times, that of the Earth, and an inestimable preponderance of force and power, is certainly more dominant than all the rest of the Solar system, and, next to the Earth, more effective upon the nature of man, no less than upon the animal and vegetable kingdoms.

The mass of the eight planets is only 2317.4+ that of the Earth. Astrologers have paid too little attention to the relative volumes and powers of the members of the Solar system, and as we shall see later (Mentality of the Solar System), to its formal, static and dynamic regions and forces.

The system advanced in this book is essentially Heliocentric. We will briefly, consider those parts of Astronomy upon which our work is based, and the relations of the bodies of the Solar system and their forces to the nature of man as an individual and as a race.

FIG. 3.

METHOD OF MAKING DELINEATIONS.

TAKE the date of the month and year, as, April 5, 1860. In the circle marked A, of Fig. 3, is seen the symbols of the twelve signs, and the days of the month on which the Sun (☉) enters and leaves each sign. The Sun enters Aries on March 21st and leaves Aries at the end of April 19th. April 5th is, therefore, in Aries (♈).

Following out this angle in the next circle, marked B, is the page number (38) on which is found the description of the Grand Division under which Aries natures are born.

In the same angle, and next circle, marked C, is the page number (45) on which begins the description of the chord, color and Responses of the Aries sign.

In the last circle, marked D, is the page number (51) of the description of the Primary or sign nature.

Following this are the twelve signs of the lunar ephemeris, in one of which the moon was on the day given. Opposite each sign in this circle space is the page number on which can be found the description of the lunar influence upon the Aries natures.

In order to know in which sign the moon was on the date given, April 5, 1860, it will be necessary to turn to that year's ephemeris in the back of the book. The lower part of the page is the moon's ephemeris for that year; April, the fourth month, is in the fourth column; running down that column until opposite the 5th day of the month, the sign ♎ (Libra) is found.

Returning to the space above noted in Fig. 3, we find that the moon in the ♎ of Aries is described on page 54.

Thus far the outline reads: April 5, 1860, sign Aries (♈), Grand Function, page 38; chords, color and Responses, page 45; Sign nature and Astronomy, page 51; Lunar influence, Libra of Aries, page 54. Or, more briefly, the index may be written—Aries, pages 38, 45, 51 and 54.

We have next to consider the influence of the planets. In this we will turn our attention to the next diagram, Fig. 4.

In the first circle, marked E, are the twelve signs of the Zodiac, each having an angle of 30°. Following outwardly, each angle crosses the circles marked F, G, H, I, J, K, and L, and each of these seven circles contains the symbol of the planets in the order given in the Ephemeris, in the same angle, and along with the symbol of the planet is the page number, upon which can be found the influence of the planet in the sign in which it is found in the Ephemeris.

Turning again to the year 1860, the first planet, Neptune (♆), is found at the top of the first column to be in Pisces (♓) during the whole year. Turning to the circle F, ♆ in ♓ is indicated as being described on page 138. In the same way Uranus (♅) in Gemini (♊) is found and indicated by circle H, in ♊ angle, as being described on page 140; Saturn is found to be in Leo (♌) until September 3d, after which date he moves into Virgo (♍); on April 5th Saturn is, therefore, yet in Leo (♌), indicated in the Leo angle, as described on page 147.

HELIOCENTRIC ASTROLOGY.

Fig. 4.

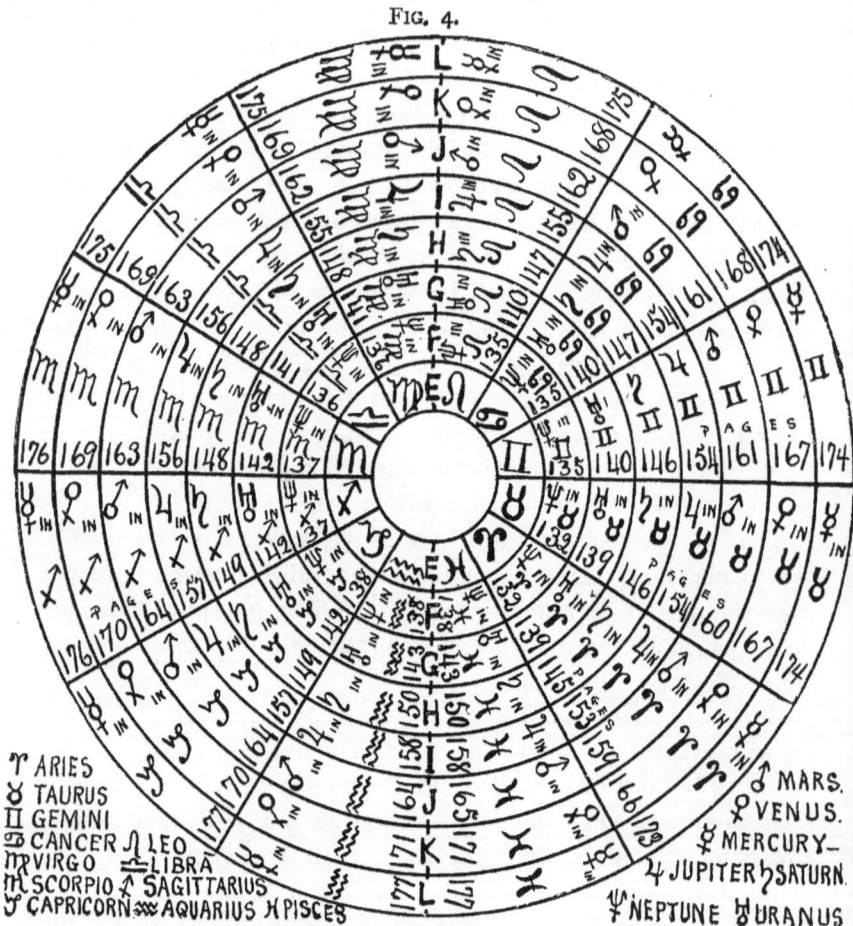

♈ ARIES
♉ TAURUS
♊ GEMINI
♋ CANCER   ♌ LEO
♍ VIRGO   ♎ LIBRA
♏ SCORPIO   ♐ SAGITTARIUS
♑ CAPRICORN   ♒ AQUARIUS   ♓ PISCES

♂ MARS.
♀ VENUS.
☿ MERCURY.
♃ JUPITER ♄ SATURN.
♆ NEPTUNE ♅ URANUS.

Jupiter (♃) is shown by the Ephemeris to have been in Virgo (♍) until May 9th, and in Libra (♎) during the rest of the year. On April 5th he was still in ♍, and the Virgo angle of circle I indicates his description in ♍ as on page 155.

At the bottom of the first column of the Ephemeris it is shown that Mars (♂) entered Scorpio (♏) on February 11th, and left it (see top of second column) on April 11th, to go into Sagittarius (♐); Mars was, therefore, in Scorpio (♏) on April 5th, and in circle J, indicated as described on page 163. Venus (♀), begins at the lower half of the second column. From March (Mh) 30th to April 16th in ♌; and Mercury (☿), given in the last four columns of planetary ephemeris, enters Libra (♎) on March 30th, leaving for Scorpio on April 8th. Venus and Mercury are shown to be described on pages 168 and 175 in the Leo angle of circle K and Libra angle of circle L.

Another method is to place the Zodiac fairly wide apart on a slip of paper, as

♈	♉	♊	♋	♌	♍	♎	♏	♐	♑	♒	♓
☉		♅		♀ ♄	♃	☽ ☿ ⊕	♂				♆

On April 5th the ☉ is in Aries, write the Sun ☉ under that sign. Turn to the ephemeris of 1860; the moon is found to have been in ♎, write it under that sign: ♆ in ♓, write it under ♓. ♅ is found in ♊, write ♅ under ♊. ♄ is found in ♌, write ♄ under ♌. ♃ was in ♍, write ♃ under ♍; ♂ in ♏, write ♂ under that sign: ♀ under the sign ♌; ☿ under the sign ♎, by the side of the ☽. The Earth was in ♎, the solar polarity of Aries, write ⊕ by the moon, under ♎.

Turning to the "Table of Contents" (or to the circular diagrams described above, as you please), Aries, of the "Twelve Great Functions," gives page 38; Chords, Responses and Colors, page 45; Twelve Signs of the Zodiac, Aries, page 51. Write these pages under Aries. ♈—☽ in ♎, page 54, write 54 under ♎. ♆ in ♓, page 138, under ♓. ♅ in ♊, page 140, under ♊; and ♄, ♃, ♂, ♀ and ☿ in the same manner. It is clearly seen that the description of the character is thus given in pages. To extend this, study the laws and equations of power on page 42; the influence of ♀ upon ♄ in ♌; the combined products of the influence upon Aries of the ⊕, ☽ and ☿ forces in ♎; the combined influence of ♄, ♀, ♃, ⊕ ☽, ☿ and ♂ in the contiguous four signs.

If the consideration is carried to the twelve laws given for the first time in this work, it will be found that ♅, ☿ and the ☽ are in (♊, ♎) chords of ♈. ♃ is in ♍, a response to ♈. April 5th is at mid-ascension of the second third, or Exaltation, of the sign, and no planets are in ♉, ♋ or ♑, the second, fourth and tenth, discords of Aries. The Solar polarity, ♎, has ☿ and the ☽. The eighth law, the Law of Restraint, is inactive. The mate was of ♎ nativity, a solar polarity, with ♃ in ♒, ♀ in ♍, ♆ in ♓, and ♂ in ♑.

ASTRONOMY.

In order to easily understand the elements of either branch of Astrology—Geocentric, or Heliocentric—it is necessary to have a general understanding of the relations of the bodies of the Solar system to, and the plan by which is ascertained their positions and directions from, each other.

The master unit, in point of power, location and force is, materially, the Sun. But our point of observation is the Earth; it is, therefore, necessary that we understand the Earth's course in order to understand our relationship, in place, to the whole solar system.

To a person in the northern hemisphere, who stands facing southward, the Earth in revolving from west to east causes the Sun by day, and the planets and constellations by night, to seem to move toward the west; to have a diurnal westward revolution.

This diurnal motion is the chief basis of calculation in the Geocentric (old) astrology.

In the Earth's annual course around the Sun, also from west to east, there is an apparent revolution of the constellations around the Earth's polar points. In reality the Earth is moving a little less than one degree of its circuit each day, and the constellations approach the meridian just that much sooner. This latter motion of the Earth, Planets and signs is the chief basis of calculation in the Heliocentric Astrology.

The Earth has a north and south pole, forming its axis of daily revolution, and these poles hold a nearly absolute relation to the fixed stars and their constellations. The poles vary through a celestial circle, 46° 54′ 48″ in diameter, in 25,670 years. If the Earth did not revolve around its poles and around the Sun, the Constellations and the Sun would appear to stand almost still. If the Earth should then begin to revolve upon its axis, evidently those parts of the heavens to which the poles point would appear to stand still, and bodies in all other directions would appear to revolve around the Earth in celestial circles parallel to the circles of latitude on the Earth.

If the Earth then began an annual revolution around the Sun, still continuing its diurnal revolution, to an observer standing on

FIG. 6.

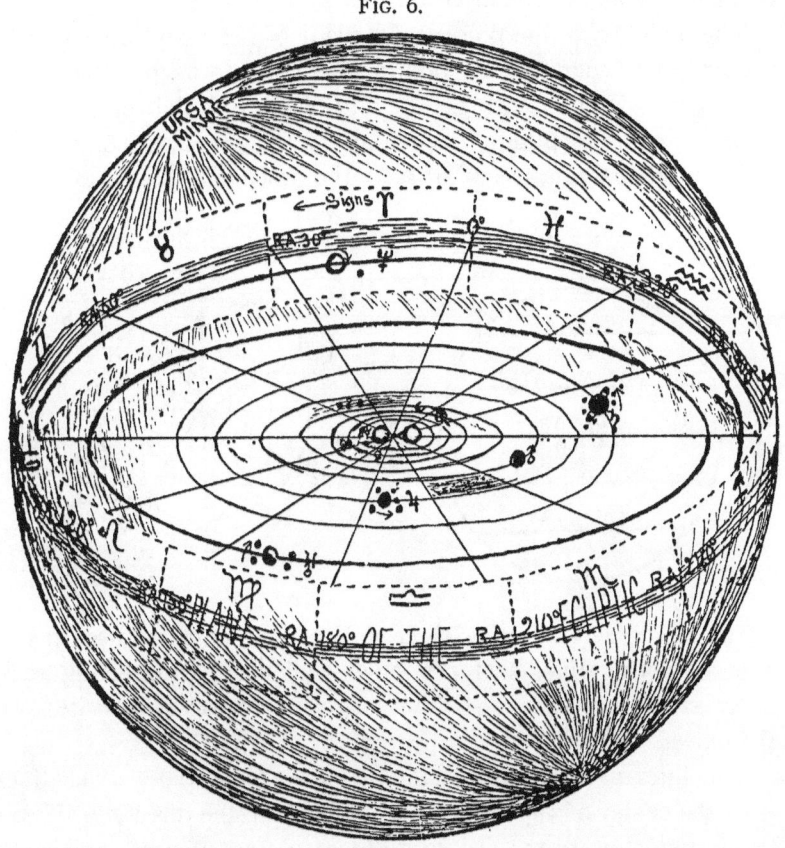

any part of the Earth and looking toward any part of the heavens during the whole year, the apparent paths of the visible constellations would maintain the same arc from east to west, their planes would incline the same toward the north or south, as though the daily motion alone was carried on, and their latitude would always seem the same. But each succeeding night throughout the year the asterisms would appear to proceed a trifle over one degree toward the westward, and stars in another four minutes of Right Ascension would appear.

By this we understand that the Earth has imaginary lines of latitude. Right lines extending from the center of the Earth through these give us Celestial latitude, generally called, in relation to the Sun and planets, declination north or south.

The obliquity of the poles to the plane of the Ecliptic complexes the apparent course of all bodies that seem to move around the Earth; we will, therefore, devote a little space to the consideration of latitude and longitude, declination and Right Ascension.

By imaginary parallels of latitude, the position of places upon the

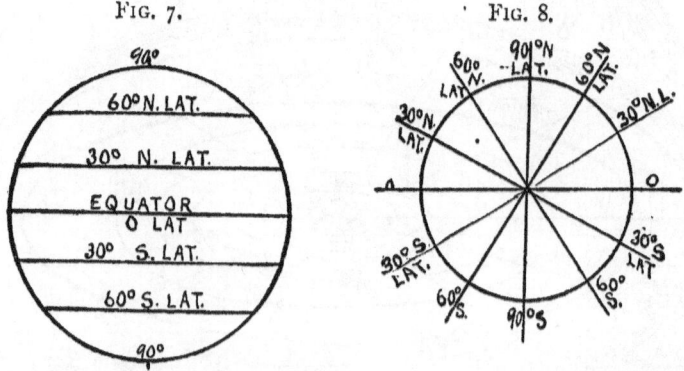

FIG. 7.   FIG. 8.

Earth can be determined with regard to their north and south distances; noting lines that run north and south intersecting each other at the poles, indicate the eastward or westward position of the object.

The lines of Fig. 7 illustrate the lines of latitude. The lines from the center of the circle, Fig. 8, indicate the direction of lines that extend toward the Celestial sphere as lines of north and south declination, and Celestial latitude.

Longitude and Right Ascension are illustrated by Figs. 9 and 10; longitude being the measurement from the Sun and from the Earth outward in degrees, minutes and seconds, and Right Ascension being the measurement of the Sun, planets, moon, and stars as seen from the Earth, in hours, minutes and seconds of time, corresponding to longitude on Earth from the First point of Aries, when measuring the Heliocentric co-ordinates from the Sun.

Because of the rate of motion of the Earth and the number of minutes in an hour, four minutes of time equal one degree.

A plane made by an imaginary line from the Sun to the Earth and extending to the limits of the Solar system, is, when it sweeps through the 360 degrees of the ellipse, called the plane of the Ecliptic (pertaining to eclipses), and all the larger and nearly all the smaller planets move in ellipses very nearly in this plane. Because of this fact we have frequent eclipses and planetary occultations.

If the poles of the Earth were at right angles to this plane, the

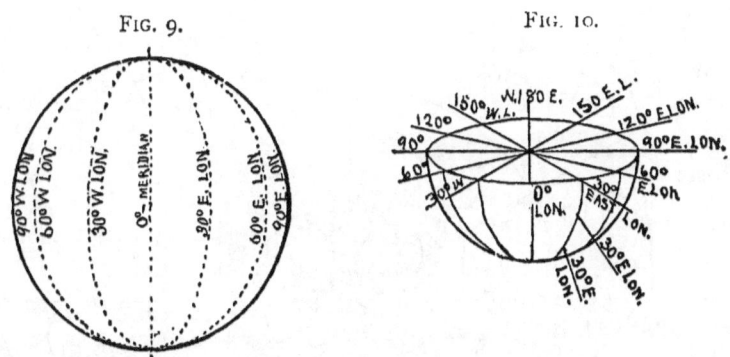

FIG. 9.   FIG. 10.

Sun would shine on any one part of the Earth from the same angle every day in the year, there would be no alternations of the seasons, no changes in the length of day and night in any latitude, and the planets would take the same courses year in and year out. But a massive fact changes all this. Instead of the north pole pointing to Omega or Psi, constellation Draco, it inclines 23° 27' 24" toward the constellations Taurus, Orion, and Gemini, that is directly toward the first point of the sign Cancer; hence it falls near the Star Polaris, in Ursa Minor. Thus it happens that the plane of the ecliptic is not the plane of the equator, and the celestial equator crosses the plane of the ecliptic midway between the points of greatest declination north and south, namely, the first point of Aries and the first point of Libra, when the Sun seems to have no decli·

nation. Half the equator will be below the plane of the ecliptic, the other half above. If the north pole inclines 23° 27′ 24″ toward Cancer, that is toward the Sun when in Cancer, the Sun will shine

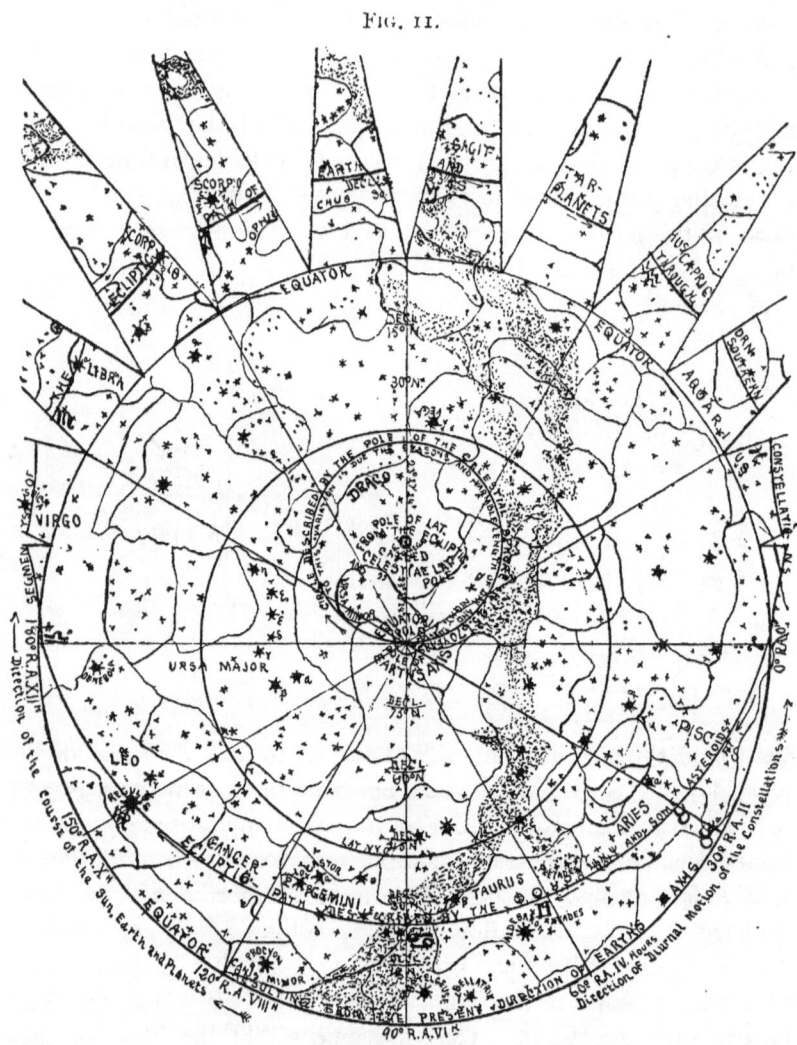

FIG. 11.

more on the northern than upon the southern hemisphere at that time. The stars, planets, Sun, and our Moon will all decline northward in day time and southward at night time in one season, and

HELIOCENTRIC ASTROLOGY. 23

the reverse at the opposite season. The inclination of the poles causes the inclination of the Equator to the ecliptic, and the changes of north and south latitude of the planets in the ecliptic.

The direct rays of the Sun's light, heat and other forces varies

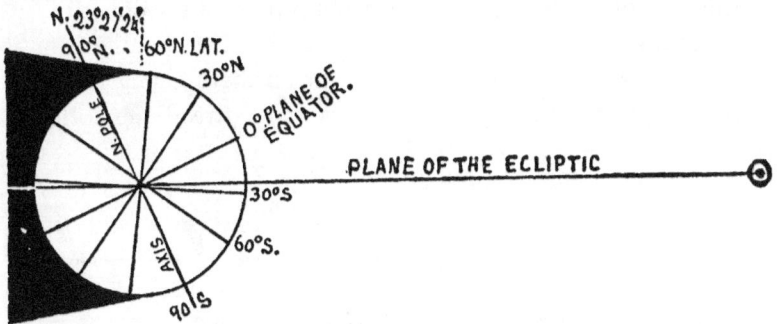

FIG. 12.

during the year an angle of 46° 54′ 48″ of the Earth's surface, one half of the angle north, the other south of the equator, producing the alternation of the seasons, and the varying length of day and night.

To make this clearer, in Fig. 12 we have drawn a circle repre-

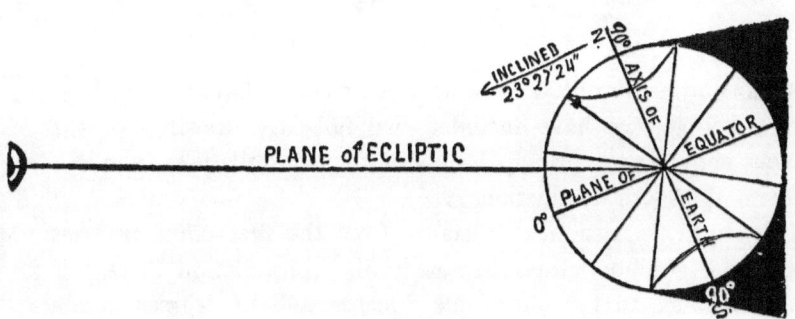

FIG. 13.

senting the latitude of the Earth and the declination of the north pole away from the Sun toward Capricorn.

In Fig. 13 we have drawn the Earth, plane of the ecliptic and Sun, as if the pole inclined to Cancer.

HELIOCENTRIC ASTROLOGY.

The general relative distances of the planets from the Sun are shown in Fig. 14; no effort was made to give proportional sizes.

In Fig. 14 the plane is drawn as an inclined broad belt, the sphere within representing the vastly extended lines of the Earth. The planes of the Earth's and the celestial equator cross the broad belt at Libra on one side and consequently at Aries on the opposite. The plane of the ecliptic is also the plain of the Zodiac; the Sun in Cancer would shine most directly upon the northern hemisphere; hence, the Tropic of Cancer; in Capricorn, most directly upon the southern.

FIG. 14.

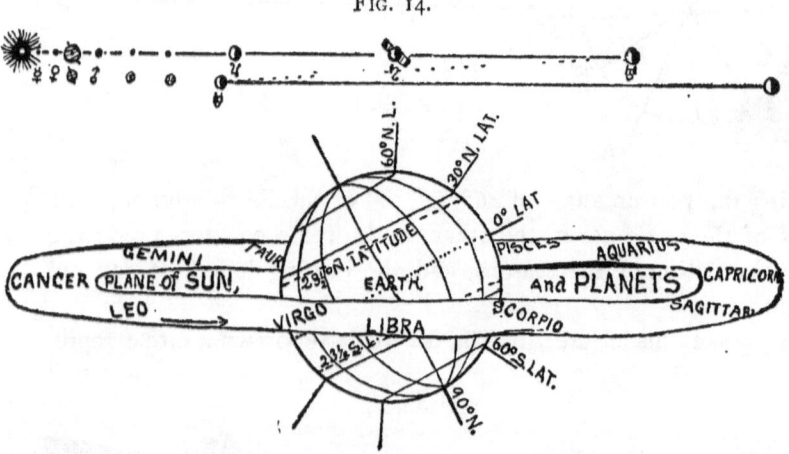

Although we have little to do with other constellations than those of the Zodiac, we have included two full-page drawings of the heavens showing the principal stars of the constellations from 45° north to 45° south declination.

The Right Ascension, or distance from the first point of Aries (the vernal equinoctial point, now in the constellation Pisces) is given in hours, to the left of the Equator, and in degrees to the right.

On the right margin of both pages is given the date on which time, about midnight, the stars along those lines of Right Ascension will pass the meridian; the stars toward the top of the page will pass earlier, those toward the bottom of the page, later (one hour

HELIOCENTRIC ASTROLOGY.

Fig. 15.

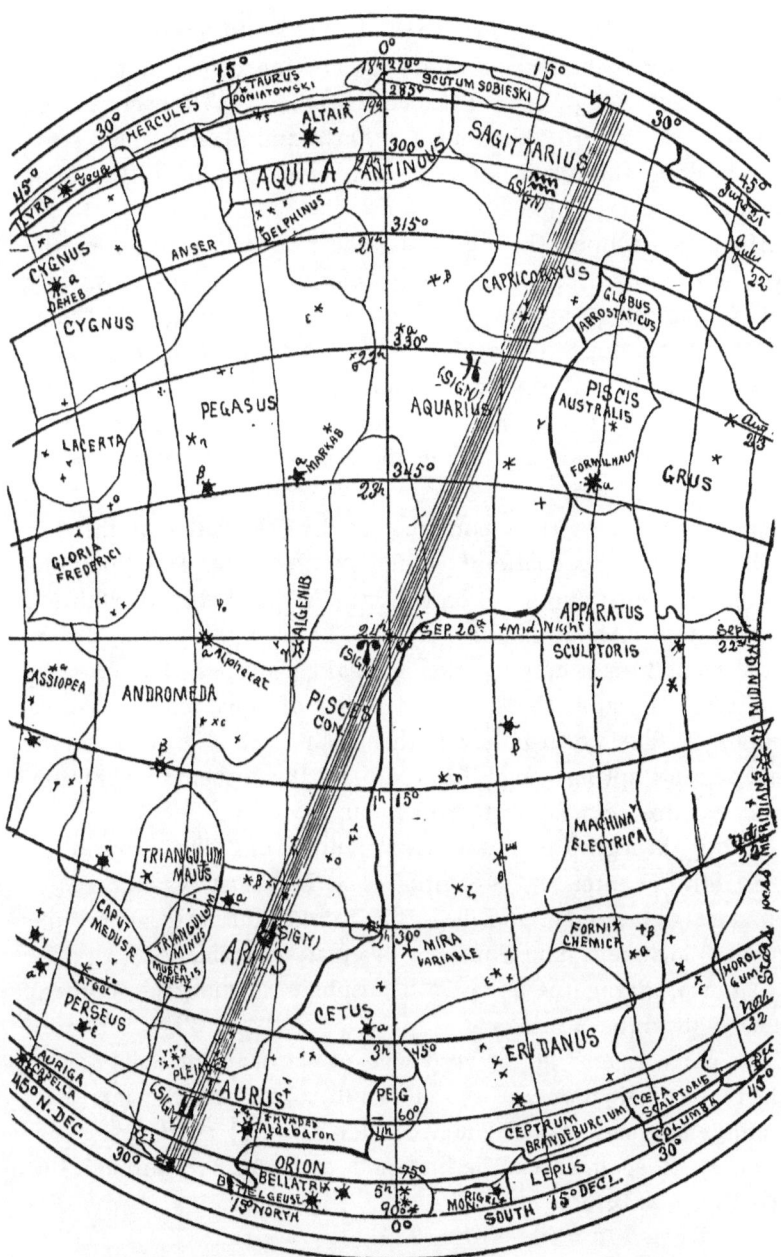

each fifteen degrees), as noted in the hours of Right Ascension along the equator.

The band of fine lines from 23° 27' 24" south, crossing the celestial equator at the first point of Aries in the center of the illustration, then to 23° 27' 24" north, in the sign Cancer, is the ecliptic. If seen from the Sun, the Earth and planets would seem to pass along this plane, and, as seen from the Earth, the Sun, Moon and planets would appear to do so.

Along this ecliptic the Earth, as seen from the Sun, enters the Sign of Capricorn, June 21st (☉ entering ♋); Aquarius, July 22d (☉ entering ♌); Pisces, August 23d (☉ entering ♍). September 22d the Earth enters Aries, the Sun being at the first point of ♎. October 22d, the Earth enters Taurus (☉ in ♏); Gemini, Nov. 22d (☉ in ♐). The Earth now passes to the constellations shown in the second map, while the Sun seems to enter those we have just considered.

The Earth enters the second map at the first minute of the sign Cancer, in the Constellation Gemini; on December 21st (☉ enters ♑); Leo, January 19th (☉ enters ♒); Virgo, February 18th (☉ entering ♓). About March 20th the Earth enters Libra, center of the second map, crossing the celestial equator, the Sun crossing the Earth's equator, the days and nights of equal length (Vernal equinox). The north pole will then lean more and more toward the Sun, and spring travel from the Earth's equator northward, blending into the most northern autumn.

Passing through Libra, the Earth enters the sign Scorpio on April 20th (☉ enters ♉); Sagittarius on May 21st (☉ enters ♌); Capricorn, June 21st, and begins with the Sun in Cancer, the Summer Solstice. The Sun is at its greatest declination (23° 27' 24") north, giving the northern hemisphere summer, the southern hemisphere winter.

The Earth is now at the very edge of the map, in Solar longitude 270°, declination 23° 27' 24" south. Stars on the meridian at midnight would have Right Ascension (R. A.) 18 Hours.

The Earth again enters the first map, and continues through the twelve signs as before.

HELIOCENTRIC ASTROLOGY.

FIG. 16.

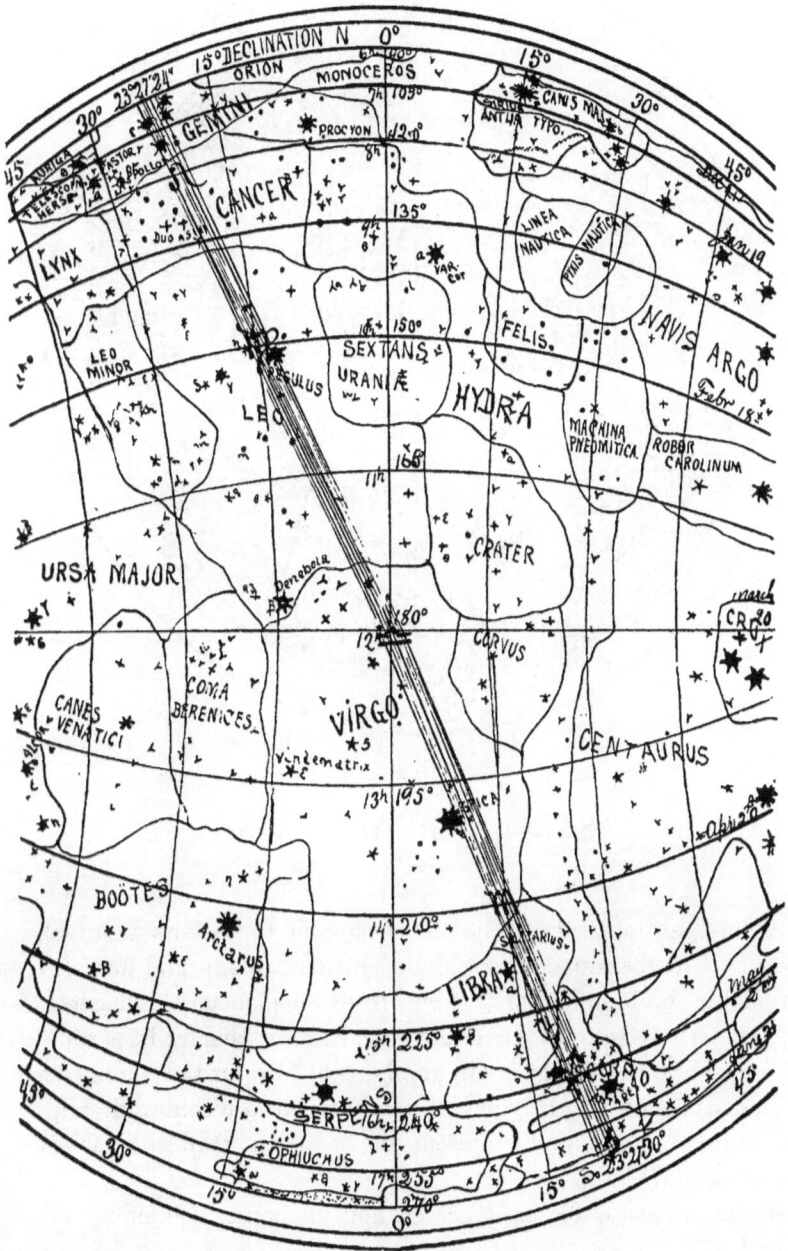

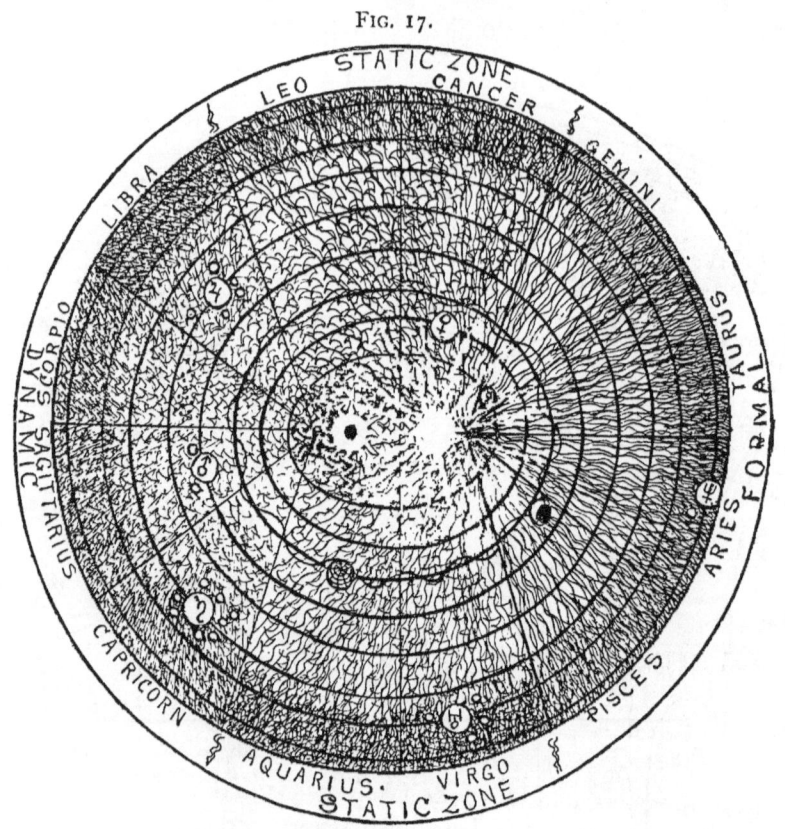

Fig. 17.

ASTROLOGICAL LAWS.

A BRIEF examination of the mental laws of the Solar system will give force to the soundness of Heliocentric astrology, and furnish a reasonable philosophy for the doctrine of planetary influences. The reader's attention is therefore called to this chapter in particular, under the belief that it will amply repay him for the time given to its consideration. It seems necessary to avoid technical description, and to more briefly present the evidence than the subject would warrant.

In Fig. 18 the circle has a center, and the bodies containing the numbers 2, 3 and 4, in order to move around the center at all times equidistant, must be governed at all times by the same amount and kind of force. If these bodies are controlled by force, any variation from these absolute paths would at once destroy all their mutual relations. We are safe in saying that this plan of action is never found to be organic. It is necessarily mechanical

In the ellipse of Fig. 18 we have placed two focusses; one formal, marked Fo, from which radiates formal energy; that is, energy that is directive and constructive. From the other center, marked Dy, radiates dynamic energy, energy that is executive and very positive.

The zone between these centers of force is a zone modified by

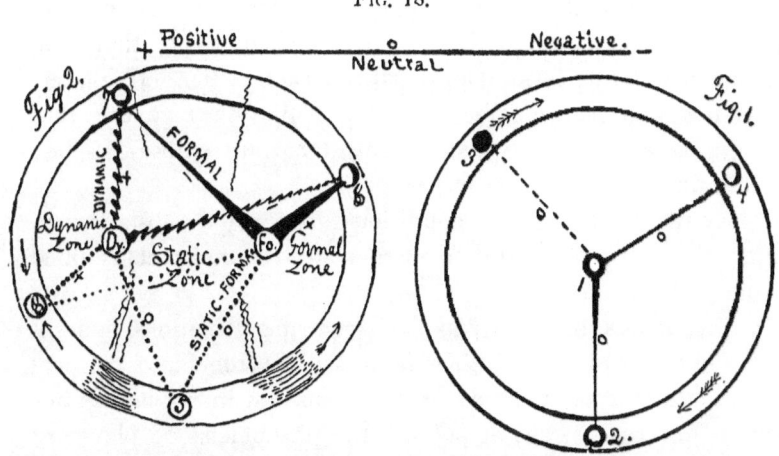

FIG. 18.

the blended formal and dynamic energies into relative neutrality, that is, giving a much more static effect than the energy of either focus.

A body under the combined influence of Fo and Dy, as at 5, is repelled by Dy, when attracted by Fo, and thus travels almost parallel to the major axis. When it passes to 6 it comes under the domination of Fo, and acts in accord to its formal forces. Propelled along its ellipse to 7, it has again crossed the static zone, but on the opposite side, and entered the dominion of Dy by which it is positively affected, and only negatively by Fo. At 5 it again comes within the more static zone of influence. Thus under the reciprocal play of positive and negative conditions, and of dynamic and formal forces, the bodies governed by the laws of vitality keep perpetually within their true sphere of action, and obey harmonic methods.

In Fig. 17, the formal forces are represented by wavy lines radiating from the formal center; the dynamic forces by angular lines, radiating from the dynamic center. The region of relative quietude, or the neutral zone, as it were, is that crossed by lines from both focuses. In one of these focuses we have the material Sun. In the other, the laws of physics and those of mentality demand another equally powerful body.

The theory of planetary motions advanced by Dr. Sivartha, and accepted by the author of this book, is in the main as follows: The law of the ellipse requires two centers of force, that from each center differing in kind and quality; each center acting alternately in a dominant degree upon the bodies they govern, thus forcing those bodies to move along paths that are ellipses, if they move at all.

It may require still other conditions, forces, and substances to compel them to move, or to perpetuate the movements once gained.

The hypothesis of centripetal and centrifugal motions, gravity government, as described by Kepler's and Newton's laws, is, perhaps, a statement of methods or of action, but in no manner accounts for or has warrant as solving the phenomena of planetary motions. And particularly is this true when we consider the relative elliptical paths of the planetary systems, and their actual epicycloidal courses through the vast realm of each star's travels.

On the other hand, the law of the ellipse, when one focus is positive and the other negative, the bodies moving around them in positive and negative states also, and all moving in a vast mass of Spirit substances the forces of which all trend toward curvilineal directions, thus keeping forever within their true sphere of activity, is ample to account for (that is, effect) the continual reign of circular law and motion throughout the Universe, likewise equal to establishing and making more and more complex the mental structure of the Solar system and supplying the substances necessary to vital and mental life upon any of the bodies of that system.

According to the discoveries of Dr. Sivartha and the corroborative evidence furnished by the investigations of Prof. Merton:

"The Universe is jointly governed by two great classes of substances, the forces and laws of each governing where it is dominant in mass, and their interaction overcoming, counterbalancing or succumbing to each other in proportion to their ever varying ratios. The dominant substance generally gives to our intelligence the impressions of its peculiar characteristics. The forces of matter (the chemical elements) are angular, inorganic, moving in right-line directions, forever trending toward decay and disintegration from complex proportions. The forces of Spirit substances are curved in body and in polarity, and propel or attract bodies along curved paths, the nature of the curve depending on the nature of the mass of substances set in motion and that of the propelling body or bodies." [HOLMES W. MERTON.]

The planetary bodies are governed by the curvilineal forces of Spirit substances, and these forces sweep the planets and satellites around their foci in elliptical paths as related to their centers, in epicycloidal paths as results of the larger ellipses of their governing bodies and the vastly greater distances of the Universe.

It is thus that the dominantly physical, and the dominantly spiritual Suns, govern the Solar System.

Under this law the planets are continually changing either the quality or the quantity of their forces as they pass through the different parts of their ellipses. These regions, as we may very properly call them, are filled with radiant forces from the centers, varying in kind and quantity with every degree of Solar longitude, and in much less marked manner with every degree of obliquity from the ecliptic.

In fact, it should seem evident to a student of physics, that the phenomena of planetary and satellitic motions are vastly different from the phenomena of matter and material forces—light, heat, gravity, chemia, magnetic and electric forces—as well as those of mechanical physics.

As far as experience goes, we have no knowledge of the motion of one natural body around one other in accordance with any law of physics, or physical philosophy.

We are thus prepared to realize that all life can be very much influenced by the organic forces of the various bodies of the Solar system, and that the major part of the energies of this and all other systems are the same in kind, although not in complexity, as those that govern the mental and vital action of all living bodies.

In Fig. 17, Aquarius and Virgo are in the static zone, the blended forces that radiate from the Solar foci toward those signs (not constellations, as these are now about 30° behind the signs) of the Zodiac are attractive, static, vital, giving a trend toward nutrition in bodily, and affection in mental action.

Toward the right (and in R. A. among the signs) is Pisces, the first of the formal, directive, intellectual region. This is followed by Aries and Taurus, the most powerful of the formal functions. The next is Gemini, the sign of Culture, the last formal region, blending gradually into the higher affections.

Cancer follows, again in the zone of calmness and attraction. This is followed by Leo, gradually blending into the dynamic and executive zone, beginning with the sign Libra, then Scorpio, Sagittarius and Capricorn.

It will be seen that the four signs just mentioned correspond to the functions of the Will.

The Intuitions of the Ancients.

The ancients named the constellations of the Zodiac (and others) and assigned to each a meaning. To each of the zodiacal signs they named a region of influence in the human body, and implied or affirmed a general mental function resulting from the influence and bodily government.

They did not realize the mastery of the brain over the body, nor the division of its functions, and that through these the influence was manifested.

About 2000 years ago, in the days of Hipparchus, the asterisms and zodiacal signs corresponded in their angles. On account of what is called the Precession of the Equinoxes (equal days and nights) the equinoctial points have gained nearly 31°, and separated the angle of 30° belonging to each sign, from their denominational constellations, hence the sign Aries now indicates the asterism Pisces, and all other signs are likewise changed.

Our study of Astrology relates essentially to the Solar system. The zodiac is but the very distant dial upon which, from our point of observation, appears delineated the paths, places and periods of time taken by the bodies of our small system moving around its central stars. The Astronomer's inquiry is vastly more extended. While confidence in material law and in the phenomena of physics fills its mission, it is apparent that these alone cannot solve problems that relate to other laws and other forces.

Fig. 19.

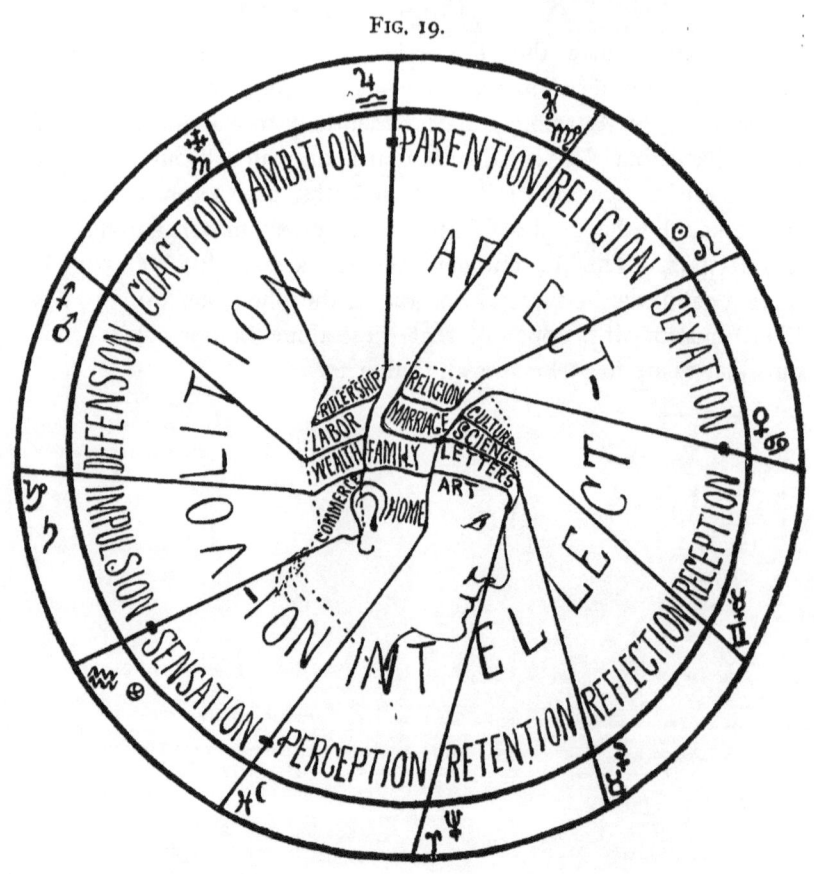

THE THREE GRAND DIVISIONS.

The analysis of Life, either with regard to its Mental functions, or to their expression in the material elements they aggregate around the spirit substances, gives us three grand divisions of forces and of functions. That is, there are three classes of powers manifested. Each class has its kind of force, of product and of organ. The first series then is Formal force, Intellectual product, the Nervous System, its organ. The second series is Static force, Affectional product, the Nutritive system, its organ. The third series is the Dynamic force, Volition product, the Muscular system, its organ.

Wisdom, Love and Will express the products in general terms.

TWELVE GRAND FUNCTIONS (SIVARTHA).

Twelve grand functions are necessary to carry on and express these divisions. Succinctly, the functions of the Intellect are Perception, to see; Retention, to retain and reawaken; Reflection, to divine, reflect and construct; Reception, to receive, to make choice.

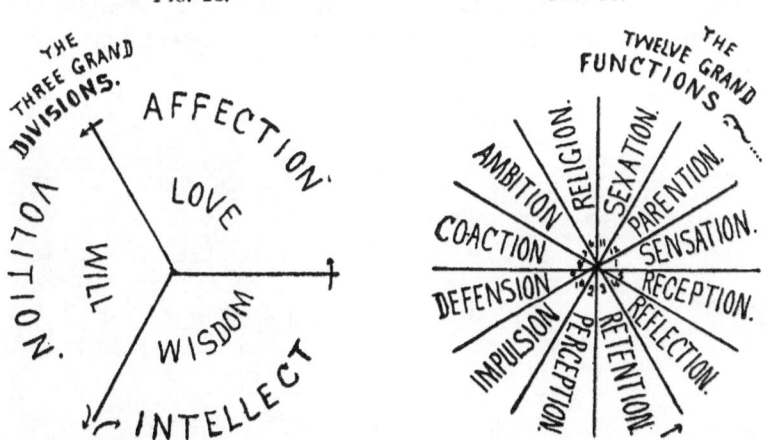

FIG. 20.   FIG. 21.

We observe, in examining the result of these functions, that their general products are Art, Letters, Science and Culture. These are vaguely symbolized, in our view of Astrology, by Pisces, Aries, Taurus and Gemini.

The functions of the Affections are Sensation, the senses of impression, feeling and of hunger; Parention, the desire and relationships of parenthood; Sexation, marriage and sex relations; Religion, harmony, human and divine unity. These are more or less clearly symbolized by Aquarius, Virgo, Cancer and Leo.

The functions of Volition, reading them downward in the order of their action, are Ambition—ruling and conservative; Coaction—industry, personal freedom; Defension—wealth and protection; Impulsion, producing commerce and mobility.

These functions are symbolized vaguely by Libra, Scorpio, Sagittarius and Capricorn. It must not be forgotton that the regional influences of these signs are not simply symbolical, but are actual influences. The fault or variation of truth is in the symbolism, not in the forces and regions.

It will be clearly seen that this system of astrology transfers the signs from representation chiefly in the body regions to the true sources of effect, that is, the brain and its mental mechanism, and thus establishes the direct relation, and also the greater equality of function, no less than the true basis of zodiacal symbolism.

Certainly this could not have been done until a true analysis of mental life was made, and many natural laws of the mental mechanism were discovered.

FIG. 22.

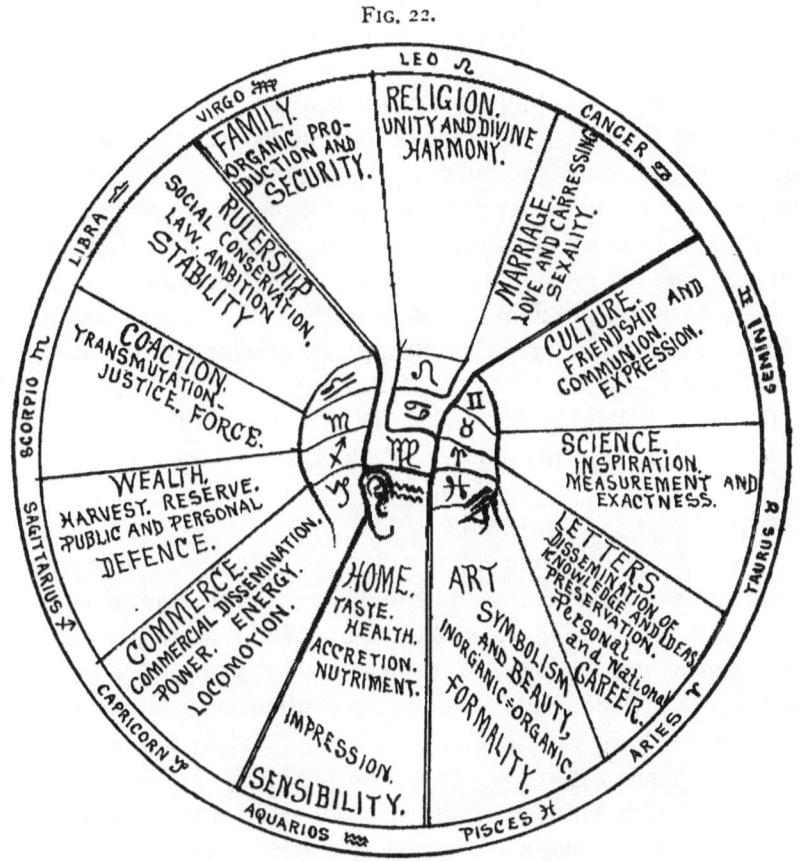

THE TWELVE GREAT FUNCTIONS.

The drawing at the head of this chapter extends the analysis of the twelve great functions into their general products, and makes clear the relation of the signs and astrological regions to the functions of the brain.

Although Pisces is the first of the formal (Intellectual) functions, we will begin with Aries, as that sign is the first in point of degrees of Heliocentric longitude and of Right Ascension.

ARIES.—The region of Aries includes the sign of 30 degrees from 0 to 30°, from the "First point of Aries," and is, in time, the first and second hour of R. A. This is also the point of the Vernal Equinox, where the Ecliptic crosses the equator.

The products of Aries may be defined by the general term Letters. The influences and forces of this region are essential to the dissemination of knowledge and ideas by language and speech ; the preservation of ideas by printing, and the various methods of recording ; and the extension of personal and national career.

The planet Neptune is in closest sympathy with the regional influences of Aries, and gives spirituality, refinement and elegance, as well as harmony, to the forces of that sign.

TAURUS.—Following the region of Aries is that of Taurus, the region of Reflection, the products of which are the Sciences. This sign has the second angle of thirty degrees along the ecliptic, and includes the 3d and 4th hour of R. A.

This is the most profound of all the regional influences ; its forces are the most directive and advancing of all the formal energies. The Taurus region is the region of inspiration, reason, measurement and exactness. In planetary sympathy, Taurus has no direct respondent. Its energies are centralizing and recipient from the true Solar pole, one of the Pleiades, and by response the energy of Venus.

GEMINI.—The products of the forces of Gemini are defined by the term Culture ; that is, refinement, friendship and elegance in expression.

In sympathy and symbolism the planet Mercury is most closely allied to Gemini and intensifies both energies whenever combined.

The longitude of this region is the third angle of 30 degrees (61° to 90°) along the ecliptic ; and in time the 5th and 6th hour of R. A.

CANCER.—The result of Cancer energies is Marriage—devotion, mating and sexuality.

The planet Venus is in closest sympathy both in force and symbolism, with the forces of this region.

The longitude is the fourth angle of 30 degrees (91° to 120°) ; the R. A. the 7th and 8th hours. At its first point is the Summer Solstice.

LEO.—The general result of Leo's energies we term Religion; its trend is toward unity and spiritual harmony. Hence, in result, it may become the highest of all the functions.

The region is most directly in sympathy with the spiritual Sun, but its planetary and bodily influences are generally accredited to the Solar Center.

The longitude of Leo is from 121° to 150°: its R. A. the 9th and 10th hour.

VIRGO.—The region of Virgo is that of Familism, and the products of its energies are organic production, security, home and tribal life.

Virgo is the home of Uranus, with which sign that planet most perfectly sympathizes and accords.

The longitude of this region is from 151° to 180°; the 11th and 12th hours of R. A. Like Cancer and Leo, Virgo is in the Static zone.

LIBRA.—Libra is the region of Rulership. It influences personal and civil government; social conservation; sense of justice, and gives dynamic force.

Libra is the home of Jupiter, the sign in which that planet finds its greatest power and sympathy.

Libra is the first and highest sign of the dynamic regions; in longitude the 30° of 181° to 210°; R. A. the 13th and 14th hours, and in time and longitude the opposite of Aries, hence it begins the Autumnal equinox.

SCORPIO.—Scorpio is the region of Coaction, or Labor. Its forces trend toward transmutation, justice and liberty. It has dynamic force of a constructive order.

The asteroids are in general sympathy with this sign. Some astrologers attribute to the region Mars influences, but this does not seem to us to be true. It is more in sympathy with Venus and Uranus than with Mars. We give the region the sympathy of the asteroids.

The region of Scorpio is the 30° from 211° to 240°; of heliocentric longitude, and its R. A. the 15th and 16th hours.

SAGITTARIUS.—The region of Wealth. Its forces are those of subsistence; reserve; caution; public and personal defence. The region trends toward preservation for purposes of utility and gain.

This region is the home of Mars, and its forces are in sympathy with the energy and symbolism of that fiery-tempered and aggressive planet.

The region of Sagittarius is the 30° of 241° to 270°, Heliocentric longitude; its R. A. the 17th and 18th hours.

CAPRICORN.—The region of Commerce. Its forces trend toward dissemination of product ; toward love of power ; destructiveness and of locomotion. It is distinctly impelling, and, when angered, repelling.

Capricorn is the home of Saturn, with which region he sympathizes most and has greatest power. Symbolically the Greek god, Cronus, and the Roman Saturnus, were both distinctly gods of commerce, of the interchange of wealth, the severest forms of government, and likewise notably interested in agriculture.

The region of Capricorn is the 30° of Heliocentric longitude from 271° to 300° ; R. A. the 19th and 20th hours.

AQUARIUS.—The region of home and Sensation. Its forces give sensibility to taste, smell, touch, psychometric sensitiveness (properly *physico-metric* sensitiveness), and nutritive power.

The Earth itself is in closest sympathy with the forces of this region, and in this is found the capacity and sympathy of the so-called physical senses.

From Aquarius (a Static Sign) the next sign is Pisces in the formal region.

The region of Aquarius is the angle from 301° to 330° ; R. A. the 21st and 22d hours.

PISCES.—The region of Perception and Art. The products of its forces are symbolism, perception of beauty, general sight, mechanical and organic ornamentation, and mechanical skill.

The region of Pisces stimulates, in a person of low organic quality, simply the capacity to see, and in a manner imitate skill and art. In a person of high organic quality it is the natural basis of artistic capacity, mathematical power, and mechanical and visual skill. The region of Pisces is the sympathetic and natural home of the Moon.

The Moon thus has greater power in awakening imagination, mental vision, and expressed emotions.

The region of Pisces is the angle of Heliocentric longitude from 331° to 360°; R. A. the 23d and 24th hours. On leaving Pisces, the next sign is Aries, and continues as before.

LAWS AND EQUATIONS OF POWER.

The equations and ratios of power are determined by a large number of conditions and laws, the principal of which are the following twelve.

The First Law.—Chords are never opponents. That is to say, they are never antagonistic in product or effect. As an illustration: The chord of Aries is Gemini; of Gemini, Aries. A planet in Gemini (*i.e.*, Saturn) cannot antagonize the result of Aries, energies; it may change the method of, but to the advantage of the Aries personality. Taurus, the next sign above, is not a chord, nor is it a response of Aries; Saturn in Taurus would adversely affect Aries; and in a less degree Mars would do so.

The Second Law.—Responses are always supporting when endowed with planets, the endowment being in quality like the planet and sign combined. As an illustration: Sagittarius is a response to Aries; and Mars in Sagittarius, the most powerful of its regions of influence, would be beneficial to Aries' success. The advantage would be marked by a more judicious economy of energy and wealth, and by aggression in opinion as well as in defence. Saturn in Sagittarius would give Aries discretion, reserve force, and a wider range of commercial insight. But Capricorn, although it is the home of Saturn, is neither a chord nor a response of Aries, hence the planet there would not fulfill the law.

The Third Law.—The solar polarity is the secondary path of action, as against any other sign. Hence, an Aries person would more easily assume the Libra nature than that of any other sign. The planet of the native sign has greater power in the solar polarity than in any other sign except its own.

The Fourth Law.—The law of Mental chord in the twelve functions. The third, seventh and ninth of any sign are in closest harmony, as are Gemini, Libra and Sagittarius with Aries.

The Fifth Law.—The law of Discords. The second, fourth and tenth are discords of any sign, as are Taurus, Cancer and Capricorn, discords of Aries.

The Sixth Law.—The law of Heredity. The nature of a person is greatly influenced by the planetary aspects governing the parents. It is always well to let such data enter into elaborate considerations.

The Seventh Law.—The law of Ascent and exaltation. The period of exaltation is the second third of the sign.

The Eighth Law.—The law of Restraint. The first third (that is, ten or eleven days) of the sign is most subject to accident, decreased power and social debasement. This depends much upon the results of the fifth and sixth laws.

The Ninth Law.—The law of Conservation and Reserve. The personality of the last third of the sign seldom experiences its maximum strength or success until very late in life. It is also often left for posterity to benefit by its efforts.

The Tenth Law.—The law of Mobility. A condition of planetary influences which depresses opportunity in mental, and exalts opportunity in physical, life, although the native sign is favorable to the former. As an illustration: Aries, with Venus and Mercury in Capricorn and Jupiter in Aquarius.

The Eleventh Law.—The law of Marriage. A state in which exaltation or depression arises from harmonious or inharmonious marriage.

The Twelfth Law.—The law of Formality. This law is in action when the planetary influences exalt opportunity in mentality, and depress it in mobility and dynamic energy. As an illustration: When the sign is Capricorn and the powerful planets are favorably located in the formal regions, as, Mercury in Pisces; Jupiter and Venus in Taurus.

Fig. 23.

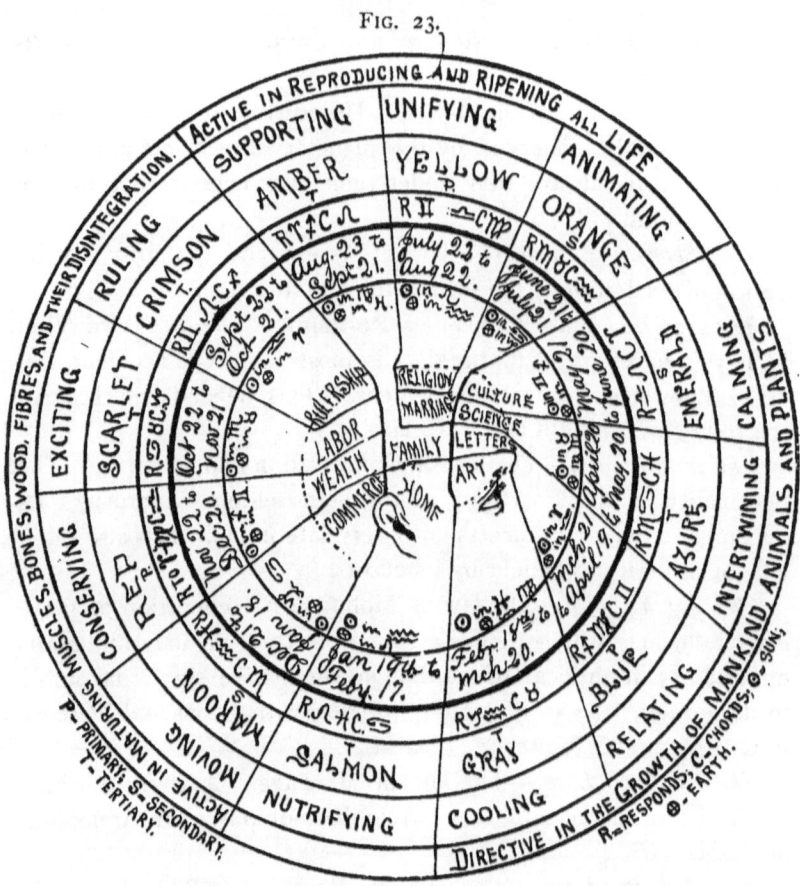

THE CHORDS, RESPONSES AND COLORS.

Pisces.—The chord of Pisces is Taurus its third above, and it is thus that "Art and Science go hand in hand," for art and skill prepare the technical instruments by which science measures; and the perceptives observe the phenomena upon which reflection founds the great sciences, for the observation of fact is the basis of science, of the discovery of law and new phenomena.

The forces of this region respond to those of Capricorn in the dynamic regions; thus art in its practical forms is closely allied to commerce. Aquarius, of the home region, is the second response of Pisces.

The color sympathy of Pisces is blue gray, and all Pisces' forces are cooling. The period of greatest power is from February 18th to March 20th, the Sun in Pisces, the Earth in Virgo.

ARIES.—This sign chords with Gemini, the region of Culture and receptivity, and thus we realize that Letters and Culture are very close chords in mentality.

Aries is the great retentive, and Gemini, its chord, the great receptive region.

The first response in force is to the accumulative region of will, Sagittarius; the latter sign aggregating wealth and ownership, while the former (Aries) accumulates knowledge, language, verbal expression and history.

In a less marked manner Aries responds to Virgo, the region of family and tribal forces, which gathers the elements of the race into families, groups and countries, establishing parental and filial love, and in the less personal form, patriotism.

The color sympathy of Aries is the primary blue. Its energies are relating in habit, as is observed in the function of memory and attention.

The period of power is from March 21st to April 19th, the Sun being in Aries, the Earth in Libra.

TAURUS.—The chord of Taurus is Pisces, as noted under that sign. Taurus elaborates the accumulated evidences, facts and impressions gathered by Pisces and those recorded by Aries, into systems, methods, rules of action, and practical results, which we call science and construction.

The first response is Scorpio in the dynamic regions, and there is great sympathy between the industry, integrity and love of liberty of that region, and the forces of Taurus. The second response of Taurus is Cancer, the region of Sexuality and organic reproduction.

In color, Taurus' forces are azure, slightly green; its forces are inter-relating and reflecting, tertiary in their blending.

The period of dominant power is from April 20th to May 20th, the Sun apparently in Taurus, the Earth in Scorpio.

GEMINI.—The forces of this sign chord with those of Aries, and the forces of one strengthen those of the other; and, as memory inter-relates ideas and connects them in series and categories, so the receptive and attractive forces of Gemini inter-relate friendly and social interests, inculcating reforms and congenial desires.

Gemini responds directly to Libra, the region of Rulership, and gives kindness to that region's forces, receiving in return energies of dignity and firmness. In less degree it responds to Leo, the region of religious energies; thus, Amity and kindness are in close accord with Hope and Love in their religious sense.

The color force of Gemini is an emerald green (the true primary, instead of blue); its effect is calming, it is the highest, but not the most powerful, of the formal energies.

The planet Mercury is in greatest sympathy with this sign. Its period of power is from May 21st to June 20th, the Sun in Gemini, the Earth in Sagittarius.

CANCER.—Its chord is Aquarius, the region of sense forces, impression and lower conjugal love. As the senses and lower affectional forces are the incentives to mating in the less advanced stages or forms of life, so the energies of cancer are the expression of and incentive to the higher forms of sex mating. The Will response of Cancer is Scorpio, and secondarily, with Taurus, as its harmonious formal energy.

The color quality of Cancer energy is the secondary orange. The nature of its energy is animating.

The planet most closely in sympathy with Cancer is Venus, and as neither of its responses (Scorpio or Taurus) are endowed with powerful planets, Venus receives responsive energy from both these signs, adding to her power unusual clearness, brilliancy and force. The period of power is from June 21st to July 21st, the Sun in Cancer, the Earth in Capricorn.

LEO.—The chord of Leo is Virgo, the region of familism, and it is evident that what familism is to kin relationships, the religious energies and unity ought to be to the race and the grander spiritual familism.

The first response of Leo is Gemini of the formal, and the second is Libra of the dynamic, regions. Thus religion responds to culture on the one hand and to rulership on the other.

The color force of Leo sympathizes with the primary yellow; its energy effect in its higher forms of purity and clearness is unifying, in its lower forms is simply to ripen and mature.

The sympathetic body to Leo energy is the primary Sun, and its period of force from July 22d to August 22d; the Sun is then in Leo, the Earth in her own home, Aquarius.

VIRGO.—The chord of Virgo is Leo, and the description of its influences can be found under that sign.

The responses of Virgo are Aries in the formal, and Sagittarius in the dynamic regions.

The energies of Virgo retain in a group the elements of the family and the tribe; its response, Aries, retains in groups and classes the order and memory associations of ideas and words; while Sagittarius makes effort to retain in mass the products of skill, energy and defence or aggression. As the energies of Virgo conserve the elements of "kith and kin," so its responses conserve those of knowledge and of wealth.

The color energy of Virgo is the tertiary amber; and the general effect of its forces are supporting. The planet Uranus is in greatest sympathy; and the Virgo period of power is from August 23d to September 21st; the Sun in Virgo, the Earth in Pisces.

LIBRA.—The chord of Libra is Sagittarius, the region of defension and wealth. The responses, as we have noted under those signs, are Gemini in the region of the Intellect and Leo in the static zone—the dominant rulership of Libra giving a more executive character to the Gemini and Leo forces of Libra.

The color sympathy of Libra is crimson, and the general trend of its forces are ruling. It is the highest of the dynamic functions, the most active in maturing muscles, bones and woody fibres.

Jupiter is the planet most in sympathy with Libra forces, and the period of Libra's greatest power is from September 22d to October 21st. The Sun is in Libra, the earth in Aries. The beginning, or first point, of Libra is the autumnal equinox, the Sun crossing the equator, southward, at that time.

SCORPIO.—The chord of Scorpio is Capricorn, the sign of impulsion and mobile commercial function. As noted under Cancer and Taurus those signs are its responses. Taurus arouses a judgment of integrity and justice in Scorpio, and Cancer, when strongly endowed, trends to marriage and family life.

The color sympathy of Scorpio is the tertiary scarlet. The orange of Cancer and maroon of Capricorn are secondaries.

The energies of Scorpio are in their general results exciting to muscularity, executive mental attitudes, and to growth in the trunks of trees and the stems of plants.

The influence of this region is greatest from October 22d to November 21st; the Sun in Scorpio, the Earth in Taurus.

Scorpio has no known planet as a sympathetic exponent, but at times accords with some of the asteroids, and with Venus of Cancer and Saturn of Capricorn (see mythology of Greek Cronus).

SAGITTARIUS.—The chord of Sagittarius is Libra; the relationship has been defined under that sign.

The presence of Mars or Jupiter in Libra of the Sagittarius nature gives firmness and a very positive undercurrent to that (♐) nature's self-esteem.

The first response of this sign is Aries in the formal regions, and by this is added a relatively powerful memory of those details that interest Sagittarius. The second response is Virgo, giving an impulse toward large family and patriotic-wealth desires.

The period of dominant power is from November 22d to December 20th. The color-sympathy is an intense red; the forces are executive and marked by energy, but conserving in tone, and trending toward defence.

Mars is in closest sympathy with this sign, and gives it martial force with aggression and caution-elements.

CAPRICORN.—The chord of Capricorn is Scorpio, as noted under that sign, and thus is closely related the energies of industry and coaction, with those of commerce and mobility, locomotion and impulsion.

The first response is Pisces, giving direction in detail and artistic skill. The second response is Aquarius, supporting in volume of nutriment and sense capacity.

The color-force of Capricorn is the secondary deep maroon,

corresponding to the color-energies of the ultra-red of the spectrum. The general tendency of its (♑) forces are impelling, moving, and in the vegetable kingdom the trend is directly toward disintegration ; and, where life-forces are low in power, toward decay.

The period of greatest power is from December 21st to January 18th ; the Sun in Capricorn, the Earth in Cancer.

The planet Saturn is in greatest sympathy with the energies of Capricorn.

AQUARIUS.—The chord of Aquarius is Cancer. The great sympathy between the energies of the principal and those of its chord is noted in the fact that in the lower forms of life, and in the lowest grades of mentality, the forces of Aquarius are the dominant elements in the preservation of the species—so considered.

The color-sympathy of Aquarius is the tertiary salmon. The dominant general direction of its forces are nutrifying, and, secondarily, those of receptive sensibility.

The period of greatest power is from January 19th to February 17th ; the Sun in Aquarius, the Earth in Leo, the static pole of Aquarius.

The planet Uranus is in greatest sympathy with this sign, and his ill-influences are largely attributed to his sensitiveness and trend toward sense-intemperance.

THE TWELVE SIGNS.

Their Symbols ; Time ; Function ; Color and Nature.

Their astronomical elements : Right Ascension ; Declination ; Latitude and Longitude ; Constellations in which the Signs are found.

A description of the character of those born under each sign ; followed by the influences of the Moon under the relationships of each of the Signs.

The relation of the Constellations of the Zodiac to the equator and ecliptic, with the principal stars in each constellation named.

Headpieces from EPHEMIRIDES, in imitation of old English woodcut.

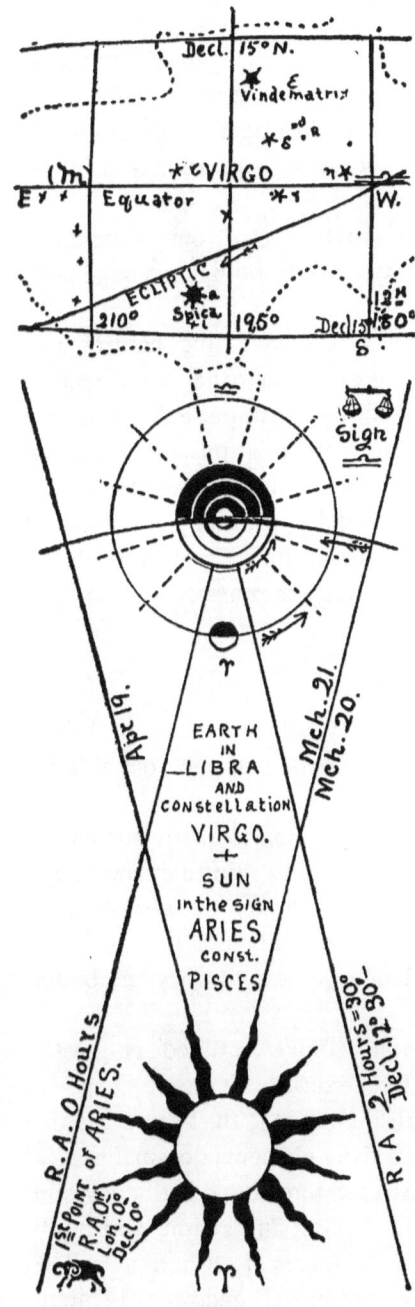

FIG. 24.

♈. ☉ in ♈, ⊕ in ♎; March 21st to April 19th. Letters; Blue; Relating.

This nature is distinguished by great retentiveness; it has a wide grasp of the course of events, remembers personalities with remarkable ease, has generally a proportionately large amount of literary ability, and, perhaps more than anything else, is noted for its capacity to disseminate knowledge of a general and useful kind.

The Aries nature is the kind that makes the proficient teacher, particularly of languages, music, and of history. It generally has a good voice, a keen sensibility to music, and a wide range of expression. Few signs have a deeper insight into the inter-relations of ideas or the natural responsibilities of human life.

(51)

This nature responds to ♃ ; thus it admires aggressiveness and wealth, or at least the presence of more than common comfort. It sympathizes with ♍, and therefore is fond of home life. It chords most finely with ♊. This last gives power to expression and intensity to friendship.

The Aries nature should marry a native of ♊ or one of its Solar polarity, ♎, as it often, if not always, needs both encouragement and governing suggestion.

It is truthfully said that ♈ natures are governing natures and natural leaders, which is true to the extent that they are directive natures, and in regard to thought and mental impulse, but not true when they turn their attention to the commercial phases of life, as they lack the defensive and impulsive forces in full strength.

The Aries nature is subject to mental oppression, often lasting two or more days, due doubtless to unusual intensity of thought or action, the remedy being rest and enforced calmness.

♈. ☽ in ♈.

This nature (unless well balanced by other planets in Aries) is not well endowed with regard to the social and generous side of the Aries nature.

The ☽ here gives Aries natures a disposition to quarrelsomeness, verbosity, and to misrepresentation in order to gain their own way. The ☽ here also gives added artistic skill, though not always practiced or put to the best use. It is wise to study and practice self-government, the judicious use of language, and to obey the better of life's impulses.

With ♃ or ♀ in Aries, the nature above outlined is greatly modified and made more frank and generous.

With ♄, ♅ or ♂ in Aries (with the moon), the nature has the sarcastic, pessimistic, and the antagonistic elements dominant.

The ☽ in this region gives the Aries nature added brilliancy and imaginative power, independence in thought and action, and in all these directions is in sympathy with the forces of ♃ and ♀. The characteristic intellectuality of Aries, when well endowed, is intensified by the ☽ when in the Aries region.

♈. ☽ in ♉.

Taurus, naturally the region of science, is also the region of intuition and imagination. Of these, the ☽ in Taurus stimulates principally the intuitive and imaginative elements, and, in a measure, gives spirituality to the Aries nature as well as exactness in details of thought and work; but it creates a somewhat restless and changeful disposition. Habits of steadiness, regularity, order and calmness should be cultivated. The disposition to overdo by spells should be governed, and the analytical method of reasoning carefully forwarded, along with the synthetic. Avoid severity, harshness and impulsiveness.

♈. ☽ in ♊.

The ☽ in Gemini gives intensity to the friendship and mimetic capacities of Aries, but its chief disposition is in the direction of added sentimentality and emotiveness.

To the directness and vividness of Aries, the ☽ in Gemini gives gracefulness, plausibility, ease of expression, and sometimes inclines the nature toward mimicry. It gives stronger love of harmony in both colors and music.

♈. ☽ in ♋.

The ☽ in Cancer gives the Aries nature more of a sense of sex-harmony than any other Lunar influence of Aries. It adds to the appreciation of delicate expression, of graceful attentions, and gives full force to the imaginative and ideal side of marriage.

The ☽ in Cancer depresses the vocal power and gives mildness to the voice; adapts the mentality to writing rather than to speaking. It also intensifies the social and religious nature of Aries. There is a slight added liability to nervous and anæmic diseases.

♈. ☽ in ♌.

The Leo nature has the religious affections dominant, the love-nature of the race for the race; it is, therefore, the impersonal region of devotion. The Moon, in its sway, gives to this nature impulses of susceptibility to emotion, to vivid imaginative habits, and to sentimentality. It increases social harmony, but not mental brilliancy, as many suppose. It produces (in Aries) religious bigotry and fanaticism unless well endowed otherwise, and sometimes gives a love of mystery, and a desire to press their views upon others, advocating maintained theories with poetic descriptions, with metaphor, simile and hyperbole.

The natural versatility of Aries makes the above manner of expression easy, while the usual directness of that character greatly varies the mental attitudes taken.

The digestive organs are usually subject to disease and weakness. The heart and arterial systems are active and enduring.

♈. ☽ in ♍.

Virgo, as we find under its description, is the region of Familism, and the ☽ in Virgo has a peculiar effect upon the Aries mentality.

Aries is not often much inclined toward familism; but here the ☽ gives great Platonic interest in children and a tender and curious love for the young of both the vegetable and animal kingdom. It instills an interest in biology and spiritual science. It leads to the study of psychological growth. It intensifies the Aries nature in its sensuousness to the world around, and gives to the male sex of that mentality somewhat of the intuitive sensitiveness of woman's. None the less, however, it adds vigor and nutritive force, and raises the power to withstand the attacks of disease and of mental oppression to which the Aries nature is often liable.

♈. ☽ in ♎.

Here the ☽ arouses in Aries a powerful sense of chivalric justice, the blending of ideality with human right. It gives a desire for political interests, and usually inspires toward a very radical social cause. The thought-action is as vivid as ever, but inclined to delay judgment; and this has led to misinterpretation by astrologers, many of whom thought the reasoning of this "polarity" was both low and slow, but intuitive. In fact the ☽ in Libra, the solar polarity of Aries (the Earth being between Aries and the Sun) gives to Aries a remarkably analytical capacity, closely allied to the Taurus nature, and a sense of equity and social justice not excelled by any other lunar influence. They are good judges, painstaking, earnest and free from personal prejudices; they abhor harshness, war and misery; love originality, dignity and elegance.

These mentalities also have great versatility in method and processes of physical accomplishment, often learning several trades or arts, and continually demonstrating great perseverance. This location intensifies the elements of sex-devotion and gives Aries greater self-control and government of temper than any other.

♈. ☽ in ♏.

This mentality is a combination of the powers of mental and physical expression and the idealistic and emotive, giving great industry when in action, and a reciprocal reaction when not under exertion.

The ☽ in this region of Aries gives energy, perseverance, executiveness, with a desire for great freedom; independence in manner and method, and an inclination toward a more practical life than is the natural Aries possession.

The larger planets more easily counteract the lunar influence in this region than in any other. There is an increased liability to diseases of the organs of circulation. It increases the muscular power in the lumbar and locomotor muscles, but in a mental direction sometimes decreases the normal expression of the Aries mentality.

♈. ☽ in ♐.

The ☽ in Sagittarius gives Aries a nativity at once aggressive, energetic, dogmatic, and often illogical as a consequence. The temper is quickened and ill-governed; there is a mixture of commercial desire, selfishness and prodigality that is rarely successful, and if financially so, is rarely happy. It is a nature that is enduring through nervous energy and muscular tone; suffers the consequences of its actions without acknowledgment of fault; is a decided enemy, but also a persistent friend as long as there can be agreement.

This mentality should, through youth, be calmly reasoned with, punished rarely, and always by denial rather than by attack or aggression, and given a thorough training in commercial arithmetic, methods and practical life.   The theory and logic will be easy deductions from experience.

This nature is liable to intemperance because of intensity, and should (by thorough explanations) be trained to avoid licentiousness and ethical obliquity.

♈.   ☽ in ♑.

Capricorn is the region of commerce, and responds to the powerful motive-faculties that move mankind in his search for interchange in the products of his labor.

The ☽ in Capricorn region of the Aries nativity combines the intense artistic influences of the ☽ with the commercial power of Capricorn, adding these to Aries, and thus gives positiveness, force and determination.   It also adds much to the ingenuity of Aries' characteristics, making that nature more money-getting in disposition, but seldom more economical in its use.

This mentality is often exacting, often severe, and in cases of opposition is very destructive to old methods or means.

When interested in reforms, this nativity is sarcastic and aggressive in attacks upon all opponents.   There is no particular liability to disease.

♈.   ☽ in ♒.

The idealizer of the home, of home life, of the beautiful, artistic and delicate—Aries, with the Moon in Aquarius. This influence of the ☽ in the Aries region is at once one of the most favorable and sympathetic of all its effects.

The ☽ here idealizes the elements of parental and of filial love. It arouses an ambition to be patriotic—even grandiloquently so.

There is often in this mentality a delightful sense of fraternity, a desire to make life a blessing to all sensuous things, to add to the pleasure of all existence.

Sometimes this nature is inclined toward intemperance in food and drink.

♈.   ☽ in ♓.

Pisces is the home of the ☽, and in the Aries nature it places the region of the two influences too close together.   But even here the ☽ gives Aries a vivid imagination and added artistic skill, capable of mastering almost any mechanical art. This nativity has usually great sensitiveness, is often quarrelsome, and generally unsuccessful in financial matters and in getting the results of their capabilities, or a due remuneration for their skill.

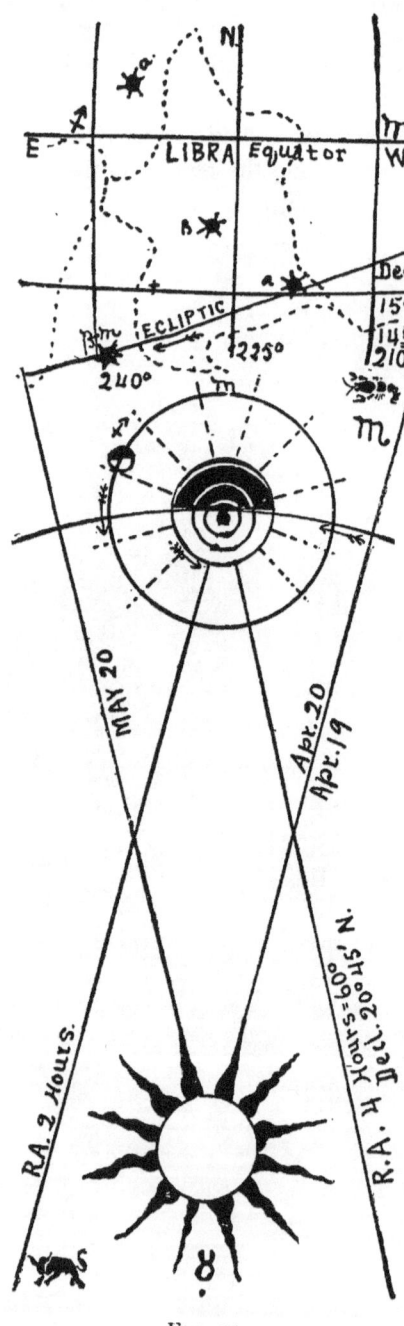

FIG. 25.

♉. ☉ in ♉, ⊕ in ♏; April 20th to May 20th. Science; Azure; Intertwining.

This nature is full of inspiration, of keen foresight, and, if endowed with ♃ in Leo, with great spirituality. But these qualities are often lost sight of in the deep trend of such a nature toward science and investigation. ☉ in Taurus nativities are noted for their exactness and their persistence in a mental struggle. But this nature often needs assistance. It is seldom capable of great financial plans, and, as it responds most easily to Scorpio, is almost always more generous with its mental and physical labors than it is able in demanding remuneration for its accomplishments.

A great range of natural sciences are within the sphere of

this nature's activity, the choice depending much upon the endowment of the parental heredity and upon the planetary polarities.

It should cultivate aggressiveness and self-defence. Responding to Cancer also, it depends much for happiness upon affection from one of the opposite sex.

This nativity should marry one born in the regions of its Solar polarity, Scorpio, or of its chord, Pisces.

This personality should exercise the greatest calmness and reserve in making choice of mate and time of marriage.

♉. ☽ in ♈.

The ☽ in Aries of the Taurus nature gives a very intense, vivid and energetic element to the cautious, scientific Taurus mentality. It adds descriptive power, and gives delicacy to the intuitions of the Taurus nature.

*Acting as a stimulant to the constructive and imaginative elements, often creates power in inventiveness, great ideality and capacity to demonstrate ideas, which usually have had a careful consideration before acceptance.

♉. ☽ in ♉.

This nature, having invariably the new ☽ and the ☉ in Taurus, is a most powerful combination of constructive energies and imaginative power; inventive in not only the mechanical, but in the philosophical range of mental conceptions. It seeks to most fully comprehend physics and philosophy, to join these by intuition and imagination; with all a very wide and sincere emotiveness. This gives to Taurus an unusual element of intense sympathy.

In fact, this combination gives to Taurus nativities much of the mentality of Aries with ♃ and ♀ influences.

The ☽ in Taurus gives also great industry, dignity, positiveness, self-control, and, if the planetary influences are favorable, pride and egotism. This stimulant gives boldness in effort, great consecutiveness, and in many ways proves a powerful resisting capacity not only in mental, but in physical self-protection. The ☽ here finds a thoroughly sympathetic region of influence; its home in Pisces is a cord of Taurus; hence an artistic sensibility, and, thus, often the power to learn a number of trades or lines of artistic work.

There is taste for landscaping, seed gardening, floriculture and horticulture. The usefully beautiful and the plainly essential are about equally blended in this nature.

In personal manners it is generally dignified and somewhat formal until exceptionally well acquainted, when there is an omission of further extreme formality.

♉. ☽ in ♊.

The Gemini nature has the forces of culture dominant, and the ☽ in this region stimulates, in a mild degree, those elements in the Taurus mentality; thus increasing the desire to illustrate and convey ideas, but, more than anything else, it adds friendliness and congeniality to the generally conservative mentality of Taurus.

The poetic element is increased, and the social instincts made more emotive and generous. In some respects this inclines Taurus toward natural science studies, but largely on account of the love of beauty and of comfort.

♉. ☽ in ♋.

This mentality is energized in the direction of home life, particularly the marriage elements; and has added idealism, imagination, artistic power and love of elegance, with increased emotion and tenderness.

The elements of this nature that are in a measure selfish, are essential; essential to overcome the natural tendency to devote time to financially unproductive investigation, and to stimulate a proper care for the protection of the home and its needs.

The reasoning organs need to be stimulated in the direction of an analytical method, as those faculties are much inclined to synthetic judgments.

In childhood this nativity needs more than ordinary tenderness in manner of government, and parents should cultivate government in their own natures in order to avoid the general irritableness so often found in the parental control of sensitive children.

♉. ☽ in ♌.

This nativity is usually overestimated by those who delineate by the various planetary methods.

Taurus with the ☽ in Leo is a severe mixture of reasoning stubbornness and ambitious orthodoxy, and, while capable, goes tc many extremes in both habits and opinions. Their appetites are acute and often voracious, but pride usually governs them in this direction. Calmness of choice and discretion in the quantity of food and drink taken is essential.

This location of the ☽ adds to the attractive faculties and strengthens the domestic affections, intensifying the love of children and generally the element of constancy toward wife or husband, as the case may be. Some other social elements are at times intensified, but seldom ungoverned.

♉. ☽ in ♍.

The regional influence over Taurus when the moon is in Virgo is almost as powerful as it is when in Libra, at which point it is almost between the ⊕ and ☉.

As we see under the nativity of Virgo, the family life and national patriotism, the new ☽ of the Taurus nature has great home provisional proclivities, is self-protecting, intuitive and keen.

These elements of force lead to self-aggrandizement, to self-upbuilding, and in every way toward acuteness and power as well as analytical judgment.

Often very successful in the scientific professions, this nature is thus seldom in sympathy with the methods of the past, generally discredits the unexamined work of others, and in many ways breaks new territory in the field of adventure.

♉. ☽ in ♎.

The powerful, but also very positive intuitions of Taurus are stimulated by this regional influence of the ☽. The mentality is therefore intuitive, sympathetic, sensitive, and yet logical.

The first opinions are intuitive, later judgment logical.

The nature is fitted, if well endowed, to take a place in the legal world; to join in political movements; to take part in practical, sometimes profound, movements toward the advancement of human society.

This personality is often minus the elements of sentiment and regard for the weak and misguided or misinformed, and expects all people to as readily understand deep problems as does its own mentality.

The liability to diseases falls principally upon the eliminative system—kidneys, skin and liver. The strict avoidance of stimulants and narcotics is advised.

♉. ☽ in ♏.

This region of the Moon's influence is the solar polarity of Taurus, being, as the ⊕ is, between the ☉ and ☽. This creates the intensest executive manner; the region of Scorpio being the region of dynamic perseverance, executive industry, self-dependence and industrial productivity.

It is because Scorpio is the sign of labor and justice, as well as of production, that that sign was so widely degraded by astrologers of earlier times, and so maintained by later ones—as their chief mode of existence depended upon the enlargement of human ills, and their skill in convincing the nobility and aristocracy that the science of astrology might keep them from the path that led to the degraded and dreaded world of human labor and the vocations of mechanics or of agriculture.

But Scorpio's influence is, as we shall see under that sign, the region of industrial integrity and co-operative power.

The ☽ and ⊕ in Scorpio, the ☉ in Taurus, gives an intensely independent, active, productive capacity, stimulating toward great utility, and turning the science of Taurus into mechanical and industrial lines.

♉. ☽ in ♐.

The elements of imaginative and constructive science as applied to commercial matters are intensified in the Taurus mentality by this location of the ☽. There is also much more self-defensive determination in commercial matters, with added economic ability.

The mentality is apt to be quick and somewhat fiery in temper, and needs to exercise calmness when under any kind of attack.

But there is less liability to any destructive tendencies, than is the case of the Capricorn lunar influence of Taurus.

The social nature of this combination is apt to be very blunt, direct and unchangeable. But under all this is an intense interest in kinship, and a set determination to protect the family and the friend.

There is an absence of flourish and of sentimentality, but the attachments of affection are usually strong and deep.

♉. ☽ in ♑.

The commercial and engineering capacities of Taurus are aroused by this regional influence of the ☽. But the severe, harsh and determined faculties of the will are most stimulated, giving that kind of temper.

There is an inclination toward emotional anger, stubborn insistence upon every personal right; and these often lead to a military career. On the other hand the lines of transportation, railroading and steamboating are often chosen as a vocation.

The mentality seeks to put its skill and thought to the most practical uses.

The nature is thus positive, determined, self-controlled in the pursuit of its own choice and desires; resistant in its forces toward the desires of others. Both sexes have that element of personal responsibility so developed that their own judgment takes precedence over the opinions of others in all cases.

The youth of this mentality should be governed by reasoning, direct statements of fact, by care not to usurp their rights, and thus by evidence carry conviction where the use of force would fail to do more than arouse antagonism.

♉. ☽ in ♒.

This regional influence gives Taurus an increased volume of sentiment and social polish, with a keen incentive toward personal elegance and diplomacy.

These nativities have much personal force and activity, and a large amount of physical strength and nutritive power.

In some ways these persons are given to extravagance in matters of appearance and like to display their taste, always desirous of making a good impression.

In the nature of women this location of the ☽ gives some characteristics of vanity and self-laudation.

The whole mentality has a supersensitiveness to the senses of taste and smell, and to the effects of foods upon the body and brain. When interested in home cares this nativity has a very capable grasp of all the details.

♉. ☽ in ♓.

Pisces is a chord of Taurus, as Art is the handmaid of Science. It is also the home region of the ☽, and thus combines in giving the normal scientific and reflective character of Taurus a gleam of artistic capacity, with vivid imagination and periodicity in habit; likewise a practical, ingenious, constructive skill. There is a tendency to dabble in too many things, to vary from one cause to another, and to lack the volume of stability needed in any branch of human endeavor in this age of forceful competition.

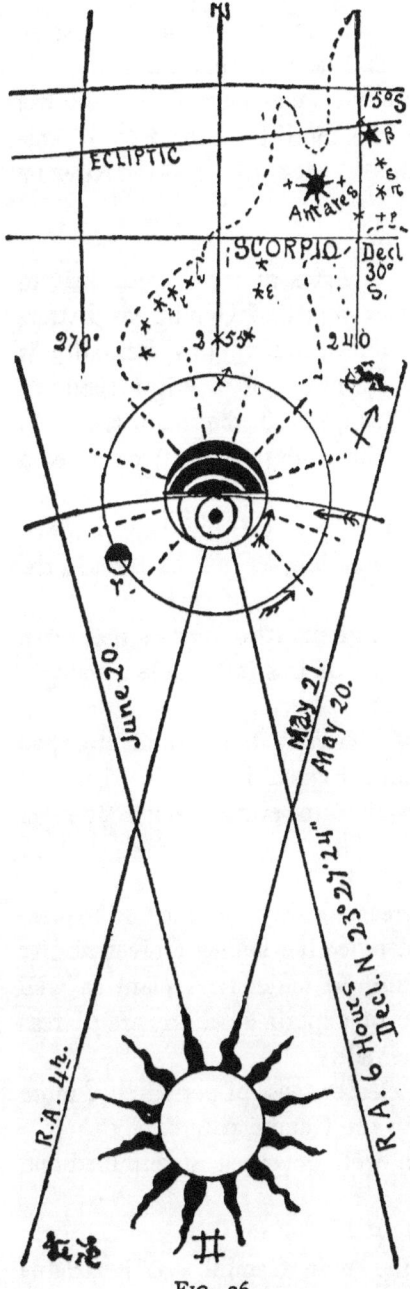

Fig. 26.

♊. ☉ in ♊, ⊕ in ♐;
May 21st to June 20th. Culture; Emerald; Calming.

This nature has as its dominant characteristics the range of friendship, and of expression. It is the personality of intense kindness and benevolence, capable in elegant gesture and graceful activities; as it responds to Libra and to Leo, is often found in political life and in the halls of legislation.

This nature is often inclined toward the various literary and legal vocations, for it is strongly influenced by its chord Aries, or its response, Libra.

Perhaps no other nativity has as wide a range of choice and of activity as this (♊), and none are less specific in vocational desire.

(65)

This mentality is the mentality of elegance of habit, just as Pisces is the mentality of elegance and taste in appointment.

This nature is generally fortunate in its marriage choice, and has little to ward against, unless badly influenced by ☋ or ♄. If feminine, this nature should mate with ♈, ♎ or with ♐ —the latter its Solar polarity.

♊. ☽ in ♈.

The regional influence of the ☽ in Aries of the Gemini nature is a sympathetic one, for Aries is a chord of Gemini, as Letters chord with Culture [Merton]. The trend of this mentality is toward the love of culture, of learning, of poetical thought, literature and idealistic study. This gives, in the main, the addition of elegance of expression to the intense attractiveness of a powerful friendship.

Well endowed hereditarily, it gives political and legal endowments; activity in the realm of instruction, as well as taste in the formulation of ideas.

This mentality loves freedom, and grants it to others; it is often radical, shunning dogmatic forms, and desires independent thought as well as natural rules of action.

Women of this endowment are generally tender and attentive mothers, but not often strong and rugged in health, therefore should have the utmost consideration in every manner of right living.

♊. ☽ in ♉.

This regional influence gives great ideality, delicacy of expression, love of science and of the reflective studies; gives ability to teach, to practice medicine, and to understand plant as well as animal life. The whole range of experimental arts are of reasonable accomplishment to this mentality.

There is an added regularity, a clearer sense of periodicity, more uniformity in effect than is usual to the Gemini nature.

To the above is often added a well governed, determined and brave will.

♊. ☽ in ♊.

The Gemini mentality, with the ☽ in Gemini, has invariably the last of the old and early part of the new phase of the ☽, with the ☉ apparently in Gemini. Hence the ☽ has here solar sympathy; the ☽ between the ☉ and ⊕ gives to Gemini but few conflicting energies and many harmonizing ones; these are the stimulated forces of intense friendship and kindness, with love for human kind and considerations that lead to generosity in opinion as well as philanthropy in matters of means and wealth.

The ☽ in Gemini gives that nature a peculiar combination of good nature, wit and kindness, mixed with a dreamy, imaginative, sensuous love of art and beauty; there is inclination toward the occult in personal life and an interest in neurology.

When finely endowed parentally there is natural capacity to understand symbolism and synchronism and to perceive the harmonies of nature.

But this mentality needs resisting force, more defence, more solidity in regard to progressive methods, and the necessary volume of economy and executiveness. That is to say, in this age there seems but little provision for the financial success of the unaggressive.

When the ☽ is accompanied by ♃ (in less degree when by ♆), there are more practical elements in the nature; ♀ gives added artistic passion; ☋ gives pensiveness, sometimes peevishness and penuriousness and disposition to futile accumulation.

♊. ☽ in ♋.

The Gemini nature, with the ☽ in Cancer, is little influenced by any of the planets in other regions. There is an added intensity of affection, and much idealistic tenderness in expressing it. It gives Gemini much of the Aquarius habit of expression.

♊. ☽ in ♌.

This influence is a combination of deep friendship, intense religious feelings, wide imagination, with emotive and poetic energies. Added to these is also more than usual perception of ethical religious truth.

The intuitive reception of truth differs widely from the reflective and scientific. The first is particularly a favorable method to this nature.

But this nativity should seek to be practical, to see the world as it is, and to make success one of positive effort rather than of negative desire. In reform, the tendency should be toward certainty and plan and avoiding the method of negative or inactive conviction.

For one of this nativity, this advice is good : Avoid all doubt as to personal success; strive to be positive, forceful, calm, self-governed and regular in method and work; the world is, to one of this nature, large or small, good, bad or indifferent, just as they make it, take it or expect it.

II. ☽ in ♍.

The ☽ in this region arouses in the Gemini mentality a powerful parental force; the energy of patriotism, of generous support, and in some ways of positivism.

There is added parental love, some increase in the love of children, added intensity of love for the opposite sex; a larger capacity to understand the needs of home and of social life. There is an increased desire for public life and a greater ambition to take part in political contests, to advance social culture, and to cultivate adaptability to the responsibilities of government.

There is often a very remarkable poetic capacity; sometimes exceptional musical or verbal talent.

The imaginative element should be kept well in hand. This mentality is orderly and elegant, careful, vivid, full of fun ; sometimes sarcastic and Socratic. In midlife should be very temperate, calm and judicious.

II. ☽ in ♎.

This mentality is a combination of great friendship, kindness, imitativeness, and philanthropy, on the one hand, and conscious dignity, self-control and force on the other.

There is added spirituality in habit and in force, a large amount of occult power, keen insight, and particularly so in regard to the nature and needs of others.

There is also in this regional influence great sensitiveness to surrounding conditions, to the physical influences of plants and mineral products, and a natural understanding of all animal life. It is very sympathetic with the Aries mentality; is quick to perceive responses of nerve force and of spiritual energies; it is in many ways given to new lines of work and to new views of human progress.

II. ☽ in ♏.

The Gemini nativity with the ☽ in Scorpio, is forced forward by the dynamic labor and executive energies of the latter region; to the tender and delicate friendship of the primary sign is added an element of positive execution much needed by the nativity.

The influence of Scorpio has often been deprecated by astrologers; there could then almost always be found a place for stress of restraint or excuse for any defect in moral or social career. That all mental faculties normally developed were essentially good was not a part of the earlier astrology any more than it was of other philosophies.

II. ☽ in ♐.

This regional influence of the ☽ brings the ☽ and ☉ in the same angle from the ⊕ and gives great commercial impetus to the mentality. It adds intensity to the wealth elements of Gemini, often makes the nature erratic in judgment and desirous of undertaking great speculative labors and problems. It is sometimes visionary, full of hypothetical schemes, and a little more excitable than is judicious in order to develop a successful character.

But this mentality often has an admirable quality and quantity of tenderness and much solicitation in the interests of family and friends. The Gemini personality, with the ☽ in Sagittarius, lives as much for others as for self.

In youth this nativity is usually oversensitive, generally nervous, full of activity and perseverance; sensitive to digestive troubles, to lack of nutritive supply, and thus requires generous treatment in many directions.

II. ☽ in ♑.

The presence of the ☽ in Capricorn of the Gemini nature gives an earnest and direct habit to all this personality. It adds commercial qualities and enlarges the judgment on methods of financial procedure, and at times gives brilliant views of business possibilities.

However, unless well endowed by parental influences and planetary forces, there will be an overplus of visionary and managerial enthusiasm.

The mentality is often much more distrustful of others than is usually the case with the Gemini nativity. There is also present a tendency toward egotism and display; sometimes over-sociability, disposition to waste time, to elaborate ideas beyond any need, and thus lose caste in friendship.

But love of travel, capacity for acute observation, with a wide range of synthetic judgments, makes their nature entertaining in manner when the time is limited to reasonable bounds.

II. ☽ in ♒.

Aquarius is the sign of home, of nutritive power, and of impression to psychometric forces. The ☽ in this region of the Gemini nativity is essentially conserving. There is a decided disposition toward agriculture, gardening, and study of pomology and botany, and their practical utilization. The influence of the ☽ in this sign of Gemini is often overestimated, and especially in regard to its financial importance and power.

II. ☽ in ♓.

This regional influence of the ☽ is one of the most powerful of those belonging to this nativity. It adds a fund of elegance and taste to the intense natural friendship, and gives full sway to the idealism and imaginative emotions of Gemini.

There is intense benevolence, generosity and hopefulness in the influence. On the other hand this combination lacks the calm judicious estimation of financial and productive efforts. It is likely to be extravagant of means at its command, fails to grasp the essential benefits of surrounding conditions, and should strive to become familiar with the problems of utility, of human economic progress, of rights and duties that devolve upon the intelligent portion of mankind.

The advice is to study ethics, justice, human natural law, practical art: to gain a vocation useful to the race and remunerative in return.

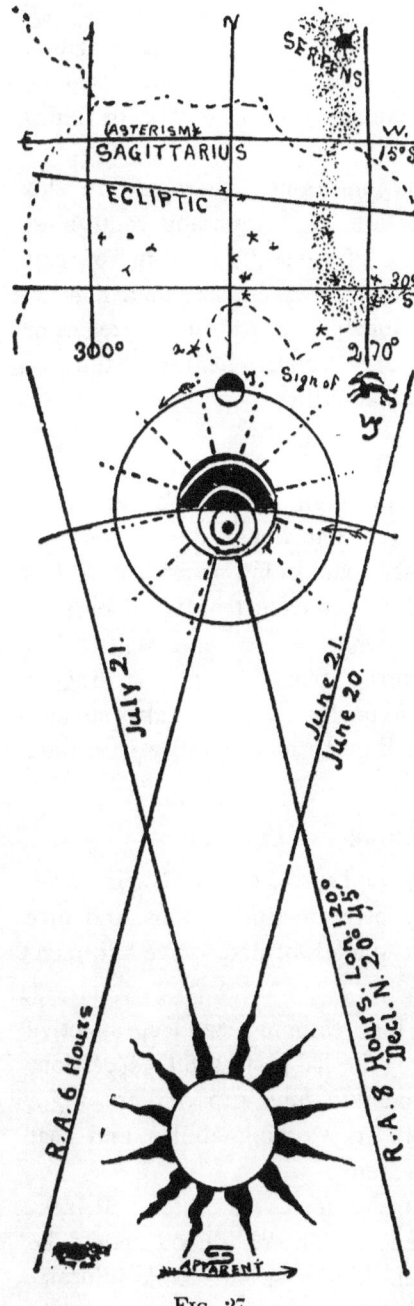

FIG. 27.

♋. ☉ in ♋, ⊕ in ♑; June 21st to July 21st. Marriage: Orange; Animating.

This nature is dominant in devotion and in family life, in strong and intense sexuality; is ardent as husband or wife.

Responding to the region of ♏ (or Co-action in Mentality), this nature is fond of work and of activity in the productive pursuits. It desires to fulfill its own measure of responsibility, to accomplish all the good possible to its strength and mental capacity.

This nature is cautious in outlays, but often discreetly generous, always just, when finely endowed with power, and particularly when ☋ is found in Capricorn, the ⊕'s place in this period of time.

This nativity responds to

(71)

Taurus, and has much of the delicate intuitions of that region; often marries the Taurus nativity, and almost as often that of Aquarius—a mental cord. For financial success, unity with Capricorn is most favorable.

As Cancer is sensitive to nervous conditions, due regard for this fact should be taken into consideration. Children and youth must be equitably governed, information of value in relation to their physical nature should be given, and care taken that their lives be made to run in useful and enjoyable paths, avoiding extremes or excess in any injurious direction. Self-government can thus be made the basis of their thought and activities.

♋. ☽ in ♈.

The influence of the ☽ in the Aries region of the Cancer nature is very marked, but not as beneficial as one would like. There are present many elements of imaginative ambition; there are desires of great personal advancement without sufficient tenacity of purpose and concentration to gain the end sought.

The wilfulness is spasmodic, quickly changed; it is lacking in consecutiveness as well as in judicial power. This mentality should, therefore, seek the combination of dignity and stability with their natural energy and intrinsic power.

♋. ☽ in ♉.

This regional influence of the ☽ in Taurus, of the Cancer nativity, gives a strong inclination to constructive professions, and love of the mechanical arts, of reflective studies, of descriptive and technical elegance.

The strong forces aroused are the reasoning and reproductive energies; the elements of regularity in habit, forceful expression, splendid digestive power, and moderate lung capacity, making a combination that varies greatly in its working ability, and that needs "humoring" to a marked extent.

This nature is sensitive to the nerve forces of others. It lacks aggressive power, or, at least, defence. The childhood should be ruled by mature judgment, counsel, kindness, and frank information on all subjects in which an interest is aroused.

♋. ☽ in ♊.

The combination of periodicity of habit and deep emotions, close friendships and intense devotion, love of children and of life, an interest in all that is beautiful, spiritual and ennobling, is present here.

But there is in this nativity a sensitiveness that needs protecting, protection by the developing of firmness, self-reliance, and by due recognition of the necessities of the age in which we live. This nature must grow self-reliant, forceful, powerful, productive and cautious.

♋. ☽ in ♋.

The ☽ in Cancer gives that sign a bright, active habit. It is generally synthetic, dislikes long analytical tasks, prefers matters of common and general interest, and often fails because of a trend toward inexactness. This nativity should cultivate attentiveness to details, should govern the affectional and emotive elements of its nature, should study economics and commercial laws, and take time to thoroughly organize its plans and work, as well as range of ideas.

There is apt to be vague conceptions of deep subjects, and a disposition to shun them because of the study required in their mastery.

♋. ☽ in ♌.

The ☽ in the region Leo, of this nature, is a powerful energy, causing much more expression of the love of race and the greater family than is usually the case in the great mass of mentalities.

The ☽ here adds humanitarian forces to those of marriage life, broadens the nature, widens the range of harmonic vision, and gives incentives toward the cultivation of moral and spiritual power.

The location of the major planets greatly influences this nativity.

♋. ☽ in ♍.

The ☽ in this region of the Cancer nativity gives a very vivid conception of beauty, love of the mysterious, weird, strange and profound, but not the kind of intellectual power that can treat of these in their scientic aspects.

The emotions are intensified, particularly so in love of family, for mate and for kindred.

In the direction of artistic sense, this nature is apt to be critical rather from intuition than from artistic study or exhaustive examination.

Love of travel, and of vocations that require movement and change, is present.

This nature appreciates elegance in movement and in form; works ceaselessly to gain the appreciation of others in matters of surroundings and personal deportment, of the home life and its associations.

♋. ☽ in ♎.

This is the ideal regional influence of the ☽ in Cancer mentality. The ☽ here gives power to the emotions, to the high organs of the brain, with intensity to the most benevolent and aspiring thoughts and feelings. It arouses the elements of rulership in the personality of the subject, gives control, firmness, power and activity to the will as well as to the affections.

We expect to find here a blending of the attainments of the intellect with the tenderness and attractiveness of the affections and the executive power of the will.

This mentality is often very capable in authorship, judgeship, and in situations requiring a well-blended character.

♋. ☽ in ♏.

The dominant influences of this position are in the direction of progressive industrial life; in the application of powerful motives in production and organization. But there is also an intense desire for justice, for sincere advancement and personal liberty.

In childhood this nativity has a great amount of self-will, is often angular and quick-tempered, suffering much under restraint; and should be governed with great moderation, generous and kindly impulses, by those who are responsible for its care and education.

♋. ☽ in ♐.

The ☽ here arouses in the Cancer nature the acutest sense of regularity in method. It creates capacity for idealistic and forceful plans, with a somewhat more intense financial and economic attitude than is usually present in the Cancer mentality.

There is a desire to give offspring a grand start in the world of contention, to provide them with financial as well as mental endowments that are required, as is supposed, to make a worldly success. Unlike the Sagittarius nature, this combined influence will not forego the pleasures of life in order merely to accumulate wealth; but it will make enjoyment arise, as far as possible, from the gaining of position and comfort.

This nativity very often mates with that of Capricorn, and thus gains the assistance of one endowed with an abundance of very active financial traits.

♋. ☽ in ♑.

The presence of the ☽ in this region of influence is always a beneficial one to Cancer, and adds to this nativity a strong inclination toward original thought in the world of enterprise and in the general conduct of life.

The ☽ induces a sense of ideality and grandeur, it gives incentives toward great purposes, it impels onward to the realm of social excellence and virtue, it finds zeal in giving the world an example of the beautiful in home life and the pleasures of successful providence.

♋. ☽ in ♒.

The Cancer mentality receives from this regional influence much of the patriotism of home life, love of social surroundings, and of kindred. It draws Cancer out of its narrowed limits and widens the view of personal life and destiny, giving broader relationships and interests, and thus makes of surroundings a more harmonious whole.

In expression this nature is often direct, very frank, and calls attention to the vital element of support or of opposition.

♋. ☽ in ♓.

The deeply affectionate nature of Cancer, with its brilliant intuitive impressiveness and spirituality, is given an added artistic capacity by this regional influence of the ☽. As art is a practical part of all mechanical and constructive work, the ☽ here arouses that group of powers, and generally turns the Cancer mentality toward mechanical arts, art work and symbolical interpretation.

The brain is always active (compared with like hereditary conditions under other influences), the senses keen, the perceptives unusually strong, and the body has great power of expression.

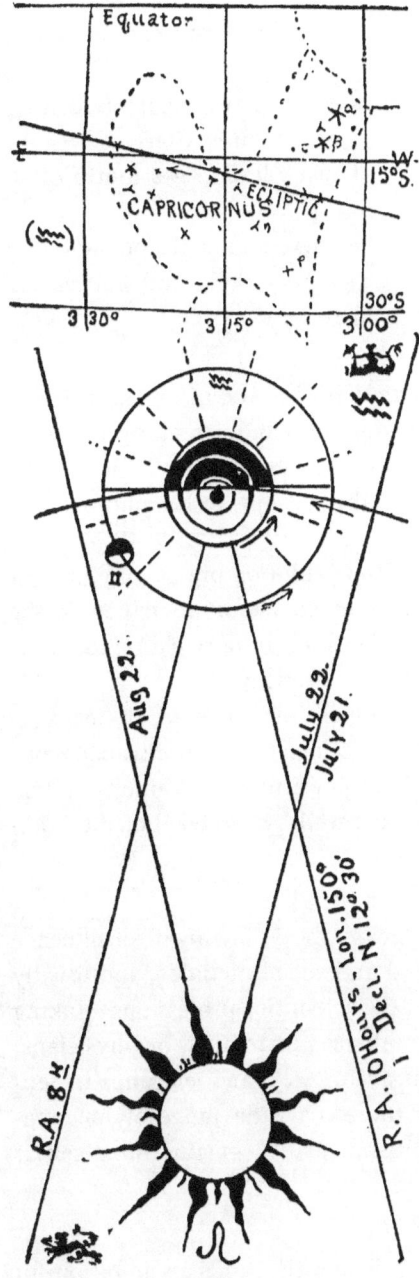

FIG. 28.

♌. ☉ in ♌, ⊕ in ♒;
July 22d to August 22d. Religion; Yellow; Unifying.

This nature is that of mental harmony: warm, sunny and genial; often endowed with great vitality and force that is used in persuasion and in corrective lines. The dominant elements of this nature are faith and confidence. In business urgent rather than aggressive, aspiring to power through eloquence and vigor.

This nature is seldom constructive. It takes things and ideas as they are found, it supports with fervor the "powers that be." It is conservative and yet responds in mental activity to Gemini in the field of culture, and to Libra in that of rulership, clinging more closely to the

(77)

latter, and using its static capacity to perpetuate and endorse social as well as personal conservatism.

This nature matures late, it sweeps over broad fields of feeling, interest and endorsement; is seldom selfish in matters of wealth, but always in matters of opinion; "Let me lead!"—a motto often seen in action.

As a whole, the activity should be mixed mental and muscular exertion, avoiding extremes of length in either, and cultivating calmness and a sense of dynamic values.

♌. ☽ in ♈.

The ☽ in Aries of the Leo mentality is a force of idealism, spontaneity, courage in opinion, but loving form and ceremony and deep distinctions in personal conduct as well as in religious beliefs. The added activity is often an excess; there is apt to be stubbornness and extreme rigidity of demand.

There is often a life conflict in the realm of philosophy, a conflict in which religion and science—the course of doctrine and the laws of nature—seem to antagonize, and, in unyielding contest, leave the aspirations in turmoil and uncertainty.

The vocation should be professional, the element of management dominant, with close relations to human social advancement.

The heart and lungs are usually powerful, the veinous system hardly adequate, the digestive organs well governed, but the brain and nervous system oversensitive.

♌. ☽ in ♉.

The Leo nature with ☽ in Taurus is always inclined to influence the world in the direction of moral and social methods, and usually adapts one of the learned, often the scientific, professions—taking as a life-work their place among biologists, naturalists or physicians.

In oratory there is often expressive power, and elegance in sentiment and movement; at times there is a wide range of imaginative power, but usually of an egotistic quality—maintaining self as the center of all plans of activity.

♌. ☽ in ♊.

This regional influence of the ☽ is one that adds an ambition for culture and high attainments, to the vigor and spontaneity of mental and physical habit of the base—Leo. But Gemini is always a general influence rather than a specific one, and hence Leo has a wide choice of life-work, but lacks in direct and distinct desires, as thus influenced by the ☽.

There is an intense element of personal freedom and personal method—a desire to be orderly in its own way—and to have others accept that order as absolute.

♌. ☽ in ♋.

The ☽ in Cancer is too much in sympathy, too near a combination with Leo to give really good results, and requires powerful planetary relations to give the mentality and body the relative amount of will and dynamic energy necessary to a complete and powerful character. ♄ in Scorpio, ♃ in Sagittarius, or ♀ in Libra would give the added energy required.

There is in this combination an over-abundance of the social nature, but a weakened tenacity, and Leo is not exact enough; the mind is inclined to be general in habit of thought, idealistic, imaginative, and dreamy.

♌. ☽ in ♌.

The ☽ and ☉ are here on the same side, in the same angle from the ⊕, and adds much that is valuable to the Leo nativity. The whole is complex and variable. There is practical power, artistic and graceful imagination. There is present vividness and convincing power. There is also in this mentality great general organizing capacity, particularly if well endowed planetarily and with good hereditary conditions. While the independence is marked, the attractions are strong. Thus, while often bigoted, will yet find deep companionship with those who hold similar views, and will work more successfully with those who are like themselves than can any other having a similar range of endowments.

These nativities will define their rights, insist upon a common method, and win by vital force where they would lose through lack of fierce will.

The planets exercise a diminished influence over the lunar forces in this sign.

♌. ☽ in ♍.

The ☽ in the ♍ region is in the chord of Leo, and adds to that broad and strong social nature distinct love of family, home, country and habitat. There is often need, however, of the practical elements of mental nature, and the person is subject to the criticism of being good, but unsuccessful.

There is need of an effort to shape life's actions to those ends which bring security and definite plan ; to exercise care in gaining a good start, a practical range of habit ; to wed a mate possessed of decision, facility in accomplishment, and a good fund of rulership.

♌. ☽ in ♎.

The regional influence of the ☽ in ♎ is that of self-rulership, but of a different order than when the ☉ is in that sign. The effect in general is to give the religious Leo habit a marked periodicity, regularity, plan and method, and thus to cause to be done in order what Leo would do in enthusiastic spontaneity if not governed or influenced.

But there is also an added element of mysticism, a love of occult views, as well as disposition to make much of every little personal incident.

This nature is in many ways adapted to religious teaching, to poetic interpretation, and to giving vivid descriptions of matters of which but a moderate amount of evidence is obtainable.

In feminine life there is more of the element of psychic insight, and a trend of thought and feeling that is decidedly emotional.

♌. ☽ in ♏.

The ☽ in Scorpio (the region of Ceres) is not a favorable location to the Leo nature, as it gives much dissatisfaction and sense of injustice inflicted, sometimes where none is intended or really exists.

But in matters of power there is no detraction. This mentality is able to lead, is full of energy, with capacity to mold others to its will.

There is independence in opinion, but little respect for dogmatic rules, and often the presence of great directive thought.

♌. ☽ in ♐.

The regional influence of the ☽ in Sagittarius, the sign region of Wealth, is one that inclines Leo to guard its interest in matters of wealth and enterprise. Leo, thus, an influence noncombative, is more aggressive, more scheming and economical; in many instances severe.

There is added imaginative power, and under extreme anger a tendency toward irrational action.

The mentality is quite hasty in judgment, synthetic in reasoning —judges by masses rather than by detail—and requires more careful training than is usual to the Leo nature.

♌. ☽ in ♑.

The ☽ in Capricorn gives the Leo nativities a wide range in commercial powers, but it is of an extremely social nature, demanding large acquaintanceships, and the opportunity to use friendships largely as a means of success.

This nativity is often a very exacting one ; it keeps close to its own methods and demands, and therefore has a plea for formality and positiveness.

Women of this nativity should seek physical freedom—bodily freedom—avoiding all worship of style and dress so far as any injurious restraint and cramping the vital functions is concerned.

♌. ☽ in ♒.

The ☽ here gives the Leo nativity a large faculty of appetite and love of luxury, with a rather unstable and in many ways ungoverned temper. The mentality needs to cultivate persistency, directness, plan and order. There should be careful consideration of all elements of success, and a clear view of the course to be taken in any predetermined direction.

Severe government of the appetites, of the nervous energies, of habits of expression, with a clear insight into the real needs as distinct from those supposed to be necessary and beneficial, are matters of greatest importance to this nature.

♌. ☽ in ♓.

The ☽, at home in Pisces, gives the Leo native a very fine and appreciative sense (perception) of the artistic and beautiful, and this, with great imaginative power and with synthetic reasoning, has the tendency to make the mentality very capable and accurate along artistic and mechanical lines.

But this nature is much more apt to be imitative than original; it lacks the elements of constancy and application, of steady trend in effort (unless so endowed by planetary regional influences), and is thus at a disadvantage in labors requiring long and persistent research and inquiry.

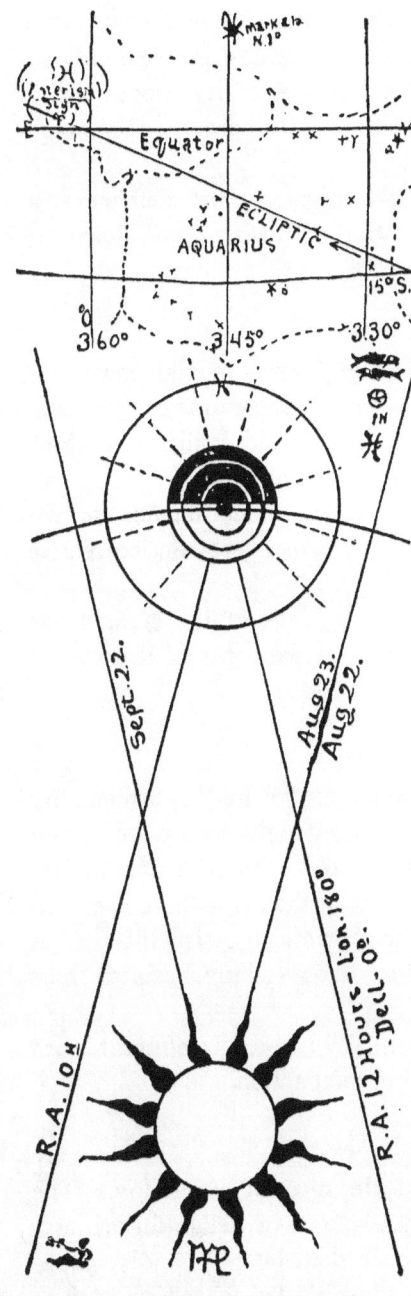

FIG. 29.

♍. ☉ in ♍, ⊕ in ♓; Aug. 23d to Sept. 22d. Familism; Amber; Supporting.

The dominant elements in this mentality are security and permanence. Trending, in this, widely to the perpetuation of the race, the wise control of its useful elements and the persistence of power. How much these comprise the aspirations of this nature can be seen by noting the responses it makes, first to Aries, the busy, active, intense and widely gainful region of the Intellect; and, second, to Sagittarius, the aggressive, defensive and fiery region of the Will. Toward both of these Virgo responds in activity, sometimes becoming almost dominant in either one or the other, but never relaxing its own fundamental field—the

(83)

family, tribal and national life. This nature often develops into the publicist, politician, often into the shrewdest business nature; and when it succeeds in uniting the activities of its responses with its chord Leo it gains great force and power to conserve the energy of others to its advantage.

Truly the combination of security, harmony and defence is a powerful one. It often unites in mating with Pisces, and joins the practical with the elegant.

♍. ☽ in ♈.

The ☽ in Aries of the Virgo nativity gives mental power, intellectuality, order, system and regularity to the efforts of that mentality. The whole nature is thus governed, and inclined to think that no action goes well unless by measured method.

But there is a lively sense of mirth, a native good-humor and wit in constant play; while all fault-finding is of a sarcastic, corrective kind, without anger.

The ☽ and ☉ are on nearly opposite sides of the ⊕, and the play of forces between them gives light to the night of this soul, a genial, spiritual, harmonic nature.

♍. ☽ in ♉.

The influence of the ☽ in Taurus adds to the Virgo mentality a complex mixture of a decided liking for the natural sciences and a wide poetic interest. It gives delicacy to the intuitive part of Reflection, and adds some foresight. But in the main there is an undercurrent of natural home love and practical desire that makes this nativity more dominant than it seems—giving business force and willfulness.

The executive side of this life is usually marked by efforts toward a plainly apparent plan and effect in useful action.

♍. ☽ in ♊.

Gemini, the region of culture, of elegance, of expression. The ☽ here adds both practical life and a volume of delightful manner.

We expect of this mentality that it shall be very kindly, good-natured, apt at portrayal of views, and well fitted for those vocations where an abundance of hospitality, friendship and enthusiasm is required.

There is an added element of fastidiousness, carefulness of appearances, calm self-control and grace that is always attractive.

♍. ☽ in ♋.

The ☽ and ☉ are, here, in quite close angles from the ⊕, the ☽ in the region of marriage, the ☉ in that of familism. Thus there is an intensifying of affectional forces to the extreme.

The result is augmented sensitiveness in affection, almost to the point of jealousy and want of confidence. To offset this there is a constant attachment to all that is loving in home life, and a desire for harmony, for exclusiveness in expression, all vieing with tenderness and sweet temper.

In business life the economic trend of Virgo is increased, and there is a decided disposition to live for family and home alone, to avoid outward pleasures, and to seek the production of family group pleasures and ease.

It is advisable to cultivate a widened view of social and civil life, to aim to create a humanitarian realm of influence, thus to see in the possible harmonic whole the future good of the single chord of paternalism.

♍. ☽ in ♌.

The ☽ in Leo, of the Virgo native, is an influence of delicate mental impulses in th realm of spiritual thought; there is an inclination toward religious enthusiasm and, after religious excitement to melancholia.

The imaginative faculties are aroused; there is ability to comprehend the profound harmonies of music and of colors; in many instances a very sensitive sensory system, recognizing odors, flavors and touch sense with great acuteness.

This nature needs to master its inclinations to any morbidity of temper or of thought; to seek congenial surroundings and companions and to avoid great emotive states.

♍. ☽ in ♍.

The sign of Virgo has, with this location, the influence of familism dominant—the love of home life, of kindred, of relationships to country and place of nativity. The familiar in location is always attractive to this regional endowment. The ☽ here arouses, to the fullest, this trend of desire, and gives with it the added inclination to sanctify the surroundings of the family group.

The sex fealty that leads to constancy is intensified; there is an increased power of expression, as well as volume of vital force.

But with all this is often found an increased sensitiveness to thought impression; the impressibility to psychometric force is greater, and with it a sensitiveness to the social nerve-auras around. The whole is often modified by extreme sensibility to conditions, and there is likely to be an erratic trend in manner unless harmonic surroundings prevail.

♍. ☽ in ♎.

The regional influence of the ☽ in Libra of the Virgo native is a very complex mixture of home life forces, imaginative art elements, mathematical power, and genial egotism. There is also self-government, control of the emotions, clear-sightedness, and a volume of ambition and wilful exactness.

These along with regularity in work, periodical brilliant thought spells, vivid portrayal of views in words, and a keen sense of appropriateness, make of them most agreeable companions and interesting as authors or investigators.

But this mentality is seldom extremely able in discoveries—it lacks the persistency and tenacity necessary to studied elaboration. It is brilliant and voluminous, rather than original and profound.

♍. ☽ in ♏.

The lunar-Scorpio influence of Virgo is a favorable one. The unity of industry and familism, of the two great co-active divisions of activity, is the serious intent to practical accomplishment and the family destiny that utilizes the results.

The Scorpio nature has an abundance of industry, the industry of combined brain and muscle. To this is here added mathematical capability; added also the vitality of good nutritive power.

There is, or may often be, lack of the graceful deportment of some polarizations of Virgo, but there is, in lieu of that, plenty of integrity, conscientious persistency, insistence upon rights, and disposition to seek their fulfilment. This author does not agree with those who would depreciate and defame every touch of Scorpio influence. The world needs more justice and less charity, more right and less duty; charity and duty breed dependence on the one hand and injustice on the other, and the ☽ in Scorpio, wherever found, counteracts these causes and tendencies.

♍. ☽ in ♐.

This regional influence of the ☽ is a very dynamic one—an influence of selfishness in regard to financial matters; it is fuller of caution, of economic plans, of combative energies and commercial activities than any other lunar influence of Virgo.

The Sagittarius influence is one of Wealth; it loves gain, ostentation, display of power; not in the direction of style or of waste, but in that of ownership.

Hence, as stated above, the conditions are such that this combination of powers trends toward family accumulation and gain, the aggregation of means and combination of forces.

There is present more than usual verbal directness, and, with the absence of delicate reserve, makes the attitude often appear harsh, which in fact is the case, but in a general way rather than in individual instances.

♍. ☽ in ♑.

The result of this influence is much nearer that so often attributed to Scorpio. The Capricorn energies of impulsion, of destructive antagonisms, are nearly always evident, when thus polarized, even in the more refined and delicate and more harmonic temperament of the Virgo nativity.

When well endowed, this nature is capable of great commercial undertakings, particularly where there is a field full of practical experience to copy from. For this region is not a realm of original methods or of original thought. It is the conservative region of Virgo forces. The tearing away of old products, of old machinery of production is not necessarily a result of radical energy; here, it is more the outcome of necessity; and this region of energies will give power to recognize the point of commercial gain with almost intuitive quickness.

♍. ☽ in ♒.

The ☽ in Aquarius gives this mentality capacity for practical conceptions of human necessity, adding social ease, personal grace, keen sensibility to the use of mechanical forces, and along with it a good-humor that wins more aid than any amount of harshness might, under the rules of order or of wages.

There is increased vitality in this influence (properly force, of course), and a personal magnetic power.

The sensibility and sympathy with poetic, rhythmical and emotional thought is increased, while there is a constancy in the happiness resulting from tender home relations.

♍. ☽ in ♓.

The ☽ in Pisces, its home region, arouses into activity the artistic elements of this mentality, and gives a very practical turn to the habits of thought and industry. If it turns toward mechanical lines, there results capable management, with ease in directive abilities, calm attitude of progressive attainment, the direction depending much upon the major planets.

There is seldom literary brilliancy, seldom profound insight; there is love of the superficial and elegant, in their lighter forms, and quite frequently a marked imitative capacity, giving taste for the stage.

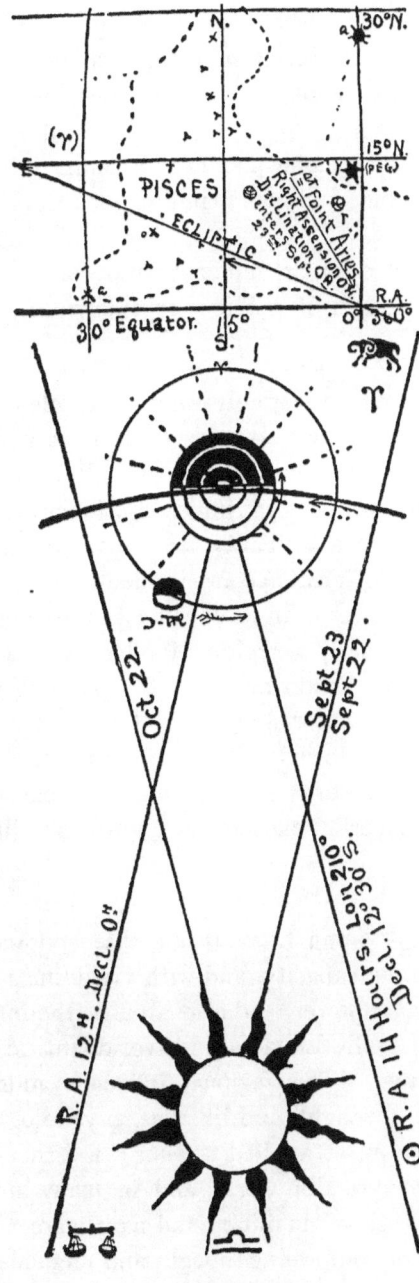

Fig. 30.

♎. ☉ in ♎, ⊕ in ♈; Sept. 23d to Oct. 22d. Rulership; Crimson; Ruling.

This nativity has as its dominating elements rulership, pride and ambition; a tendency toward severe conservatism and worshipfulness for law.

It is seldom varied by others' opinions or desires except by choice; seldom yields to mental or physical force, without severe resistance.

Libra responds to Gemini because its ambition is to seek higher planes of power, and in order to gain the aid of the formal intellect, to give keener direction. With high endowments this nature adds to its forces the full volume of stability, and is to the community around it an element of firmness and power.

(89)

It chords with Sagittarius; hence, when not carrying out the vocations that cluster around rulership in action, it seeks association with energetic mentalities in the fields of business reserve—the accumulation of wealth.

Of this nativity are many soldiers, commanders and commercial organizers. They love power, but find it often difficult to obey others of higher rank.

Sometimes Librans are attracted to the regional nature of Leo, and assume a place in the directorates of religious organizations.

♎. ☽ in ♈.

The presence of the ☽ in this sign, invariably a full ☽, is one of great power, particularly in this nativity. It adds to Libra a vast amount of distinct and useful imaginative ability, with clear conception of methods and progress in matters under consideration. It gives the constant Libra nature a brilliancy and regularity in application that is the foundation of great accomplishment.

The combination is almost as powerful in its effects as if the signs were transposed. Libra is essentially a region of rulership, and the ☽ in Aries gives it the formal power necessary to completely sense the analytical phases of every undertaking.

Many great chemists are thus endowed. There is often a masterly control of the voice, and of gesture. The muscular system is quick and always at ease, with superior capacity to co-ordinate in complex movements.

♎. ☽ in ♉.

The influence of the Taurus ☽ upon Libra is one that endows that nature with practical reflective capacity, and with vivid imagination; constructive thought and power, and also arouses the intuitive spirituality of Libra. Usually Libra is positive, dogmatic, certain, logical, but not sensitive. This regional influence adds sensitiveness; gives inspiration, foresight, and likewise, psychological power. It is able at invention, at applied science; is generally so in building and heavy construction work; and in many instances this influence forms the basis of a military and naval career.

The presence of imagination, of conforming thought and methods of specific utility that are often noted in this endowment (when blended with fine prenatal conditions), may reach a grandeur of purpose worthy of great admiration.

♎. ☽ in ♊.

The endowment of the Gemini ☽ in Libra is one of varied effect, depending much upon the influence of the planets.

It usually adds quickness of action and kindness of temper to the more rigid and persistent Libra force. It trends toward ideality; imagery; the sensuous expression of admiration. It gives mental government and pliability in bodily movement.

In some combinations, this influence gives a somewhat fantastic intensity to the self-laudatory elements of the Libra nature, and thus depreciates or modifies some of that sign's forces of dignity.

In the direction of oratory, in the government of the masses by thought and feeling, in power to influence the rules of social conduct, few natures can excel this one.

♎. ☽ in ♋.

The nature of the lunar influence, here, is to increase the love of home surroundings, and the desire to gain quietude that is so lacking in the Libra nature.

It makes the paternal feelings more vivid, the maternal more delicate and intense.

In some mentalities it arouses a desire to enter business life with definite plans, and with no other ambition than to succeed commercially.

♎. ☽ in ♌.

The ☽ in Leo of the Libra forces is an influence of sensitiveness, spirituality and refinement. The conception of delicate and refined ideas, of strong moral forces, belong to this nature. There is love for the classics, for the masterpieces of music, and all that symbolizes or interprets the mysteries of the ages. There is a realm of conservative interests here blended with the irrepressible impulses of the age; and all that satisfies the receptive faculties, and yet belongs to the past, as an evolution of thought, touches a chord in this nature.

♎. ☽ in ♍.

This nature is influenced by human forces along the same lines as those of the ☽ in ♌, only in an accentuated degree. There is here the climax of family government and of social control from the standpoint of affection blended with will. The deepest antagonisms of tyrannical planets (♄ and ♂) cannot instil into this nature their forces to offset the tenderness of filial love or of parental devotion.

The ☽ in Virgo also gives a delicacy and sincerity to expression, as well as to physical action, that is very attractive. It is a regional influence typified by the graces of family association.

♎. ☽ in ♎.

The ☽ in Libra of the Libra nature is not as harmonious in influence and effect as one would expect. It is too closely drawn in the elements of rulership. There is apt to be egotism running rampant, self-laudation in extreme, a philosophy of ego-greatness that depreciates many good qualities, and neutralizes power that might be better exerted.

There is apt to be an unconscious, or semi-conscious, grasping at others' rights; an absorption of possible pleasures that belong to others, even when no deep benefit is derived by the aggressor. The imagination swims in visions of power and importance, and in daydreams of grand achievements, without a question as to the mastery of self or the exertion of mental power required to gain that aim. And all these likely to change by the whim of an incident's effect.

When Libra is highly endowed by the warlike planets, the Moon in Libra adds to this nature the elements of keen perception (sight memory), and mathematical capacity; it gives artistic desires and grace, with an intense interest in regularity and precision.

This nature is often fascinated with military and naval affairs. It is subject to calumny in a small way; in danger of being misunderstood or viciously abused by jealously inclined persons.

The mentality possesses a great amount of stoical resistance and determination to hold its own, and to gain, along its own course, its preconceived design.

♎. ☽ in ♏.

The ☽ here is not a particularly favorable influence, but it does give Libra an added mathematical and industrial impulse. It adds power to the capacity to rule others by strategy, by determination and by application of the doctrine of "practice what you preach." It leads in activity, and others must either do or be undone. It will brook no laziness, condone no laggardly process; will build great plans, mentally, and struggle with Herculean efforts to effect them.

Often considered severe, it yet believes in justice. It demands success and is ready to grant to others the title earned, and in home life is seldom extremely congenial, is generally direct, prompt, unevasive, but is successful in gaining a part of its enlarged ambitions.

♎. ☽ in ♐.

The ☽ in Sagittarius of Libra is a chord of Libra, and a forceful one, at that. Its forces are always practical; the nature that results grasps and utilizes opportunity, calculates costs and products, plans deep plans, and requires a very powerful volume of anti-force to overcome it.

The aim may be an agricultural plan, a plan of mechanics, of trade, or of labor-vocation; but, whatever it is, there is with it an uncompromising attitude of successful approach, and the industry of motion, of physical and nerve-force application that seldom fails to gain fair success.

♎. ☽ in ♑.

The influence of the ☽ in the Capricorn region of Libra gives a very imaginative business nature, and one that leads to very speculative habits.

The mentality has mathematical power and likes to build schemes of great importance, but if well endowed, will combine original methods with a sense of justice and rapid action.

♎. ☽ in ♒.

The Aquarius influence of the ☽ is one that is but mildly felt in Libra mentalities; generally adds a volume of nutritive and absorptive capacity to physical life; keen senses of smell and taste, and remarkable psychometric powers. The psychometric ability must not be confused with that of intuition and foresight, as they are altogether different.

"The psychometric organ (Impression) receives and senses quality and quantity of force, either nerve-force, organic (vital) force, or inorganic (chemic) forces. Intuition and foresight are capacities by which the intellectual faculty of Inspiration determines the meaning of an idea radiated by another mentality as spiritual thought-force. In other words, psychometry is rather the resonance of mentality to matter, than of mentality to mental force. Inspiration is the receptive organ of spiritonic ideas."—[HOLMES W. MERTON, Lectures on Mentology, 1886.]

♎. ☽ in ♓.

The lunar influences of Pisces on the Libra nativity are desirable and very valuable influences. Libra needs the artistic, mathematical and materially orderly capacities aroused. This, the intensing of the Libra-Pisces energy does, and there is an added interest in mathematics, mechanical art and exactness, as well as a more luminous imagination, constructive insight, love of colors and elegant forms. There is a resonance to physical forces similar to that aroused by the lunar-Aquarius influence.

But the whole trends to make a nature thus endowed more practical and in many ways more skillful in the use of material and physical properties. It also lessens the egotism and willfulness of Libra.

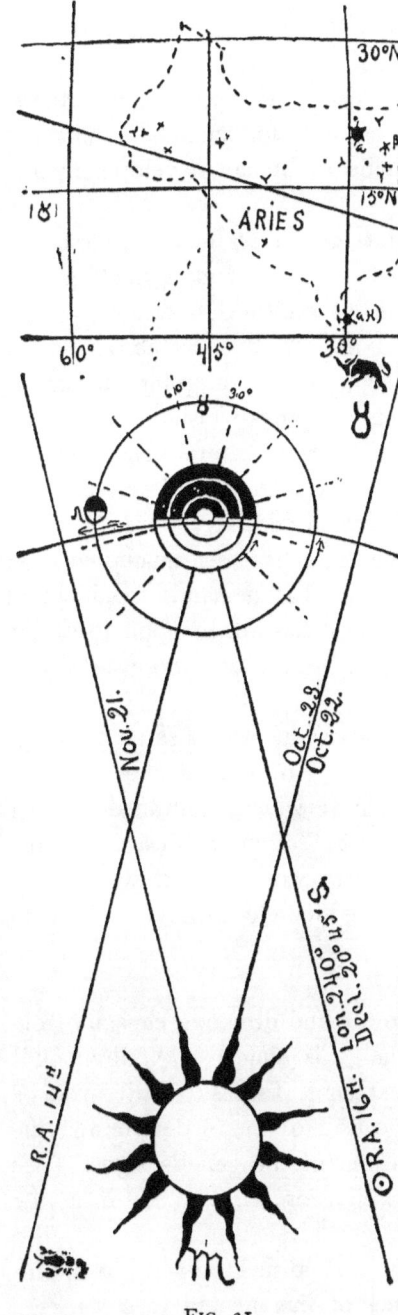

FIG. 31.

♏. ☉ in ♏, ⊕ in ♉;
October 23d to November 21st.
Co-action ; Labor ; Scarlet ; Exciting.

This nature, the most markedly dynamic of all natures, is severely earnest in the production of things to satisfy human requirements, and in the transmutation of energy in productive methods. It is the great perfecting mentality. This is an endowment of love of labor, activity, of intense interest in justice ; intent on giving due reward for all benefits received, and on paying bounty for bounty ; on returning element for element. There is skill given, in conserving inorganic forces to the use of mankind.

Scorpio responds to Cancer, hence this nature usually marries early in life, and, despite its presumed severity and ill-nature,

(95)

almost always lives happily, so far as the marriage relations are concerned.

This nature responds also to Taurus, its solar pole in force, therefore is in sympathy with, and has capacity for science, manufacturing, and the more materialistic side of human development and advancement.

Therefore, a native of this sign is generally found interested in mechanical trades, as tradesmen, mechanics, and agriculturalists, or may often find a place in systems of transportation.

Scorpio chords with Capricorn, and in this, as above noted, comes the interest in railroad, telegraph and shipping industries; when severely endowed, the planets in oppressive signs, there is an inclination to force others to do the Scorpio nature's share of the work of the world, chiefly because it has sufficient directive power to make its employment in that direction necessary.

Scorpio, from the nature of the sign, has been much maligned and illy credited. This nature is one that demands freedom and will struggle for liberty. In so doing it has drawn upon itself the enmity and prejudice both of those in power and those seeking to control.

The supposed harshness of Scorpio is due to its sense of integrity, justice, and desire for freedom. In the days of military power, of serfdom and monarchical slavery (still continued in other but less apparent forms) it was almost a crime to desire freedom and personal liberty. Astrologers were wont to find signs of reproof, and aspects by which those freedom elements could be condemned.

♏. ☽ in ♈.

The Scorpio nature receives power and directive capacity from this lunar regional influence. The ☽ is almost a "full moon" here, and the ⊕ itself is in the next sign, Taurus; for it must be remembered that the apparent location of the ☉ determined the question, or rather the nomenclature, of the genesis sign. (See statement at head of each regional division, viz.: ♏. ☉ in ♏, ⊕ in ♉, etc.)

The ☽ here adds intellectuality, and formal capacity to the industry, forcefulness and perseverance of this mentality.

Parents should remember distinctly, in governing children of this endowment, that there is a vast difference between stubbornness and perseverance. The first is, generally, objectless resistance; the latter, generally, restless desire to accomplish. This nature requires genial direction rather than angular repression.

♏. ☽ in ♉.

The dominant influence of this region is in the direction of applied science, physics and mechanical power. In some instances it turns the cast of mental activities toward art expressions, inclines the thoughts into channels of illustrative activity and public work.

There is generally much determination to succeed by exercise of mental power, and to use the perceptive powers as an aid to ease, and short-paths in matters of energy-use or muscular exertion.

The mind is practical, capable of doing the best work possible in proportion to the quality of brain fibre possessed.

In highly organized mentalities there is a marked desire to gain power and affluence as well as competence. The whole has dominating industry.

♏. ☽ in ♊.

The lunar-Gemini influence on Scorpio is one of variable quality, and one that depends much upon the relative position of the planets. Scorpio natures are generally made more genial and intense in friendship, with greater interest in amusement and conviviality.

The descriptive capacity is usually much increased, language expression more vivid and fluent, while there is, in a mild degree, an increase in the imaginative powers, and in the direction of careless benevolence.

♏. ☽ in ♋.

The ♏ is here in a region that responds to Scorpio; there is a beneficial influence from the ☽ and its regional influence here. The marriage faculties of a person born with this endowment of force are calmer, more constant, and in many ways made more expressive.

Fidelity, sex fealty, and sex affection are, thus, more easily expressed by the Scorpio nature; and, while it may not always be greatly deepened by this influence, the more frequent "testifying" by words and gentle acts, gives happiness and security to the mate.

So far as financial life is concerned, or the impulses of mentality toward occupation, this regional influence of the ☽ has very little significance.

♏. ☽ in ♌.

The lunar influence of Scorpio with the ☽ in Leo is one that somewhat closely blends the forces of the two signs, and adds to Scorpio a sense of human unity, of social inter-relations, that in many ways modifies the dynamic power of the major sign, and gives it sentiments of religious emotions, philanthropy, congeniality, of social concern, that are apart from the industrial impulses of Scorpio.

The ☽ does not depreciate the power of consecutive application, but it, in a marked degree, blends the energies in more sympathetic forms.

In marriage relationships this location of the ☽ trends to give freedom of expression; it is less guarded and less severe than the usual attitude of the dynamic signs—Libra, Scorpio, Sagittarius and Capricorn.

♏. ☽ in ♍.

The ☽ here arouses all the home love of Scorpio. It gives an intense desire for comfort and for plenty of food of rich quality; it also gives management and impressibility to the conditions around, that warrant improvement. There is thus a capacity to manage real estate, agriculture undertakings; the arrangement of power and structural work by which there is a saving of labor, time, or money.

As there is an increased patriotism, this may lead to self-laudation and an egotistic plausibility.

♏. ☽ in ♎.

The regional influence of the ☽ in Libra gives to Scorpio natures an added, and generally high, ambition; it supplies firmness and perseverance to their industry and productive energy. These natures are truly willful; they have a dominating individuality that is marked in manner and in processes of execution.

This endowment almost always gives commercial sagacity, and a keen sense of values; and to the extent, or in proportion to the demand, there is an interest in the practical sciences. This author has not found the influence of the ☽ in Libra of Scorpio very much inclined toward the metaphysical, but has found that it was almost invariably too positive in its forces to have the desired sensitiveness.

♏. ☽ in ♏.

The ☽, here, gives the Scorpio nature a vast amount of system and orderly attainment, making periodicity in effort, and even in mental work, almost a necessity. It has been said that this nature is hasty, spasmodic and passionate; but this author has found it rather inclined to fretful energy, disliking restraint, and very much disturbed by any interruption in its plans.

Scorpio is never, under any planetary influence, pleased with dictation—it likes suggestion, grasps utilizable ideas, and loves improvements—and it is even less so inclined when the ☽ is present in that sign. When so situated there is an increase in imaginative power and added artistic skill; a desire to travel; to assume responsibility, and to stand the consequences as well as take all the credit for its success.

♏. ☽ in ♐.

The lunar influence in the Sagittarius of Scorpio is one of keen business interests, of clear appreciation of values, and an insight into the relation of opportune times and places. There is added to Scorpio the instincts of business and economic procedure, often also increased legal capacity, a fund of general information, but a desire to avoid any vocation where repetition of labor or action is very great. In this way, the ☽ here reverses much of the Scorpio nature, and adds decidedly new attitudes of thought.

The nature, as a whole, needs calm advice more than arbitrary government, and should be given freedom of action to an extent not usually granted.

♏. ☽ in ♑.

The aroused Capricorn element in Scorpio is an energy of executive power, it is ambitious for gain and accumulation, and in

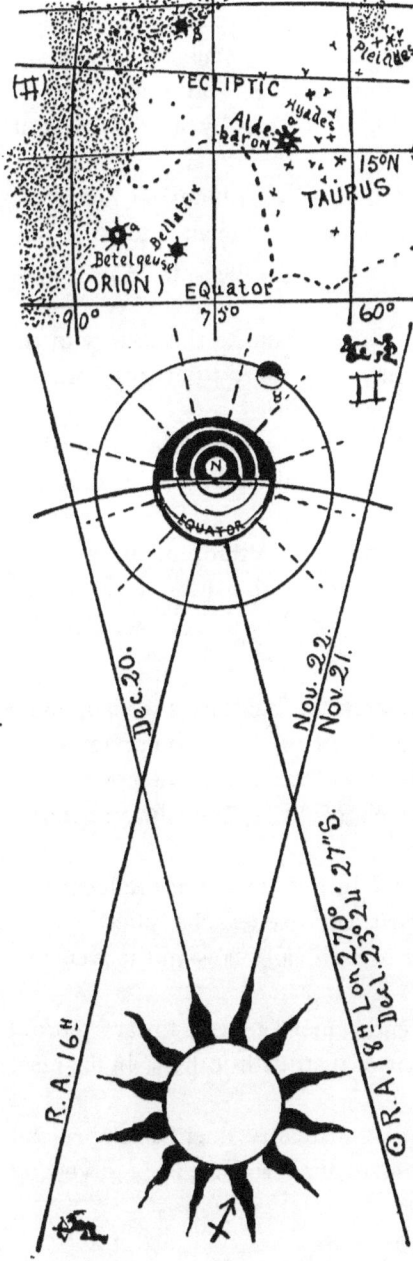

FIG. 32.

♐. ☉ in ♐, ⊕ in ♊;
November 22d to December
20th. Wealth; Red; Conserving.

The mentality born under this sign is dominant in Defension. It generally has the desire, power and directiveness necessary to defend itself, to care for others, and to accumulate wealth.

This mentality is cautious, brave, courageous; its nature is to prepare for emergencies, both in personal matters and in those of interest to the public. It is conservative of wealth, just as Libra is of ideas, forms and laws. In fact this nature chords with Libra, and furnishes the material as well as the antagonism necessary to all severe self-protection.

This mentality aims at the accumulation of wealth, and develops under favorable conditions into the commercial magnate—the financial monitor. In this capacity often saving wealth for times of famine, and more often contributing to distress by shrewd manipulations of others' rights.

Perhaps no other region of mentality contributes so much dynamic and direct force to both sides of human life—the successful side and the miserable side—as does this. It has great responsibilities.

This nature responds to Aries, and is awake to the history of the past and the habits of the present; it is alert to every advantage and aroused by every change of human effort.

Sagittarius is in response to Virgo, and is therefore inclined to provide for all future emergencies and requirements of its descendants "Unto the third and fourth generation."

This mentality usually finds a mate in Virgo, or in its solar polarity, Gemini. Occasionally it mates with a Libra or an Aquarius nativity.

1. ☽ in ♈.

The impulsive, energetic, fiery nature of Sagittarius is made more eccentric and intellectual when endowed with the lunar forces in Aries. It has directive capacity as well as executive power. In many cases this nature makes much of little, but always reaches the climax of its capacity.

There is nothing slow or "logy" in the lunar Aries influence on Sagittarius; and the economic spirit is aroused to the fullest extent, with plenty of the reserve nature to make all plans and movements secret.

Occasionally there is in this endowment a trend toward morbid fear of failure, with a large amount of distrust in others, in financial directions.

It would be well to study ethics, spirituality, mental science and government; also to take up a natural science as a diverting element.

1. ☽ in ♉.

This influence leads the accumulative nature of Sagittarius into the field of scientific commercial pursuits, and gives an inclination toward structural and architectural trades or business.

There is, noticeably, an increase in the imaginative powers, with a keen perception of the trend of advancing values.

This mentality will therefore often turn toward real-estate speculation, or investment ; and, if only moderately educated, may take up the primary forms of natural sciences, as stock-raising, fruit-growing, landscape gardening, etc.

In general the judgment is synthetic and quick, not easily changed, often considered a stubborn disposition, and intense in its advocacy of the views taken.

♐. ☽ in ♊.

The play of lunar-Gemini forces on the Sagittarius nature is one that gives congeniality, gracefulness and love of culture to that otherwise very practical nature. The cautious and defensive elements are less prominent, and at times there is a generous turn in the commercial field.

In general this nature is intense and aggressive, with more than ordinary bluntness of action and of speech. The ☽ in Gemini gives eccentricity when associated with ♄ and ♅ ; it gives intellectual brilliancy when found in this sign with ♃ or with ♀. When these are not present, there is liability to extreme exertion, and nervous exhaustion.

♐. ☽ in ♋.

The Sagittarius mentality is aroused in home matters, has a much stronger attachment for a local region of activity, and generally inclines to a solid and non-speculative business, when endowed with the ☽ in this region.

The marriage faculties are stimulated, and there is an increased expression of sexality, parental tenderness, and the romantic side of married life.

It is well for this nature to calmly consider and calmly act upon all matters relating to sex-devotion ; there is liability to hasty judgments, and to hasty temper displays, both of which may lead to misery and distrust.

♐. ☽ in ♌.

Sagittarius with ☽ in Leo is a bundle of contraries; often blamed for unintentional injuries, faults and actions, yet much inclined to self-defence.

Saving, emotional, vivid in expression, generous when aroused by misery, but uncompromising when angered. It is difficult to describe in its various moods the intense and variable nature of this influence.

In marriage there is an expression of general kindness, but present an individuality that is not fully realized or appreciated by the mate.

♐. ☽ in ♍.

The ☽ in Virgo of Sagittarius is a calming and in every way beneficial influence, leading to love of home and family life, and, in all, adding parental solicitation. In patriotism and politics this nature is extremely conservative. The political economy of established forms, protected wealth, and home investments, is the kind in which this combined influence is interested.

It is evident, in the characters under this influence, that they are interested in the establishment of permanent family households, and in the accumulation of local power in both matters of wealth and of social influence.

♐. ☽ in ♎.

The ☽ in Libra endows Sagittarius with great ambition, firmness and perseverance; it gives calm force, of an executive nature, and pride in carrying out all plans seriously entered into.

The ☽ has here a moderate amount of idealistic force, but not as much as is usually accredited to it. There is a fine volume of practical government, both of personality and over others, and along with this a moderate interest in science and physics.

The physical nature is generally a powerful one, with strong back and arm muscles, and a very great amount of endurance.

♐. ☽ in ♏.

The wealth instincts of Sagittarius are turned into the channels of physical labor, and largely given to personal comfort by this regional influence of the ☽.

There is also an endowment of physical strength, ability to resist disease and to revive quickly from its effects.

The large sense of justice, desire for personal liberty, and the culmination of aggressive and persevering energy, gives power to continued work, of any order, engaged in, and the constant desire to defend rights and property.

♐. ☽ in ♐.

The ☽ in Sagittarius of Sagittarius nature gives that mentality a congenial and social responsiveness that it does not usually possess, and influences it to spend time and money in accumulating objects of beauty or adornment, and for ornamentation of surroundings.

Sagittarius so endowed (with the ☽) has an increased amount of regularity in work, is more apt at mental arithmetic, and is in every way interested in orderly business methods. It can be very agreeable, and is exceptionally entertaining when interested in descriptions of mercantile problems, or objects, bric-a-brac, or in the elements of architecture.

There is a remarkably keen perception of all that transpires near it, and while apparently indifferent to surroundings, sees clearly the course of events or result of actions. Sagittarius and Taurus are both lunar sympathetic regions.

This influence upon the mentality is one of a conservative nature—it is independent force added to caution and economy.

A person so endowed will take care of the financial responsibilities of the home, will guard against waste, and will work with industry and ease.

But there is (under great disappointment) danger and liability to morbid fears of failure; in this all tendency toward miserliness and financial despondency should be guarded against.

A sense of security should be gained from experience and study, and an effort made to master more than one branch of a vocation.

♐. ☽ in ♑.

This regional influence of the ☽ is one that stimulates the business capacity of Sagittarius. It makes it very impulsive and forceful in either mental or physical directions; and is essentially an industrial combination of influences. These seldom leading to professional life, but often giving the spirit of personal freedom, and love of physical labor, above these the individual finds it difficult to rise.

But when highly endowed by parental conditions, and possessed of a fine nervous organization, there is a wide range of activities open to choice, with ability to make the most of them, or at least of the one chosen.

1. ☽ in ♒.

The ☽ here endows the mentality with a vivid ideality in regard to home affairs, and creates love for the family, its surroundings and pleasures.

The dominantly defensive nature of Sagittarius is modified into a much calmer and less aggressive habit by this endowment. With finely located planetary influences, this mentality will succeed in the more general business, and in agriculture. It is also inclined toward the intemperate impulses; overeating, intemperate drinking, excessive seasoning of foods, and negligence in protection from inclement weather, are all matters to be guarded against

1. ☽ in ♓.

This is essentially an artistic and mathematical endowment, and with it a degree of what may be called secondary executive ability —carrying out the instructions of others. The impressionable faculties are seldom acute, excepting the sense of sight, and generally this sense must be guarded by due periods of rest.

There is liability of severe temper, unrestrained self-defence, a disposition to be quarrelsome and meddlesome, that needs restraining.

The digestive organs are rarely strong or efficient, and need care.

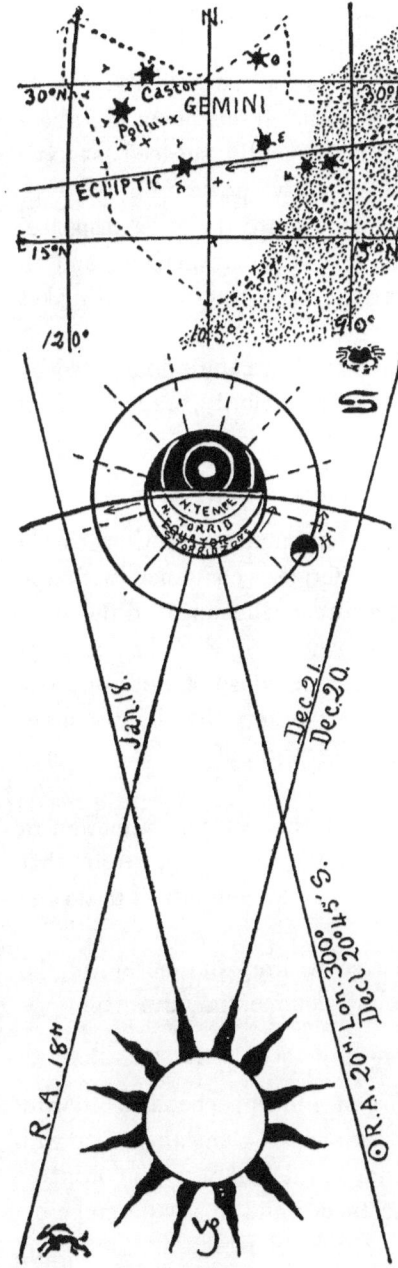

FIG. 33.

♑. ☉ in ♑, ⊕ in ♋.
December 21st to January 18th.
Commerce; Maroon; Moving.

This mentality has a wide field of action and is disposed to take care of its own interests, to accept all kinds of commissions (as a factor) from others, and when acting as an agent is always capable, exact and quick.

The commercial instincts of this nature are essentially those of movement and travel, of desire for wide and great acquaintanceship.

This mentality has great reserve power; it seldom demonstrates its full capacity; it often lacks pride and ambition, and when that is the case is satisfied to do a normal amount of work for a moderate remuneration. When highly endowed it is full of fire and force; when attacked

(107)

is destructive and revengeful; when badgered is sarcastic, severe, and rigid in judgment.

This nature responds to Pisces, and, hence, can use the arts to great practical purpose; is often very able at mathematics, at accounting, and at recording. It can frequently succeed at civil engineering and in the management of motive power.

When the nature is feminine it trends toward the other response, Aquarius, and glories in the home and its management, and in minimizing the waste of energy, while, on the other hand, it makes every effort count.

In marriage this personality usually weds a nature dominated by Aquarius forces, or by those of its solar polarity, Cancer. It is seldom unhappy in marriage.

♑. ☽ in ♈.

Capricorn, with ☽ in Aries, has the influence of Capricorn's commercial capacity and directive energies, combined with the formulating powers of Aries, and the direct scheming and imaginative forces derived from the ☽ in its own energies. The result is an endowment of managing power, a wide grasp of necessary demands, and a controlling influence over others that is absolutely necessary to large enterprises and the execution of all heavy working plans.

True, the natural tendency is to omit the personal attention to details, not because details are unnecessary, but for the reason that persons of this endowment find it cheaper to get others to do the details than to do them themselves.

Capricorn is a defensive, executive nature, and here has the power to plan its processes of gain and commercial advantage.

♑. ☽ in ♉.

The ☽ in Taurus of Capricorn is an influence bending toward executive exactness and science in commerce. This mentality will often lead to engineering, railroading, naval and marine construction; to the commercial arts and sciences; and in a wide range of applied physics will find an enjoyable field of labor.

There are imaginative forces enough for the practical business life; tenderness enough to make home enjoyable : and vigor enough to urge the completion of financial and mechanical plans.

Sometimes, as may be seen by planetary endowments, there will be destructive and antagonistic forces in excess. These should be governed by the Intellect, and brought into useful submission.

♑. ☽ in ♊.

The ☽ in Gemini of the Capricorn nativity is a beneficial one, giving that severe nature a congeniality that is necessary to it, and that will bridge over many rough places in life.

There is also an added gracefulness, a trend toward philanthropy, and a clearer view of artistic beauty and utility.

The field of artistic commercial activities is best suited to the mentality developed under this combination of influences, and particularly if ♃ or ♀ are also in Capricorn, or if in Pisces.

♑. ☽ in ♋.

The ☽ here intensifies the marriage forces and the devotional tenderness of Capricorn. It also arouses a strong love for home comforts, and for the exercise of caution in making provision for any financial setback that may befall the head of the household.

It does not intensify the economic faculties as much as it does the general cautionary nature; but the result is indirectly the same.

The spirituality of the nature is enlarged and made more sensitive, the expression more graceful and congenial, while there is an attitude of calmer deliberation in all this person does, than would be the case with the ☽ in more dynamic regions.

♑. ☽ in ♌.

The lunar-Leo influence on the Capricorn nature is one of mixed forces, giving a changeable nature and one that goes to extremes of kindness and of severity. There is a leaning toward dogmatism, arbitrary religious methods, generosity in case of vested power, and restricted interests where that power is withheld.

"Give me my way and I will be generous" is a motto this nature generally acts upon. It is forceful either in its support or its opposition, and seldom neutral in any matter that in any way bears, however indirectly, upon its interests.

♑. ☽ in ♍.

The ☽ in Virgo affects the social nature of Capricorn much more than the intellectual. Indirectly it inclines the mentality toward a love of art and poetry, though it seldom gives the required power of expression.

The home life is usually one of intense enjoyment, particularly so when the person so endowed is a parent and has children to inspire his efforts, or to give enthusiasm to the desire to make life a success.

This nature is often deeply interested in politics, public education, in civil reforms, and in the display of patriotism. These, in connection with an interest in business and community growth, lead to speculative enterprises, real-estate investments, and the various forms of local enterprise of a permanent financial nature.

♑. ☽ in ♎.

The mentality thus endowed has self-rulership in abundance, with dignity, stability, seriousness, and commercial aptitude in the ascendant. If the hereditary conditions are poor there will be a struggle for attainments of an ordinary order, but still clearly above the plane of life upon which the personality seems placed.

With fine, prenatal conditions the nature is capable of high attainments, commercial power, leadership in the affairs of life, and a sensitiveness to the dominant demands of the age.

♑. ☽ in ♏.

The presence of the ☽ in this sign of Capricorn gives that nature a deeper sense of justice and of personal responsibility. It gives imagination, regularity, periodicity in methods, and ease in expression.

This influence gives the Capricorn mentality a tendency to physical exertion, and love of an active rather than a sedentary life.

There is an added element of self-government, much needed by

Capricorn, and especially so if ♄ or ♅ or ♆ are also in the sign. These, there, are apt to add angularity, and need calming.

♑. ☽ in ♐.

Capricorn and Sagittarius are both in the executive regions, and are essentially commercial and money-making—if highly endowed —or, under less favorable conditions, are given to manual labor. The ☽ here stimulates Capricorn in whichever may be the direction the main body of mentality trends. It always gives directness, bluntness, and temper to its primary when found in Sagittarius. In temperament this endowment is one of severity, haste, and defensiveness. It will seldom compromise its opinions, and will rather contest a doubtful case than modify its course.

♑. ☽ in ♑.

The ☽ in Capricorn gives a disposition to lead a political or semi-public life; is fortunate in clerkships and office work; generally a good accountant, capable in executing the orders of others; is quick in planning methods of action; is careful in looking after property and details in business.

This temperament is subject to much depressing sensitiveness; to periods of despondence, and has an inclination to fret; it will yield unnecessarily to the angry intents and purposes of others.

A person thus endowed should avoid egotistic impulses; try to gain self-control; master nerves quivering under the lash of ignorant oppression, and, by this, make conditions less and less depressing. Seek pleasure in Art, or artistic business; in study of the beautiful and in pleasure-giving domestic surroundings.

♑. ☽ in ♒.

The lunar-Aquarius influence on Capricorn is one that varies greatly with planetary endowments.

With ♀ in Capricorn it gives intensity to conjugal life, vivifies the love of children, and makes more mental and spiritual the sex-associations. With ♃ in Capricorn the nature has much egotism, self-laudation, energy, and varied mental capacity.

With ♄ in the sign, there is an abundance of mild sarcasm and of rather severe wit.

With ☋ in the sign, the ☽ and ☋ combine to give the mentality a quick temper, plenty of warlike imagination, a disposition to plan larger schemes than it can execute, and then to blame the innocent for the failure.

♑. ☽ in ♓.

The lunar-Pisces influence upon Capricorn is generally a practical one, but not always of a high order. It will give the industrious mentality facility in perceptive lines, and in the direction of manual skill.

It sometimes turns the attention to military matters, and to a love of sport or destructive pleasures.

If highly endowed by planetary forces, there is often mechanical skill of a successful quality. In home affairs there is love of display and of personal ease.

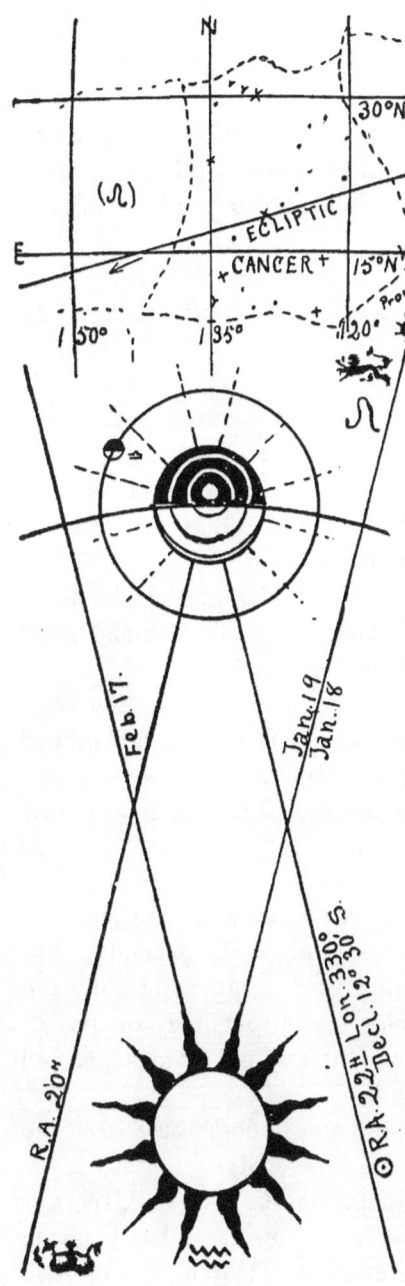

FIG. 34.

♒. ☉ in ♒, ⊕ in ♌. January 19th to February 17th. Home; Salmon; Nutrifying.

This nature is dominant in taste, sensitiveness, impression, and in all that appertains to the congeniality of the home and its comforts. It is often strongly endowed with the acute perception of Pisces and the deep religious nature of Leo, both of which are responses to Aquarius.

The mental chord of Aquarius is Cancer, and by this is added much of the deep devotion of the marriage faculties.

There is a wide range of social functions, and, under a natural form of government, the capacity for economic management natural to this endowment could be exercised with great benefit to society, as well as to the home life of the person so endowed.

8 113)

This mentality is sensitive to the wide range of desires arising from the impressible mental faculties, and easily understands the wants of others.

In many ways this nature is adapted to minor business pursuits, but it seldom has enough of the Sagittarius and Capricorn forces to be able to master great financial plans, or to organize massive industrial bodies.

This nature inclines in marriage toward its solar polarity, Leo, and, in a less degree, toward a mate from the realm of its formal response, Pisces.

♒. ☽ in ♈.

This regional influence of the ☽ is one of intellectuality in the Aquarius nature, but essentially practical. It increases the verbal capacity of the person so endowed, and adds love of music, rhythm, and poetry. It gives intense application, as well as intense attention to all that the mentality is interested in.

Very often there is an endowment of delicate psychometric power, and also keen intuitions. The senses of touch and smell are extremely acute, and nutritive capacity good.

Generally this nature takes home life in a matter-of-fact way, enjoys social surroundings, likes to take part in all neighborhood activities; is seldom inclined toward a confining and severe profession, choosing rather a business life or a trade as a source of income.

♒. ☽ in ♉.

This combination of Solar-Lunar-Earth forces is the most intensely sensitive of all endowments, and while generally very strongly endowed vitally, is yet often very negative mentally and nervously, with extreme sensitiveness to surrounding conditions; easily impressed by the nerve auras of others, and by geologic and mineral energies.

This nativity is interested in mining and in floriculture, seems to understand nature with great ease and little study.

When too negative to act in financial matters with ease, there is a tendency toward pessimistic reserve, or, on the other hand, to clairvoyance and mediumistic professions. There is need of positiveness and determination.

♒. ☽ in ♊.

This endowment gives grace, ease, and tenderness. There is a volume of genial imagination, with a disposition to over-laudation in praise of friends, and in attention to children. The mentality has much of the mimetic capacity, and, with large amiability, finds pleasure in the theatrical profession. When ♀ is found in Aries, there is generally vocal power, and musical capacity. With ☿ in Capricorn, the tendency is toward employment where the " Light fantastic toe " has a plea for activity.

In home life this nature is genial, affectionate, but not as constant as might be desired.

♒. ☽ in ♋.

The Moon's influence in Cancer of the Aquarius nature is one that intensifies Aquarius, gives imaginative bearing to all efforts, leads to an economical habit, and to more constancy.

But it does not widen the general range of ambitions, nor stimulate the mentality toward higher attainments than those which accompany the idea of necessity.

This influence, therefore, needs the support of powerful beneficial planets in both the intellectual regions and in the upper will regions, as ♃ in Libra, or, in the first instance, ♀ in Aries ; ♀ in Gemini or in Pisces. These would give a balance of power that would be highly beneficial.

♒. ☽ in ♌.

The Lunar-Leo influence is one of great value to Aquarius, giving high motives, direct incentives to activity, and a positive nerve-force, with a clear avoidance of the despondence Aquarius mentalities are so apt to gradually drift into. The combination is one that predicates hopefulness, good cheer, graceful ambitions, foresight, and security.

In the world of activity a useful and practical career should be found ; and the determination to make life a competent success be taken as the basis of thought and action.

♒. ☽ in ♍.

The ☽ in Virgo is not a favorable location in the Aquarius nativity, and tends to draw the nature too closely into the realm of vitality and the affections, thereby leaving static energies dominant, and an absence of sufficient will force or power to establish an equipoise of mentality.

The field of industry open to this nature is generally one of every-day activity, and, unless well endowed hereditarily, and by planetary influences, will hardly have ambition enough to gain expert capacity in any wide field, or in the professions.

The mentality is often intense in feeling, with home interests very dominant, and with an inclination toward intemperance, extreme appetites, and passionate sexuality.

♒. ☽ in ♎.

The Moon in the Libra region of Aquarius gives energy, force and determination. The nature is apt to be positive in habit and decisive incidents; but, when opportunity admits of delay will be so inclined. There is often a fair amount of intuition; a disposition to generalize and avoid specific utterances. The ☽ here also gives a slight tendency toward melancholia and hopelessness when unfavorable conditions befall the person. Self-confidence is a necessity to success in the natures thus endowed.

♒. ☽ in ♏.

The Moon in Scorpio of the Aquarius mentality gives it a strong mechanical tendency, but not inventive power, as Aquarius seldom is inventive. In a minor way it gives business capacity and political aspirations, but this is so tempered with changeable opinions and by variable temper that the influence is scarcely prolonged enough to accomplish a favorable end in political life.

The successes of this endowment depend much upon the hereditary quality of nerve structure. But as a whole the trend is toward the trades, agriculture and the smaller lines of business venture.

If the Planets are much opposed to this influence they will prevail in greatly modifying it.

♒. ☽ in ♐.

The Moon in the Sagittarius of an Aquarius mentality gives that mentality a much more favorable financial capacity than its natural endowment. It is a beneficial influence when governed by Reason and a sense of calm procedure. The Moon's endowment gives imagination and vivid expression; it also arouses the defensive and aggressive elements of the Aquarius mind. In matters of importance this endowment gives directness, executive power, caution, and persistence; sometimes it is excitable and irascible under moderate provocation, needing good self-government and favorable planetary forces to bring the best results.

Let it be remembered that any single adverse quality or habit can be overcome by the combination of good faculties opposed to the bad one.

♒. ☽ in ♑.

The Moon in Capricorn is, to the Aquarius mentality, a favorable force. It gives judicious commercial attributes and forces, and a sense of commercial freedom not usual to Aquarius.

The patriotism of this mentality finds a means of vivid expression; there is an added impulsiveness that, when well controlled, adds successful power. The Lunar-Capricorn energy is quite synthetic; loves to deal with masses and generalities, and, in this direction, should seek exactness and accuracy. Investigating every proposition presented for action is good advice for this mentality to act upon.

♒. ☽ in ♒.

This influence of the Moon is closely blended with the solar influence, and Aquarius under this combination has an intensified family, religious and patriotic disposition; it is inclined to accept a business life, or one in which close social relations are the dominant feature. This nature is generally very sensitive, more than usually intuitive, is confiding to friends, given to suffer greatly from disappointment, and also to magnifying small injuries into large ones, making matters appear to themselves worse than they really are.

All tendency toward morbid imagination, lack of confidence, or supersensitiveness, should be avoided as harmful. Religious and emotional enthusiasm is reacting, to an injurious degree, to a person thus endowed.

♒. ☽ in ♓.

The Lunar-Pisces influence on Aquarius is very largely one of perceptive power; it gives capability in art criticism, in mechanical drawing and in engraving; it arouses an interest in nature, and institutes a clear pride in personal appearance and in the ability to execute whatever matters of skill it essays to take an interest in. There is a generous fund of mathematical capacity, and with it the habit of exacting details in money matters.

In the main this nature is selfish, and often distinctly so in small affairs. The author has found that this endowment is inclined to miss opportunity, and it fails to grasp the full importance of its capabilities. The Aquarius mentality so endowed must seek to broaden its better nature, cultivate enthusiasm, forcefulness and **breadth of view.**

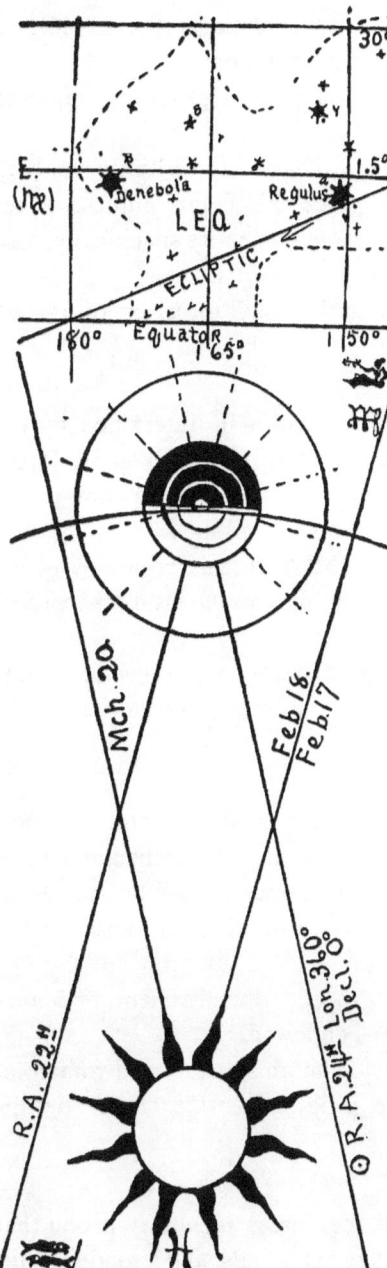

FIG. 35.

♓. ☉ in ♓, ⊕ in ♍;
February 18th to March 20th.
Art; Gray; Cooling.

This nature is the most capable, and finds natural ability in the arts; particularly in those arts that express symbolism, beauty, and the elements of form. There is an aptitude in these, and in most of the mechanical trades. The perceptions are wide awake, remember clearly anything seen in which an interest is taken.

When other vocations are chosen, it is usually in the line of manual labor, or the lighter forms of trade.

This nature responds to Capricorn and is thus of great use to commerce, quick in accounting, retentive to forms and methods.

In its response to Aquarius

(119)

it is interested in beautifying the home, in elegant surroundings, and its temperament is essentially calm in action.

In its chord with science it finds its greatest pleasures, enjoying the artistic elements of nature.

The Pisces mentality is disposed to have large vitality, and, if ♀ is in the region of Aquarius, it gives this nature intense affections. The planets influence this mentality more specifically than than they do any other.

Pisces natures should marry a native of Taurus, or of Pisces solar polarity, Virgo.

♓. ☽ in ♈.

The Pisces artistic and mechanical nature is intensified by the lunar influence in Aries; this latter combination also gives Pisces mentalities more directive capacity, more force in direction of application and in line of practical results.

To a highly endowed personality the ☽ in this region gives literary tastes, expression in verbal directions, and great mathematical memory.

It is found that this influence gives more tenderness and constancy to the affections, and increases the love of home life.

♓. ☽ in ♉.

To Pisces, the ☽ in Taurus adds love of science and of exactness. There is often deep interest in higher mechanics and in mathematics; it leads to study of architecture, building, construction work, and, when opportunities are wanting in these, to the manual branches.

Civil engineers, mechanical engineers, draughtsmen, and analytical chemists, are very often thus endowed.

The faculties of marriage are made more spiritual and romantic. There is an added interest in the progressive side of life by this regional influence.

♓. ☽ in ♊.

The Lunar-Gemini influence on the Pisces mentality is one that leads to artistic elegance, verbal descriptiveness, and a tendency toward extreme sociability.

There are forces that demand artistic expression in movement more directly than in lines of illustration. But the mental capacity often runs in both, with elocutionary power added.

A technical education is always best for persons of this endowment, and in the lines of trade and commercial work. If inclined to portraiture, landscape painting, or to caricature, they are liable to financial failure, and to become improvident.

With ♀ and ♃ in the same sign, or in Pisces, this latter tendency is much modified.

♓. ☽ in ♋.

The energy playing upon Pisces from this aroused region is beneficial in the direction of home matters; it gives constancy and tenderness to the affections.

In the field of action it inclines to outdoor exertion, to agriculture, floriculture, to stock raising. The reflective nature is synthetic; it judges by generalities, dislikes consecutive examination and persistent study of a single phase. There is not, then, the capacity for scientific research, nor for prolonged educational study.

The endowment necessitates a careful attention to regularity in work, and an effort to avoid all waste of time and energy.

♓. ☽ in ♌.

The Lunar-Leo influence on Pisces is apt to lead to erratic methods, to conflicting opinions, changeable views, and to excessive emotions.

There will be extreme sensibility to nervous and climatic impressions, generally some clairvoyant power, and vague and idealistic imagination.

A person thus endowed should avoid building too great "castles in the air," and should seek to take a practical view of all essential matters; to look at the world as it really is and as it ought to be. The choice of an occupation that employs the mental nature in an enjoyable way, and that gives pleasure as it gives product, is an essential to this nature.

♓. ☽ in ♍.

The endowment of Virgo forces, through the Moon's position, is a beneficial one to Pisces, as it gives calmness, security, home and family interests, and adds, besides, a clear volume of spiritual force that Pisces usually needs.

This endowment also stimulates the nature to a more analytical trend of thought, and with it a desire for the practical application of the perceptive talents that the Pisces region of influence gives.

With ♀ or ♃ in Pisces there is added a clear and vivid imagination, with power to more forcefully rule the habits of life, and govern associates and members of the family.

♓. ☽ in ♎.

The forces of the regions of Pisces and of Libra are in many ways discordant, unsympathetic and asynchronous. The result of this in the person so endowed is an unsatisfied, unsteady and variable mental state much of the time. When highly organized there is more than usual clearness of thought, directness, willful carrying out of plans, and a trend of previsional intuition that serves many good purposes.

The materialistic tendency of Pisces natures is much decreased, and there is usually an added nervousness, with more pride, perseverance and positiveness when in good health.

♓. ☽ in ♏.

The ☽ in Scorpio of the Pisces nature adds to that mentality directness, industry, positive forces, and a disposition to direct other people's course in life or in industry.

In many ways this influence is a beneficial one. It gives a keen insight into the uses of mechanical instruments, aids in understanding the laws of physics and their application. It gives permanence to the plan and policy of the mental life, and in a measure adds economy, self-reliance, and a desire to gain a competence.

♓. ☽ in ♐.

The Lunar-Sagittarius forces are not harmonic with those of Pisces, and there is a constant pessimistic feeling and thought in persons thus endowed. The influence of the greater planets may overcome much of this ill influence, and give sufficient aggression to make a successful nature.

The tendency is to irregularity in effort, to be variable in temper, and to compromise success by rash action at vital points.

The prime caution should be to study mastery and moderation in judgment and action, and to take particular notice of all the conditions bearing upon the project at hand.

In social and marital affairs to avoid extremes, haste, and irrational expression.

♓. ☽ in ♑.

To the Pisces native, the influence of the ☽ in Capricorn (a response of Pisces) is one of great promise and benefit, giving determined energy, impulse to execute desires entertained as valuable, and, with this, enough motor forces to endure the heavier tasks. The choice of vocation is, in range, a wide one, of a most practical class, and generally leads to moderate success.

The position of the major planets is of much consequence, and determines in marked manner the course of life and its results.

In marriage this mentality should mate with one of calm and equable temperament—perhaps a Taurus, Virgo or Libra native.

♓. ☽ in ♒.

The Lunar-Aquarius forces are a favorable endowment to the Pisces nature, but needs the presence of powerful planetary influences, and high power hereditary texture, to reach a marked place in industrial and social life.

The needs of this mentality are more dignity, persistency, executive force, and aggressiveness.

In marital matters their natures are extreme and variable, needing self-government and constancy, with a thorough regard for the impulse of fidelity and filial love.

♓. ☽ in ♓.

Pisces is the home of the Moon, and if it exerts a powerful influence anywhere it is in this region.

In the mentality of the Pisces nature it exerts its influence toward the love of all that is strange, weird, and phenomenal, giving the mentality an interest in the widest scope of decorative art and in all kinds of fanciful home surroundings. It adds periodicity and exactness to methods, and formulates habits which are not easily set aside.

If ♃ is also in Pisces (with the ☽) at birth, it will trend toward the natives having an inclination toward scientific art, or, properly, the display of art in natural science illustration. As Taurus is the chord of Pisces, this becomes easy when so influenced.

The presence of ♅ with the ☽ in Pisces often gives inclination toward historical painting and sculpture.

FIG. 36.

Apollo Musagetes (Vatican, Rome).

HELIOCENTRIC ASTROLOGY.

Fig. 37.

Apollo and the Muses, G. Romano (Florence).

HELIOS, OR SOL.

The physical phenomena of the Sun, including the orb, was represented among the ancient Greeks by the god Helios. But as light was at the same time an emblem of mental illumination, truth, right, and moral purity, a distinction was made in earlier times between the physical and mental attributes of the Sun. The latter series was represented by the oracular god Phœbus Apollo, who throws light on the dark ways of the future, who by knowledge and goodness brought peace and plenty, joy and freedom, quickened life; and determined in many ways the nature of many living things.

The myth of Apollo was of purely Greek origin, and he was the personification of many ideals, of many objects. The god of youth and beauty, of earthly blessings, of the herds of the field, of medicine, music, and of oracles which reveal the secrets of the future. He had eternal youth, great strength and loved athletics.

Apollo, and his twin sister, Artemis, were children of Zeus and Leto (Latona). In later times the Greeks made no distinction between Apollo and the Sun-god Helios, nor did the Romans distinguish between Apollo and Sol.

Fig. 38.

Monday, Luna (Raphael).

THE MOON, OF PISCES REGION.

Originally, in Greek mythology, the divine personification of the moon was Artemis, a sister of Apollo, the Sun. But as in the case of the Sun, so of the Moon, there gradually grew in the popular mind a distinction between the goddess of the orb and the goddess of the nature of the Moon.

Selene, or Luna, then became goddess of the orb.

Artemis, or Diana, was the goddess of the influence of the Moon upon natural life and vegetation, and as sister of Apollo was believed to share his deepened spiritual qualities.

The quickening influence of the cool night and the falling dew increased the fertility of the southern dry land. The clear calm light of the Moon was thought to cool the hot night air and to congeal the dew.

Artemis was believed to roam by night over fields and vales, in gardens and orchards, and by the rivulets, near fountains, to breathe upon the valleys and to shine down upon all with a silvery light that gave to the dewy blades gems of wondrous hues, as illusive and as spiritual as the source from which they came.

She was worshiped as a goddess of the female productive power in nature, and therefore as the guardian of childbirth, caretaking and nursing of children ; as the goddess of youth ; and, as her name implies, Artemis, the "Modest, spotless goddess," may well be called the goddess of "Strict upbringing, of good fame, of upright mind, and of sensibility in affairs of ordinary life."

Fig. 39.

Artemis. (Vatican, Rome.)

As the patron goddess of huntsmen, she had the title of Agrotera. Under the form of a bear, called Calleste, she was worshiped by the Arcadians. As the goddess Dictynna, or Britomartis, she protected the occupation of fishermen.

The Asteroids, of Scorpio Region.

We know how Jupiter and Neptune and Hera controlled the heavens, sky, and sea. Pluton (Pluto) or Aïdes (Hades) as he was also called, was a son of Cronus and Rhea, and was, on the dethronement of his father, entitled to a share in the management of

Fig. 40.

Ceres. (Vatican, Rome.)

the world; a share equal to that of his brothers Zeus and Poseidon and his sister Hera (Juno). The brothers cast lots: to Pluton fell the dominion of the lower world. There, it is said, in that dark realm rested the shades of the dead, and the invisible demons of evil. Shall we admit that that realm was a region only of evil? That all good dwelt in the kingdoms of Zeus, Poseidon, or of

Hera? Forbid it. Were there not, hidden in that dominion of darkness, the gems and precious metals? Jewels, gold, iron, brass, and copper? But more than all these, far more, were the vital forces that impelled all plant life upward : from which sprang forth the subsistence of all earthly creatures!

What, then, if in the heavens there shone no star for Pluton? In mythology his home was the realm of darkness, extending to the unfathomable abyss beneath, far beyond the doomful river, Styx, from beyond where grim Charon might with mystic oar bring back the soul ; or, failing to win dread Cerberus' consent, it might wander by the Acheron, river of eternal woe ; by Pyriphlegethon, Cocytus, or Lethe, rivers of " Fire," " Weeping and wailing," and of " Forgetfulness."

But this was not all.

From his possessions came the metals of the Arts, of manufacture, the elements of color, aye, the very marble from which were hewn the worshiped images of his brother gods and sister goddesses, and the mighty pillars of their temples.

May we not say that the cycle of the heavens where floats the asteroids, to the eye dark, in which there whirls no visible luminary, the allotted space of one grand body, shattered into elements by a mighty cataclysm, faded, the one into many ; lightless, forevermore, is the realm of Pluton?

Neptune, of Aries Region.

The Titans failing to restore to Cronus his throne, the government of the world was divided by lot among his three sons, Zeus (Jupiter), Poseidon (Neptune), and Hades (Pluto), and to Poseidon fell the control of the element of water. As a god his character and actions were reflected in the phenomena of that element ; his nature was like the vast ocean, ever changing yet ever the same, bearing the commerce of the world or destroying the fleets of nations ; the storm cloud, the mists and the rain that gave fertility to the earth, in that it might bring forth plenty.

As the horse was likened to the storm—impetuous, wild and powerful—and to the rushing river, Neptune was the first to train and employ him, and the horse was taken as a suitable symbol of his power in war and in labor—swift in flight, controllable, beautiful, and spiritual in ambition.

Neptune was worshiped as the god of the fountain, the river, and the sea; in some places as a physician (among the Romans as Neptunus, father of streams): as the protector and creator of human sustenance; his honor was celebrated by festivals, feasts, and games. His rightful wife was Amphitrite, a daughter of Oceanus and Tethys: according to others, daughter of Nereus and Doris.

♆. Neptune in Aries.

♈ is the home of ♆, and in this sign that distant planet exercises his greatest influence. This (Aries-Neptune) nature is full of vivid impulses toward the correction of human ills; it gives an inclination to eradicate every idea it does not sympathize with, and a persistence in demonstration far beyond that of the ordinary kind.

♆ in ♈ also gives incentive toward a national career, and a desire to become of great political importance and power.

With ♀ in ♈ this (Aries-Neptune-Venus) nature has great intellectual sympathy with its mate, and tenderness in expressions of affection and friendship.

With ♃ in ♈ this (Aries-Neptune-Jupiter) nature has a brilliant spirituality (provided there were favorable hereditary signs also), and a wide-awake ethical trend of thought.

♆ in ♉.

This element added to the Taurus nature gives an active desire to distribute scientific knowledge and to popularize it as far as possible, and seeks to make the truth known in the easiest possible way, and to carry forward the philosophies and occult side of the production of the Taurus nature.

It has in it a love of the strange and weird, seeks pleasure in unusual lines of investigation: it studies to gain insight into natural phenomena, and to undo the doctrines of materialism.

But this (♆-♉) nature often lacks certainty and persistence in gaining the common pleasures of life. It sometimes sees a vision of the course of human progress years in advance of the age, but

FIG. 41.

Neptune, of Aries Region.

fails to understand the severe trend of the present. It is this nature that fathoms mental futurity.

♆ in Taurus also gives a tendency toward psychical states, a disposition toward negation, receptivity without executiveness, and a decided inclination toward the imaginative and mysterious.

♆ in ♊.

Neptune in Gemini gives the Gemini nature greater verbal capacity, extreme conversational disposition, and a tendency to poetic and philosophical investigation and occult inquiry.

At times, this nature professes extreme friendships and promises more than it can fulfill, but not consciously or maliciously, or with any intent to mislead, but simply through excessive geniality.

This mentality is much interested in elocution and the dramatic arts, often in fiction and in comedy, and in wide traveling for friendship's sake.

If ♄ and ♅ are present in the sign the nature will have spells of despondence and of extreme depression, erratic changes of thought and desire, and will very likely gain the reputation of eccentricity. ♀ with ♆ gives the nature an exceedingly happy disposition.

♆ in ♋.

The planet Neptune in the Cancer region throws around this nativity an influence of great delicacy and refinement, giving the more spiritual organs power and added brilliancy.

The trend of married life is an elevated one; the growth toward constancy and harmony; there is an added love of nature in her purer forms, and a deep and clear perception of natural law that seems inspirational.

With long study and examination into the natural sciences, this nature may become exceptionally brilliant in all that pertains to social elegance.

In the main, it is expected that this influence should give spirituality, elegance of thought, calmness of will, and a very graceful form.

♆ in ♌.

Neptune in Leo—the climax of spirituality in the forces of religion.

This endowment should certainly give an intense religious nature, a nature that would hunt throughout the realm of intelligence to find spiritual truth, and to advance the cause it once decides to favor.

The only fault to be found is the fact of Neptune's great distance, and the consequent liability of other nearer planets exercising a counteracting force; but even if this were true, this mentality should have a delicacy of expression, an intuitive and sensitive foresight, as well as keen emotional force, that would distinguish the Neptune in Leo parts of a matured mind.

Intense attention to the higher emotions, with power to poetic interpretation of human feelings, must be prime elements in this person's disposition.

♆ in ♍.

Neptune in Virgo brings to the nativity a distinctly intellectual spirituality, and deep and profound home ties, as a basis of family life.

It gives gentleness and constancy, a just patience (all patience is not just by any means), and fullness in its expression.

The influence of ♆ in Virgo is much less in natures of a coarser and denser quality than in those where hereditary conditions are of the higher kind—where the parentage was fine-textured and well-endowed.

The influence of ♆ in Virgo gives added power to the Aries and Sagittarius signs of the nativity, sometimes to Leo. Its weakest force is in the Virgo of Capricorn, Scorpio, and Taurus. It intensifies Gemini's love of children, and romantic thought. It discords very much with ♄ when in the same sign. It is made more sensitive by ☊ or ♃ in Virgo with it.

♆ in ♎.

Neptune in the Libra region of a nativity gives keener memory, mental accuracy, a pride in ancestral reputation; the capacity to speak directly on the point at issue, and a fair degree of mental focus. ♆ also brings an added chance of good fortune, a disposition to gain by lucky incident along with the preservation of activity in a career that yields honor and reputation.

♄ with ♆ in this region gives a disposition to arbitrary judgment, harsh command and haughtiness.

When ♄ is present, with ♆ in Libra, the cast of the whole influence is much changed and inclines to a boastful and arrogant demeanor (except Libra of Capricorn), to being extremely severe, and aims to defeat the success of others, sometimes when there is no necessity for so doing.

♆ in ♏.

Neptune in the Scorpio of the higher dynamic and formal signs gives its possessor a strong desire to extend the arts of mechanical and organic production over as wide a range of human effort as it is possible to reach, and to blend the doctrine of ethics and essential good with those of practical use. ♆ in the Scorpio of Scorpio and of Leo, gives a practical spirituality with an extreme sense of justice; in that of Taurus, Pisces and Capricorn, it gives a desire to make the history and experience of the race one of practical effort and utility.

♆ in the Scorpio of Aries, Taurus, Sagittarius and Libra mentalities, adds memory of useful knowledge, sense of right freedom, desire for industrial advancement, particularly in publishing, telegrapic and commercial communication, in advancing political reforms, social progress and personal uprightness.

♆ in ♐.

Neptune in Sagittarius, the home of Mars, is in the house of a friend, and whatever ethical dominance, enduring memory, vivid perception and keen mental vision can do toward the accumulation of wealth, that assistance ♆ forces will make effort to give.

Sagittarius, always brave, aggressive, keen in finance, and economic in both energy and means, loses nothing of its own and gains much by the endowment of ♆; and, unless the nativity to which it belongs is very much influenced by depressed hereditary conditions, it will give much power.

If with this planet ♃ is also found in the Sagittarius of its chords or responses (Libra, Aries or Virgo) there will be bravery and justice commingled with aggression and caution.

♆ in ♑.

Neptune in Capricorn gives a nature of great industrial aptitude, one that has resources of many kinds; it is capable of argument, swift in application of thought to action, and also quick in gaining the understanding necessary for execution. This is the true commercial nature mixed with mental sincerity and endowed with attainments of the widest variety; noted for skill in railroading, in agriculture, and in the cornering of products for speculative purposes. But often has much more of the ethical and congenial spirituality than is generally found in the Capricorn nature, unless ♃ or ♀ are in the region.

This nature is generally successful, particularly in business and in the home life; at home it has need to be calm and self-controlled.

♆ in ♒.

The influence of Neptune on the Aquarius nature is a remote one, and it has been many (about sixty-six) years since that planet was in that sign, and it will be eighty-six years before it will again enter Aquarius. As Neptune is now, 1899, in Gemini, and in 1901 enters Cancer, and in 1915 enters Leo, it is not necessary here to dwell at length upon its aspect to Aquarius natures.

When in that nature's sign, it adds spirituality, refinement and delicacy to all the mental functions.

♆ in ♓.

The home of Neptune is Aries, and its nature is to accentuate the faculties of attention, of historic elements, and of expression in the more inorganic (mechanical) forms. Hence ♆ in Pisces gives literary taste, delicacy of subject, disposition to treat art ideas and the subjects in art work with historical accuracy, and to give force and character to all the nature's activity. It also adds a mental elegance and responsiveness to the nature that is very attractive. ♆ in Pisces has a marked effect in reducing the ill effects of ☊ and ♄. It adds spirituality to expression.

Uranus, of Virgo.

Uranus, personification of the firmament of the heavens, was produced by the power of the Gæa (Earth), and, at the instance of Eros (Cupid), god of love, was mated with Gæa : and these peopled the Earth with a vast host of beings, beings of great physical frame and strength. Chaos was brought to order at the instance of Love. An older myth accords the creation of the Earth and Heavens to Oceanus and his wife Tethys.

But in the usually accepted mythology of the Greeks, Uranus was rated as the first of the gods. As the husband of the Earth, bringing to it warmth and moisture, giving vigor and life to its prime objects, his nature was in sympathy with his early origin.

Uranus was succeeded by his son, who on his part was also succeeded by his sons, Zeus (Jupiter), Poseidon (Neptune), and Pluto (Hades). To his grandchildren was given even more direct worship than to himself. The astrologers have generally debased the power of Uranus.

♅ in ♈.

Uranus is said to be a mildly evil planet, an infortune, and disposed to cause trouble.

With ♅ in ♈, the nature is somewhat vacillating, changeable, and easily varied from its course. It may depress the nature so that it is simply unsuccessful along lines usually ably followed.

This planet in Aries gives a liking for vocations that are clerical and semi-literary, secretaryships, keeping records, etc.

This nature has a strong interest in home and home life ; is particularly interested in children, oftener from a mental or intellectual standpoint than from the affectionate side of its nature.

♂ in ♈ with ♅ gives the nature recklessness and a speculative drift. These may be neutralized by other planets.

♅ in ♉.

This nature is seldom fortunate. Its energies are often wasted upon futile problems, upon riddles, the solution of which are of minor importance. When no other planet is in the Taurus region with it ♅ inclines the nature to family love, but fails to supply the kind of energy required to take care of the family.

This nature should struggle for competence, first; that won, then seek glory and honor as it choses to. To withstand grave opposition, and to wrest its own from the world around, it needs security.

With ♃ or with ♂ also in Taurus, ♅ receives the support necessary to give it some successful power, and make it more practical. In matters pertaining to family life ♅ gives constancy.

♅ in ♊.

Uranus in Gemini inclines the nature to great variability, to eccentricity in friendship and in expression.

It gives the calm and congenial (♊) nature a cast of uncertainty and a tinge of distrust quite different from its normal disposition.

The planet has force toward love of children and the family life, and hence gives the nature variable kindness in that direction; but it is seldom controlled by deep and prolonged attachments, except for its own offspring.

♅ in ♋.

The influence of Uranus in Cancer is one of marked selfish desires, and an inclination to gain every pleasure for the personality so endowed.

There may be other influences to modify the regional influence. But there is a tendency to exactitude, to quite plain commands; and, while there is a powerful desire to gain advantage for the home life, there should be cautious care to avoid selfishness, excess, dominance, and in some states, if uncontrolled by other influences, the presence of pessimistic views and melancholia.

Under favorable surroundings, there is an added love of children, and sometimes great patriotism, self-protection for national purposes, and a clear grasp of economics.

♅ in ♌.

Uranus in Leo. The mentality that has this endowment has much that is extremely industrious in its aspirations, yet it may be physically disposed to great moderation.

The ill effects of ♅ in many of the signs is in a large measure neutralized in Leo, where the presence of a dominant religious force affects the lack of spirituality in that planet's influences.

Where ♅ in Leo is alone, and ♀ at home or in Virgo, it creates a desire for a large family if the person is married, and a keen interest in the care and material welfare of the young.

☋ with ♅ in Leo gives a proselyting disposition. ♄ with ♅ in Leo gives the mentality a money-making, covetous and bigoted orthodoxy, and a desire to rule faith with the sword.

♅ in ♍.

Uranus in Virgo is in its own region, and intensifies family love (filial love in particular), patriotism, and adds clannishness to family habits and to nationality. ♅ here increases the desire for security, to gain comforts, to make the most of the productive capacity in manufacturing and other enterprises in which this nature is likely to have interests.

♅ in Virgo often gives a fascination for outdoor life, for agricultural pursuits, stock raising, and horticulture. This is particularly true in the Virgo of Capricorn, Scorpio, Aquarius and Pisces.

It must be remembered that a planet's influence is better in its home region; it also intensifies the nature of that region rather than its own power.

♅ is static and earthly, just as ♀ is static and spiritual.

♅ in ♎.

Uranus in Libra depreciates the natural uprightness of the Libra forces whenever the action relates to others than the native's family. To the world at large the impulse of this endowment is to gain advantage by every scheme at hand, and if it is the Libra of Taurus, Sagittarius, Capricorn (sometimes of Virgo), these are coupled with a life of policy and of political methods. In the Libra of the Libra nativity with ♅ in that sign, the nature is much more selfish, personal and grasping than with any other combination of planets.

When ♃ and ♅ are present in Libra, ♅ loses power by the intervention of Jupiterian beneficence, and the region again assumes its dignified attitude.

♅ invests minds of a low order with cunning and bossism, when it is in the regions of the Will.

♅ in ♏.

Uranus in Scorpio intensifies the activity of its possessor toward self-advancement and personal gain. But ♅ in Scorpio of the Scorpio nativity makes it more selfish and depreciates the integrity of Scorpio, and of the dynamic signs in general. In the static signs it arouses a desire to shirk responsibility and to avoid a due amount of labor.

With ♄ in Scorpio with ♅, there is danger of malicious attacks from others, and of personal injury as a result of willful persistence in opposition to generally accepted views.

♅ both pessimistic and seeking greater freedom, ♄ planning to gain undue advancement, gives a restless, changeful temperament. ♄ and ♅ give resentment and severity in this sign, and, when ☿ is present with either ♄ or ♅ in the Scorpio of a mentality, there is danger of duplicity, cunning, and a garnish of elegant presumption.

♅ in ♐.

Uranus in the Sagittarius of nearly all the signs is in an unhappy region, and there is apt to be much contention. As far as the Uranus-Sagittarius forces are concerned they give an unhappy temperament seldom satisfied with its surroundings. A nature thus endowed should cultivate self-control, should avoid the disposition to extreme caution, and the tendency to imagine the existence of dangers that may never appear.

To take the world easier, to live freer from useless fear, to calmly pursue a course of usefulness, and, above all, to seek happiness in the interests of family life, is a policy necessary to the success of a nativity with ♅ in Sagittarius.

♀ in Sagittarius with ♅ does much to beautify and give it security.

♅ in ♑.

Uranus in Capricorn gives a drastic and sometimes very critical nature, one that generally reserves to itself all the advantages that surround it. But it has many good qualities, and an intense love for home life ; is a cautious, earnest and sympathetic parent, and is forceful in protection, of both family and country. This nature is patriotic, is given to politics for the purpose of ruling, and many times manages others (who act as agents) to gain the end sought. However strong may be the desire to enjoy life, gaiety and traveling, this nature still seeks security, and unless depressed by sickness is full of energy and perseverance.

With ♃ in Capricorn there is an influence that trends to ward off the worst effects of ♅ (which is tentatively supposed to be un- fortunate in his nature).

♅ in ♒.

Uranus in Aquarius is an influence that leads to supersensitive nerves. It gives quickness in forming judgments and a certain extreme activity in physical movements that is a stress upon health, as well as upon endurance.

Uranus in many ways works against a successful career when found in this sign of a nativity, and requires the presence of a steadying force. The cultivation of moderation, stability, perse- verance in undertakings, and, in the other extreme, more of a dis- position to lightheartedness.

♅ in ♓.

Uranus in Pisces gives that nature intensified affection and family desires, adds to the control of children, and to the nature's pa- triotic and home life. But in the commercial direction gives a disposition to use skill in illegal ways, to turn to artistic and finan- cial trickery, which should be guarded against. Jupiter in Libra, or ♆ in Taurus, have good control over ♅ in Pisces. ♀ in Pisces gives a guiding and retarding influence, and a unifying effect; for ♅ has a disposition toward dispersing the efforts of Pisces natures. Observe the effect of good planets over the evil ones in each nativity.

Fig. 42.

Saturday, Saturn (Raphael).

SATURN, OF CAPRICORN.

Saturnus, among the early Romans, was a god of agriculture, gardening, and fruit growing; and, by instruction and the incentives he gave the people, raised them from a rude, almost barbarous condition to one of order and peace, of plenty, gladness, innocence, freedom and joy. During his joint reign with Janus, was the golden age of Rome. Once a year, in December, the Romans held a festival lasting from five to ten days, called Saturnalia, in his honor. Saturnus was not worshiped as a Greek god; but Greek mythology also had its golden age. This is said to have occurred during the reign of Cronus, and thus the identification of Saturnus and Cronus as apparently the same, although there was a vast difference in their characters.

The name of Saturn's wife was Ops; the name of Cronus' wife was Rhea, a daughter of Gæa.

Cronus was called "The ripener, the harvest god;" but he is said to have devoured five of his children because it was rumored that he would, like his father, be dethroned by them. He had irremediably wounded his father with a sickle presented to him by his mother Gæa (Earth), because of her grief at the hard fate of her offspring.

Cronus was severe, harsh, ambitious, and often destructive, either directly or indirectly; and we see that the astrological nature of the planet Saturn is much more nearly typified by Cronus of the Greeks than by Saturnus of the Romans, and that the Roman Saturnus in character is much more like the Greek Neptune than the Greek Saturnus.

FIG. 43.

Cronus.

♄ in ♈.

This nature is inclined toward a career of commercial literary piracy and sharp business sagacity, using talent for others' success, and often failing to realize the results of native brilliancy.

As Saturn (♄) glories in commerce and in transportation, he is almost certain, when in any region, to give that region the impulse of his nature. In Aries, ☿ is the only planet that can neutralize this ♄ force. It is well to observe this fact.

Sometimes, when other planets in other regions give directive power, this nature becomes a powerful publishing force, disseminating vast amounts of knowledge, yet with the financial incentive the chief thought. This nature is predisposed to lung troubles.

♄ in ♉.

♄ in Taurus gives the Taurus nature a logical commercial force, stubborn in its desire to mould matters to its own course, and disposed to compel others to follow this (♄ - ♉) nature's arbitrary rule.

When inclined most toward the scientific side of life, it is more successful in agricultural and horticultural pursuits than in the direction of mechanics.

As this nature, so often dogmatic in method, may become perverse and sullen through disappointment, it should strive to keep the attention on the brighter side of life, and to seek enjoyment where there is freedom from constraint and antagonism.

The presence of another planet in the Taurus region has much less influence upon the power of ♄ than it would have in any other region. The reason is plain, for ♄ - ♉ depends much upon reason, upon the general course of events. It lacks the impressive nature, and in place of the emotions it has installed impulse and materialistic force. It needs to cultivate that intuitive energy that attracts, and to study the more delicate phases of insight and mental foresight.

This nativity has a fair self-assurance; it critically and often cynically observes the faults and failings of others; and, with some wide divisions of force, is compelled, by its severity, to do more than is necessary in order to accomplish its aims.

♄ in ♊.

Saturn in Gemini loses much of his general malignant nature, being in the opposite region from his own, and where the influence of Mercury is dominant.

But ♄ here gives a commercial attitude to the nature, and the suave and persuasive forces of the agent and the promoter of enterprises.

This mentality is often troubled by matters pertaining to contracts, by legal actions, and by having overstated values, of painted opportunities into highly-colored views. It lacks the persistency necessary to accomplish great gains and the success that its talents would seem to warrant.

With ♂ also in the sign with ♄, there is a necessity for controlling the nature against the disposition to deceive.

♄ in ♋.

The influence of ♄ in the Cancer region is not a favorable one. It incites to sensuality, to extremes in the appetites; it even trends toward the use of stimulants and narcotics; and, while it gives strength and physical endurance, these are often wasted through misappropriation and poor application.

There is need of self-control, of study in personal rights—the rights of others as related to those of self.

There should be cautious care to not allow dissensions, as, once started, ♄ here is apt to perpetuate them. Avoid any cause for jealousy, and also avoid the supposition of its appearance.

It is thus seen that ♄ in Cancer is a very contrary force, and needs government; those who have it will not easily see their own faults.

♄ in ♌.

Saturn in Leo of a nativity gives physical intensity, severe generalizations in opinion, a dominant commercial spirit, and variable emotions of a higher order, and alternating with those less to be desired; at times exceedingly generous, at others very exacting and aggressive.

The endowment gives a large amount of grace, flexibility, virility and vital motive power. It is destructive when antagonized, cautious under the slightest suspicion of danger, confident in an attack, and believes more in force than in skill or diplomacy.

With all the natural capacity of the nature thus endowed, it is seldom happy, and often quite irritable and hard to keep under sufficient self-restraint.

♂ in the sign with ♄ adds an angular and severe element, with a desire to profit through the failure of others.

♄ in ♍.

The home of Saturn is Sagittarius, a chord of Virgo, and in this region, with Virgo influence aroused by that planet, there is an aggressive spirituality; the energies are turned toward the practical side of life, and there is a constant struggle for prominence and power of a very mundane order; the attitude being much inclined to gain wealth and family influence, the nepotism of planetary influence is here shown in its most dominant manner.

The result of this regional influence is always toward the improvement of circumstances. When badly endowed by ♂ and ♀, or by ♃, there is apt to be inter-family troubles, angular expression in useless antagonism among kinships, with a relentless persistency in maintaining a position once taken, or an opinion once passed. This personality should study the rights of others.

♄ in ♎.

Saturn in Libra of a nativity adds the severely commercial spirit to Libra elements; has small fear of destructive results, nor cares how much others suffer when the possible satisfaction of governing with an iron rule exists. It is thus that it often happens that antagonists to this nature become unmerciful and go to extremes to severely punish ♄ in Libra natures. It is well that this mentality exerts self-restraint and caution, and avoids legal contentions or personal controversies.

♄ in the Libra of Taurus, Leo, Sagittarius and Scorpio, adds impulsion and angularity, sometimes rigor and pessimistic aversion.

♄ in the Libra of Aries, Gemini, Cancer and Capricorn is somewhat neutralized by the forces of those regions and their harmony with Libra.

♄ with ♅, ♆ and ☿ in Libra gives erratic, variable temperament, and weakened judgment.

♄ in ♏.

Saturn alone in Scorpio of the greater number of the nativities, may be considered a very bad combination, giving an evil temper to low quality mentalities, with a quarrelsome and violent disposition, seldom at rest or satisfied

♄ gives to the Scorpio influence a wider commercial impulse than the normal force, and adds some destructive forces, a full share of doubt, fear, aversion or antipathy, depending upon the conditions.

The home of ♄ chords with Scorpio, and there is a sympathy between the boldness of ♄ and the industry and hardihood of Scorpio.

With ♃ in Scorpio with ♄ , there is contention, vacillation, and changes from the extremes of integral goodness and beneficent assistance to the harsh antagonism of competition and doubt. ♄ and ♃ are never in sympathy, and particularly in the domain of Saturn's stronger influences.

♄ in ♐.

Saturn in Sagittarius is in a fairly sympathetic region, but not in one of greatest power. The nature so endowed, unless well counterbalanced, will have a severe strain of asceticism in it, along with a calm and determined desire to put all opposition out of the way. It will make due preparation for a contest, and, when once aroused to the attack, seldom retreat. In business ventures, and where open contention enters into the game of fortune, this nature is full of sagacity, resource, resistance, and when apparently necessary as a last resort, of destructiveness.

When crossed, this nature is easily angered and is difficult to appease. Unless it tries hard to exercise self-control, there is danger of rash acts and loss of friends.

♄ in Sagittarius natures should study the impulses of Gemini and Libra.

♄ in ♑.

Saturn in Capricorn is at home, that is in his own region, and gives power to that region, so that there is an accelerated commercial capacity and rapidity of action; a fiercer judgment.

This is the nature fully adapted to commerce; the energetic, mobile nature; always alert in guarding its own interests.

There is a degree of severity in this mentality that requires modifying; it needs to look toward the higher, more spiritualized range of thought; to turn its ambitions to promote the nobler aims of life, and thus exert those influences and disseminate those truths, that the less aggressive and less financially successful natures cannot spread because of lack of means.

This nature will not brook injury, insult or oppression; it needs and seeks freedom; it forces co-operation. It rules the weak and enjoins the powerful to its advantage.

♄ in ♒.

This is often a favorable force, giving attention to financial and provisional matters, and causing the person to exercise economy, where needed, caution in personal habits and in general expression, and, with this, giving some positiveness.

When ☿ is also in Aquarius there is apt to be a clash of impulses, more carelessness, and unnecessary severity when aroused to anger.

A careful supervision of studies, aims, capacities and temperament may be valuable, and effort made to arouse in the young who are under this influence a series of worthy ambitions.

♄ in ♓.

Saturn in Pisces brings from Capricorn a disposition toward shrewd observation, keen perception, a trend toward making a living by simply knock-about methods, sometimes by war—as soldiers —and in favorite military positions.

In humbler walks of life, or at least in the natures of ignorant persons, the influence of ♄ is toward intemperance, variable temper and inclination to indifferent workmanship.

When fine qualitied, this mentality is active, sometimes very restless, and should always seek to carry a firm, steady hand and head, and gain personal control over ill-temper or injudicious desire.

With ☿ in Gemini and ♃ in Aries or Taurus, these forces will much reduce the ill-effects of ♄ in Pisces. This personality may become very brilliant in artistic skill; in symbolic art and accomplishments with brush and palette.

HELIOCENTRIC ASTROLOGY. 151

FIG. 44.

Thursday, Jupiter (Raphael).

JUPITER, OF LIBRA.

Cronus swallowed his first five children, but his wife, Rhea, by strategy, succeeded in saving the sixth, which was conveyed to the island of Crete, where nymphs tended him, the goat Amathia supplied him with milk, and bees gathered honey for him.

The baby Zeus, who was in the future to wisely organize the affairs of the Universe, thus began life.

Zeus succeeded his father, Cronus, and was undoubtedly the most widely worshiped of all the gods of Greece and Rome.

As his name implies, he was god of the broad light of the day, the phenomena of the heavens, and all the general interests of human affairs.

He had many titles; the Storm-king, Cloud-gatherer, the Everlasting, the Thunderer. These and many others.

The eagle was sacred to him, the mountain peaks favorite places of worship. The wind rustling the leaves of the sacred oak told his desire to speak to men, and the priesthood of Selli were the interpreters.

He was worshiped as the highest god, as the ruler and preserver of men; endowed with wisdom, always just; unlimited in his goodness and love; the promoter of natural law, protector of kings and rulers and the poor.

Fig. 45.

Jupiter Verospi (Vatican, Rome).

Zeus is accused of being untrue to his marriage vows; his first wife is said to have been Metis (Cleverness), the daughter of Titian

Oceanus. Metis he swallowed. Next he is said to have married Themis (Justice), and became the father of Astræ and Horæ. But he loved Hera (Juno), the mother of Hebe, Ares (Mars), and Hephæstus (Vulcan). Zeus is said not to have remained constant in marriage even to Hera; and thus Demeter (Ceres) bore him Perséphonē. Leto became the mother of Apollo and Artemis (Diana); and Dionē, the mother of Aphrodite (Venus). So, too, Mnemosynē, the mother of the muses; Eurynomē, of the Charities (Graces); Semelē, of Dionysus (Bacchus); Maia, of Hermes (Mercury); Alcmene, of Heracles; and some of the demigods were also sons.

But it is probable that, in different localities, there was a confusion of the names of his true wife, and as the worship spread, and the established favorites did not correspond in personification to the local desire, new favorites, with new dominant powers, were found to have descended to them.

Thus in the long periods of changing peoples, and varied language, under the reign of ideas demanding other sons and other gods, Zeus was associated with the same wife, but under several names, just as there was often a change or confusion of godly power or function.

Mighty and costly statues were in many places, made in his honor. One by Pheidias, placed on the plain of Olympia, was forty feet in height, and was called one of the seven wonders of the world.

♃ in ♈.

An almost ideal combination, with powerful inclinations toward creative thought; with capacity for literary and imaginative visions, and with a self-command that is admirable. Jupiter's home is in ♎, the Solar polarity of ♈, and when in Aries gives a deep sense of honor and worth, and an intense desire for grand achievements and literary fame. Included in this is a love of legislative power and legal accomplishments.

This nature is seldom subject to accident (unless ♄ and ♅ are also in ♈), and therefore has great confidence in carrying out its plans.

♃ and ♀ in ♈ gives poetic talent, dramatic instincts and sometimes talent for dramatic authorship.

This nature may gain wealth and military honors, but will seldom crave the latter unless there is great activity in the direction of war.

♃ in ♉.

♃ adds to the Taurus nature a volume of powerful energies. The nature becomes more hopeful, more vivid, and in general more spiritual in thought. As a whole, it is full of prophetic instincts, of sensitive mental impulses, and of the sense of mastership in whatever it essays to attempt.

♃ brings into full play the inspiration of Taurus, and gives clearness to the thoughts and activity of this nature. At the same time that it inclines the (♃-♉) mind toward exactness in practical matters, it forces forward the broad and synthetic view of human necessity.

If ♀ is also in Cancer, the nature is sensuous, full of romance, sensitive to the pathetic and inclined to great generosity. If ♂ is in Taurus (with ♃) there is a culmination of war talent and severity in opinion.

♃ in ♊.

Jupiter in Gemini indicates a very enjoyable nature, full of kindness, bravery and good humor. It intensifies the grace and elegance of the Gemini mentality, and makes dominant the desire to do justly and kindly by every one. Jupiter also gives great versatility in conveying ideas, fullness of thought, expression, and ease in mastering the resources of surrounding associations.

To the nature it gives power to suggest to others matters of advantage to them, and to foresee the probable political action of the populace. This nature smiles a challenge at the shadow of adversity. It conquers by friendship.

The presence of ♄ with ♃ makes the nature aggressive and inclined toward political and social self-advancement, and makes in many ways enthusiastic public servants—not forgetting in the least their own interests.

♃ in ♋.

The home of ♃ is in Libra, and there is a remarkably desirable effect in the influence of ♃ in Cancer.

This regional influence intensifies the mental attractions of marriage, it makes the realm of marriage more spiritual and more ruled, better governed, better tempered. The nature is freer; there is an added elegance and brilliancy; there is a deep sense of justice, and also added industry.

At times, to nativities of Sagittarius, Capricorn and Scorpio, ♃ in this sign gives pride and a little boastfulness, some tendency toward wit and humor, and a vivid interest in new enterprises.

With ♄ also in Cancer there is a tendency toward selfish family interests, and an inclination toward clannishness.

With ♄ in Scorpio, the nature thus endowed trends toward incessant labor and productivity both of a material and mental order.

♃ in ♌.

Jupiter in Leo is a very favorable endowment, one giving great mental harmony. A personality thus endowed is generous, self-ruling, well controlled, matures early in life, gains through forcefulness the handling of relatively large responsibilities, and nearly always has a large amount of vitality to aid in carrying forward any work at hand.

When the native sign is dynamic (will) there is a strong disposition to dominate the course of others, and, at times, this should be carefully considered, or others' rights will be decidedly infringed. The presence of other planets in Leo with ♃ may very much modify or greatly increase the harmony.

♄ causes coldness and sternness; ♂ gives this endowment greater intensity and passionate vitality. ♀ adds delicacy, imagination and spiritual gracefulness.

♃ in ♍.

Jupiter in Virgo arouses the elements of Rulership, and thus increases the stability and perseverance of the Virgo nature.

It gives more brilliancy and social desires in the broadest sense of that term. It decreases personal and clannish selfishness, and thus awakens a fund of harmony in civil efforts, in matters that relate to the needs of the community.

Jupiter in this region incites to personal egotism, the egotism of dress and display, of self-laudation, often to an extreme, and sometimes causes an overestimation of individual capacity, importance and responsibility. In poorly endowed natures this causes trouble; the personality is braggart and boastful. In moderately endowed mental organizations there is a stimulated energy. In highly organized natures the result is a somewhat overexerted nervous system, with high accomplishments.

♃ in ♎.

Jupiter in Libra, and in the nativity of Libra, gives a culmination of self-government, dignity and justice. In the Libra of Aries, Taurus, Gemini, Scorpio, Leo, and Sagittarius, it praises whatever it sees worthy of praise, compliments the struggling, protects the weak, and glories in checking the overbearing and abusive. In these nativities it is generally able and forceful, mild in temper unless greatly aggravated, forgiving when there is warrant for so being, esteemed, and generally well loved.

♃ in Libra of Libra, Cancer, Leo and Aquarius adds generosity and kindness in all friendships. In signs most generously endowed it would be well to exercise unusual care and discretion in business matters, avoiding a disposition to overconfidence in others' integrity, and to see that burdens based upon "duty" do not accumulate to the obliteration of justice in some other direction. No other planet greatly depreciates Libra with ♃ at home.

♃ in ♏.

Jupiter in Scorpio of any nativity adds to the love of freedom, and an intent to carry out that nativity's desires unrestricted and unopposed, and adds the motive to force others to act in accord therewith.

♃ in Scorpio of that nativity is a beneficent force. If the Scorpio is that of a Capricorn, Sagittarius or Pisces nativity it inclines to shrewd, crafty and unnecessarily severe methods.

In the Scorpio of all the nativities ♃ accomplishes much but unevenly; it raises their power in detail and courage to a high pitch and sometimes falls from its eminence by its own dominance.

In law matters ♃ gains cases but loses the benefits that might accrue. In commercial matters this influence finds success, but with struggles due to mental discords that defeat much of the possible pleasure.

Many of the asteroids are at home in Scorpio, and ♃ disseminates or scatters their forces.

♃ in ♐.

Jupiter in Sagittarius gives the mentality in which it is found that ruling element under which the influence of Sagittarius is more uniform in its effects. There is an added interest in public and official business; in military matters; in overseeing the many branches of manufacturing and building.

The mentality under this influence seeks direct results; it is fierce in competition when there is danger of failure. In some ways this nature is apt, because of its power, to overreach and in midlife lose some of its rapidly accumulated advantages.

A proper weight should be given to the cautionary elements of Sagittarius, and these balanced by the best forces of the Gemini sign.

Sagittarius chords with Libra, the region of Jupiter, and makes ♃ dominant over all the planets except ♂.

♃ in ♑.

Jupiter in Capricorn modifies the Capricorn forces, and at the same time brightens, beautifies it, and makes the mentality more graceful and idealistic; less severe, and less destructive to others' ambitions.

♃ lends to this mentality a disposition toward benevolence, and brings some interest to bear on the getting and enjoyment of wealth by others.

The ♃ endowment is here toward humane and magnanimous actions; it gives agreeability, winsomeness and expression of strong attractions for those less successful. It is apparent that ♃ in Capricorn of most nativities gives power in argument, and an interest in the financial results of politics; aims at fostering home enterprises and in building up superb surroundings. This nature glories in wealth; it is seldom extremely covetous, unless ♄ is in the same region.

♃ in ♒.

When Aquarius has Jupiter as its stimulating planet, there is almost always found an intense social ambition, a desire to gain society honors, and a tendency to neglect the affairs of utility in the household, or in business life.

The ambitions are always in evidence. There is a desire to govern, and with it, generally, political aspirations.

The nature thus endowed will many times succeed with less capacity than is thought necessary by others, and will take success easy, as if it were due.

The tendency of persons thus endowed is to sow their "wild oats" while comparatively young.

♃ in ♓.

Jupiter in Pisces gives to a mentality a grander conception of artistic elements, and a disposition toward enduring work which no other planet and only our ☽ can equal.

In natures of high quality this placement of ♃ gives persistence and efficiency; it adds endurance in research; desire for minute accuracy. It makes the nature capable of that elegance of expression and manner that is so attractive, and instills ambition to excel.

To mentalities of less delicate quality, ♃ gives power in practical utility; manual dexterity; a generous disposition to use energy for the benefit of others.

♃ combats ♄ with marked effect in this sign.

☿ adds to ♃'s power in the Pisces sign; and if ♂ is also in the sign with ♃ it is an evidence of military prowess.

HELIOCENTRIC ASTROLOGY.

Fig. 46.

Tuesday, Mars (Raphael).

Mars, or Sagittarius.

Ares, or Mars, was a son of Zeus (Jupiter) and Hera (Juno), originally god of the storm, tempest and hurricane; later the god of turmoil, strife and war, most fierce and terrible, with love of aggression, slaughter and massacre. He had great prowess, physical strength and valor. Worshiped in Greece but little, in Thrace more, and in Rome next to Jupiter, as a guardian of the state.

Fatal Strife (Eris), Dread and Alarm (Deimos and Phobos), were usually by his side, or attending his footsteps.

In Thebes, Aphrodite (Venus) was often worshiped as his proper wife, symbolizing, probably, the peace and quiet that followed the rancor and struggle of war.

♂ in ♈.

Mars in Aries fires that nature with aggressive energies, and very often leads it toward research and exploration, but generally with view to conquest or to commercial advantages. It is this nature that seeks distinction and fame in pioneer work of all kinds, and in the various plans for defence, or for the accumulation of new territory.

♂ adds much of a domineering element to the Aries nature, and particularly if ♄ is also in the region; the same is true in less degree if ♅ is present; in the latter case there is apt to be a vein of boastfulness and egotistic familiarity in business and public affairs.

♀ and ♂ neutralize the influence of each other when both are

Fig. 47.

Ares, or Mars (Villa Ludovisi, Rome).

in the Aries region; the presence of ☿, however, restores the influence of Venus.

♂ in ♉.

♂ in Taurus—war and science combined; destruction, defence, and love of wealth, mixed with science, progress and discovery—is the combination in this nature. It may be that quality and texture of the mentality will not sustain both lines, or raise the whole into prominence; nevertheless there will be force, and to the extent the personal capacity will admit.

♂ upholds the constructive side of the ♂ in Taurus nature, just as ♆ upholds and intensifies the intuitive, or as ♃ inclines it toward brilliancy and exactness.

♄ with ♂ in Taurus gives the nature pessimistic and lethargic qualities that are otherwise foreign to the nature in which ♂ is found in Taurus.

♂ in ♊.

Mars in Gemini seeks every possible gain by plausible and friendly competition, and to outgeneral all opposition by means of pen and voice. It is often most aggravating to opponents, calmly challenging their methods or their views, and then when the point at issue is decidedly close, just as calmly ridiculing their seriousness.

This nature, calm outwardly, is always intense, often very successful in scientific research, and likewise in the accumulation of wealth by profitable trading; in real estate and in manufacturing general commodities; for very heavy manufacturing there is hardly enough of the elements of consecutive and sustained effort to succeed well.

This mentality seeks large freedom, varies much, has great independence in matters of small importance, or of apparent opinion; while in heavier fields of action it will yield to the advice as well as to the rights of others. This personality is, therefore, an agreeable but often provoking companion, putting up barriers everywhere and then suavely taking them down again; often suggesting cataclysms of opinion and then with its own breath blowing them away.

♂ in ♋.

The influence of ♂ in Cancer is one of forcefulness and aggressive power. It is often inclined toward mild deception, but seldom deepens into injury. ♂ in this region adds strength to the constitution, gives courage in the defence of home life, and added boldness.

But the influence of ♂ in this region acts very differently upon different nativities, and must therefore be harmonized with the particular powers at work.

In the affectional signs ♂ is modified much, and in the Cancer of the Will signs he is strengthened; in that of the thought signs, ♂ becomes supporting and aids in giving caution and defence.

♂ in ♌.

Mars in Leo detracts from rather than adds to the Leo endowment. Especially is this true of the Leo nativity. In all nativities there is a disposition to utilize the labors and energies of others for this nature's selfish purposes. It gives Leo, Virgo and Pisces greater intensity, power to drive business and to carry on its warfare in the direction of its native sign. To the Leo of Libra, Scorpio, Sagittarius and Capricorn it gives caution, fearlessness, self-protection and defence. In most of the signs it watches and uses social advantages for monetary reasons and against surprise. It loves argument, but for contest rather than for information.

A person so endowed should exercise government over temper, avoid useless contention, seek to make others happy and contented, rather than to arouse their fears or take away their opportunity. Much depends upon the places of the other planets.

♂ in ♍.

Mars in Virgo is not a favorable location, nor often a pleasure-giving influence. The kind of positive force exerted by ♂ disturbs and detracts from the smooth harmony of Virgo energies; it leads to deception in social affairs, and causes loss of constant interest in the affairs of personal life.

Unless well governed by other planetary (and by hereditary) conditions, this influence will give angularity, hasty temper, an idle love for contest, and a disposition to gluttony, sometimes ungoverned intemperance, and along with it an utter disregard for financial obligations.

When the whole organization is highly endowed, with ♃ in Aries, Taurus, or Libra, there is a far better result, and may have a wide range of competency.

♂ in ♎.

Mars brings to Libra regional forces a great amount of courage and caution, and a mentality thus endowed will not be easily imposed upon nor easily defeated.

To the Libra of Scorpio, Sagittarius, Capricorn, and, to a less marked degree, Aries nativities, ♂ in Libra adds sagacity, inclination to be aggressive, positive, dogmatic, exact, and, when aroused to anger, revengeful.

♂ in Libra of Libra nativities causes them to seek government positions, military commands, and, when modified by planets in Aries or Taurus, captaincies of ships. In Libra of other signs, it finds enjoyment in overseeing, construction, etc., etc.

☿ in Libra with ♂ adds social power and gracefulness, as well as intellectual aptitude.

With ♄ and ♂ in Libra of Libra, Aries (and even Leo), it often gives Herculean power, though severe, changeable, erratic, kind or protective by spasmodic impulses, and generally reaps severe defeat in early life, only to learn a lesson and rise stronger later on.

♂ in ♏.

Mars in Scorpio adds wealth and war forces to the energetic coactive impulses of Scorpio. In this, ♂ gives endurance, courage, daring and economic caution. In the Scorpio of the cosmic signs and that of Aries and Taurus, sometimes that of Pisces, ♂ in times of peace institutes productive habits and energy, constructiveness and interest in manufacturing enterprises. In times of war he arouses aggression, and instigates severe action.

♀ in Scorpio with ♂ acts as a modifier, and softens the harshness of its severer attitudes. ♄ aggravates the whole, giving angularity, destructiveness and revenge.

♅ with ♂ in Scorpio arouses a moody taciturnity, and particularly in the nativities of the static regions.

♅ and ♂ with ♄ in the Scorpio of a Leo native is a very depressing, pessimistic, despondent and melancholy-creating influence.

♂ in ♐.

Mars is at home in Sagittarius, and his warlike powers, fierce temper, indomitable courage are in control. This endowment is therefore keenly alive to the accumulation of wealth, to gaining security for self and those dependent upon it; it is economical except when there is a prospect of great gain, or an advantage in business. This nature is boastful by action rather than by words, and almost always for a purpose. It can hold subordinate positions, but desires freedom to execute its will, and the least restraint possible. ♃ in Sagittarius with ♂ gives great boldness and bravery. ♀ with ♂ gives this nature intense interest in family life, love of mate, and a fund of brilliant sarcasm.

♄ with ♂ intensifies the desire for wealth, and gives the nature a necessity for guarding against criminal desires of a civil order.

♂ in ♑.

Mars in Capricorn is the presence of the war god in the domain of commerce, and there is a fiery, energetic, forceful, diligent, and extremely aggressive nature as a result, unless much modified by other favorable planets.

This nature is exact, it forces order, is shrewd and calculating, affable where it has interests, indifferent where it has none or is in doubt.

This mentality makes many friends, holds them well when there is only social interests at stake, and often loses them when business intervenes, because it is too exact and demands large profits. There is apt to be reaction in business by those who are outwitted, and there is a necessity for both frankness and careful contracts on the part of both parties. Generally successful.

♂ in ♒.

Mars in Aquarius gives an incentive toward financial and trade organization, economic study, precautionary thought, and a disposition to rule in a moderate way by citing incentives instead of arousing antagonism.

But when aroused, it will cause trouble in social affairs, and sometimes study the processes of revenge with much interest.

It is always well for persons thus endowed to act with calm discretion, to keep free from any entanglements that may easily cause discord.

♄ in ♓.

Mars in Pisces adds to the nativity of any sign increased perceptive energy ; a disposition to go to extremes in the observation of possible danger ; but does not add artistic skill. It forces the Pisces and Gemini mentality to a more martial spirit than is supposed to belong to the artistic temperament.

♄ in the Pisces of Intellectual signs gives them a critical and somewhat aggravating trend ; in the Pisces of the Will signs, and when unrestrained, makes them more severe and accumulative, and particularly if in the last days of the Pisces sign.

According to the geocentric system, Mars in Pisces gives rather an ugly temper ; is controversial, deceitful, easily angered, not easily imposed upon ; besides this, is also hypercritical in religion, and loves to exercise authority. This author has found that ♄ in Pisces increases ambition, pride and constructiveness.

FIG. 48.

Friday, Venus (Raphael).

VENUS, OF CANCER.

Venus (Aphrodite) was the goddess of love in its widest sense—the love thought to be the cause of productiveness in all nature. In her character we find the noble, good and beautiful, and often, with these, much that was debasing and ignoble, as a result of passion and licentiousness. Beauty, luxury and voluptuousness were attributed to results of her power.

Many of her characteristics are said to have been derived from the Phœnicians, who had, in the personification Astartē, a similar goddess. She is described by the Greeks as a daughter of Zeus (Jupiter) and Dionē, and thus, through her mother, was associated with the ancient worship of Dodona. She was supposed to preside over married life and its ceremonies.

♀ in ♈.

The nature of Venus is fortunate, and, when in power, she symbolizes a very wide range of elegance, and of intense activity and feeling. ♀ adds to the Aries nature a disposition toward extreme congeniality, graceful friendship, and intensifies the desire for companionship in thought and in the struggles of life. But the Aries nature is then very apt to have confidence in unsuccessful plans, to overestimate the possibilities of a course of action; there is often an absence of business sagacity in even trifling financial matters, and none the less in larger ones.

♄ in Capricorn aids with business shrewdness. ♆ in Scorpio indicates great struggles and losses, as well as waste of energy.

♂ in Sagittarius (with ♀ in ♈) aids much to overcome financial carelessness, or the ill effects of ♄ or ♆ as above stated.

♀ in ♉.

Venus in Taurus gives calmness, spiritual intensity, ennobling aims, persistence in action, and love of grace and elegance. But it may also add all kinds of passion when the nature is not well endowed hereditarily, or when some other disturbing element enters the region.

When the ☽ and ♀ are both in Taurus the nature may be exceedingly fond of compliments, be easily turned from its purposes by even insincere laudation, by flattery that would be easily fathomed by the nature under other influences.

The mentality is successful, congenial, vivid, full of variety of thought and expression, often very emotive in feelings, but severe in anger.

FIG. 49.

Venus. (Capitol, Rome.)

♀ in ♊.

Venus in Gemini gives this nature lightness of heart and delicacy of expression markedly its own; sometimes a rather playful buoyancy. It intensifies the devotion of Gemini, creating a great amount of romantic inclination and a disposition to express fondness and attachment.

♀ in Gemini gives great hereditary force, and the descendants will much resemble the parents, maintaining deep chararteristics several generations.

♆ in Gemini with ♀ gives this nature a very happy, usually also a contented disposition. ♃ with ♀ gives brilliancy and constructive power, and adds to the mentality endurance and courage. When ♄ is present the nature lacks marital constancy.

♀ in ♋.

Venus is at home in Cancer. All that is supposed to be beautiful and elegant, brilliant or powerful in the influence of ♀ upon life, is here at its maximum. The mentality in which ♀ has a Cancer regional influence will find every other ill influence modified, and often completely neutralized. The nature will have added sexality, sex fealty and tenderness; there will be modified any inclination to sensuality caused by some locations of either ♅, ♄ or the ☽.

The nature that is endowed with exceptional artistic power will find an increased tenderness of expression; and in the realm of devotion clear and tranquil attractiveness will be the chief influence.

♀ in ♌.

Venus in Leo gives the natives of Leo, Cancer, Aquarius and Pisces regions more delicacy and vividness of thought, but it also often adds sensuality. Sometimes these natures are inclined to strong appetites.

In nearly all the signs, ♀ in Leo gives an inclination to variableness, changing from intense spiritual thought and refined expression to petulant self-defence; from hopeful and confident attitudes under slight successes to equally as morose and despondent states under very moderate reverses or failures.

The nature thus endowed needs to accumulate personal force, hardihood, independence, stability and steadiness, and, finding a useful and congenial vocation, gain the equipoise needed to dignified sway of circumstances. Often other planets in other signs bring about this effect.

♀ in ♍.

Venus in Virgo greatly intensifies the forces of sex association, and gives to the nature so endowed an exalted opinion of the marriage relations, and of what constitutes the home life; there is great love for children, a sense of tenderness toward those who are unprotected, and a very prominent interest in all that is considered educational.

In some nativities (Gemini, Cancer, Aries and Capricorn, with ♀ in Virgo) there is generally an added gracefulness in movement, with marked elegance in expression and gesture.

With ♀ in Virgo of Scorpio and Sagittarius there is a constant desire to give pleasure to children, as well as to make pets of young animals. In old age, there is an inclination toward jealousy when favors are shown to others.

♀ in ♎.

Venus in Libra adds calmness, gentleness, compassion and spirituality to nearly all the nativities in which it is so found. It gives dignity and extreme attentiveness to social details, and to the requirements of etiquette and the gracious expression of interest in enjoyable accomplishments.

The influence of ♀ in Libra of the dynamic regions is toward virility, vigor, mobility, and plausibility without affectation. In Libra of the formal regions (at least of Aries, Taurus and Gemini) it gives ease, beauty in expression, firmness, and love of praise from others. It also freely approves merit.

♀ in the Libra of Aquarius gives a tinge of boastfulness; in Virgo, family pride and patriotic ostentation; in Cancer, added stability and permanence, with increased romantic devotion. In the Libra of Pisces it inclines to variability and egotism, but adds talent and imagination.

♀ in ♏.

Venus in the Scorpio of a Scorpio nativity gives a keen, deep and penetrating mind, that can utilize opportunity, and gain insight into the aims of others.

Scorpio responds to Cancer, the home of ♀, and increases the intensity of devotion in either sign, and adds reflective as well as intuitive power to both regions.

In all signs the presence of ♀ in the Scorpio region adds much to the elements of wit, versatility, and, in a measure, to mechanical ingenuity.

☿ with ♀ in Scorpio gives intensity and lasting quality to friendship, and a much greater volume of personal liberty than is the case in their absence.

♀ and ♆ are congenial aids to Scorpio forces when there is no other anti-♆ force at work.

♀ in ♐.

Venus in Sagittarius is a blending of the forces of wealth, devotion, and grace, the result being an accomplished and thoroughly pleasing nature, devoid of the penuriousness of Sagittarius force, but holding its energy, force of character and ability to gain the aims it most desires. This nature is, when well endowed hereditarily, a very able one, and possesses many poetical intuitions, is apt at law and in oratory, but its efforts are essentially accumulative. The desires for social accomplishments are often with a view to place in the world of affairs. The home life of this nature is with few exceptions successful and happy, and where it is not, is because of the lack of confidence of others. There is apt to be both jealousy and lack of confidence.

♀ in ♑.

Venus in Capricorn of the Intellectual realm gives a nature admirably adapted to teaching and governing those who need controlling, and where a wide general knowledge is needed. This gives a kind and pleasing disposition (when ♄ is not present in the region of Capricorn), and is often very graceful in movement; quick in gaining an insight into natural science ; profits by intuition, and by a broad and appreciative interest in financial problems.

With ☿ in Pisces this nature has mental elegance, artistic appreciation, capacity to illustrate ideas. With ♄ at home, in Capricorn, there is more severity, more use of the arts of dissimulation, and some need of self-government.

There is danger of fickleness in affection, a tendency to emotive dabbling in literature, and of insincere practice of the higher professions.

♀ in ♒.

Venus in Aquarius blends marriage and home life into a very close and constant harmony, and makes the family life one of extreme happiness in so far as the person so endowed can bring about that result.

This planet also adds artistic tastes, makes the mental vision of usefulness harmonize with that of dainty attractiveness, and in both art and music finds a deep interest.

It gives the nature cheerfulness, mimicry, wit, and generosity. These are often found associated with a dreamy quaintness that is much enjoyed by companions.

♀ in ♓.

Venus, when in Pisces, adds the elements of intense affection, or, when not well governed, may increase the disposition toward licentiousness or voluptuousness, and arouse an interest in the more passionate forms of art and literature. The calm and personal self-complacency of Pisces forces, and the disposition toward dilettante artistic graces, are often increased when ♀ is the sole planet in Pisces, but when ♃ is also in this sign with ♀, the nature is generally (subject to the other planets in a degree) more brilliant and more intense.

When ♀ is accompanied by ♄ in Pisces the natural influence of ♄ is inclined to give trickery to the love nature of ♓, and to some other signs, and thus mix their love affairs in many tangled interests.

FIG. 50.

Wednesday, Mercury (Raphael).

MERCURY, OF GEMINI.

Hermes, or Mercury, was a son of Zeus and Maia; the myth of his nature varied much from time to time, and in different regions.

At first it was considered that to him was due the prolificness of the animal kingdom. As civilization advanced, he was supposed to extend trade and to act as the guardian of commerce. From these latter tasks he grew, in time, shrewd, prudent, and cunning, accredited with great "persuasive speech," and finally with oratory.

He was chosen a messenger of the gods, was a special favorite of Zeus, carrying messages between heaven and earth, even having access to the under world. Familiar thus with the worlds above and below, he became an interpreter of dreams. Apollo, his brother, gave him a golden divining-rod and the power of prophecy.

As a messenger, an athlete of great fleetness, familiar with all countries, he was a splendid guide, and travelers invoked his aid. To aid them he is said to have inspired the erecting of guide-posts.

It was Hermes who taught Palamēdēs to express words in writing, and being also a musician of renown, invented Apollo's lyre. He is described as being of youthful figure, but athletic, wearing a *petasus* and carrying a *caduceus*.

☿ in ♈.

As Mercury finds home in Gemini, the sign of culture, refinement, communication and expression, when in Aries (the chord of Gemini) he creates a wonderful incentive toward learning and literary capacity. This mentality has the capacity to interest others in new ideas, in carrying out new theories, in the widening of

FIG. 51.

Hermes, or Mercury.

ethical life, and in gaining a clearer view of poetic interpretation of natural law and the laws of the beautiful.

This nature needs the influence of strong planets (♃ and ☋), and is cautioned against too great confidence in the success of any element of knowledge that may seem or be new and original—is warned to anticipate delay in radical reforms.

The presence of ♄ in Aries with ☿ inclines the nature toward crafty political and literary activity.

☿ in ♉.

☿ brings to the ☿ in Taurus mentality an immense volume of platonic love, pure friendship, and leads this nature to seek the field of social and ethical life. This combination of energies is that required of the greatest teachers, and of the expressors of culture in the ethical and psychological branches of human knowledge. To this is added the desire to communicate ideas, and to publish political and ethical doctrines.

When ☋ joins ☿ in Taurus the struggle for mastery between conflicting energies often brings great disappointments, perverse actions, variable temper, and lack of steadiness.

There is still worse contentions when ♄ or ♅ are present with ☿. All study should then be toward self-mastery.

☿ in ♊.

Mercury in Gemini is at home, and hence there is a compounding of the culture elements to the highest pitch. The faculties of congenial personality are at their maximum, but it is the element of conviviality and good humor that dominates; there is present the philosophy of ease and gentility, the desire for the luxuries of the Intellect, for fine dress, elegant apartments, fine art.

This mentality is also greatly inclined toward the distribution of intelligence, to authorship and personal correspondence. There are strong undercurrents of wit and of vigorous fun indicated by this combination. ♃ adds sarcasm and criticism. ♄ adds irony and ridicule. With ☿, ♄ and ☋ in Gemini there is a tendency toward dissimulation, sarcasm and ironical jest, to carry severity too far, as it would be less expected from this general nature.

☿ in ♋.

The influence of ☿ in Cancer is that of impassioned love and tendency toward intemperate habit in sex relationships; there is an added brilliancy in social life of the individual, love of style and elegance, and often an earnest struggle for the highest attainments in culture and gracefulness.

This influence seldom leads to a scientific profession; it demands a vocation where the march of personal advantage is rather rapid; where display and formalities have much to do with success.

The nutritive powers are often increased, there being an element of roundness and smoothness and flexibility to the bodily form.

☿ in ♌.

Mercury in Leo originates a combination of forces greatly modified by other planets in the same region, or even in those near by. The combination of hasty frankness and greatly individualized personality, with the moderate, harmonizing, and sometimes passionate Leo force, gives a mixture of self-assurance, animation, congeniality and desire to control others, that can scarcely be defined in any description independent of surrounding circumstances.

♆ in Leo adds to this nature self-control and sensitiveness. ♅ adds independence and a disposition to torment. ♄ makes the nature far more selfish and rash in action. ♃ gives self-control, ambition, often a great amount of pride, even to extreme egotism. ☋ adds cool calculation, and ♀ intensifies the affections.

☿ in ♍.

The energies aroused by Mercury in Virgo, when the nativity sign is of Pisces, Aries or Taurus, causes vivid imagination and constructive ability; there is increased capacity to govern children, and in physical life a very much better arterial circulation than when Mercury is in either Leo or Libra.

Mercury in Virgo with ♄ leads to some deceit, and to deep plans of self-betterment.

Mercury, with ♃ increases the love for children and the family life, and gives a judicious government in home affairs.

Mercury, with ♅ in Virgo, is an influence toward the Peter-Pindar-like story-teller, and increases the political trend of Virgo forces.

☿ in ♎.

Mercury in Libra is a force of many varieties of expression, and of characteristics widely different in the Libra of different nativities. The chief effects of the endowment in the Libra of Aries, Taurus, Gemini, Leo, Cancer, Virgo and Libra, is the tendency to humorous and witty expression, toward widening the range of friendship, and to elaborate correspondence with absent friends.

♄ in Libra with ☿ adds a disposition toward sarcasm and moodiness.

♃ and ☿ in Libra gives great anticipations, and a somewhat enthusiastic struggle to gain eminence. When the Libra is a segment of the dynamic signs there is increased pride, self-esteem, with desire for much approbation. In the Libra of the formal signs, there is added brilliancy, keenness and force in practical lines, including the friendliness noted above of ☿ alone in Libra.

☿ in ♏.

Mercury in the Scorpio sign and nativity brings much that is graceful, elegant and refined. It lightens the solid thought and heaviness of the Scorpio mentality. In the Scorpio of signs that respond (Cancer and Taurus, also of Gemini), it intensifies the social nature and makes it more eloquent. It adds warmth and congeniality to the Scorpio forces of nearly all the signs of which it may be a part.

☿ in Scorpio is but a moderately successful financial endowment. In the Scorpio of Sagittarius, Libra, and Aquarius, ☿ is inclined to be selfish and fretful. It makes these nativities somewhat careless in matters of detail, and in constancy. To the Scorpio of Capricorn it gives a desire to travel and to commercial pursuits.

☿ and the ☽ in Scorpio gives an imaginative, mechanical and inventive turn to thought and ambition.

☿ in ♐.

Mercury in Sagittarius gives a combination out of which grows a great variety of characteristics, depending largely upon the signnature of which it forms a part. It even swings the same mentality from one extreme to another. It will influence close companionship, intense feeling, friendship; again, it will go to the opposite extreme of severe accountability toward those around, close calculation in financial matters, and harsh defense when aroused.

The mentality is subject to hasty conclusions and rapid judgment;

it suffers loss through changing the course of its activity, and by not being constant.

There is a strong inclination to superstitious fear; unwise changes are made because of this.

In general, the nature thus endowed would be more successful if it had more self-control and a more uniform habit.

☿ in ♑.

Mercury in Capricorn lends to the mentality a combination of intense friendship, fickle ambition, wayward and non-malicious fun, and a struggling, often unsuccessful effort at wealth accumulation.

☿ in the Capricorn of the formal signs is an influence that forgives easily, overlooks ill-usage; is kind to friends; gets angry and over being so with remarkable ease, and then pays the penalty of others' displeasure because they do not overlook its faults and make allowance for them.

There are forces in this mental influence that effect undercurrents of superstition that amuse friends; tendencies to change from one vocation to another without due consideration; but with this is a capacity to carry out the plans of others better than it can its own.

A nature with ☿ in Capricorn needs extra caution in selecting a mate.

☿ in ♒.

This planet varies much in this sign, depending upon the major sign, the one under which the person is born.

In the Aquarius of Aries it gives intensity to the love of home comforts and intense friendships.

In the Aquarius of Libra it adds a disposition to extreme boastfulness and directness.

In the Sagittarius and Capricorn signs there is a trend toward subterfuge and trickery.

In Aquarius major sign it gives versatility and capacity to master conventionalities, methods, and much intuitive foresight into probable events.

☿ in ♓.

Mercury in Pisces arouses in the Pisces influence a clearer blending of art talent and the capacity for the dissemination of art ideas;

the trend toward graceful expression and motions, and the ability to make symbolism reveal ideas and portray mental states.

☿ in Pisces also adds intense love of beauty in organic forms, in wild life, and interest in the weird of nature's scenery.

Such natures are apt to be great travelers and gatherers of curios. They love to take long walks, and find it hard to choose between companionship, or their own unrestricted desires to do as they please, and venture where they will, without consulting others' wishes.

APPENDIX.

EXPLANATION OF ASTRONOMICAL SYMBOLS.

Signs of the Zodiac.

0. ♈ Aries, ...	0°	VI. ♎ Libra, . . .	180°
I. ♉ Taurus, . . .	30	VII. ♏ Scorpio, . . .	210
II. ♊ Gemini, . . .	60	VIII. ♐ Sagittarius, . .	240
III. ♋ Cancer, . . .	90	IX. ♑ Capricornus, .	270
IV. ♌ Leo, ...	120	X. ♒ Aquarius, . . .	300
V. ♍ Virgo, ...	150	XI. ♓ Pisces, ...	330

The Sun, ... ☉   A Star, ... ✱

☌ Conjunction.
□ Quadrature.
☍ Opposition.
h. Hours.
m. Minutes of Time.
s. Seconds of Time.

° Degrees.
′ Minutes of Arc.
″ Seconds of Arc.
R. A., Right Ascension.
Dec$^{l.}$ D., or δ, Declination.
N. P. D., North-polar Distance.

Greek Alphabet, used in naming the Stars.

α	Alpha.	ι	Iota.	ρ	Rho.
β	Beta.	κ	Kappa.	σ	Sigma.
γ	Gamma.	λ	Lambda.	τ	Tau.
δ	Delta.	μ	Mu.	υ	Upsilon.
ε	Epsilon.	ν	Nu.	φ	Phi.
ζ	Zeta.	ξ	Xi.	χ	Chi.
η	Eta.	ο	Omicron.	ψ	Psi.
θ	Theta.	π	Pi.	ω	Omega.

Major Planets.

☿ Mercury. ♃ Jupiter.
♀ Venus. ♄ Saturn.
⊕ or ♁ The Earth. ♅ Uranus.
♂ Mars. ♆ Neptune.

The Sun.

The Sun's mean distance from the Earth is 92,700,000 miles; his diameter is 865,000 miles; his density, as compared with water, is 1.4; his ellipticity is insensible; he rotates on his axis in a period between 25 and 26 days. The inclination of the Sun's axis to Plane of Ecliptic (for 1850) 82° 45'; his volume, the Earth's taken as 1, is about 1,245,000; his mass about 315,000.

The Moon.

The Moon's mean distance from the Earth is 239,000 miles. The diameter of the Moon is 2,160 miles; her density, as compared with water, is 3.5. The time of revolution around the earth is 27.322 days. Daily geocentric motion 13° 10' 35". Volume, Earth's as 1,0.02012.

ELEMENTS OF THE MAJOR PLANETS.

Planet.	Distance from the Sun in Millions of Miles.			Periodic Time in Days.	Mean Diameter in Miles.	Density Compared with Water
	Mean.	Least.	Greatest.			
Mercury	35.9	28.6	43.3	87.969	2,992	6.85
Venus	67.0	66.6	67.5	224.70	7,660	4.81
Earth	92.7	91.1	94.6	365.26	7,918	5.66
Mars	141.	128.	155.	686.98	4,200	4.0
Jupiter	482.	459.	505.	4,332.6	87,300	1.38
Saturn	884.	834.	936.	10,759.	71,000	0.75
Uranus	1780.	1700.	1860.	30,687.	31,700	1.28
Neptune	2780.	2760.	2810.	60,127.	34,500	1.15

SATELLITES OF MARS.

Name.	Mean distance from centre of Mars.	Periodic time.		
		H.	M.	S.
Phobos,	5,800	7	39	14
Deimos,	14,500	30	17	54

SATELLITES OF JUPITER.

Name.	Mean distance.		Periodic time.		
Bernard,	112,500	0	11	57	22.6
I. (Io),	262,000	1	18	27	34.
II. (Europa),	417,000	3	13	13	42.
III. (Ganymede),	664,000	7	3	42	33.
IV. (Callisto),	1,170,000	16	16	32	11.

SATELLITES OF SATURN.

Name.	Mean distance from centre of $\hbar$.		Periodic time.		
		D.	H.	M.	S.
Mimas,	118,000	0	22	37	27.9
Enceladus,	152,000	1	8	53	6.7
Thethys,	188,000	1	21	18	25.7
Dione,	241,000	2	17	41	8.9
Rhea,	337,000	4	12	25	10.8
Titan,	771,000	15	22	41	25.2
Hyperion,	946,000	21	7	7	40.8
Japetus,	2,280,000	79	7	54	40.4

Satellites of Uranus.

		Periodic time; days.
Ariel, ...	119,000	2.520+
Umbriel, ...	166,000	4.144+
Titania, ...	272,000	8.705+
Aberon, ...	363,000	13.463

Satellite of Neptune.

Satellite, ...	220,000	5.876+

EPHEMERIS OF

♆, ♅, ♄, ♃, ☋, ♀, ☿, AND THE ☽

FROM

1830 TO 1913

1830—EPHEMERIS OF THE PLANETS AND THE MOON—1830

♆	♂	♀	☿	☿	☿	☿
Ja 1 ♑	Ja 13 ♏	Ap 23 ♐	Ja 1 ♑	Ap 1 ♒	Jul 7 ♓	Oc 4 ♓
De 31 ♑	Mh 12 ♐	Ma 11 ♑	" 4 ♒	" 10 ♓	" 13 ♈	" 10 ♈
♅	Ma 1 ♑	" 30 ♒	" 13 ♓	" 16 ♈	" 19 ♉	" 16 ♉
Ja 1 ♒	Ju 24 ♒	Ju 18 ♓	" 19 ♈	" 22 ♉	" 25 ♊	" 21 ♊
De 31 ♒	Au 10 ♓	Jul 6 ♈	" 25 ♉	" 28 ♊	" 30 ♋	" 26 ♋
♄	Se 26 ♈	" 26 ♉	" 31 ♊	Ma 3 ♋	Au 4 ♌	" 31 ♌
Ja 1 ♌	No 15 ♉	Au 14 ♊	Fe 5 ♋	" 7 ♌	" 10 ♍	No 5 ♍
De 31 ♌	♀	Se 1 ♋	" 10 ♌	" 13 ♍	" 16 ♎	" 13 ♎
♃	Ja 1 ♊	" 20 ♌	" 15 ♍	" 19 ♎	" 25 ♏	" 21 ♏
Ja 1 ♐	" 19 ♋	Oc 8 ♍	" 22 ♎	" 28 ♏	" " "	De 1 ♐
" 30 ♑	Fe 7 ♌	" 26 ♎	" " "	" " "	" " "	" 12 ♑
De 30 ♒	" 25 ♍	No 14 ♏	Mh 1 ♏	Ju 7 ♐	Se 4 ♐	" 22 ♒
♂	Mh 16 ♎	De 2 ♐	" 13 ♐	" 18 ♑	" 15 ♑	" 30 ♓
Ja 1 ♎	Ap 4 ♏	" 21 ♑	" 22 ♑	" 28 ♒	" 25 ♒	" 31 ♓

Day	Jan.	Feb.	Mch.	Apr.	May	June	July	Aug	Sept.	Oct.	Nov.	Dec.
1	♈	♉	♊	♌	♍	♎	♏	♑	♒	♈	♉	♋
2	..	♊	..	..	..	♏	♐	..	♓	..	♊	..
3	♉	..	♋	..	♎	..	..	♒	..	..	..	♌
4	..	♋	..	♍	..	♐	♑	..	♈	♉	♋	..
5	♊	..	♌	..	..	..	..	♓	..	..	..	..
6	..	♌	..	♎	♏	..	..	..	♉	♊	♌	♍
7	♋	..	♍	..	..	♑	♒	..	..	..	..	..
8	..	♍	..	♏	♐	..	..	♈	♊	♋	♍	♎
9	..	..	..	..	..	..	♓	..	..	..	..	..
10	♌	♎	♎	..	..	♒	..	♉	..	♌	..	♏
11	..	..	..	♐	♑	..	..	..	♋	..	♎	..
12	♍	..	♏	..	..	♓	♈	♊	..	♍	..	..
13	..	♏	..	♑	♒	..	..	..	♌	..	♏	♐
14	♎	..	..	..	..	♈	♉	♋	..	♎	..	..
15	..	♐	♐	..	..	..	..	..	♍	..	♐	♑
16	♏	..	..	♒	♓	♉	♊	♌	..	..	..	..
17	..	..	♑	..	..	..	..	..	♎	♏	..	..
18	..	♑	..	♓	♈	♊	♋	♍	..	..	♑	♒
19	♐	..	..	..	..	..	..	..	♏	♐	..	..
20	..	♒	♒	..	♉	♋	♌	..	..	..	♒	♓
21	♑	..	..	♈	..	..	..	♎	..	♑	..	..
22	..	..	♓	..	♊	♌	♍	..	♐	..	..	..
23	..	♓	..	♉	..	..	..	♏	..	..	♓	♈
24	♒	..	♈	..	♋	..	♎	..	♑	♒	..	..
25	..	♈	..	♊	..	♍	..	♐	..	..	♈	♉
26	♓	..	♉	..	♌	..	..	..	..	♓	..	..
27	..	♉	..	♋	..	♎	♏	..	♒	..	♉	♊
28	♈	..	♊	..	♍	..	..	♑	..	..	..	..
29	.		..	♌	..	♏	♐	..	♓	♈	♊	..
30	..		♋	..	..	..	..	♒	..	..	..	♋
31	♉		..		♎		..	..		♉		..

1831—EPHEMERIS OF THE PLANETS AND THE MOON—1831

♆	♂	♀	☿	☿	☿	☿
Ja 1 ♑	Mh 6 ♋	Ma 2 ♌	Ja 1 ♓	Ap 2 ♈	Jul 5 ♉	Oc 1 ♉
De 31 ♑	Ma 6 ♌	" 20 ♍	" 5 ♈	" 8 ♉	" 11 ♊	" 6 ♊
♅	Jul 18 ♍	Ju 9 ♎	" 10 ♉	" 13 ♊	" 16 ♋	" 11 ♋
Ja 1 ♒	Se 22 ♎	" 29 ♏	" 15 ♊	" 18 ♋	" 21 ♌	" 16 ♌
De 31 ♒	No 27 ♏	Jul 16 ♐	" 20 ♋	" 23 ♌	" 26 ♍	" 22 ♍
♄	De 31 ♏	Au 4 ♑	" 25 ♌	" 28 ♍	Au 2 ♎	" 29 ♎
Ja 1 ♌	♀	" 22 ♒	" 30 ♍	Ma 5 ♎	" 10 ♏	No 6 ♏
Dc 31 ♌	Ja 1 ♑	Se 11 ♓	Fe 7 ♎	" 15 ♏	" 20 ♐	" 16 ♐
♃	" 9 ♒	" 30 ♈	" 15 ♏	" 25 ♐	" 31 ♑	" 27 ♑
Ja 1 ♒	" 28 ♓	Oc 18 ♉	" 25 ♐	" " "	" " "	De 8 ♒
De 30 ♓	Fe 16 ♈	No 6 ♊	" " "	Ju 5 ♑	" " "	" 16 ♓
♂	Mh 7 ♉	" 24 ♋	Mh 8 ♑	" 15 ♒	Se 10 ♒	" 22 ♈
Ja 1 ♉	" 27 ♊	De 13 ♌	" 18 ♒	" 23 ♓	" 19 ♓	" 28 ♉
" 7 ♊	Ap 14 ♋	" 31 ♌	" 26 ♓	" 30 ♈	" 26 ♈	" 31 ♉

Day	Jan.	Feb	Mch.	April	May	June	July	Aug.	Sept.	Oct.	Nov.	Dec.
1	♌	♍	♏	♏	♐	♑	♓	♈	♊	♋	♍	♎
2	..	♎	♎	..	..	♒	..	♉	..	♌	..	♏
3	..	..	..	♐	♑	..	..	..	♋	..	♎	..
4	♍	..	♏	..	..	♓	♈	♊	..	♍	..	..
5	..	♏	..	♑	♒	..	..	..	♌	..	♏	♐
6	♎	..	..	..	..	♈	♉	♋	..	♎	..	..
7	..	♐	♐	..	..	.	..	..	♍	.	♐	♑
8	♏	..	..	♒	♓	♉	♊	♌	..	.	..	..
9	..	..	♑	..	..	..	..	..	♎	♏	..	..
10	..	♑	..	♓	♈	..	♋	♍	..	..	♑	♒
11	♐	..	..	..	.	♊	..	..	♏	♐	..	..
12	..	♒	♒	..	♉	..	♌	..	..	..	♒	♓
13	..	..	..	♈	..	♋	..	♎	..	♑	..	..
14	♑	..	♓	..	♊	..	♍	..	♐	..	..	..
15		♓	..	♉	..	♌	..	♏	..	..	♓	♈
16	♒	..	♈	..	♋	..	♎	..	♑	♒	..	..
17	..	♈	..	♊	..	♍	..	♐	..	..	♈	♉
18	♓	.	♉	..	♌	..	..	..	..	♓	..	..
19	..	♉	..	♋	..	♎	♏	..	♈	..	♉	♊
20	..	..	..	..	..	..	..	♑	..	..	..	..
21	♈	♊	♊	♌	♍	♏	♐	..	♓	♈	♊	♋
22	..	..	..	..	..	..	.	♒	..	..	..	..
23	♉	♋	♋	♍	♎	..	..	.	..	♉	..	♌
24	..	..	..	..	..	♐	♑	..	♈	..	♋	..
25	♊	♌	♌	♎	♏	..	..	♓	..	♊	..	♍
26	..	..	..	..	..	♑	♒	..	♉	..	♌	..
27	♋	..	♍	..	..	..	..	♈	..	♋	..	♎
28	..	♍	..	♏	♐	..	..	..	♊	..	♍	..
29	♌		♎	..	..	♒	♓	..	..	♌	..	♏
30	..		..	♐	♑	..	..	♉	♋	..	♎	..
31	♍		♏		..		♈	..		..		♐

1832—EPHEMERIS OF THE PLANETS AND THE MOON—1832

	♆	♂	♀	☿	♃	☿	☿
Ja	1 ♑	Ja 25 ♐	Ap 22 ♓	Ja 1 ♉	Ap 4 ♋	Jul 1 ♋	Oc 2 ♌
De	20 ♒	Mh 19 ♑	Ma 10 ♈	" 2 ♊	" 9 ♌	" 6 ♌	" 7 ♍
"	31 ♒	Ma 12 ♒	" 30 ♉	" 7 ♋	" 14 ♍	" 11 ♍	" 14 ♎
♅		Ju 25 ♓	Ju 18 ♊	" 12 ♌	" 21 ♎	" 18 ♎	" 23 ♏
Ja	1 ♒	Au 12 ♈	Jul 6 ♋	" 17 ♍	" 30 ♏	" 27 ♏	No 3 ♐
De	31 ♒	Se 30 ♉	" 24 ♌	" 24 ♎	Ma 10 ♐	Au 6 ♐	" 13 ♑
♄		No 24 ♊	Au 12 ♍	Fe 2 ♏	" 21 ♑	" 16 ♑	" 24 ♒
Ja	1 ♍	♀	" 30 ♎	" 12 ♐	" 31 ♒	" 27 ♒	De 1 ♓
De	31 ♍	Ja 1 ♍	Se 18 ♏	" 23 ♑	" " "	" " "	" 8 ♈
♃		" 18 ♎	Oc 6 ♐	Mh 4 ♒	" " "	Se 4 ♓	" 14 ♉
Ja	1 ♓	Fe 6 ♏	" 26 ♑	" 12 ♓	Ju 8 ♓	" 11 ♈	" 19 ♊
No	24 ♈	" 24 ♐	No 12 ♒	" 19 ♈	" 15 ♈	" 17 ♉	" 24 ♋
♂		Mh 14 ♑	De 1 ♓	" 25 ♉	" 21 ♉	" 22 ♊	" 29 ♌
Ja	1 ♏	Ap 2 ♒	" 22 ♈	" 30 ♊	" 26 ♊	" 27 ♋	" 31 ♌

Day	Jan.	Feb.	Mch.	April	May	June	July	Aug.	Sept.	Oct.	Nov.	Dec.
1	♐	♒	♒	♈	♉	♋	♌	♎	♏	♑	♒	♓
2	♑	..	♓	..	..	..	..	♐	..	..	..	..
3	..	♓	..	♉	♊	♌	♍	♏	..	♒	♓	♈
4	♒	..	..	..	..	..	..	..	♑	..	..	..
5	..	♈	♈	..	♋	♍	♎	..	..	♓	♈	♉
6	..	..	..	♊	..	..	..	♐	..	..	..	..
7	♓	..	♉	..	♌	♎	♏	..	♒	..	..	♊
8	..	♉	..	♋	..	..	..	♑	..	♈	♉	..
9	♈	..	♊	..	♍	♏	♐	..	♓	..	..	..
10	..	♊	..	♌	..	..	..	♒	..	♉	♊	♋
11	♉	..	..	..	..	♐	..	..	..	..	..	..
12	..	♋	♋	♍	♎	..	♑	..	♈	..	♋	♌
13	..	..	..	..	..	♑	..	♓	..	♊	..	..
14	♊	♌	♌	♎	♏	..	♒	..	♉	..	..	♍
15	..	..	..	..	..	..	..	♈	..	♋	♌	..
16	♋	♍	♍	♏	♐	♒	..	..	..	..	..	♎
17	..	..	..	..	..	..	♓	..	♊	♌	♍	..
18	♌	♎	♎	♐	♑	♓	..	♉	..	..	..	♏
19	..	..	..	..	..	..	♈	..	♋	♎	..	..
20	♍	♏	♏	♒	♒	..	..	♊	..	♍	♏	♐
21	..	..	..	♑	..	♈	..	..	♌	..	♏	..
22	♎	..	♐	..	..	..	♉	..	♎	..	..	..
23	..	♐	..	♒	♓	♉	..	♋	♍	..	♐	♑
24	♏	..	♑	..	..	..	♊	..	..	♏	..	..
25	..	♑	..	..	♈	..	..	♌	♎	..	♑	♒
26	♐	..	..	♓	..	♊	♋	..	♏	♐	..	♓
27	..	..	♒	..	..	..	♍	♏	..	..	..	♓
28	..	♒	..	♈	♉	♋	♌	..	..	♑	♒	..
29	♑		♓	..	..	..	♎	♐	..	..	..	..
30	..		..	♊	..	♍	..	..	..	..	♓	♈
31	♒		..		♊		♏	..		♒		..

187

1833—EPHEMERIS OF THE PLANETS AND THE MOON—1833

♆	♂	♀	☿	☿	☿	☿
Ja 1♒	Ja 23♋	Ap 30♏	Ja 1♌	Ap 1♍	Jul 5♎	Oc 1♎
De 31♒	Mh 26♌	Ma 18♐	" 4♍	" 8♎	" 14♏	" 9♏
♅	Ju 1♍	Ju 6♑	" 10♎	" 17♏	" 24♐	" 19♐
Ja 1♒	Au 10♎	" 25♒	" 18♏	" 27♐	Au 4♑	" 30♑
De 31♒	Oc 5♏	Jul 15♓	" 28♐	Ma 8♑	" 14♒	No 9♒
♄	De 13♐	Au 3♈	Fe 8♑	" 18♒	" 22♓	" 18♓
Ja 1♍	♀	" 23♉	" 18♒	" 26♓	" 29♈	" 25♈
Au 20♎	Ja 1♈	Se 10♊	" 26♓	" " "	" " "	De 1♉
De 31♎	" 10♉	" 28♋	" " "	Ju 2♈	" " "	" 6♊
♃	" 28♊	Oc 16♌	Mh 5♈	" 8♉	Se 4♉	" 11♋
Ja 1♈	Fe 17♋	No 2♍	" 11♉	" 13♊	" 9♊	" 16♌
Oc 19♉	Mh 7♌	" 21♎	" 16♊	" 18♋	" 14♋	" 22♍
♂	" 25♍	De 10♏	" 21♋	" 23♌	" 19♌	" 29♎
Ja 1♊	Ap 11♎	" 30♐	" 26♌	" 29♍	" 24♍	" 31♎

Day	Jan.	Feb	Mch.	April	May	June	July	Aug.	Sept.	Oct.	Nov.	Dec.
1	♈	♊	♋	♍	♎	♐	♑	♓	♈	♉	♋	♌
2	♉	♋	♌	..	♏	..	♒	..	♉	♊	..	..
3	..	..	..	♎	..	♑	..	♈	..	..	♌	♍
4	♊	..	♍	..	♐	..	♓	..	..	♋	..	..
5	..	♌	..	♏	..	♒	..	..	♊	..	♍	♎
6	♋	..	♎	..	♑	..	..	♉	..	..	..	..
7	..	♍	..	♐	..	♓	♈	..	♋	♌	♎	♏
8	♌	..	♏	..	♒	..	..	♊	..	..	..	..
9	..	♎	..	♑	..	..	♉	..	♌	♍	♏	♐
10	♍	..	♐	..	..	♈	..	..	..	..	..	..
11	..	♏	..	♒	♓	.	..	♋	..	♎	♐	♑
12	♎	..	♑	..	..	♉	♊	..	♍	..	..	..
13	..	♐	..	♓	♈	..	..	♌	..	♏	♑	♒
14	♏	..	..	..	..	..	♋	..	♎	..	..	..
15	..	♑	♒	..	.	♊	..	♍	..	♐	..	♓
16	..	..	..	♈	♉	..	..	..	♏	..	♒	..
17	♐	..	♓	..	..	♋	♌	♎	..	♑	..	..
18	..	♒	..	..	♊	..	..	..	♐	..	♓	♈
19	♑	..	..	♉	..	♌	♍	♏	..	♒	..	..
20	..	♓	♈	..	..	..	..	..	♑	..	♈	♉
21	♒	..	..	♊	♋	♍	♎	♐	..	..	..	..
22	..	♈	♉	..	..	..	..	..	♒	♓	.	..
23	..	.	..	♋	♌	..	♏	♑	..	..	♉	♊
24	♓	♉	..	..	..	♎	..	..	♓	♈	..	..
25	..	..	♊	..	♍	..	♐	..	..	..	♊	♋
26	♈	♊	..	♌	..	♏	.	♒	..	..	..	..
27	..	..	♋	..	♎	..	♑	.	♈	♉	..	..
28	..	♋	..	♍	..	♐	..	♓	..	..	♋	♌
29	♉	..	..	..	♏	..	♒	..	♉	♊	..	..
30	..		♌	♎	..	♑	..	..	..	..	♌	♍
31	♊		..		♐		..	♈	.	..	..	..

1834—EPHEMERIS OF THE PLANETS AND THE MOON—1834

♆	♂	♀	☿	☿	☿	☿
Ja 1 ♒	Mh 26 ♒	Ma 11 ♋	Ja 1 ♎	Ap 4 ♏	Jul 10 ♐	Oc 6 ♐
De 31 ♒	Ma 13 ♓	" 30 ♌	" 5 ♏	" 14 ♐	" 21 ♑	" 17 ♑
♅	Ju 31 ♈	Ju 16 ♍	" 15 ♐	" 24 ♑	" 31 ♒	" 27 ♒
Ja 1 ♒	Au 18 ♉	Jul 6 ♎	" 26 ♑	Ma 4 ♒	Au 10 ♓	No 6 ♓
De 31 ♒	Oc 12 ♊	" 23 ♏	Fe 6 ♒	" 13 ♓	" 17 ♈	" 12 ♈
♄	De 8 ♋	Au 12 ♐	" 14 ♓	" 20 ♈	" 21 ♉	" 17 ♉
Ja 1 ♎	♀	" 31 ♑	" 21 ♈	" 26 ♉	" 26 ♊	" 22 ♊
De 31 ♎	Ja 1 ♐	Se 19 ♒	" 28 ♉	" 31 ♊	" 31 ♋	" 27 ♋
♃	" 18 ♑	Oc 8 ♓	" " "	" " "	" " "	" " "
Ja 1 ♉	Fe 6 ♒	" 27 ♈	Mh 4 ♊	Ju 5 ♋	" " "	De 2 ♌
Se 14 ♊	" 25 ♓	No 15 ♉	" 9 ♋	" 10 ♌	Se 5 ♌	" 9 ♍
♂	Mh 16 ♈	De 2 ♊	" 14 ♌	" 15 ♍	" 12 ♍	" 16 ♎
Ja 1 ♐	Ap 4 ♉	" 22 ♋	" 19 ♍	" 22 ♎	" 18 ♎	" 23 ♏
Fe 4 ♑	" 23 ♊	" 31 ♋	" 26 ♎	" 30 ♏	" 26 ♏	" 31 ♏

Day	Jan.	Feb.	Mch.	Apr.	May	June	July	Aug.	Sept.	Oct.	Nov.	Dec.
1	♎	♐	♐	♒	♒	♈	♉	♋	♌	♎	♏	♑
2	..	..	..	..	♓	♉	♊	..	♍	..	♐	..
3	♏	..	♑	..	..	..	..	♌	..	♏	..	♒
4	..	♑	..	♓	♈	♊	♋	..	♎	..	♑	..
5	♐	..	♒	..	..	..	..	♍	..	♐	..	♓
6	..	♒	..	♈	..	..	..	..	♏	..	♒	..
7	♑	..	♓	..	♉	♋	♌	..	..	♑	..	..
8	..	♓	..	♉	..	..	..	♎	♐	..	♓	♈
9	♒	..	..	..	♊	♌	♍	..	..	..	..	..
10	..	♈	♈	..	..	..	..	♏	..	♒	♈	♉
11	..	..	..	♊	..	..	♎	..	♑	..	..	..
12	♓	..	♉	..	♋	♍	..	♐	..	♓	..	..
13	..	♉	..	..	..	..	..	..	♒	..	♉	♊
14	♈	..	..	♋	♌	♎	♏	♑	..	♈	..	..
15	..	♊	♊	..	..	..	..	..	..	..	♊	♋
16	♉	..	..	♌	..	♏	♐	♒	♓	..	..	..
17	..	..	♋	..	♍	..	..	..	..	♉	..	..
18	..	♋	..	♍	..	♐	♑	♓	♈	..	♋	♌
19	♊	..	..	..	♎	..	..	..	..	♊	..	..
20	..	♌	♌	..	..	♑	♒	♈	♉	..	♌	..
21	♋	..	..	♎	♏	..	..	..	..	..	..	♍
22	..	♍	♍	..	..	♒	♓	..	..	♋	..	..
23	..	..	..	♏	♐	..	..	♉	♊	..	♍	♎
24	♌	..	♎	..	..	♓	♈	..	..	♌	..	..
25	..	♎	..	♐	♑	..	..	♊	♋	..	♎	..
26	♍	..	♏	..	..	..	..	..	..	♍	..	♏
27	..	♏	..	♑	♒	♈	♉	..	..	..	♏	..
28	♎	..	♐	..	..	..	..	♋	♌	..	..	♐
29	..		..	..	♓	♉	♊	..	..	♎	♐	..
30	♏		♑	♒	..	..	..	♌	♍	..	..	♑
31	..		..		♈	..	..	..	..	♏		..

1835—EPHEMERIS OF THE PLANETS AND THE MOON—1835

♆	♂	♀	☿	☿	☿	☿
Ja 1 ♒	Ap 19 ♍	Ma 20 ♓	Ja 1 ♏	Ap 11 ♑	Jul 8 ♑	Oc 4 ♑
De 31 ♒	Ju 29 ♎	Ju 8 ♈	" 2 ♐	" 21 ♒	" 18 ♒	" 14 ♒
♅	Au 31 ♏	" 26 ♉	" 13 ♑	" 30 ♓	" 27 ♓	" 23 ♓
Ja 1 ♒	Oc 30 ♐	Jul 15 ♊	" 23 ♒	Ma 7 ♈	Au 3 ♈	" 30 ♈
De 31 ♓	De 23 ♑	Au 3 ♋	Fe 1 ♓	" 12 ♉	" 8 ♉	No 4 ♉
♄	♀	" 21 ♌	" 8 ♈	" 17 ♊	" 13 ♊	" 9 ♊
Ja 1 ♎	Ja 1 ♋	Se 9 ♍	" 13 ♉	" 22 ♋	" 18 ♋	" 14 ♋
De 31 ♎	" 9 ♌	" 27 ♎	" 18 ♊	" 27 ♌	" 23 ♌	" 19 ♌
♃	" 27 ♍	Oc 16 ♏	" 23 ♋	" 31 ♍	" 29 ♍	" 25 ♍
Ja 1 ♊	Fe 14 ♎	No 4 ♐	" 28 ♌	" " "	" " "	" " "
Au 25 ♋	Mh 5 ♏	" 22 ♑	Mh 4 ♍	" " "	Se 5 ♎	De 2 ♎
♂	" 24 ♐	De 11 ♒	" 13 ♎	Ju 9 ♎	" 13 ♏	" 10 ♏
Ja 1 ♋	Ap 12 ♑	" 30 ♓	" 21 ♏	" 17 ♏	" 29 ♐	" 20 ♐
Fe 11 ♌	Ma 1 ♒	" 31 "	" 31 ♐	" 27 ♐	" " "	" 31 ♑

Day	Jan.	Feb.	Mch.	April	May	June	July	Aug.	Sept.	Oct.	Nov.	Dec.
1	♒	♓	♈	♉	♊	♌	♍	♏	♐	♒	♓	♈
2	..	♈	..	♊	..	..	♎	..	♑	..	♈	♉
3	♓	..	..	..	♋	♍	..	♐	..	♓	..	..
4	..	♉	♉	..	..	..	..	..	♒	..	..	♊
5	♈	..	..	♋	♌	♎	♏	♑	..	..	♉	..
6	..	..	♊	..	..	..	..	..	♓	♈	..	..
7	..	♊	..	♌	♍	♏	♐	..	..	..	♊	♋
8	♉	..	..	..	..	..	..	♒	♈	♉	..	..
9	..	♋	♋	..	♎	♐	♑	..	..	..	♋	♌
10	♊	..	..	♍	..	..	..	♓	..	..	..	..
11	..	♌	♌	..	♏	♑	♒	..	♉	♊	..	..
12	..	..	..	♎	..	..	..	♈	..	..	♌	♍
13	♋	..	♍	..	♐	..	♓	..	♊	♋	..	..
14	..	♍	..	♏	..	♒	..	♉	..	..	♍	♎
15	♌	..	♎	..	♑	..	..	..	..	..	..	..
16	..	♎	..	♐	..	♓	♈	..	♋	♌	..	♏
17	♍	..	♏	..	♒	..	..	♊	..	..	♎	..
18	..	♏	..	♑	..	♈	♉	..	♌	♍	..	♐
19	♎	..	♐	..	♓	..	..	..	..	..	♏	..
20	..	♐	..	♒	..	..	..	♋	..	♎	..	♑
21	..	..	♑	..	..	♉	♊	..	♍	..	♐	..
22	♏	♑	..	♓	♈	..	..	♌	..	♏	..	♒
23	..	..	..	..	..	♊	♋	..	♎	..	♑	..
24	♐	♒	♒	..	♉	..	..	♍	..	♐	..	♓
25	..	..	..	♈	..	..	..	..	♏	..	♒	..
26	♑	..	♓	..	..	♋	♌	♎	..	♑	..	♈
27	..	♓	..	♉	♊	..	..	..	♐	..	♓	..
28	♒	..	♈	..	..	♌	♏	♏	..	♒	..	..
29	..		..	..	♋	..	..	..	♑	..	♈	♉
30	♓		♉	♊	..	♍	♎	..	..	..	..	..
31	..		..		..		..	♐		♓		♊

1836—EPHEMERIS OF THE PLANETS AND THE MOON—1836

♆	♂	♀	☿	☿	☿	☿
Ja 1 ♒	Fe 11 ♒	Ap 20 ♍	Ja 1 ♑	Ap 7 ♒	Jul 4 ♒	Oc 9 ♓
De ♒	Mh 30 ♓	Ma 9 ♎	" 10 ♒	" 16 ♓	" 13 ♓	" 15 ♈
♅	Ma 17 ♈	" 27 ♏	" 19 ♓	" 23 ♈	" 20 ♈	" 21 ♉
Ja 1 ♓	Ju 5 ♉	Ju 15 ♐	" 26 ♈	" 28 ♅	" 25 ♉	" 26 ♊
De 31 ♓	Au 28 ♊	Jul 4 ♑	" 31 ♉	Ma 3 ♊	" 30 ♊	" 31 ♋
♄	Oc 25 ♋	" 23 ♒	Fe 5 ♊	" 8 ♋	Au 4 ♋	No 5 ♌
Ja 1 ♎	De 29 ♌	Au 11 ♓	" 10 ♋	" 13 ♌	" 9 ♌	" 11 ♍
Fe 20 ♏	♀	" 30 ♈	" 15 ♌	" 19 ♍	" 15 ♍	" 17 ♎
De 31 ♏	Ja 1 ♓	Se 18 ♉	" 21 ♍	" 25 ♎	" 21 ♎	" 26 ♏
♃	" 18 ♈	Oc 7 ♊	" 28 ♎	" " "	" 30 ♏	" " "
Ja 1 ♋	Fe 6 ♉	" 25 ♋	" " "	Ju " "	" " "	De 6 ♐
Au 21 ♌	" 25 ♊	No 13 ♌	Mh 7 ♏	" 3 ♏	Se 9 ♐	" 17 ♑
♂	Mh 14 ♋	De 1 ♍	" 17 ♐	" 13 ♐	" 20 ♑	" 27 ♒
Ja 1 ♑	Ap 2 ♌	" 20 ♎	" 28 ♑	" 24 ♑	" 30 ♒	" 31 "

Day	Jan.	Feb.	Mch.	Apr.	May	June	July	Aug.	Sept.	Oct.	Nov.	Dec.
1	♊	♋	♌	♎	♏	♑	♒	♈	♊	♊	♌	♍
2	..	♌	♍	..	♐	..	♓	..	..	♋	..	♎
3	♋	..	..	♏	..	♒	..	♉	..	..	..	..
4	..	..	♎	..	♑	..	..	..	♋	♌	♍	..
5	♌	♍	..	♐	..	♓	♈	..	..	..	..	♏
6	..	..	..	..	♒	..	..	♊	..	..	♎	..
7	..	♎	♏	♑	..	♈	..	..	♌	♍	..	♐
8	♍	..	..	..	♓	..	♉	♋	..	..	..	..
9	..	..	♐	♒	..	..	..	..	♍	♎	♏	♑
10	♎	♏	..	..	♈	♉	♊	..	..	..	..	..
11	..	..	♑	♓	♈	..	..	♌	..	♏	♐	♒
12	♏	♐	..	..	..	♊	..	..	♎	..	..	..
13	..	..	♒	..	♉	..	♋	♍	..	♐	♑	♓
14	♐	♑	..	♈	..	..	..	..	♏	..	..	..
15	..	..	♓	..	..	♋	♌	♎	..	..	♒	♈
16	♑	♒	..	♉	♊	..	..	..	♐	♑	..	..
17	..	..	♈	..	..	♌	..	..	..	..	♓	..
18	♒	♓	..	..	♋	..	♍	♏	♑	♒	..	♉
19	..	..	..	♊	..	..	..	..	..	..	♈	..
20	♓	♈	♉	..	..	♍	♎	♐	♒	♓	..	♊
21	..	..	..	♋	♌	..	..	..	..	..	♉	..
22	..	♉	♊	..	..	♎	♏	♑	♓	♈	..	..
23	♈	..	..	♍	..	..	..	♒	..	..	♊	♋
24	..	..	♋	..	♏	..	♐	..	♈	♉	..	♌
25	♉	♊	♋	..	..	♐	..	♓	..	..	♋	♌
26	..	..	..	♍	♎	♐	..	..	♉	..	..	..
27	..	♋	♌	..	..	♑	..	♈	..	♊	..	..
28	♊	..	..	♎	♏	..	♒	..	..	..	♌	♍
29	..	♌	..	..	♑	♒	..	♉	♊	♋	..	..
30	♋	.	♍	♏	♐	..	♓	..	..	..	♍	♎
31	..		..		♓	..	..	♉		..		..

1837—EPHEMERIS OF THE PLANETS AND THE MOON—1837

♆	♂	♀	☿	☿	☿	☿
Ja 1 ♒	Mh 6 ♍	Ap 30 ♉	Ja 1 ♒	Ap 3 ♓	Jul 6 ♈	Oc 2 ♈
De 31 ♒	Ma 14 ♎	Ma 19 ♊	" 5 ♓	" 9 ♈	" 12 ♉	" 8 ♉
♅	Ju 18 ♏	Ju 7 ♋	" 11 ♈	" 15 ♉	" 17 ♒	" 13 ♊
Ja 1 ♓	Se 16 ♐	" 25 ♌	" 17 ♉	" 20 ♊	" 22 ♋	" 18 ♋
De 31 ♓	No 9 ♑	Jul 14 ♍	" 22 ♊	" 25 ♋	" 27 ♌	" 23 ♌
♄	De 30 ♒	Au 1 ♎	" 27 ♋	" 30 ♌	Au 1 ♍	" 28 ♍
Ja 1 ♏	♀	" 20 ♏	Fe 1 ♌	Ma 5 ♍	" 8 ♎	No 4 ♎
De 31 ♏	Ja 1 ♎	Se 8 ♐	" 7 ♍	" 12 ♎	" 17 ♏	" 13 ♏
♃	" 7 ♏	" 27 ♑	" 13 ♎	" 21 ♏	" 27 ♐	" 23 ♐
Ja 1 ♌	" 26 ♐	Oc 16 ♒	" 22 ♏	" 31 ♐	" " "	De 4 ♑
De 5 ♍	Fe 14 ♑	No 3 ♓	" " "	" " "	" " "	" 14 ♒
" 31 ♍	Mh 5 ♒	" 23 ♈	Mh 4 ♐	Ju 11 ♑	Se 7 ♑	" 22 ♓
♂	" 21 ♓	De 11 ♉	" 15 ♑	" 21 ♒	" 17 ♒	" 29 ♈
Ja 1 ♌	Ap 12 ♈	" 30 ♊	" 25 ♒	" 30 ♓	" 26 ♓	" 31 ♈

Day	Jan.	Feb	Mch.	April	May	June	July	Aug.	Sept.	Oct.	Nov.	Dec.
1	♎	♐	♐	♒	♓	♉	♊	♌	♎	♏	♐	♑
2	♏	♑	♑	♓	♈	♊	♋	..	..	..	♑	♒
3	..	..	..	..	..	..	..	♍	..	..	..	..
4	♐	♒	♒	♈	♉	..	♌	..	♏	♐	♒	♓
5	..	..	..	..	..	♋	..	..	..	..	..	..
6	♑	♓	♓	♉	♊	..	..	♎	..	♑	..	♈
7	..	..	..	..	..	♌	♍	..	♐	..	♓	..
8	♒	♈	♈	..	♋	..	..	♏	..	♒	..	♉
9	..	..	..	♊	..	..	♎	..	♑	..	♈	..
10	♓	..	♉	..	..	♍	..	♐	..	♓	..	♊
11	..	♉	..	♋	♌	..	..	..	♒	..	♉	..
12	♈	..	♊	..	..	♎	♏	♑	..	♈	..	..
13	..	♊	..	..	♍	..	..	..	♓	..	♊	♋
14	♉	..	..	♌	..	..	♐	♒	..	♉	..	..
15	..	♋	♋	..	..	♏	..	..	♈	..	♋	♌
16	..	..	..	♍	♎	..	♑	♓	..	..	..	..
17	♊	..	♌	..	..	♐	..	..	♉	♊	..	..
18	..	♌	..	..	♏	..	♒	♈	..	..	♌	♍
19	♋	..	..	♎	..	♑	..	..	♊	♋	..	..
20	..	♍	♍	..	♐	..	♓	..	..	..	♍	♎
21	..	..	..	♏	..	♒	..	♉	..	♌	..	..
22	♌	..	♎	..	♑	..	♈	..	♋	..	..	..
23	..	♎	..	♐	..	♓	..	♊	..	..	♎	♏
24	♍	..	..	..	..	..	..	..	♌	♍	..	..
25	..	♏	♏	♑	♒	♈	♉	♋	..	..	♏	♐
26	..	..	..	..	..	..	..	..	..	♎	..	..
27	♎	..	♐	♒	♓	♉	♊	..	♍	..	♐	♑
28	..	♐	..	..	..	..	..	♌	..	..	..	..
29	♏		♑	♓	♈	..	♋	..	♎	♏	..	♒
30	..		..	..	..	♊	..	♍	..	..	♑	..
31	♐		♒		♉	..	..	..		♐		♓

1838—EPHEMERIS OF THE PLANETS AND THE MOON—1838

♆	♂	♀	☿	☿	☿	☿
Ja 1 ♒	Ap 4 ♈	Ma 9 ♑	Ja 1 ♈	Ap 2 ♉	Jul 4 ♊	Oc 5 ♋
De 31 ♒	Ma23 ♉	" 28 ♒	" 4 ♉	" 7 ♊	" 9 ♋	" 10 ♌
♅	Jul 15 ♊	Ju 16 ♓	" 9 ♊	" 12 ♋	" 14 ♌	" 15 ♍
Ja 1 ♓	Se 12 ♋	Jul 5 ♈	" 14 ♋	" 17 ♌	" 19 ♍	" 22 ♎
De 31 ♓	No 15 ♌	" 24 ♉	" 19 ♌	" 22 ♍	" 26 ♎	" 31 ♏
♄	De 30 ♍	Au 12 ♊	" 24 ♍	" 29 ♎	Au 4 ♏	No 10 ♐
Ja 1 ♏	♀	" 30 ♋	" 31 ♎	Ma 8 ♏	" 14 ♐	" 21 ♑
De 31 ♐	Ja 1 ♊	Se 18 ♌	Fe 9 ♏	" 18 ♐	" 25 ♑	" " "
♃	" 18 ♋	Oc 6 ♍	" 19 ♐	" 29 ♑	" " "	De 1 ♒
Ja 1 ♍	Fe 5 ♌	" 25 ♎	" " "	" " "	Se 4 ♒	" 9 ♓
Oc 2 ♎	" 23 ♍	No 12 ♏	Mh 2 ♑	Ju 8 ♒	" 12 ♓	" 16 ♈
♂	Mh14 ♎	De 1 ♐	" 12 ♒	" 16 ♓	" 19 ♈	" 22 ♉
Ja 1 ♒	Ap 2 ♏	" 20 ♑	" 20 ♓	" 23 ♈	" 25 ♉	" 27 ♊
Fe 15 ♓	" 20 ♐	" 31 ♑	" 27 ♈	" 29 ♉	" 30 ♊	" 31 ♊

Day	Jan.	Feb.	Mch.	Apr.	May	June	July	Aug.	Sept.	Oct.	Nov.	Dec.
1	♓	♉	♉	♋	♌	♍	♏	♐	♒	♓	♉	♊
2	♈	..	♊	..	..	♎	..	♑	..	..	..	..
3	..	♊	..	♌	♍	..	..	..	♓	♈	♊	♋
4	♉	..	♋	..	..	♏	♐	..	..	..	..	..
5	..	♋	..	..	..	..	..	♒	♈	♉	♋	♌
6	..	..	..	♍	♎	..	♑	..	..	..	..	..
7	♊	..	♌	..	..	♐	..	♓	♉	♊	..	♍
8	..	♌	..	♎	♏	..	♒	..	..	..	♌	..
9	♋	..	♍	..	..	♑	..	♈	♊	♋	..	..
10	..	♍	..	..	♐	..	..	..	..	..	♍	♎
11	♌	..	..	♏	..	♒	♓	♉	..	♌	..	..
12	..	..	♎	..	..	..	..	..	♋	..	..	♏
13	..	♎	..	♐	♑	♓	♈	♊	..	..	♎	..
14	♍	..	♏	..	..	..	..	..	♌	♍	..	..
15	..	♏	..	♑	♒	♈	♉	♋	..	..	♏	♐
16	♎	..	..	..	..	..	..	..	..	♎	..	..
17	..	..	♐	..	♓	..	♊	..	♍	..	..	♑
18	..	♐	..	♒	..	♉	..	♌	..	..	♐	..
19	♏	..	♑	..	♈	..	♋	..	♎	♏	..	♒
20	..	♑	..	♓	..	♊	..	♍	..	..	♑	..
21	♐	..	♒	..	♉	..	..	..	..	♐	..	..
22	..	♒	..	♈	..	♋	♌	..	♏	..	♒	♓
23	♑	..	♓	..	♊	..	..	♎	..	..	..	..
24	..	♓	..	♉	..	♌	♍	..	♐	♑	♓	♈
25	♒	..	♈	..	..	..	..	♏	..	..	..	..
26	..	♈	..	♊	♋	..	..	..	♑	♒	..	♉
27	♓	..	♉	..	..	♍	♎	..	..	..	♈	..
28	..	♉	..	♋	♌	..	..	♐	..	♓	..	♊
29	♈		..	..	..	♎	♏	..	♒	..	♉	..
30	..		♊	..	♍	..	..	♑	..	..	..	♋
31	..		..		..		♐	..		♈		..

1839—EPHEMERIS OF THE PLANETS AND THE MOON—1839

♆	♂	♀	☿	☿	☿	☿
Ja 1 ♒	Mh 31 ♎	Ap 30 ♌	Ja 1 ♊	Ap 4 ♌	Jul 1 ♌	Oc 2 ♍
De 1 ♒	Ju 5 ♏	Ma 19 ♍	" 1 ♋	" 9 ♍	" 6 ♍	" 9 ♎
♅	Au 4 ♐	Ju 6 ♎	" 6 ♌	" 16 ♎	" 13 ♎	" 18 ♏
Ja 1 ♓	Se 27 ♑	" 25 ♏	" 11 ♍	" 25 ♏	" 22 ♏	" 28 ♐
De 31 ♓	No 16 ♒	Jul 14 ♐	" 18 ♎	Ma 5 ♐	Au 1 ♐	No 8 ♑
♄	De 31 ♒	Au 2 ♑	" 27 ♏	" 16 ♑	" 12 ♑	" 18 ♒
Ja 1 ♐	♀	" 21 ♒	Fe 6 ♐	" 26 ♒	" 22 ♒	" 26 ♓
De 31 ♐	Ja 1 ♑	Se 9 ♓	" 17 ♑	" " "	" 30 ♓	De 3 ♈
♃	" 8 ♒	" 22 ♈	" 27 ♒	" " "	" " "	" 9 ♉
Ja 1 ♎	" 27 ♓	Oc 16 ♉	Mh 7 ♓	Ju 3 ♓	Se 6 ♈	" 14 ♊
No 3 ♏	Fe 15 ♈	No 4 ♊	" 14 ♈	" 10 ♈	" 12 ♉	" 19 ♋
♂	Mh 6 ♉	" 23 ♋	" 20 ♉	" 16 ♉	" 17 ♊	" 24 ♌
Ja 1 ♌	" 24 ♊	De 11 ♌	" 25 ♊	" 21 ♊	" 22 ♋	" 29 ♍
" 22 ♍	Ap 12 ♋	" 30 ♍	" 30 ♋	" 26 ♋	" 27 ♌	" 31 ♍

Day	Jan.	Feb.	Mch.	April	May	June	July	Aug.	Sept.	Oct.	Nov.	Dec.
1	♌	♍	♍	♏	♐	♒	♓	♈	♊	♌	♍	♎
2	..	♎	♎	..	..	..	..	♉	♋	..	..	♏
3	..	..	..	♐	♑	..	♈	..	..	..	♎	..
4	♍	..	♏	..	..	♓	..	♊	♌	♍	..	..
5	..	♏	..	..	♒	..	♉	..	..	..	♏	♐
6	♎	..	..	♑	..	♈	..	♋	..	♎	..	..
7	..	..	♐	..	..	..	♊	..	♍	..	..	♑
8	..	♐	..	♒	♓	♉	..	♌	..	..	♐	..
9	♏	..	♑	..	..	..	♋	..	♎	♏	..	..
10	..	♑	..	♓	♈	♊	..	♍	..	..	♑	♒
11	♐	..	..	..	..	..	..	..	♏	♐	..	..
12	..	♒	♒	♈	♉	♋	♌	..	..	..	♒	♓
13	..	..	..	..	..	..	..	♎	..	..	..	..
14	♑	♓	♓	♉	♊	♌	♍	..	♐	♑	..	♈
15	..	..	..	..	..	..	..	♏	..	..	♓	..
16	♒	♈	♈	♊	♋	..	♎	..	♑	♒	..	♉
17	..	..	..	..	..	♍	..	..	..	..	♈	..
18	♓	♉	♉	♋	♌	..	..	♐	..	♓	..	♊
19	..	..	..	..	..	♎	♏	..	♒	..	♉	..
20	♈	..	♊	..	♍	..	..	♑	..	..	..	♋
21	..	♊	..	♌	..	..	♐	..	♓	♈	♊	..
22	♉	..	♋	..	..	♏	..	♒	..	..	..	..
23	..	♋	..	♍	♎	..	..	..	♈	♉	♋	♌
24	♊	..	♌	..	..	♐	♑	..	..	..	..	..
25	..	♌	..	♎	♏	..	..	♓	♉	♊	♌	♍
26	♋	..	..	..	..	♑	♒	..	..	..	..	..
27	..	♍	♍	..	..	..	..	♈	♊	♋	♍	♎
28	..	..	..	♏	♐	..	♓	..	..	..	..	..
29	♌		♎	..	..	♒	..	♉	♋	♌	..	..
30	..		..	♐	♑	..	♈	..	..	..	♎	♏
31	♍		..		..		..	♊		♍		..

1840—EPHEMERIS OF THE PLANETS AND THE MOON—1840

♆	♂	♀	☿	☿	☿	☿
Ja 1 ♒	Ja 3 ♓	Ap 20 ♓	Ja 1 ♍	Ap 2 ♎	Jul 7 ♏	Oc 3 ♏
De 31 ♒	Fe 19 ♈	Ma 9 ♈	" 5 ♎	" 11 ♏	" 18 ♐	" 14 ♐
♅	Ap 9 ♉	" 28 ♉	" 14 ♏	" 21 ♐	" 29 ♑	" 25 ♑
Ja 1 ♓	Ju 1 ♊	Ju 16 ♊	" 24 ♐	Ma 2 ♑	Au 8 ♒	No 4 ♒
De 31 ♓	Jul 30 ♋	Jul 4 ♋	Fe 4 ♑	" 12 ♒	" 16 ♓	" 12 ♓
♄	Oc 2 ♌	" 23 ♌	" 14 ♒	" 20 ♓	" 23 ♈	" 19 ♈
Ja 1 ♐	De 9 ♍	Au 10 ♍	" 22 ♓	" 27 ♈	" 29 ♉	" 25 ♉
De 31 ♐	☿	" 29 ♎	" 29 ♈	" " "	" " "	" 30 ♊
♃	Ja 1 ♍	Se 16 ♏	" " "	Ju 2 ♉	" " "	De 4 ♋
Ja 1 ♏	" 17 ♎	Oc 5 ♐	Mh 6 ♉	" 7 ♊	Se 3 ♊	" 9 ♌
No 27 ♐	Fe 5 ♏	" 24 ♑	" 11 ♊	" 11 ♋	" 7 ♋	" 15 ♍
De 31 ♐	" 23 ♐	No 12 ♒	" 16 ♋	" 16 ♌	" 12 ♌	" 22 ♎
♂	Mh 13 ♑	De 1 ♓	" 20 ♌	" 22 ♍	" 18 ♍	" 30 ♏
Ja 1 ♒	Ap 1 ♒	" 20 ♈	" 26 ♍	" 29 ♎	" 25 ♎	" 31 ♏

Day	Jan.	Feb.	Mch.	April	May	June	July	Aug.	Sept.	Oct.	Nov.	Dec.
1	♐	♑	♒	♈	♉	♋	♌	♍	♏	♐	♑	♓
2	..	♒	..	..	..	..	..	♎	..	..	♒	..
3	..	..	♓	..	♊	♌	♍	..	♐	♑	..	♈
4	♑	..	..	♉	..	..	..	♏	..	..	♓	..
5	..	♓	♈	..	♋	..	♎	..	..	♒	..	..
6	♒	..	..	♊	..	♍	..	..	♑	..	♈	♉
7	..	♈	♉	..	♌	..	..	♐	..	..	..	..
8	♓	..	..	♋	..	♎	♏	..	♒	♓	♉	♊
9	..	♉	♊	..	♍	..	..	♑	..	..	..	..
10	..	..	..	♌	..	♏	♐	..	♓	♈	..	♋
11	♈	♊	♋	..	..	..	..	..	..	..	♊	..
12	..	..	..	♍	♎	♐	..	♒	..	♉	..	♌
13	♉	♋	..	..	..	..	♑	..	♈	..	♋	..
14	..	..	♌	♎	♏	♑	..	♓	..	♊	..	♍
15	♊	♌	..	..	..	..	♒	..	♉	..	♌	..
16	..	..	♍	..	..	..	..	♈	..	♋	..	♎
17	♋	..	..	♏	♐	♒	..	..	♊	..	♍	..
18	..	♍	♎	..	..	..	♓	..	..	♌	..	..
19	♌	..	..	♐	♑	♓	..	♉	♋	..	♎	♏
20	..	♎	..	..	..	..	♈	..	..	♍	..	..
21	♍	..	♏	..	..	..	..	♊	♌	..	♏	♐
22	..	♏	..	♑	♒	♈	♉	..	..	..	..	..
23	♎	..	♐	..	..	..	..	♋	..	♎	..	..
24	..	..	..	♒	♓	♉	♊	..	♍	..	♐	♑
25	..	♐	..	..	..	..	..	♌	..	♏	..	..
26	♏	..	♑	..	♈	♊	♋	..	♎	..	♑	♒
27	..	♑	..	♓	..	..	..	♍	..	..	..	..
28	♐	..	♒	..	♉	♋	♌	..	♏	♐	..	♓
29	..	..	..	♈	..	..	..	♎	..	..	♒	..
30	..		♓	..	♊		..	..	♐	♑	..	..
31	♑		..		..		♍	♏	..	..		♈

1841—EPHEMERIS OF THE PLANETS AND THE MOON—1841

♆	♂	♀	☿	☿	☿	☿
Ja 1 ♒	Fe 15 ♎	Ap 29 ♏	Ja 1 ♏	Ap 8 ♐	Jul 5 ♐	Oc 1 ♐
De 31 ♒	Ap 22 ♏	Ma 18 ♐	" 10 ♐	" 18 ♑	" 15 ♑	" 10 ♑
♅	Ma 21 ♐	Ju 6 ♑	" 20 ♑	" 29 ♒	" 26 ♒	" 21 ♒
Ja 1 ♓	Au 14 ♑	" 25 ♒	" 31 ♒	Ma 7 ♓	Au 3 ♓	" 30 ♓
De 31 ♓	Oc 3 ♒	Jul 14 ♓	Fe 8 ♓	" 14 ♈	" 10 ♈	No 6 ♈
♄	No 20 ♓	Au 2 ♈	" 15 ♈	" 20 ♉	" 16 ♉	" 12 ♉
Ja 1 ♐	♀	" 20 ♉	" 21 ♉	" 25 ♊	" 21 ♊	" 17 ♊
Ju 27 ♑	Ja 1 ♈	Se 8 ♊	" 26 ♊	" 29 ♋	" 25 ♋	" 21 ♋
De 31 ♑	" 8 ♉	" 27 ♋	" " "	" " "	" 30 ♌	" 26 ♌
♃	" 26 ♊	Oc 15 ♌	Mh 2 ♋	" " "	" " "	De 2 ♍
Ja 1 ♐	Fe 14 ♋	No 3 ♍	" 7 ♌	Ju 3 ♌	" " "	" 9 ♎
De 8 ♑	Mh 4 ♌	" 21 ♎	" 13 ♍	" 9 ♍	Se 5 ♍	" 17 ♏
♂	" 22 ♍	De 10 ♏	" 20 ♎	" 16 ♎	" 12 ♎	" 28 ♐
Ja 1 ♍	Ap 10 ♎	" 29 ♐	" 28 ♏	" 24 ♏	" 20 ♏	" 31 ♐

Day	Jan.	Feb.	Mch.	April	May	June	July	Aug.	Sept.	Oct.	Nov.	Dec.
1	♈	♊	♊	♌	♍	♏	♐	♒	♓	♈	♊	♋
2	♉	..	♋	..	♎	..	..	..	..	♉	..	♌
3	..	♋	..	♍	..	♐	♑	..	♈	..	♋	..
4	♊	..	♌	..	♏	..	..	♓	..	♊	..	♍
5	..	♌	..	♎	..	..	♒	..	♉	..	♌	..
6	♋	..	♍	..	..	♑	..	♈	..	..	..	..
7	..	♍	..	♏	♐	..	..	..	♊	♋	♍	♎
8	♌	..	..	..	..	♒	♓	..	..	..	..	..
9	..	♎	♎	♐	♑	..	..	♉	♋	♌	♎	♏
10	♍	..	..	..	..	..	♈	..	..	..	..	..
11	..	♏	♏	..	..	♓	..	♊	♌	♍	♏	♐
12	♎	..	..	♑	♒	..	♉	..	..	..	..	..
13	..	..	♐	..	..	♈	..	♋	..	♎	♐	♑
14	..	♐	..	♒	..	..	..	..	♍	..	..	..
15	♏	..	..	..	♓	♉	♊	♌	..	♏	..	..
16	..	♑	♑	..	..	..	..	..	♎	..	♑	♒
17	♐	..	..	♓	♈	♊	♋	♍	..	♐	..	..
18	..	..	♒	..	..	..	..	..	♏	..	♒	♓
19	..	♒	..	♈	♉	♋	♌	♎	..	..	..	..
20	♑	..	..	..	..	..	..	..	♐	♑	..	..
21	..	♓	♓	..	♊	♌	♍	♏	..	..	♓	♈
22	♒	..	..	♉	..	..	..	..	♑	♒	..	..
23	..	..	♈	..	♋	♍	♎	..	..	..	..	♉
24	..	♈	..	♊	..	..	..	♐	..	..	♈	..
25	♓	..	♉	..	♌	..	♏	..	♒	♓	..	..
26	..	♉	..	♋	..	♎	..	♑	..	..	♉	♊
27	♈	..	♊	..	♍	..	♐	..	♓	♈	..	..
28	..	♊	..	♌	..	♏	..	..	..	..	♊	♋
29	..		♋	..	♎	..	..	♒	..	..	..	..
30	♉		..	♍	..	♐	♑	..	♈	♉	♋	♌
31	..		..		..		..	♓		..		..

1842—EPHEMERIS OF THE PLANETS AND THE MOON—1842

♆	♂	♀	☿	☿	☿	☿
Ja 1♒	Fe 25♉	Ma 9♋	Ja 1♐	Ap 5♑	Jul 2♑	Oc 8♒
De 31♒	Ap 19♊	" 28♌	" 7♑	" 15♒	" 12♒	" 17♓
♅	Ju 17♋	Ju 15♍	" 17♒	" 24♓	" 21♓	" 24♈
Ja 1♓	Au 20♌	Jul 4♎	" 26♓	Ma 1♈	" 28♈	" 29♉
De 31♓	Oc 27♍	" 22♏	Fe 2♈	" 6♉	Au 2♉	No 3♊
♄	De 31♍	Au 10♐	" 7♉	" 11♊	" 7♊	" 8♋
Ja 1♑	♀	" 29♑	" 13♊	" 16♋	" 12♋	" 13♌
De 31♑	Ja 1♐	Se 17♒	" 17♋	" 21♌	" 17♌	" 19♍
♃	" 16♑	Oc 6♓	" 22♌	" 27♍	" 23♍	" 26♎
Ja 1♑	Fe 4♒	" 25♈	" 28♍	" " "	" 30♎	" " "
N 30♒	" 23♓	No 13♉	" " "	" " "	" " "	De 4♏
♂	Mh14♈	De 1♊	Mh 7♎	Ju 3♎	Se 7♏	" 14♐
Ja 1♓	Ap 2♉	" 20♋	" 15♏	" 11♏	" 17♐	" 25♑
" 6♈	" 21♊	" 31♋	" 25♐	" 21♐	" 28♑	" 31♑

Day	Jan.	Feb.	Mch.	Apr.	May	June	July	Aug.	Sept.	Oct.	Nov.	Dec.
1	♍	♎	♏	♐	♒	♓	♈	♊	♋	♍	♎	♐
2	..	♏	..	♑	..	♈	♉	..	♌	..	♏	..
3	♎	..	♐	..	..	..	..	♋	..	♎	..	♑
4	..	♐	..	♒	♓	..	..	..	♍	..	♐	..
5	♏	..	♑	..	..	♉	♊	♌	..	♏	..	..
6	..	♑	..	..	♈	..	..	..	♎	..	♑	♒
7	♐	..	..	♓	..	♊	♋	♍	..	♐	..	..
8	..	♒	♒	..	..	..	..	♏	..	..	♒	♓
9	..	..	..	♈	♉	..	♌	♎	..	..	..	..
10	♑	..	♓	..	..	♋	..	..	♐	♑	..	..
11	..	♓	..	♉	♊	..	♍	♏	..	..	♓	♈
12	♒	..	..	..	..	♌	..	♏	♑	♒	..	..
13	..	..	♈	..	♋	..	♎	..	..	..	♈	♉
14	..	♈	..	♊	..	♍	..	♐	..	..	..	..
15	♓	..	♉	..	♌	..	♏	..	♒	♓	..	..
16	..	♉	..	♋	..	♎	..	♑	..	..	♉	♊
17	♈	..	..	..	..	..	..	..	♓	♈	..	..
18	..	♊	♊	♌	♍	♏	♐	..	..	..	♊	♋
19	..	..	..	..	..	..	♒	..	..	..	..	..
20	♉	..	♋	♍	♎	♐	♑	..	♈	♉	..	♌
21	..	♋	..	..	..	..	..	♓	..	..	♋	..
22	♊	..	♌	♎	♏	..	♒	..	♉	♊	..	♍
23	..	♌	..	..	..	♑	..	..	..	♌	..	..
24	♋	..	♍	♏	♐	..	♓	♈	..	..	♍	♎
25	..	♍	..	..	..	♒	♓	..	♊	..	..	..
26	♌	..	♎	..	♑	..	♉	..	..	♍	..	♏
27	..	♎	..	♐	..	..	♈	..	♋	♌	♎	..
28	♍	..	♏	..	..	♓	..	..	..	..	..	..
29	..		..	♑	♒	..	..	♊	♌	♍	♏	♐
30	♎		♐	..	..	♈	♉	..	..	..	..	..
31	..		..		♓		♋	..		♎		♑

1843—EPHEMERIS OF THE PLANETS AND THE MOON—1843

♆	♂	♀	♀	☿	☿	☿
Ja 1 ♒	Ja 3 ♎	Ap 11 ♑	De 30 ♓	Mh 23 ♑	Jul 8 ♓	Oc 4 ♓
De 31 ♒	Mh 10 ♏	" 30 ♒	☿	Ap 2 ♒	" 15 ♈	" 11 ♈
♅	Ma 8 ♐	Ma 19 ♓	Ja 1 ♑	" 11 ♓	" 20 ♉	" 16 ♉
Ja 1 ♓	Jul 2 ♑	Ju 7 ♈	" 4 ♒	" 18 ♈	" 25 ♊	" 21 ♊
Au 25 ♈	Au 21 ♒	" 25 ♉	" 13 ♓	" 23 ♉	" 30 ♋	" 26 ♋
♄	Oc 8 ♓	Jul 14 ♊	" 20 ♈	" 28 ♊	Au 4 ♌	" 31 ♌
Ja 1 ♑	No 24 ♈	Au 1 ♋	" 25 ♉	Ma 3 ♋	" 10 ♍	No 6 ♍
De 31 ♑	♀	" 26 ♌	" 30 ♊	" 8 ♌	" 17 ♎	" 12 ♎
♃	Ja 1 ♋	Se 8 ♍	Fe 4 ♋	" 14 ♍	" 25 ♏	" 21 ♏
Ja 1 ♒	" 8 ♌	" 26 ♎	" 9 ♌	" 21 ♎	" " "	" " "
No 7 ♓	" 26 ♍	Oc 15 ♏	" 15 ♍	" 29 ♏	" " "	De 2 ♐
De 31 ♓	Fe 14 ♎	No 3 ♐	" 22 ♎	Ju 8 ♐	Se 4 ♐	" 12 ♑
☊	Mh 4 ♏	" 22 ♑	Mh 2 ♏	" 19 ♑	" 15 ♑	" 22 ♒
Ja 1 ♍	" 24 ♐	De 11 ♒	" 12 ♐	" 30 ♒	" 25 ♒	" 31 ♓

Day	Jan.	Feb.	Mch.	April	May	June	July	Aug.	Sept.	Oct.	Nov.	Dec.
1	♑	♓	♓	♈	♊	♋	♌	♎	♐	♑	♓	♈
2	..	..	..	♉	..	♌	..	♏	..	♒	..	..
3	♒	♈	♈	..	..	..	♍	..	♑	..	..	♉
4	..	..	..	♊	♋	♍	..	♐	..	..	♈	..
5	♓	..	♉	..	..	..	♎	..	♒	♓	..	..
6	..	♉	..	♋	♌	..	..	♑	..	..	♉	♊
7	♈	..	..	..	..	♎	♏	..	♓	♈	..	..
8	..	♊	♊	..	♍	..	..	..	..	..	♊	♋
9	..	..	..	♌	..	♏	♐	♒	♈	..	..	..
10	♉	..	♋	..	♎	..	..	..	..	♉	..	♌
11	..	♋	..	♍	..	♐	♑	♓	..	..	♋	..
12	♊	..	♌	..	♏	..	..	..	♉	♊	..	..
13	..	♌	..	♎	..	♑	..	♈	..	..	♌	♍
14	♋	..	♍	..	♐	..	♒	..	..	♋	..	..
15	..	♍	..	♏	..	♒	..	..	♊	..	..	♎
16	♌	..	♎	..	♑	..	♓	♉	..	..	♍	..
17	..	♎	..	♑	..	♓	..	..	♋	♌	..	♏
18	..	..	♏	..	..	..	♈	♊	..	..	♎	..
19	♍	♏	..	♐	♒	..	..	..	♌	♍	..	♐
20	..	..	♐	..	..	♈	♉	..	..	..	♏	..
21	♎	♐	..	♒	♓	..	..	♋	..	♎	..	♑
22	..	..	..	..	..	♉	♊	..	♍	..	♐	..
23	♏	♑	♑	..	♈	..	..	♌	..	♏	..	♒
24	..	..	..	♓	..	..	♋	..	♎	..	♑	..
25	♐	..	♒	..	..	♊	..	♍	..	♐	..	..
26	..	♒	..	♈	♉	..	..	..	♍	..	♒	♓
27	♑	..	♓	..	..	♋	♌	♎	..	♑	..	..
28	..	♓	..	..	..	..	..	..	♐	..	♓	♈
29	♒		..	♉	♊	♌	♍	..	..	..	..	..
30	..		♈	..	..	..	..	♏	♑	♒	..	♉
31	..		..		♋		♎	..		..		..

1844—EPHEMERIS OF THE PLANETS AND THE MOON—1844

♆	♂	♀	☿	☿	☿	☿
Ja 1 ♒	Mh 6 ♊	Ma 27 ♏	Ja 1 ♓	Ap 4 ♈	Jul 6 ♉	Oc 2 ♉
De 31 ♒	Ma 4 ♋	Ju 14 ♐	“ 7 ♈	“ 9 ♉	“ 11 ♊	“ 7 ♊
♅	Jul 7 ♌	Jul 3 ♑	“ 12 ♉	“ 14 ♊	“ 16 ♋	“ 12 ♋
Ja 1 ♈	Se 13 ♍	“ 22 ♒	“ 17 ♊	“ 19 ♋	“ 21 ♌	“ 17 ♌
De 31 ♈	No 20 ♎	Au 10 ♓	“ 22 ♋	“ 24 ♌	“ 27 ♍	“ 23 ♍
♄	♀	“ 29 ♈	“ 27 ♌	“ 30 ♍	Au 2 ♎	“ 29 ♎
Ja 1 ♑	Ja 1 ♓	Se 17 ♉	Fe 2 ♍	Ma 6 ♎	“ 11 ♏	No 7 ♏
Mh 18 ♒	“ 17 ♈	Oc 6 ♊	“ 8 ♎	“ 15 ♏	“ 21 ♐	“ 17 ♐
♃	Fe 5 ♉	“ 21 ♋	“ 17 ♏	“ 25 ♐	“ “ “	“ 28 ♑
Ja 1 ♓	“ 24 ♊	No 12 ♌	“ 27 ♐	“ “ “	“ “ “	De 8 ♒
Oc 2 ♈	Mh 13 ♋	“ 30 ♍	“ “ “	Ju 5 ♑	Se 1 ♑	“ 17 ♓
♂	Ap 1 ♌	De 19 ♎	Mh 9 ♑	“ 15 ♒	“ 11 ♒	“ 23 ♈
Ja 1 ♈	“ 19 ♍	“ “ “	“ 19 ♒	“ 24 ♓	“ 20 ♓	“ 29 ♉
“ 13 ♉	Ma 8 ♎	“ 31 ♎	“ 28 ♓	“ 30 ♈	“ 26 ♈	“ 31 ♉

Day	Jan.	Feb.	Mch.	April	May	June	July	Aug.	Sept.	Oct.	Nov.	Dec.
1	♉	♋	♌	♍	♎	♐	♑	♓	♉	♊	♋	♌
2	♊	..	..	♎	♏	♑	♒	♈	..	..	♌	♍
3	..	♌	..	..	..	..	..	..	..	..	..	..
4	♋	..	♍	♏	♐	♒	♓	..	♊	♋	..	♎
5	..	♍	..	..	..	..	..	♉	..	..	♍	..
6	..	..	♎	♐	♑	♓	♈	..	♋	♌	..	♏
7	♌	♎	..	..	..	..	..	♊	..	..	♎	..
8	..	..	♏	♑	♒	..	♉	..	..	♍	..	♐
9	♍	♏	..	..	..	♈	..	..	♌	..	♏	..
10	..	..	♐	♒	♓	..	..	♋	..	♎	..	♑
11	♎	..	..	..	..	♉	♊	..	♍	..	♐	..
12	..	♐	♑	..	♈	..	..	♌	..	..	..	♒
13	♏	..	..	♓	..	..	..	..	♎	♏	♑	..
14	..	♑	♒	..	..	♊	♋	..	..	..	..	..
15	♐	..	..	♈	♉	..	..	♍	♏	♐	♒	♓
16	..	♒	..	..	..	♋	♌	..	..	..	..	..
17	♑	..	♓	..	♊	..	..	♎	♐	♑	♓	♈
18	..	♓	..	♉	..	..	♍	..	..	..	..	..
19	..	..	♈	..	..	♌	..	♏	♑	♒	..	♉
20	♒	..	..	♊	♋	..	..	..	..	..	♈	..
21	..	♈	♉	..	..	♍	♎	♐	..	♓	..	..
22	♓	..	..	..	♌	..	..	..	♒	..	♉	♊
23	..	♉	..	♋	..	♎	♏	♑	..	♈	..	..
24	♈	..	♊	..	..	..	..	..	♓	..	..	♋
25	..	..	..	♌	♍	♏	♐	♒	..	..	♊	..
26	..	♊	♋	..	..	..	..	..	♈	♉	..	..
27	♉	..	..	♍	♎	♐	♑	♓	..	..	♋	♌
28	..	♋	..	..	..	..	..	..	♉	♊	..	..
29	♊	..	♌	..	♏	♑	♍	..	..	..	..	♍
30	..		..	♎	..	..	..	♈	..	..	♌	..
31	..		♍		♐		♓	..		♋		..

1845—EPHEMERIS OF THE PLANETS AND THE MOON—1845

♆	♂	♀	☿	☿	☿	☿
Ja 1 ♒	Mh 25 ♐	Ap 30 ♉	Ja 1 ♉	Ap 1 ♊	Jul 3 ♋	Oc 4 ♌
De 31 ♒	Ma 19 ♑	Ma 18 ♊	" 3 ♊	" 6 ♋	" 8 ♌	" 9 ♍
♅	Jul 8 ♒	Ju 6 ♋	" 8 ♋	" 11 ♌	" 13 ♍	" 16 ♎
Ja 1 ♈	Au 25 ♓	" 24 ♌	" 13 ♌	" 16 ♍	" 20 ♎	" 26 ♏
De 31 ♈	Oc 11 ♈	Jul 13 ♍	" 18 ♍	" 23 ♎	" 29 ♏	No 4 ♐
♄	No 30 ♉	" 31 ♎	" 25 ♎	Ma 2 ♏	" " "	" 15 ♑
Ja 1 ♒	♀	Au 19 ♏	Fe 3 ♏	" 12 ♐	Au 8 ♐	" 25 ♒
De 31 ♒	Ja 1 ♎	Se 7 ♐	" 13 ♐	" 23 ♑	" 19 ♉	" " "
♃	" 6 ♏	" 26 ♑	" 24 ♑	" " "	" 29 ♒	De 3 ♓
Ja 1 ♈	" 25 ♐	Oc 15 ♒	" " "	Ju 2 ♒	Se 6 ♓	" 10 ♈
Au 26 ♉	Fe 13 ♑	No 3 ♓	Mh 6 ♒	" 10 ♓	" 13 ♈	" 16 ♉
♂	Mh 4 ♒	" 22 ♈	" 15 ♓	" 17 ♈	" 19 ♉	" 21 ♊
Ja 1 ♎	" 23 ♓	De 10 ♉	" 22 ♈	" 23 ♉	" 24 ♊	" 26 ♋
" 24 ♏	Ap 11 ♈	" 29 ♊	" 27 ♉	" 28 ♊	" 29 ♋	" 31 ♌

Day	Jan.	Feb	Mch.	April	May	June	July	Aug.	Sept.	Oct.	Nov.	Dec.
1	♎	♐	♐	♒	♓	♉	♊	♋	♍	♎	♐	♑
2	..	..	..	..	..	..	..	♌	..	..	..	..
3	♏	♑	♑	♓	♈	..	♋	..	♎	♏	♑	♒
4	..	..	..	..	..	♊	..	..	..	..	..	..
5	♐	♒	♒	♈	♉	..	..	♍	..	♐	..	♓
6	..	..	..	..	..	♋	♌	..	♏	..	♒	..
7	♑	♓	♓	..	♊	..	..	♎	..	♑	..	♈
8	..	..	..	♉	..	..	♍	..	♐	..	♓	..
9	♒	..	♈	..	..	♌	..	♏	..	♒	..	♉
10	..	♈	..	♊	♋	..	..	..	♑	..	♈	..
11	♓	..	♉	..	..	♍	♎	..	..	♓	..	..
12	..	♉	..	..	♌	..	..	♐	♒	..	♉	♊
13	♈	..	..	♋	..	..	♏	..	..	..	..	..
14	..	♊	♊	..	..	♎	..	♑	♓	♈	..	♋
15	..	..	..	♌	♍	..	♐	..	..	..	♊	..
16	♉	..	♋	..	..	♏	..	♒	♈	♉	..	..
17	..	♋	..	..	♎	..	♑	..	..	..	♋	♌
18	♊	..	..	♍	..	♐	..	♓	♉	♊	..	..
19	..	♌	♌	..	♏	..	♒	..	..	..	♌	♍
20	..	..	..	♎	..	♑	..	♈	..	..	..	..
21	♋	..	♍	..	♐	..	♓	..	♊	♋	..	..
22	..	♍	..	♏	..	♒	..	♉	..	..	♍	♎
23	♌	..	♎	..	♑	..	♈	..	♋	♌	..	..
24	..	♎	..	♐	..	♓	..	♊	..	..	♎	♏
25	..	..	..	..	♒	..	..	..	..	..	..	..
26	♍	♏	♏	♑	..	♈	♉	..	♌	♍	..	♐
27	..	..	..	..	..	..	..	♋	..	..	♏	..
28	♎	♐	♐	♒	♓	♉	♊	..	♍	♎	..	♑
29	..		..	..	..	..	..	♌	..	..	♐	..
30	♏		♑	♓	♈	..	..	..	..	♏	..	♒
31	..		..		..		♋	..		..		..

1846—EPHEMERIS OF THE PLANETS AND THE MOON—1846

♆	♂	♀	☿	☿	☿	☿
Ja 1 ♒	Mh 22 ♋	Ma 27 ♒	Ja 1 ♌	Ap 3 ♍	Jul 7 ♎	Oc 3 ♎
De 31 ♒	Ma 25 ♌	Ju 15 ♓	" 5 ♍	" 10 ♎	" 16 ♏	" 12 ♏
♅	Au 1 ♍	Jul 4 ♈	" 12 ♎	" 19 ♏	" 26 ♐	" 22 ♐
Ja 1 ♈	Oc 8 ♎	" 23 ♉	" 21 ♏	" 29 ♐	Au 6 ♑	No 2 ♑
De 31 ♈	De 12 ♏	Au 11 ♊	" 31 ♐	Ma 10 ♑	" 16 ♒	" 12 ♒
♄	♀	" 29 ♋	Fe 11 ♑	" 20 ♒	" 24 ♓	" 20 ♓
Ja 1 ♒	Ja 1 ♊	Se 17 ♌	" 21 ♒	" 28 ♓	" 31 ♈	" 27 ♈
No 9 ♓	" 17 ♋	Oc 5 ♍	" " "	" " "	" " "	De 3 ♉
♃	Fe 4 ♌	" 24 ♎	Mh 1 ♓	Ju 4 ♈	" " "	" 8 ♊
Ja 1 ♉	" 23 ♍	No 11 ♏	" 8 ♈	" 10 ♉	Se 6 ♉	" 13 ♋
Jul 25 ♊	Mh 13 ♎	" 30 ♐	" 14 ♉	" 15 ♊	" 11 ♊	" 18 ♌
♂	Ap 1 ♏	De 19 ♑	" 19 ♊	" 20 ♋	" 16 ♋	" 23 ♍
Ja 1 ♉	" 19 ♐	" " "	" 24 ♋	" 25 ♌	" 21 ♌	" 30 ♎
" 22 ♊	Ma 8 ♑	" 31 ♑	" 29 ♌	" 30 ♍	" 26 ♍	" 31 ♎

Day	Jan.	Feb.	Mch.	Apr.	May	June	July	Aug.	Sept.	Oct.	Nov.	Dec.
1	♒	♈	♉	♊	♌	♍	♎	♐	♑	♒	♈	♉
2	..	..	..	♋	..	♎	♏	..	♒	♓	..	♊
3	♓	♉	..	..	..	..	♑	..	..	..	♉	..
4	..	..	♊	♌	♍	..	..	..	♓	♈	..	♋
5	..	♊	..	..	..	♏	♐	..	..	..	♊	..
6	..	..	♋	♍	♎	..	..	♒	..	♉	..	♌
7	♉	..	..	..	..	♐	♑	..	♈	..	♋	..
8	..	♋	♌	..	..	..	..	♓	..	♊	..	♍
9	♊	..	..	♎	♏	..	..	..	♉	..	♌	..
10	..	♌	♍	..	..	♑	♒	♈	..	♋	..	♎
11	♋	..	..	♏	♐	..	..	..	♊	..	♍	..
12	..	♍	♎	..	..	♒	♓	..	..	♌	..	..
13	♌	..	..	..	..	..	..	♉	♋	..	♎	♏
14	..	♎	..	♐	♑	..	♈	..	..	..	..	..
15	..	..	♏	..	..	♓	..	♊	♌	♍	..	♐
16	♍	..	..	♑	♒	..	♉	..	..	..	♏	..
17	..	♏	♐	..	..	♈	..	♋	♍	♎	..	..
18	♎	..	..	♒	♓	..	♊	..	..	..	♐	♑
19	..	♐	♑	♒	..	♉	..	♌	♎	..	..	..
20	♏	..	..	..	..	♊	..	..	♎	♏	..	♒
21	..	..	..	♓	♈	♊	♋	♍	..	..	♑	..
22	..	♑	♒	..	..	♋	..	♏	♐	..	..	♓
23	♐	..	♒	♈	♉	♋	♌	♎	..	♑	♒	♓
24	..	♒	♓	..	..	..	..	..	..	♑	..	..
25	♑	..	..	♉	♊	♌	♍	..	♐	..	♓	♈
26	..	♓	..	..	..	..	♏	..	..	♒	..	..
27	..	..	♈	♊	♋	♍	♎	..	♑	♒	..	♉
28	♒	..	..	..	..	..	♐	..	..	..	♈	..
29	..		♈	♉	♋	♌	..	♏	..	..	♓	..
30	♓	..	..	..	♌	♎	..	..	♒	..	♉	♊
31	..		♊		♍	..	♑	..		♈		..

1847—EPHEMERIS OF THE PLANETS AND THE MOON—1847

♆	♂	♀	☿	☿	☿	☿
Ja 1 ♒	Ap 6 ♑	Ap 29 ♌	Ja 1 ♎	Ap 5 ♏	Jul 2 ♏	Oc 8 ♐
Ap 23 ♓	Ma 26 ♒	Ma 18 ♍	" 7 ♏	" 15 ♐	" 12 ♐	" 19 ♑
♅	Ju 13 ♓	Ju 5 ♎	" 17 ♐	" 26 ♑	" 23 ♑	" 29 ♒
Ja 1 ♈	Au 29 ♈	" 23 ♏	" 28 ♑	Ma 6 ♒	Au 2 ♒	No 6 ♓
De 31 ♈	Oc 18 ♉	Jul 12 ♐	Fe 7 ♒	" 15 ♓	" 11 ♓	" 13 ♈
♄	De 10 ♊	" 31 ♑	" 16 ♓	" 21 ♈	" 17 ♈	" 19 ♉
Ja 1 ♓	♀	Au 19 ♒	" 23 ♋	" 27 ♉	" 23 ♉	" 24 ♊
De 31 ♓	Ja 1 ♑	Se 13 ♓	" 28 ♉	" " "	" 28 ♊	" 29 ♋
♃	" 7 ♒	" 26 ♈	" " "	" " "	" " "	" " "
Ja 1 ♊	" 26 ♓	Oc 15 ♉	Mh 5 ♊	Ju 1 ♊	Se 2 ♋	De 4 ♌
Jul 6 ♋	Fe 18 ♈	No 2 ♊	" 10 ♋	" 6 ♋	" 7 ♌	" 9 ♍
♂	Mh 6 ♉	" 21 ♋	" 15 ♌	" 11 ♌	" 12 ♍	" 16 ♎
Ja 1 ♏	" 23 ♊	De 9 ♌	" 21 ♍	" 17 ♍	" 19 ♎	" 25 ♏
Fe 10 ♐	Ap 11 ♋	" 28 ♍	" 28 ♎	" 23 ♎	" 28 ♏	" 31 ♏

Day	Jan	Feb.	Mch.	April	May	June	July	Aug.	Sept.	Oct.	Nov.	Dec.
1	♋	♌	♍	♎	♏	♑	♒	♈	♊	♋	♌	♎
2	..	♍	..	♏	♐	..	♓	..	..	..	♍	..
3	♌	..	..	..	..	♒	..	♉	♋	♌	..	..
4	..	♎	♎	..	♑	..	♈	..	..	..	♎	♏
5	♍	..	..	♐	..	♓	..	♊	..	♍	..	..
6	..	..	♏	..	..	..	♉	..	♌	..	..	♐
7	..	♏	..	♑	♒	♈	..	♋	..	..	♏	..
8	♎	..	..	..	..	..	..	..	♍	♎	..	..
9	..	♐	♐	♒	♓	♉	♊	♌	..	..	♐	♑
10	♏	..	..	..	..	..	..	..	..	♏	..	..
11	..	♑	♑	♓	♈	♊	♋	..	♎	..	..	♒
12	♐	..	..	..	..	..	..	♍	..	..	♑	..
13	..	..	♒	♈	♉	♋	♌	..	♏	♐	..	♓
14	..	♒	..	..	..	..	..	♎	..	..	♒	..
15	♑	..	♓	♉	♊	..	..	..	..	♑	..	♈
16	..	♓	..	..	..	♌	♍	..	♐	..	♓	..
17	♒	..	♈	♊	♋	..	..	♏	..	..	..	..
18	..	♈	..	..	..	♍	♎	..	♑	♒	♈	♉
19	♓	..	♉	..	♌	..	..	♐	..	..	..	..
20	..	♉	..	♋	..	..	..	..	♒	♓	♉	♊
21	♈	..	♊	..	..	♎	♏	..	..	..	..	..
22	..	♊	..	♌	♍	..	..	♑	♓	♈	♊	♋
23	♉	..	♋	..	..	♏	♐	..	..	..	..	..
24	..	♋	..	..	♎	..	..	♒	♈	♉	♋	♌
25	♊	..	..	♍	..	..	♑	..	..	..	..	..
26	..	♌	♌	..	..	♐	..	♓	♉	♊	..	♍
27	..	..	..	♎	♏	..	♒	..	..	..	♌	..
28	♋	..	♍	..	..	♑	..	♈	♊	♋	..	..
29	..		..	..	♐	..	♓	..	..	..	♍	♎
30	♌		..	♏	..	♒	..	♉	..	♌	..	..
31	..		♎		..		..	..		..		♏

1848—EPHEMERIS OF THE PLANETS AND THE MOON—1848

♆	♂	♀	☿	☿	☿	☿
Ja 1 ♓	Fe 6 ♋	Ma 8 ♈	Ja 1 ♏	Ap 1 ♐	Jul 9 ♑	Oc 5 ♑
De 31 ♓	Ap 11 ♌	" 26 ♉	" 4 ♐	" 12 ♑	" 19 ♒	" 15 ♒
♅	Ju 17 ♍	Ju 14 ♊	" 15 ♑	" 22 ♒	" 27 ♓	" 23 ♓
Ja 1 ♈	Au 24 ♎	Jul 3 ♋	" 25 ♒	" 30 ♓	Au 3 ♈	" 30 ♈
De 31 ♈	Oc 29 ♏	" 21 ♌	Fe 2 ♓	Ma 7 ♈	" 9 ♉	No 5 ♉
♄	De 28 ♐	Au 9 ♍	" 9 ♈	" 13 ♉	" 14 ♊	" 10 ♊
Ja 1 ♓	♀	" 27 ♎	" 15 ♉	" 18 ♊	" 19 ♋	" 15 ♋
De 31 ♓	Ja 1 ♍	Se 15 ♏	" 20 ♊	" 23 ♋	" 24 ♌	" 20 ♌
♃	" 15 ♎	Oc 3 ♐	" 25 ♋	" 28 ♌	" 29 ♍	" 25 ♍
Ja 1 ♋	Fe 3 ♏	" 22 ♑	" " "	" " "	" " "	" " "
Ju 30 ♌	" 22 ♐	No 10 ♒	Mh 1 ♌	Ju 2 ♍	" " "	De 2 ♎
De 31 ♌	Mh 12 ♑	" 29 ♓	" 6 ♍	" 9 ♎	Se 5 ♎	" 11 ♏
♂	" 31 ♒	De 18 ♈	" 13 ♎	" 18 ♏	" 14 ♏	" 21 ♐
Ja 1 ♊	Ap 19 ♓	" 31 ♈	" 22 ♏	" 28 ♐	" 24 ♐	" 31 ♐

Day	Jan.	Feb.	Mch.	April	May	June	July	Aug.	Sept.	Oct.	Nov.	Dec.
1	♏	♐	♑	♓	♈	♊	♋	♍	♎	♏	♑	♒
2	..	♑	♒	..	♉	..	♌	..	♏	♐	..	..
3	♐	..	..	♈	..	♋	..	♎	..	..	♒	♓
4	..	♒	♓	..	♊	..	♍	..	..	♑	..	..
5	♑	..	..	♉	..	♌	..	..	♐	..	♓	♈
6	..	♓	♈	..	♋	..	..	♏	..	..	..	..
7	♒	..	..	♊	..	♍	♎	..	♑	♒	..	♉
8	..	♈	♉	..	♌	..	..	♐	..	..	♈	..
9	..	..	..	♋	..	..	♏	..	♒	♓	..	♊
10	♓	♉	♊	..	..	♎	..	..	..	..	♉	..
11	..	..	..	♌	♍	..	..	♑	..	♈	..	♋
12	♈	♊	..	..	..	♏	♐	..	♓	..	♊	..
13	..	..	♋	♍	♎	..	..	♒	..	♉	..	♌
14	♉	♋	..	..	..	..	♑	..	♈	..	♋	..
15	..	..	♌	..	..	♐	..	♓	..	♊	..	♍
16	♊	..	..	♎	♏	..	..	..	♉	..	♌	..
17	..	♌	♍	..	..	♑	♒	♈	..	♋	..	..
18	♋	..	..	..	♐	..	..	..	♊	..	♍	♎
19	..	♍	..	♏	..	♒	♓	♉	..	♌	..	..
20	♌	..	♎	..	..	..	..	..	♋	..	♎	♏
21	..	♎	..	♐	♑	..	♈	..	..	..	..	..
22	..	..	♏	..	..	♓	..	♊	♌	♍	..	..
23	♍	..	..	..	♒	..	♉	..	..	..	♏	♐
24	..	♏	..	♑	..	♈	..	♋	♍	♎	..	..
25	♎	..	♐	..	♓	..	♊	..	..	..	♐	♑
26	..	♐	..	♒	..	♉	..	♌	..	..	..	..
27	..	..	♑	..	..	..	♋	..	♎	♏	..	..
28	♏	..	..	♓	♈	♊	..	♍	..	..	♑	♒
29	..	♑	..	..	..	..	..	..	♏	♐	..	..
30	♐		♒	♈	♉	♋	♌	..	..	..	♒	♓
31	..				..	..	..	♎		..		..

1849—EPHEMERIS OF THE PLANETS AND THE MOON—1849

♆	♂	♀	☿	☿	☿	☿
Ja 1 ♓	Fe 20 ♑	Ap 9 ♎	De 27 ♐	" 30 ♑	Jul 6 ♒	Oc 2 ♒
De 31 ♓	Ap 11 ♒	" 27 ♏	♂	Ap 9 ♒	" 14 ♓	" 10 ♓
⛢	Ma 29 ♓	Ma 16 ♐	Ja 1 ♑	" 17 ♓	" 21 ♈	" 17 ♈
Ja 1 ♈	Jul 16 ♈	Ju 4 ♑	" 11 ♒	" 24 ♈	" 27 ♉	" 23 ♉
De 31 ♈	Se 8 ♉	" 23 ♒	" 19 ♓	" 30 ♉	Au 1 ♊	" 28 ♊
♄	Oc 26 ♊	Jul 12 ♓	" 26 ♈	Ma 5 ♊	" 6 ♋	No 2 ♋
Ja 1 ♓	De 24 ♋	" 31 ♈	Fe 1 ♉	" 10 ♋	" 11 ♌	" 7 ♌
Ma 15 ♈	♀	Au 19 ♉	" 6 ♊	" 15 ♌	" 16 ♍	" 12 ♍
De 31 ♈	Ja 1 ♈	Se 6 ♊	" 11 ♋	" 20 ♍	" 23 ♎	" 19 ♎
♃	" 6 ♉	" 25 ♋	" 16 ♌	" 27 ♎	" " "	" 28 ♏
Ja 1 ♌	" 25 ♊	Oc 14 ♌	" 21 ♍	" " "	" " "	" " "
Jul 14 ♍	Fe 12 ♋	No 1 ♍	" 28 ♎	Ju 5 ♏	Se 1 ♏	De 8 ♐
♂	Mh 3 ♌	" 19 ♎	Mh 9 ♏	" 15 ♐	" 11 ♐	" 19 ♑
Ja 1 ♐	" 21 ♍	De 8 ♏	" 19 ♐	" 26 ♑	" 22 ♑	" 29 ♒

Day	Jan.	Feb.	Mch.	Apr.	May	June	July	Aug.	Sept.	Oct.	Nov.	Dec.
1	♈	♉	♊	♌	♍	♎	♏	♑	♒	♈	♉	♋
2	..	♊	..	..	♏	♐	..	♓	..	♊	..
3	♉	..	♋	..	♎	..	♒	..	..	..	♌
4	..	♋	..	♍	..	♐	♑	..	♈	♉	♋	..
5	♊	..	♌	..	..	..	..	♓	..	..	..	..
6	..	♌	..	♎	♏	..	..	..	♉	♊	♌	♍
7	♋	..	♍	..	..	♑	♒	..	..	..	..	..
8	..	♍	..	♏	♐	..	..	♈	♊	♋	♍	♎
9	..	..	..	..	..	♓	..	..	..	..	..
10	♌	♎	♎	..	..	♒	..	♉	..	♌	..	♏
11	..	..	..	♐	♑	..	..	..	♋	..	♎	..
12	♍	..	♏	..	..	♓	♈	♊	..	♍	..	..
13	..	♏	..	♑	♒	..	..	..	♌	..	♏	♐
14	♎	..	..	..	..	♈	♉	♋	..	♎	..	..
15	..	♐	♐	..	..	..	..	..	♍	..	♐	♑
16	♏	..	..	♒	♓	♉	♊	♌	..	..	..	..
17	..	..	♑	..	..	..	..	..	♎	♏	..	..
18	..	♑	..	♓	♈	♊	♋	♍	..	..	♑	♒
19	♐	..	♒	..	..	..	..	..	♏	♐	..	..
20	..	♒	..	♈	♉	♋	♌	..	..	..	♒	♓
21	♑	..	..	♈	..	..	..	♎	..	♑	..	..
22	..	..	♓	..	♊	♌	♍	..	♐	..	..	..
23	..	♓	..	♉	..	..	..	♏	..	♒	♓	♈
24	♒	..	♈	..	♋	..	♎	..	♑	♒	..	..
25	..	♈	..	♊	..	♍	..	♐	..	..	♈	♉
26	♓	..	♉	..	♌	..	..	..	♒	♓	..	..
27	..	♉	..	♋	..	♏	♐	..	..	..	♉	♊
28	♈	..	♊	..	♍	..	♑	♒	..	..	..	..
29	..		..	♌	..	♏	♐	..	♓	♈	♊	..
30	..		♋	..	..	..	♒	..	..	..	..	♋
31	♉		..		♎		..			♉		..

1850—EPHEMERIS OF THE PLANETS AND THE MOON—1850

♆	♂	♀	☿	☿	☿	☿
Ja 1 ♓	Ma 5 ♍	Ma 26 ♌	Ja 1 ♒	Ap 4 ♓	Jul 1 ♓	Oc 4 ♈
De 31 ♓	Jul 12 ♎	Ju 14 ♍	" 6 ♓	" 11 ♈	" 3 ♈	" 10 ♉
♅	Se 16 ♏	Jul 2 ♎	" 13 ♈	" 17 ♉	" 14 ♉	" 15 ♊
Ja 1 ♈	No 15 ♐	" 21 ♏	" 19 ♉	" 22 ♊	" 19 ♊	" 20 ♋
De 31 ♈	" " "	Au 8 ♐	" 24 ♊	" 27 ♋	" 24 ♋	" 25 ♌
♄	♀	" 27 ♑	" 29 ♋	Ma 2 ♌	" 29 ♌	" 30 ♍
Ja 1 ♈	Ja 1 ♐	Se 16 ♒	Fe 3 ♌	" 7 ♍	Au 3 ♍	No 6 ♎
De 31 ♈	" 15 ♑	Oc 4 ♓	" 8 ♍	" 14 ♎	" 10 ♎	" 15 ♏
♃	Fe 3 ♒	" 23 ♈	" 15 ♎	" 23 ♏	" 19 ♏	" 25 ♐
Ja 1 ♍	" 22 ♓	No 11 ♉	" 24 ♏	" " "	" 29 ♐	" " "
Au 11 ♎	Mh 12 ♈	" 30 ♊	" " "	" " "	" " "	De 6 ♑
♁	" 31 ♉	De 18 ♋	Mh 6 ♐	Ju 2 ♐	Se 9 ♑	" 16 ♒
Ja 1 ♋	Ap 20 ♊	" " "	" 17 ♑	" 13 ♑	" 19 ♒	" 24 ♓
Fe 6 ♌	Ma 8 ♋	" 31 ♊	" 27 ♒	" 23 ♒	" 27 ♓	" 31 ♈

Day	Jan.	Feb.	Mch.	April	May	June	July	Aug.	Sept.	Oct.	Nov.	Dec.
1	♌	♍	♏	♏	♐	♑	♓	♈	♊	♋	♍	♎
2	..	♎	♎	..	..	♒	..	♉	..	♌	..	♏
3	..	..	..	♐	♑	..	..	..	♋	..	♎	..
4	♍	..	♏	..	..	♓	♈	♊	..	♍	..	..
5	..	♏	..	♑	♒	..	..	..	♌	..	♏	♐
6	♎	..	..	..	..	♈	♉	♋	..	♎	..	♑
7	..	♐	♐	..	..	..	..	..	♍	..	♐	♑
8	♏	..	..	♒	♓	♉	♊	♌	..	..	..	..
9	..	..	♑	..	..	..	..	..	♎	♏	..	..
10	..	♑	..	♓	♈	..	♋	♍	..	..	♑	♒
11	♐	..	..	..	..	♊	..	..	♏	♐	..	..
12	..	♒	♒	..	♉	..	♌	..	..	..	♒	♓
13	..	..	..	♈	..	♋	..	♎	..	♑	..	..
14	♑	..	♓	..	♊	..	♍	..	♐	..	..	..
15	..	♓	..	♉	..	♌	..	♏	..	..	♓	♈
16	♒	..	♈	..	♋	..	♎	..	♑	♒	..	..
17	..	♈	..	♊	..	♍	..	♐	..	..	♈	♉
18	♓	..	♉	..	♌	..	..	..	♒	♓	..	..
19	..	♉	..	♋	..	♎	♏	♐	..	..	♉	♊
20	..	..	..	..	..	..	♑	..	..	..	..	..
21	♈	♊	♊	♌	♍	♏	♐	..	♓	♈	♊	♋
22	..	..	..	..	..	..	♒	..	..	..	..	..
23	♉	♋	♋	♍	♎	..	..	♑	..	♉	♋	♌
24	..	..	..	..	..	♐	♑	..	♈	..	♋	♍
25	♊	♌	♌	♎	♏	..	♓	..	♉	♊	..	♍
26	..	..	..	..	..	♑	♒	..	..	♌	..	♎
27	♋	..	♍	..	..	..	..	♈	♊	..	..	♎
28	..	♍	..	♏	♐	..	..	..	..	♊	♍	..
29	♌		♎	..	..	♒	♓	♉	..	♌	..	♏
30	..		..	♐	♑	..	..	..	♋	..	♎	..
31	♍		♏	..			♈	..				♐

1851—EPHEMERIS OF THE PLANETS AND THE MOON—1851

♆	♂	♀	☿	☿	☿	☿
Ja 1 ♓	Fe 27 ♒	Ap 28 ♒	Ja 1 ♈	Ap 4 ♉	Jul 1 ♉	Oc 2 ♊
De 31 ♓	Ap 16 ♓	Ma 17 ♓	" 6 ♉	" 9 ♊	" 6 ♊	" 6 ♋
♅	Ju 3 ♈	Ju 5 ♈	" 11 ♊	" 13 ♋	" 10 ♋	" 11 ♌
Ja 1 ♈	Jul 22 ♉	" 24 ♉	" 16 ♋	" 18 ♌	" 15 ♌	" 17 ♍
Mh 19 ♉	Se 13 ♊	Jul 13 ♊	" 21 ♌	" 22 ♍	" 19 ♍	" 24 ♎
♄	No 13 ♋	" 31 ♋	" 26 ♍	Ma 1 ♎	" 28 ♎	No 1 ♏
Ja 1 ♈	♀	Au 19 ♌	Fe 2 ♎	" 9 ♏	Au 5 ♏	" 11 ♐
Se 30 ♉	Ja 1 ♋	Se 6 ♍	" 10 ♏	" 20 ♐	" 16 ♐	" 22 ♑
♃	" 6 ♌	" 25 ♎	" 21 ♐	" 30 ♑	" 26 ♑	De 2 ♒
Ja 1 ♎	" 24 ♍	Oc 13 ♏	" " "	" " "	" " "	" 11 ♓
Se 11 ♏	Fe 12 ♎	No 1 ♐	Mh 3 ♑	" " "	Se 5 ♒	" 18 ♈
♂	Mh 2 ♏	" 20 ♑	" 14 ♒	Ju 10 ♒	" 14 ♓	" 24 ♉
Ja 1 ♐	" 21 ♐	De 9 ♒	" 22 ♓	" 18 ♓	" 21 ♈	" 29 ♊
" 8 ♑	Ap 9 ♑	" 28 ♓	" 29 ♈	" 25 ♈	" 27 ♉	" 31 ♊

Day	Jan.	Feb.	Mch.	April	May	June	July	Aug.	Sept.	Oct.	Nov.	Dec.
1	♐	♒	♒	♈	♉	♋	♌	♎	♏	♑	♒	♓
2	♑	..	♓	..	..	..	..	..	♐	..	..	..
3	..	♓	..	♉	♊	♌	♍	♏	..	♒	♓	♈
4	♒	..	..	..	..	..	..	..	♑	..	..	..
5	..	♈	♈	..	♋	♍	♎	..	..	♓	♈	♉
6	..	..	..	♊	..	..	..	♐	..	..	..	..
7	♓	..	♉	..	♌	♎	♏	..	♒	..	..	♊
8	..	♉	..	♋	..	..	..	♑	..	♈	♉	..
9	♈	..	♊	..	♍	♏	♐	..	♓	..	..	..
10	..	♊	..	♌	..	..	..	♒	..	♉	♊	♋
11	♉	..	..	..	..	♐	..	..	..	..	..	..
12	..	♋	♋	♍	♎	..	♑	..	♈	..	♋	♌
13	..	..	..	..	..	♑	..	♓	..	♊	..	..
14	♊	♌	♌	♎	♏	..	♒	..	♉	..	..	♍
15	..	..	..	..	..	..	..	♈	..	♋	♌	..
16	♋	♍	♍	♏	♐	♒	..	..	..	..	..	♎
17	..	..	..	..	..	..	♓	..	♊	♌	♍	..
18	♌	♎	♎	♐	♑	♓	..	♉	..	..	..	♏
19	..	..	..	..	..	..	♈	..	♋	..	♎	..
20	♍	♏	♏	..	♒	..	..	♊	..	♍	..	♐
21	..	..	..	♑	..	♈	..	..	♌	..	♏	..
22	♎	..	♐	..	..	..	♉	..	..	♎	..	..
23	..	♐	..	♒	♓	♉	..	♋	♍	..	♐	♑
24	♏	..	♑	..	..	..	♊	..	..	♏	..	..
25	..	♑	..	..	♈	..	..	♌	♎	..	♑	♒
26	♐	..	..	♓	..	♊	♋	..	..	♐	..	..
27	..	..	♒	..	..	..	..	♍	♏	..	..	♓
28	..	♒	..	♈	♉	♋	♌	..	..	♑	♒	..
29	♑		♓	..	..	..	..	♎	♐	..	..	..
30	..		..	..	♊	..	♍	..	..	..	♓	♈
31	♒		..		..		..	♏		♒		..

1852—EPHEMERIS OF THE PLANETS AND THE MOON—1852

♆	♂	♀	☿	☿	☿	☿
Ja 1 ♓	Mh 22 ♍	Ma 25 ♏	Ja 1 ♊	Ap 4 ♌	Jul 1 ♌	Oc 3 ♍
De 31 ♓	Ma 29 ♎	Ju 13 ♐	" 2 ♋	" 16 ♍	" 7 ♍	" 10 ♎
♅	Au 2 ♏	Jul 2 ♑	" 7 ♌	" 17 ♎	" 14 ♎	" 18 ♏
Ja 1 ♉	Se 30 ♐	" 21 ♒	" 13 ♍	" 25 ♏	" 22 ♏	" 28 ♐
De 31 ♉	No 25 ♑	Au 8 ♓	" 20 ♎	Ma 5 ♐	Au 1 ♐	No 8 ♑
♄	♀	" 27 ♈	" 28 ♏	" 16 ♑	" 12 ♑	" 18 ♒
Ja 1 ♉	Ja 1 ♓	Se 15 ♉	Fe 7 ♐	" 26 ♒	" 22 ♒	" 27 ♓
De 31 ♉	" 15 ♈	Oc 4 ♊	" 18 ♑	" " "	" 31 ♓	De 4 ♈
♃	Fe 4 ♉	" 22 ♋	" 28 ♒	" " "	" " "	" 9 ♉
Ja 1 ♏	" 22 ♊	No 10 ♌	Mh 8 ♓	Ju 4 ♓	Se 7 ♈	" 14 ♊
Oc 5 ♐	Mh 12 ♋	" 28 ♍	" 15 ♈	" 11 ♈	" 13 ♉	" 19 ♋
♂	" 31 ♌	" " "	" 21 ♉	" 17 ♉	" 18 ♊	" 24 ♌
Ja 1 ♋	Ap 18 ♍	De 17 ♎	" 26 ♊	" 22 ♊	" 22 ♋	" 30 ♍
" 14 ♌	Ma 6 ♎	" 31 ♎	" 31 ♋	" 27 ♋	" 27 ♌	" 31 ♍

Day	Jan.	Feb.	Mch.	April	May	June	July	Aug.	Sept.	Oct.	Nov.	Dec.
1	♈	♊	♋	♍	♎	♐	♑	♓	♈	♉	♋	♌
2	♉	♋	♌	..	♏	..	♒	..	♉	♊	..	..
3	..	..	..	♎	..	♑	..	♈	..	..	♌	♍
4	♊	..	♍	..	♐	..	♓	..	..	♋	..	..
5	..	♌	..	♏	..	♒	..	..	♊	..	♍	♎
6	♋	..	♎	..	♑	..	..	♉	..	..	..	..
7	..	♍	..	♐	..	♓	♈	..	♋	♌	♎	♏
8	♌	..	♏	..	♒	..	..	♊	..	..	..	..
9	..	♎	..	♑	..	..	♉	..	♌	♍	♏	♐
10	♍	..	♐	..	..	♈	..	..	..	..	..	..
11	..	♏	..	♒	♓	..	..	♋	..	♎	♐	♑
12	♎	..	♑	..	..	♉	♊	..	♍	..	..	..
13	..	♐	..	♓	♈	..	..	♌	..	♏	♑	♒
14	♏	..	..	..	..	..	♋	..	♎	..	..	..
15	..	♑	..	..	..	♊	..	♍	..	♐	..	♓
16	..	..	..	♈	♉	..	..	..	♏	..	♒	..
17	♐	..	♓	..	..	♋	♌	♎	..	♑	..	..
18	..	♒	..	..	♊	..	..	..	♐	..	♓	♈
19	♑	..	..	♉	..	♌	♍	♏	..	♒	..	..
20	..	♓	♈	..	..	..	..	..	♑	..	♈	♉
21	♒	..	..	♊	♋	♍	♎	♐	..	..	..	..
22	..	♈	♉	..	..	..	..	..	♒	♓	..	..
23	..	..	..	♋	♌	..	♏	♑	..	..	♉	♊
24	♓	♉	..	..	..	♎	..	..	♓	♈	..	..
25	..	..	♊	..	♍	..	♐	..	..	..	♊	♋
26	♈	♊	..	♌	..	♏	..	♒	..	..	..	..
27	..	..	♋	..	♎	..	♑	..	♈	♉	..	..
28	..	♋	..	♍	..	♐	..	♓	..	..	♋	♌
29	♉	..	..	..	♏	..	♒	..	♉	♊	..	..
30	..		♌	♎	..	♑	..	..	..	..	♌	♍
31	♊		..		♐		..	♈		..		..

1853—EPHEMERIS OF THE PLANETS AND THE MOON—1853

♆	♂	♀	☿	☿	☿	☿
Ja 1 ♓	Mh 3 ♓	Ap 28 ♉	Ja 1 ♍	Ap 4 ♎	Jul 1 ♎	Oc 5 ♏
De 31 ♓	Ap 19 ♈	Ma 17 ♊	" 6 ♎	" 12 ♏	" 9 ♏	" 15 ♐
♅	Ju 8 ♉	Ju 4 ♋	" 14 ♏	" 22 ♐	" 19 ♐	" 26 ♑
Ja 1 ♉	Jul 31 ♊	" 23 ♌	" 24 ♐	Ma 3 ♑	" 30 ♑	No 5 ♒
De 31 ♉	Se 28 ♋	Jul 11 ♍	Fe 4 ♑	" 13 ♒	Au 9 ♒	" 14 ♓
♄	De 1 ♌	" 30 ♎	" 14 ♒	" 22 ♓	" 18 ♓	" 21 ♈
Ja 1 ♉	♀	Au 17 ♏	" 23 ♓	" 29 ♈	" 25 ♈	" 26 ♉
De 31 ♉	Ja 1 ♎	Se 5 ♐	" " "	" " "	" 30 ♉	" " "
♃	" 5 ♏	" 24 ♑	Mh 2 ♈	" " "	" " "	De 6 ♊
Ja 1 ♐	" 23 ♐	Oc 13 ♒	" 7 ♉	Ju 3 ♉	Se 4 ♊	" 6 ♋
Oc 15 ♑	Fe 11 ♑	No 1 ♓	" 12 ♊	" 8 ♊	" 9 ♋	" 11 ♌
♂	Mh 2 ♒	" 20 ♈	" 17 ♋	" 13 ♋	" 14 ♌	" 17 ♍
Ja 1 ♑	" 21 ♓	De 9 ♉	" 22 ♌	" 18 ♌	" 20 ♍	" 23 ♎
" 14 ♒	Ap 9 ♈	" 27 ♊	" 28 ♍	" 24 ♍	" 26 ♎	" 31 ♎

Day	Jan.	Feb.	Mch.	Apr.	May	June	July	Aug.	Sept.	Oct.	Nov.	Dec.
1	♎	♐	♐	♒	♒	♈	♉	♋	♌	♎	♏	♑
2	..	..	..	..	♓	♉	♊	..	♍	..	♐	..
3	♏	..	♑	..	..	..	..	♌	..	♏	..	♒
4	..	♑	..	♓	♈	♊	♋	..	♎	..	♑	..
5	♐	..	♒	..	..	..	..	♍	..	♐	..	♓
6	..	♒	..	♈	..	..	..	..	♏	..	♒	..
7	♑	..	♓	..	♉	♋	♌	..	..	♑	..	..
8	..	♓	..	♉	..	..	..	♎	♐	..	♓	♈
9	♒	..	..	..	♊	♌	♍	..	..	..	..	..
10	..	♈	♈	..	..	..	..	♏	..	♒	♈	♉
11	..	..	..	♊	..	..	♎	..	♑	..	..	..
12	♓	..	♉	..	♋	♍	..	♐	..	♓	..	..
13	..	♉	..	..	..	..	..	..	♒	..	♉	♊
14	♈	..	..	♋	♌	♎	♏	♑	..	♈	..	..
15	..	♊	♊	..	..	..	..	..	..	..	♊	♋
16	♉	..	..	♌	..	♏	♐	♒	♓	..	..	..
17	..	..	♋	..	♍	..	..	..	..	♉	..	..
18	..	♋	..	♍	..	♐	♑	♓	♈	..	♋	♌
19	♊	..	..	..	♎	..	..	..	..	♊	..	..
20	..	♌	♌	..	..	♑	♒	♈	♉	..	♌	..
21	♋	..	..	♎	♏	..	..	..	..	..	..	♍
22	..	♍	♍	..	..	♒	♓	..	..	♋	..	..
23	..	..	..	♏	♐	..	..	♉	♊	..	♍	♎
24	♌	..	♎	..	..	♓	♈	..	..	♌	..	..
25	..	♎	..	♐	♑	..	..	♊	♋	..	♎	..
26	♍	..	♏	..	..	..	..	..	..	♍	..	♏
27	..	♏	..	♑	♒	♈	♉	..	..	..	♏	..
28	♎	..	♐	..	..	..	..	♋	♌	..	..	♐
29	..		..	..	♓	♉	♊	..	..	♎	♐	..
30	♏		♑	♒	..	..	..	♌	♍	..	..	♑
31	..		..		♈	..	..	..	..	♏		..

1854—EPHEMERIS OF THE PLANETS AND THE MOON—1854

♆	♂	♀	☿	☿	☿	☿
Ja 1 ♓	Ap 16 ♎	Ma 26 ♒	Ja 1 ♏	Ap 9 ♐	Jul 6 ♐	Oc 2 ♐
De 31 ♓	Ju 20 ♏	Ju 14 ♓	" 11 ♐	" 20 ♑	" 17 ♑	" 13 ♑
♅	Au 19 ♐	Jul 2 ♈	" 22 ♑	" 30 ♒	" 27 ♒	" 23 ♒
Ja 1 ♉	Oc 13 ♑	" 21 ♉	Fe 1 ♒	Ma 9 ♓	Au 5 ♓	" 31 ♓
De 31 ♉	De 2 ♒	Au 9 ♊	" 10 ♓	" 16 ♈	" 11 ♈	No 7 ♈
♄	♀	" 28 ♋	" 17 ♈	" 21 ♉	" 17 ♉	" 13 ♉
Ja 1 ♉	Ja 1 ♊	Se 15 ♌	" 22 ♉	" 26 ♊	" 22 ♊	" 18 ♊
" 4 ♓	" 15 ♋	Oc 4 ♍	" 27 ♊	" 31 ♋	" 27 ♋	" 23 ♋
♃	Fe 2 ♌	" 22 ♎	" " "	" " "	" " "	" 28 ♌
Ja 1 ♑	" 21 ♍	No 10 ♏	Mh 4 ♋	" " "	" " "	De 2 ♍
Oc 8 ♒	Mh 11 ♎	" 28 ♐	" 9 ♉	Ju 5 ♌	Se 1 ♌	" 10 ♎
♂	" 30 ♏	De 17 ♑	" 15 ♍	" 11 ♍	" 6 ♍	" 19 ♏
Ja 1 ♌	Ap 18 ♐	" " "	" 21 ♎	" 17 ♎	" 31 ♎	" 29 ♐
Fe 7 ♍	Ma 7 ♑	" 31 "	" 30 ♏	" 26 ♏	" 22 ♏	" 31 "

Day	Jan.	Feb.	Mch.	April	May	June	July	Aug.	Sept.	Oct.	Nov.	Dec.
1	♒	♓	♈	♉	♊	♌	♍	♏	♐	♒	♓	♈
2	..	♈	..	♊	..	..	♎	..	♑	..	♈	♉
3	♓	..	..	..	♋	♍	..	♐	..	♓	..	..
4	..	♉	♉	..	..	..	..	..	♒	..	..	♊
5	♈	..	..	♋	♌	♎	♏	♑	..	..	♉	..
6	..	..	♊	..	..	..	..	..	♓	♈	..	..
7	..	♊	..	♌	♍	♏	♐	..	..	..	♊	♋
8	♉	..	..	..	..	..	..	♒	♈	♉	..	..
9	..	♋	♋	..	♎	♐	♑	..	..	..	♋	♌
10	♊	..	..	♍	..	..	..	♓	..	..	..	..
11	..	♌	♌	..	♏	♑	♒	..	♉	♊	..	..
12	..	..	..	♎	..	..	..	♈	..	..	♌	♍
13	♋	..	♍	..	♐	..	♓	..	♊	♋	..	..
14	..	♍	..	♏	..	♒	..	♉	..	..	♍	♎
15	♌	..	♎	..	♑	..	..	..	..	..	..	..
16	..	♎	..	♐	..	♓	♈	..	♋	♌	..	♏
17	♍	..	♏	..	♒	..	..	♊	..	..	♎	..
18	..	♏	..	♑	..	♈	♉	..	♌	♍	..	♐
19	♎	..	♐	..	♓	..	..	..	..	..	♏	..
20	..	♐	..	♒	..	..	..	♋	..	♎	..	♑
21	..	..	♑	..	..	♉	♊	..	♍	..	♐	..
22	♏	♑	..	♓	♈	..	..	♌	..	♏	..	♒
23	..	..	..	..	..	♊	♋	..	♎	..	♑	..
24	♐	♒	♒	..	♉	..	..	♍	..	♐	..	♓
25	..	..	..	♈	..	..	..	..	♏	..	♒	..
26	♑	..	♓	..	..	♋	♌	♎	..	♑	..	♈
27	..	♓	..	♉	♊	..	..	..	♐	..	♓	..
28	♒	..	♈	..	..	♌	♏	♏	..	♒	..	..
29	..		..	..	♋	..	..	..	♑	..	♈	♉
30	♓		♉	♊	..	♍	♎	..	..	..	..	..
31	..		..		..		..	♐		♓		♊

1855—EPHEMERIS OF THE PLANETS AND THE MOON—1855

♆	♂	♀	☿	☿	☿	☿
Ja 1 ♓	Mh 7 ♈	Ap 28 ♌	Ja 1 ♐	Mh 17 ♏	Jul 4 ♑	Oc 11 ♒
De 31 ♓	Ap 26 ♉	Ma 17 ♍	" 10 ♑	" 27 ♐	" 14 ♒	" 19 ♓
♅	Ju 19 ♊	Ju 4 ♎	" 20 ♒	Ap 8 ♑	" 23 ♓	" 26 ♈
Ja 1 ♉	Au 17 ♋	" 25 ♏	" 29 ♓	" 18 ♒	" 30 ♈	No 1 ♉
De 31 ♉	Oc 21 ♌	Jul 12 ♐	Fe 4 ♈	" 26 ♓	Au 6 ♉	" 5 ♊
♄	De 24 ♍	" 30 ♑	" 10 ♉	Ma 3 ♈	" 11 ♊	" 10 ♋
Ja 1 ♊	♀	Au 19 ♒	" 15 ♊	" 9 ♉	" 14 ♋	" 15 ♌
De 31 ♊	Ja 1 ♑	Se 8 ♓	" 19 ♋	" 14 ♊	" 19 ♌	" 21 ♍
♃	" 5 ♒	" 25 ♈	" 24 ♌	" 19 ♋	" 25 ♍	" 29 ♎
Ja 1 ♒	" 25 ♓	Oc 15 ♉	Mh 2 ♍	" 24 ♌	" " "	" " "
Se 17 ♓	Fe 14 ♈	No 2 ♊	" 9 ♎	" 29 ♍	Se 1 ♎	De 6 ♏
♂	Mh 4 ♉	" 20 ♋	" " "	Ju 5 ♎	" 10 ♏	" 16 ♐
Ja 1 ♒	" 23 ♊	De 10 ♌	" " "	" 14 ♏	" 21 ♐	" 25 ♑
" 19 ♓	Ap 10 ♋	" 29 ♍	" " "	" 24 ♐	" 30 ♑	" 31 "

Day	Jan.	Feb.	Mch.	Apr.	May	June	July	Aug	Sept.	Oct.	Nov.	Dec.
1	♊	♋	♌	♎	♏	♑	♒	♈	♊	♊	♌	♍
2	..	♌	♍	..	♐	..	♓	..	..	♋	..	♎
3	♋	..	..	♏	..	♒	..	♉	..	..	..	..
4	..	..	♎	..	♑	..	..	..	♋	♌	♍	..
5	♌	♍	..	♐	..	♓	♈	..	..	..	..	♏
6	..	..	..	..	♒	..	..	♊	..	..	♎	..
7	..	♎	♏	♑	..	♈	..	..	♌	♍	..	♐
8	♍	..	..	..	..	..	♉	♋	..	..	..	..
9	..	..	♐	♒	♓	..	..	..	♍	♎	♏	♑
10	♎	♏	..	..	..	♉	♊	..	..	..	..	..
11	..	..	♑	♓	♈	..	..	♌	..	♏	♐	♒
12	♏	♐	..	..	..	♊	..	..	♎	..	..	..
13	..	..	♒	..	♉	..	♋	♍	..	♐	♑	♓
14	♐	♑	..	♈	..	..	..	..	♏	..	..	..
15	..	..	♓	..	..	♋	♌	♎	..	..	♒	♈
16	♑	♒	..	♉	♊	..	..	..	♐	♑	..	..
17	..	..	♈	..	..	♌	..	..	..	..	♓	..
18	♒	♓	..	..	♋	..	♍	♏	♑	♒	..	♉
19	..	..	..	♊	..	..	..	..	..	..	♈	..
20	♓	♈	♉	..	..	♍	♎	♐	♒	♓	..	♊
21	..	..	..	♋	♌	..	..	..	..	..	♉	..
22	..	♉	♊	..	..	♎	♏	♑	♓	♈	..	..
23	♈	..	..	..	♍	..	..	..	..	..	♊	♋
24	..	..	..	♌	..	♏	..	♒	..	♉	..	..
25	♉	♊	♋	..	..	..	♐	..	♈	..	♋	♌
26	..	..	..	♍	♎	♐	..	♓	..	..	..	..
27	..	♋	♌	..	..	..	♑	..	♉	♊	..	..
28	♊	..	..	♎	♏	♑	..	♈	..	..	♌	♍
29	..		..	..	..	..	♒	..	♊	♋	..	..
30	♋		♍	♏	♐	♒	..	♉	..	..	♍	♎
31	..		..		..		♓	..		..		..

1856—EPHEMERIS OF THE PLANETS AND THE MOON—1856

♆	♂	♀	☿	☿	☿	☿
Ja 1 ♓	Ja 1 ♍	Ap 18 ♓	Ja 1 ♑	Ap 2 ♒	Jul 1 ♒	Oc 5 ♓
De 31 ♓	Mh 3 ♎	Ma 8 ♈	" 6 ♒	" 11 ♓	" 9 ♓	" 12 ♈
♅	Ma 9 ♏	" 26 ♉	" 15 ♓	" 19 ♈	" 16 ♈	" 18 ♉
Ja 1 ♉	Jul 7 ♐	Ju 14 ♊	" 22 ♈	" 24 ♉	" 21 ♉	" 22 ♊
De 31 ♉	Au 30 ♑	Jul 2 ♋	" 29 ♉	" 29 ♊	" 26 ♊	" 28 ♋
" " "	Oc 18 ♒	" 21 ♌	Fe 2 ♊	Ma 4 ♋	Au 1 ♋	No 2 ♌
♄	De 6 ♓	Au 8 ♍	" 7 ♋	" 9 ♌	" 6 ♌	" 8 ♍
Ja 1 ♊	♀	" 27 ♎	" 12 ♌	" 15 ♍	" 11 ♍	" 14 ♎
Mh 22 ♋	Ja 1 ♍	Se 15 ♏	" 18 ♍	" 22 ♎	" 18 ♎	" 22 ♏
De 31 ♋	" 15 ♎	Oc 3 ♐	" 24 ♎	" 30 ♏	" 26 ♏	" " "
♃	Fe 3 ♏	" 22 ♑	" " "	" " "	" " "	De 2 ♐
Ja 1 ♓	" 22 ♐	No 10 ♒	Mh 3 ♏	" " "	Se 6 ♐	" 13 ♑
Au 12 ♈	Mh 11 ♑	" 30 ♓	" 14 ♐	Ju 10 ♐	" 16 ♑	" 23 ♒
De 31 ♈	" 30 ♒	De 18 ♈	" 24 ♑	" 20 ♑	" 26 ♒	" 31 ♒

Day	Jan.	Feb.	Mch.	April	May	June	July	Aug.	Sept.	Oct.	Nov.	Dec.
1	♎	♐	♐	♒	♓	♉	♊	♌	♎	♏	♐	♑
2	♏	♑	♑	♓	♈	♊	♋	..	..	..	♑	♒
3	..	..	..	..	..	..	..	♍	..	..	..	..
4	♐	♒	♒	♈	♉	..	♌	..	♏	♐	♒	♓
5	..	..	..	..	..	♋	..	..	..	..	..	..
6	♑	♓	♓	♉	♊	..	..	♎	..	♑	..	♈
7	..	..	..	..	..	♌	♍	..	♐	..	♓	..
8	♒	♈	♈	..	♋	..	♏	..	♒	..	..	♉
9	..	..	..	♊	..	..	♎	♑	..	..	♈	..
10	♓	..	♉	..	♌	..	♐	..	♓	..	..	♊
11	..	♉	..	♋	♌	..	..	♒	..	♉	..	..
12	♈	..	♊	..	♎	♏	♑	..	♈	..	..	..
13	..	♊	..	..	♍	..	..	..	♓	..	♊	♋
14	♉	..	..	♌	..	..	♐	♒	..	♉	..	..
15	..	♋	♋	..	..	♏	..	♓	♈	..	♋	♌
16	..	..	..	♍	♎	..	♑	♓	..	..	..	..
17	♊	..	♌	..	..	♐	..	..	♉	♊	..	..
18	..	♌	..	..	♏	..	♒	♈	..	..	♌	♍
19	♋	..	..	♎	♑	..	..	..	♊	♋	..	..
20	..	♍	♍	..	♐	♒	♓	..	..	..	♍	♎
21	..	..	..	♏	♒	..	..	♉	♌	..	..	..
22	♌	..	♎	..	♑	..	♈	..	♋	..	..	..
23	..	♎	..	♐	..	♓	..	♊	..	..	♎	♏
24	♍	..	..	..	..	..	..	♌	♍	..	..	..
25	..	♏	♏	♑	♒	♈	♉	♋	..	..	♏	♐
26	..	..	..	..	..	..	..	..	♎	..	..	..
27	♎	..	♐	♒	♓	♉	♊	..	♍	..	♐	♑
28	..	♐	..	..	..	..	..	♌	..	..	..	♒
29	♏		♑	♓	♈	..	♋	..	♎	♏	..	♒
30	..		..	..	..	♊	..	♍	..	..	♑	..
31	♐		♒		♉	..	..	..		♐		♓

211

♆	♂	♀	☿	☿	☿	☿
Ja 1 ♓	Ja 23 ♈	Ap 27 ♏	Ja 1 ♓	Ap 6 ♈	Jul 3 ♈	Oc 4 ♉
De 31 ♓	Mh 13 ♉	Ma 16 ♐	“ 6 ♈	“ 11 ♉	“ 8 ♉	“ 16 ♊
♅	Ma 6 ♊	Ju 4 ♑	“ 13 ♉	“ 16 ♊	“ 13 ♊	“ 15 ♋
Ja 1 ♉	Jul 3 ♋	“ 22 ♒	“ 18 ♊	“ 21 ♋	“ 18 ♋	“ 20 ♌
De 31 ♉	Se 4 ♌	Jul 12 ♓	“ 23 ♋	“ 26 ♌	“ 22 ♌	“ 25 ♒
♄	No 11 ♍	“ 31 ♈	“ 28 ♌	Ma 2 ♍	“ 29 ♍	No 1 ♎
Ja 1 ♋	♀	Au 18 ♉	Fe 3 ♍	“ 9 ♎	Au 6 ♎	“ 7 ♏
De 31 ♋	Ja 1 ♈	Se 6 ♓	“ 10 ♎	“ 17 ♏	“ 14 ♏	“ 19 ♐
♃	“ 6 ♉	“ 25 ♋	“ 18 ♏	“ 26 ♐	“ 25 ♐	“ 30 ♑
Ja 1 ♈	“ 24 ♊	Oc 13 ♌	“ 28 ♐	“ “ “	“ “ “	“ “ “
Jul 7 ♉	Fe 12 ♋	No 1 ♍	“ “ “	“ “ “	Se 4 ♑	De 10 ♒
De 31 ♉	Mh 2 ♌	“ 20 ♎	Mh 12 ♑	Ju 7 ♑	“ 14 ♒	“ 18 ♓
♂	“ 21 ♍	De 9 ♏	“ 21 ♒	“ 17 ♒	“ 22 ♓	“ 26 ♈
Ja 1 ♓	Ap 8 ♎	De 26 ♐	“ 30 ♓	“ 26 ♓	“ 28 ♈	“ 31 ♈

Day	Jan.	Feb.	Mch.	Apr.	May	June	July	Aug.	Sept.	Oct.	Nov.	Dec.
1	♓	♉	♉	♋	♌	♍	♏	♐	♒	♓	♉	♊
2	♈	..	♊	..	..	♎	..	♑	..	..	..	..
3	..	♊	..	♌	♍	..	..	..	♓	♈	♊	♋
4	♉	..	♋	..	..	♏	♐	..	..	..	..	..
5	..	♋	..	..	..	..	..	♒	♈	♉	♋	♌
6	..	..	..	♍	♎	..	♑	..	..	..	..	..
7	♊	..	♌	..	..	♐	..	♓	♉	♊	..	♍
8	..	♌	..	♎	♏	..	♒	..	..	..	♌	..
9	♋	..	♍	..	..	♑	..	♈	♊	♋	..	..
10	..	♍	..	..	♐	..	..	..	..	..	♍	♎
11	♌	..	..	♏	..	♒	♓	♉	..	♌	..	..
12	..	..	♎	..	..	..	..	..	♋	..	..	♏
13	..	♎	..	♐	♑	♓	♈	♊	..	..	♎	..
14	♍	..	♏	..	..	..	..	..	♌	♍	..	..
15	..	♏	..	♑	♒	♈	♉	♋	..	..	♏	♐
16	♎	..	..	..	..	..	..	..	..	♎	..	..
17	..	..	♐	..	♓	..	♊	..	♍	..	..	♑
18	..	♐	..	♒	..	♉	..	♌	..	..	♐	..
19	♏	..	♑	..	♈	..	♋	..	♎	♏	..	♒
20	..	♑	..	♓	..	♊	..	♍	..	..	♑	..
21	♐	..	♒	..	♉	..	..	..	..	♐	..	..
22	..	♒	..	♈	..	♋	♌	..	♏	..	♒	♓
23	♑	..	♓	..	♊	..	..	♎	..	..	..	..
24	..	♓	..	♉	..	♌	♍	..	♐	♑	♓	♈
25	♒	..	♈	..	..	..	..	♏	..	..	..	..
26	..	♈	..	♊	♋	..	..	..	♑	♒	..	♉
27	♓	..	♉	..	..	♍	♎	..	..	..	♈	..
28	..	♉	..	♋	♌	..	..	♐	..	♓	..	♊
29	♈		..	..	..	♎	♏	..	♒	..	♉	..
30	..		♊	..	♍	..	..	♑	..	..	..	♋
31	..		..		..		♐	..		♈		..

1858—EPHEMERIS OF THE PLANETS AND THE MOON—1858

♆	♂	♀	♀	☿	☿	☿
Ja 1 ♓	Ja 1 ♍	Ap 1 ♉	De 18 ♋	Mh 28 ♉	Jul 5 ♋	Oc 1 ♋
De 31 ♓	“ 20 ♎	“ 19 ♊	☿	Ap 3 ♊	“ 10 ♌	“ 6 ♌
♅	Mh 25 ♏	Ma 8 ♋	Ja 1 ♉	“ 8 ♋	“ 16 ♍	“ 11 ♍
Ja 1 ♊	Ma 26 ♐	“ 26 ♌	“ 5 ♊	“ 13 ♌	“ 22 ♎	“ 19 ♎
Jul 22 ♊	Jul 18 ♑	Ju 13 ♍	“ 10 ♋	“ 19 ♍	“ 31 ♏	“ 28 ♏
De 31 ♊	Se 6 ♒	Jul 2 ♎	“ 15 ♌	“ 26 ♎	Au 10 ♐	No 6 ♐
♄	Oc 24 ♓	“ 20 ♏	“ 21 ♍	Ma 4 ♏	“ 21 ♑	“ 17 ♑
Ja 1 ♋	De 11 ♈	Au 8 ♐	“ 28 ♎	“ 14 ♐	“ 31 ♒	“ 27 ♒
Ju 1 ♌	♀	“ 27 ♑	Fe 5 ♏	“ 25 ♑	Se 8 ♓	De 6 ♓
De 31 ♌	Ja 1 ♐	Se 15 ♒	“ 15 ♐	Ju 4 ♒	“ “ “	“ 12 ♈
♃	“ 9 ♑	Oc 4 ♓	“ 26 ♑	“ 13 ♓	“ “ “	“ 18 ♊
Ja 1 ♉	Fe 2 ♒	“ 23 ♈	Mh 8 ♒	“ 19 ♈	“ 15 ♈	“ 23 ♋
Ju 5 ♊	“ 22 ♓	No 11 ♉	“ 17 ♓	“ 25 ♉	“ 21 ♉	“ 28 ♌
De 31 ♊	Mh 12 ♈	“ 30 ♊	“ 22 ♈	“ 30 ♊	“ 26 ♊	“ 31 ♌

Day	Jan.	Feb.	Mch.	April	May	June	July	Aug.	Sept.	Oct.	Nov.	Dec.
1	♌	♍	♍	♏	♐	♒	♓	♈	♊	♌	♍	♎
2	..	♎	♎	..	..	..	..	♉	♋	..	..	♏
3	..	..	..	♐	♑	..	♈	..	..	..	♎	..
4	♍	..	♏	..	..	♓	..	♊	♌	♍	..	..
5	..	♏	..	..	♒	..	♉	..	..	..	♏	♐
6	♎	..	..	♑	..	♈	..	♋	..	♎	..	..
7	..	..	♐	..	..	..	♊	..	♍	..	..	♑
8	..	♐	..	♒	♓	♉	..	♌	..	..	♐	..
9	♏	..	♑	..	..	..	♋	..	♎	♏	..	..
10	..	♑	..	♓	♈	♊	..	♍	..	..	♑	♒
11	♐	..	..	..	..	..	..	..	♏	♐	..	..
12	..	♒	♒	♈	♉	♋	♌	..	..	..	♒	♓
13	..	..	..	..	..	..	..	♎	..	..	..	..
14	♑	♓	♓	♉	♊	♌	♍	..	♐	♑	..	♈
15	..	..	..	..	..	..	..	♏	..	..	♓	..
16	♒	♈	♈	♊	♋	..	♎	..	♑	♒	..	♉
17	..	..	..	..	..	♍	..	..	..	..	♈	..
18	♓	♉	♉	♋	♌	..	..	♐	..	♓	..	♊
19	..	..	..	..	..	♎	♏	..	♒	..	♉	..
20	♈	..	♊	..	♍	..	..	♑	..	..	..	♋
21	..	♊	..	♌	..	..	♐	..	♓	♈	♊	..
22	♉	..	♋	..	..	♏	..	♒	..	..	..	..
23	..	♋	..	♍	♎	..	..	..	♈	♉	♋	♌
24	♊	..	♌	..	..	♐	♑	..	..	..	..	..
25	..	♌	..	♎	♏	..	..	♓	♉	♊	♌	♍
26	♋	..	..	..	..	♑	♒	..	..	..	..	..
27	..	♍	♍	..	..	..	..	♈	♊	♋	♍	♎
28	..	..	..	♏	♐	..	♓	..	..	..	..	..
29	♌		♎	..	..	♒	..	♉	♋	♌	..	..
30	..		..	♐	♑	..	♈	..	..	..	♎	♏
31	♍		..		..		..	♊		♍		..

1859—EPHEMERIS OF THE PLANETS AND THE MOON—1859

♆	♂	♀	☿	☿	☿	☿
Ja 1 ♓	Ja 30 ♉	Ap 28 ♒	Ja 1 ♋	Ap 6 ♍	Jul 3 ♍	Oc 6 ♎
De 31 ♓	Mh 24 ♊	Ma 17 ♓	" 3 ♌	" 12 ♎	" 9 ♎	" 15 ♏
♅	Ma 22 ♋	Ju 4 ♈	" 9 ♍	" 21 ♏	" 18 ♏	" 25 ♐
Ja 1 ♊	Jul 24 ♌	" 23 ♉	" 14 ♎	Ma 2 ♐	" 28 ♐	No 4 ♑
De 31 ♊	Se 31 ♍	Jul 12 ♊	" 22 ♏	" 12 ♑	Au 8 ♑	" 14 ♒
♄	De 7 ♎	" 31 ♋	Fe 2 ♐	" 22 ♒	" 18 ♒	" 22 ♓
Ja 1 ♌	♀	Au 18 ♌	" 13 ♑	" 30 ♓	" 26 ♓	" 29 ♈
De 31 ♌	Ja 1 ♋	Se 6 ♍	" 23 ♒	" " "	" " "	" " "
♃	" 6 ♌	" 25 ♎	Mh 3 ♓	" " "	Se 2 ♈	De 5 ♉
Ja 1 ♊	" 24 ♍	Oc 13 ♏	" 10 ♈	Ju 5 ♈	" 8 ♉	" 10 ♊
Ma 13 ♋	Fe 12 ♎	No 1 ♐	" 16 ♉	" 11 ♉	" 13 ♊	" 15 ♋
De 31 ♋	Mh 2 ♏	" 19 ♑	" 21 ♊	" 16 ♊	" 18 ♋	" 20 ♌
ƨ	" 21 ♐	De 8 ♒	" 26 ♋	" 21 ♋	" 23 ♌	" 25 ♍
Ja 1 ♈	Ap 9 ♑	" 29 ♓	" 31 ♌	" 26 ♌	" 29 ♍	" 31 ♍

Day	Jan.	Feb.	Mch.	April	May	June	July	Aug.	Sept.	Oct.	Nov.	Dec.
1	♐	♑	♒	♈	♉	♋	♌	♍	♏	♐	♑	♓
2	..	♒	..	..	..	..	..	♎	..	..	♒	..
3	..	..	♓	..	♊	♌	♍	..	♐	♑	..	♈
4	♑	..	..	♉	..	..	..	♏	..	..	♓	..
5	..	♓	♈	..	♋	..	♎	..	..	♒	..	..
6	♒	..	..	♊	..	♍	..	..	♑	..	♈	♉
7	..	♈	♉	..	♌	..	..	♐	..	..	..	..
8	♓	..	..	♋	..	♎	♏	..	♒	♓	♉	♊
9	..	♉	♊	..	♍	..	..	♑	..	..	..	..
10	..	..	..	♌	..	♏	♐	..	♓	♈	..	♋
11	♈	♊	♋	..	..	..	..	..	..	..	♊	..
12	..	..	..	♍	♎	♐	..	♒	..	♉	..	♌
13	♉	♋	..	..	..	..	♑	..	♈	..	♋	..
14	..	..	♌	♎	♏	♑	..	♓	..	♊	..	♍
15	♊	♌	..	..	..	..	♒	..	♉	..	♌	..
16	..	..	♍	..	..	..	..	♈	..	♋	..	♎
17	♋	..	..	♏	♐	♒	..	..	♊	..	♍	..
18	..	♍	♎	..	..	..	♓	..	..	♌	..	..
19	♌	..	..	♐	♑	♓	..	♉	♋	..	♎	♏
20	..	♎	..	..	..	..	♈	..	..	♍	..	..
21	♍	..	♏	..	..	..	..	♊	♌	..	♏	♐
22	..	♏	..	♑	♒	♈	♉	..	..	..	..	..
23	♎	..	♐	..	..	..	..	♋	..	♎	..	..
24	..	..	..	♒	♓	♉	♊	..	♍	..	♐	♑
25	..	♐	..	..	..	..	..	♌	..	♏	..	..
26	♏	..	♑	..	♈	♊	♋	..	♎	..	♑	♒
27	..	♑	..	♓	..	..	..	♍	..	..	..	..
28	♐	..	♒	..	♉	♋	♌	..	♏	♐	..	♓
29	..	..	..	♈	..	..	..	♎	..	..	♒	..
30	..		♓	..	♊		..	..	♐	♑	..	..
31	♑		..		..		♍	♏	..	..		♈

1860—EPHEMERIS OF THE PLANETS AND THE MOON—186

♆	♂	♀	☿	☿	☿	☿
Ja 1 ♓	Ap 11 ♐	Ma 6 ♎	Ja 1 ♍	Ap 8 ♏	Jul 4 ♏	Oc 11 ♐
De 31 ♓	Ju 3 ♑	" 25 ♏	" 2 ♎	" 17 ♐	" 14 ♐	" 21 ♑
♅	Jul 23 ♒	Ju 12 ♐	" 10 ♏	" 28 ♑	" 25 ♑	" 31 ♒
Ja 1 ♊	Se 11 ♓	Jul 1 ♑	" 20 ♐	Ma 8 ♒	Au 5 ♒	No 9 ♓
De 31 ♊	Oc 28 ♈	" 20 ♒	Fe 1 ♑	" 16 ♓	" 13 ♓	" 15 ♈
♄	De 16 ♉	Au 8 ♓	" 11 ♒	" 23 ♈	" 19 ♈	" 22 ♉
Ja 1 ♌	♀	" 27 ♈	" 18 ♓	" 29 ♉	" 25 ♉	" 27 ♊
Se 3 ♍	Ja 1 ♓	Se 15 ♉	" 26 ♈	" " "	" 30 ♊	" " "
♃	" 17 ♈	Oc 4 ♊	Mh 3 ♉	" " "	" " "	De 2 ♋
Ja 1 ♋	Fe 3 ♉	" 23 ♋	" 8 ♊	Ju 3 ♊	Se 5 ♋	" 7 ♌
Ma 9 ♌	" 22 ♊	No 10 ♌	" 13 ♋	" 8 ♏	" 10 ♌	" 12 ♍
♂	Mh 13 ♋	" 28 ♍	" 18 ♌	" 13 ♌	" 15 ♍	" 18 ♎
Ja 1 ♎	" 30 ♌	De 18 ♎	" 23 ♍	" 18 ♍	" 22 ♎	" 27 ♏
Fe 11 ♏	Ap 17 ♍	" " "	" 29 ♎	" 25 ♎	" 30 ♏	" 31 ♏

Day	Jan.	Feb.	Mch.	April	May	June	July	Aug.	Sept.	Oct.	Nov.	Dec.
1	♈	♊	♊	♌	♍	♏	♐	♒	♓	♈	♊	♋
2	♉	..	♋	..	♎	..	..	..	..	♉	..	♌
3	..	♋	..	♍	..	♐	♑	..	♈	..	♋	..
4	♊	..	♌	..	♏	..	..	♓	..	♊	..	♍
5	..	♌	..	♎	..	..	♒	..	♉	..	♌	..
6	♋	..	♍	..	..	♑	..	♈	..	..	..	..
7	..	♍	..	♏	♐	..	..	..	♊	♋	♍	♎
8	♌	..	..	..	..	♒	♓	..	..	..	..	..
9	..	♎	♎	♐	♑	..	..	♉	♋	♌	♎	♏
10	♍	..	..	..	..	..	♈	..	..	..	..	..
11	..	♏	♏	..	..	♓	..	♊	♌	♍	♏	♐
12	♎	..	..	♑	♒	..	♉	..	..	..	..	..
13	..	..	♐	..	..	♈	..	♋	..	♎	♐	♑
14	..	♐	..	♒	..	..	..	..	♍	..	..	..
15	♏	..	..	..	♓	♉	♊	♌	..	♏	..	..
16	..	♑	♑	..	..	..	..	..	♎	..	♑	♒
17	♐	..	..	♓	♈	♊	♋	♍	..	♐	..	..
18	..	..	♒	..	..	..	..	..	♏	..	♒	♓
19	..	♒	..	♈	♉	♋	♌	♎	..	..	..	..
20	♑	..	..	..	..	..	..	..	♐	♑	..	..
21	..	♓	♓	..	♊	♌	♍	♏	..	..	♓	♈
22	♒	..	..	♉	..	..	..	..	♑	♒	..	..
23	..	..	♈	..	♋	♍	♎	..	..	..	..	♉
24	.	♈	..	♊	..	..	..	♐	..	..	♈	..
25	♓	..	♉	..	♌	..	♏	..	♒	♓	..	..
26	..	♉	..	♋	..	♎	..	♑	..	..	♉	♊
27	♈	..	♊	..	♍	..	♐	..	♓	♈	..	..
28	..	♊	..	♌	..	♏	..	..	..	..	♊	♋
29	..	..	♋	..	♎	..	..	♒	..	..	..	..
30	♉		..	♍	..	♐	♑	..	♈	♉	♋	♌
31	..		..		..		..	♓		..		..

1861—EPHEMERIS OF THE PLANETS AND THE MOON—1861

♆	♂	♀	☿	☿	☿	☿
Ja 1♓	Ap 8♋	Ma 16♊	Ja 1♏	Ap 4♐	Jul 1♐	Oc 8♑
Au 26♈	Ju 10♌	Ju 4♋	" 7♐	" 14♑	" 12♑	" 18♒
♅	Au 15♍	" 22♌	" 16♑	" 25♒	" 22♒	" 27♓
Ja 1♋	Oc 25♎	Jul 11♍	" 27♒	Ma 3♓	" 30♓	No 2♈
De 31♋	De 29♏	" 22♎	Fe 4♓	" 10♈	Au 6♈	" 7♉
♄	♀	Au 17♏	" 9♈	" 16♉	" 12♉	" 12♊
Ja 1♍	Ja 1♎	Se 5♐	" 16♉	" 21♊	" 17♊	" 17♋
De 31♍	" 4♏	" 23♑	" 22♊	" 26♋	" 21♋	" 22♌
♃	" 23♐	Oc 13♒	" 27♋	" 31♌	" 26♌	" 27♍
Ja 1♌	Fe 11♑	" 31♓	" " "	" " "	" " "	" " "
Ma 23♍	" 23♒	No 19♈	Mh 4♌	" " "	Se 7♍	De 5♎
☊	Mh 21♓	De 8♉	" 9♍	Ju 5♍	" 8♎	" 13♏
Ja 1♉	Ap 9♈	" 27♊	" 16♎	" 12♎	" 17♏	" 24♐
Fe 25♊	" 28♉	" " "	" 25♏	" 21♏	" 27♐	" 31♐

Day	Jan.	Feb.	Mch.	Apr.	May	June	July	Aug.	Sept.	Oct.	Nov.	Dec.
1	♍	♎	♏	♐	♒	♓	♈	♊	♋	♍	♎	♐
2	..	♏	..	♑	..	♈	♉	..	♌	..	♏	..
3	♎	..	♐	..	..	..	..	♋	..	♎	..	♑
4	..	♐	..	♒	♓	..	..	..	♍	..	♐	..
5	♏	..	♑	..	..	♉	♊	♌	..	♏	..	..
6	..	♑	..	..	♈	..	..	..	♎	..	♑	♒
7	♐	..	..	♓	..	♊	♋	♍	..	♐	..	..
8	..	♒	♒	..	..	..	..	♏	..	..	♒	♓
9	..	..	..	♈	♉	..	♌	♎	..	..	..	..
10	♑	..	♓	..	..	♋	..	..	♐	♑	..	..
11	..	♓	..	♉	♊	..	♍	..	..	..	♓	♈
12	♒	..	..	..	..	♌	..	♏	♑	♒	..	..
13	..	..	♈	..	♋	..	♎	..	..	..	♈	♉
14	..	♈	..	♊	..	♍	..	♐	..	..	..	..
15	♓	..	♉	..	♌	..	♏	..	♒	♓	..	..
16	..	♉	..	♋	..	♎	..	♑	..	..	♉	♊
17	♈	..	..	..	..	..	..	♓	♈	..	..	..
18	..	♊	♊	♌	♍	♏	♐	..	..	..	♊	♋
19	..	..	..	..	..	..	♒	..	..	..	..	..
20	♉	..	♋	♍	♎	♐	♑	..	♈	♉	..	♌
21	..	♋	..	..	..	..	♓	..	..	♋	..	..
22	♊	..	♌	♎	♏	..	♒	..	♉	♊	..	♍
23	..	♌	..	..	..	♑	..	♈	..	..	♌	..
24	♋	..	♍	♏	♐	..	♓	..	♊	♋	♍	♎
25	..	♍	..	..	..	♒	♓	♉	..	..	..	..
26	♌	..	♎	..	♑	..	..	..	♋	♌	..	♏
27	..	♎	..	♐	..	..	♈	..	♌	..	♎	..
28	♍	..	♏	..	..	♓	..	♊	..	♍	..	..
29	..	..	..	♑	♒	..	♉	♌	♍	♏	♐	
30	♎		♐	..	..	♈	♉	..	..	..	♎	♑
31	..		..		♓	..	..	♋		♎		♑

1862—EPHEMERIS OF THE PLANETS AND THE MOON—1862

♆	♂	♀	☿	☿	☿	☿
Ja 1 ♈	Fe 2 ♐	Ap 17 ♐	Ja 1 ♐	Ap 2 ♑	Jul 8 ♒	Oc 4 ♒
De 31 ♈	Ap 22 ♑	Ma 6 ♑	“ 3 ♑	“ 11 ♒	“ 17 ♓	“ 13 ♓
♅	Ju 12 ♒	“ 25 ♒	“ 14 ♒	“ 20 ♓	“ 25 ♈	“ 20 ♈
Ja 1 ♊	Jul 30 ♓	Ju 13 ♓	“ 22 ♓	“ 27 ♈	“ 30 ♉	“ 26 ♉
De 31 ♊	Se 15 ♈	Jul 2 ♈	“ 29 ♈	Ma 3 ♉	Au 4 ♊	“ 31 ♊
♄	No 2 ♉	“ 21 ♉	Fe 3 ♉	“ 8 ♊	“ 9 ♋	“ “ “
Ja 1 ♍	De 22 ♊	Au 8 ♊	“ 9 ♊	“ 13 ♋	“ 14 ♌	No 4 ♋
De 31 ♍	♀	“ 27 ♋	“ 13 ♋	“ 17 ♌	“ 19 ♍	“ 9 ♌
♃	Ja 1 ♊	Se 15 ♌	“ 18 ♌	“ 23 ♍	“ 26 ♎	“ 15 ♍
Ja 1 ♍	“ 15 ♋	Oc 3 ♍	“ 24 ♍	“ 31 ♎	“ “ “	“ 22 ♎
Ju 20 ♎	Fe 2 ♌	“ 22 ♎	“ “ “	“ “ “	“ “ “	“ 30 ♏
De 31 ♎	“ 21 ♍	No 9 ♏	Mh 3 ♎	Ju 7 ♏	Se 3 ♏	De 10 ♐
☋	Mh 12 ♎	“ 28 ♐	“ 12 ♏	“ 17 ♐	“ 14 ♐	“ 21 ♑
Ja 1 ♏	“ 30 ♏	De 18 ♑	“ 23 ♐	“ 28 ♑	“ 25 ♑	“ 31 ♑

Day	Jan.	Feb.	Mch.	April	May	June	July	Aug.	Sept.	Oct.	Nov.	Dec.
1	♑	♓	♓	♈	♊	♋	♌	♎	♐	♑	♓	♈
2	..	..	..	♉	..	♌	..	♏	..	♒	..	..
3	♒	♈	♈	..	..	..	♍	..	♑	..	..	♉
4	..	..	..	♊	♋	♍	..	♐	..	..	♈	..
5	♓	..	♉	..	..	..	♎	..	♒	♓	..	..
6	..	♉	..	♋	♌	..	..	♑	..	..	♉	♊
7	♈	..	..	..	..	♎	♏	..	♓	♈	..	..
8	..	♊	♊	..	♍	..	..	..	..	..	♊	♋
9	..	..	..	♌	..	♏	♐	♒	♈	..	..	..
10	♉	..	♋	..	♎	..	..	..	..	♉	..	♌
11	..	♋	..	♍	.	♐	♑	♓	..	..	♋	..
12	♊	..	♌	..	♏	..	..	..	♉	♊	..	..
13	..	♌	..	♎	..	♑	..	♈	..	..	♌	♍
14	♋	..	♍	..	♐	..	♒	..	..	♋	..	..
15	..	♍	..	♏	..	♒	..	..	♊	..	..	♎
16	♌	..	♎	..	♑	..	♓	♉	..	..	♍	..
17	..	♎	..	♑	..	♓	..	..	♋	♌	..	♏
18	..	..	♏	..	..	..	♈	♊	..	..	♎	..
19	♍	♏	..	♐	♒	..	..	..	♌	♍	..	♐
20	..	..	♐	..	..	♈	♉	..	..	..	♏	..
21	♎	♐	..	♒	♓	..	..	♋	..	♎	..	♑
22	..	..	..	..	..	♉	♊	..	♍	..	♐	..
23	♏	♑	♑	..	♈	..	..	♌	..	♏	.	♒
24	..	..	..	♓	..	..	♋	..	♎	..	♑	..
25	♐	..	♒	..	..	♊	..	♍	..	♐	..	..
26	..	♒	..	♈	♉	..	..	..	♍	..	♒	♓
27	♑	..	♓	..	..	♋	♌	♎	..	♑	..	..
28	..	♓	..	..	..	..	..	..	♐	..	♓	♈
29	♒		..	♉	♊	♌	♍	..	..	..	..	..
30	..		♈	..	..	..	..	♏	♑	♒	..	♉
31	..		..		♋		♎	..		..		..

1863—EPHEMERIS OF THE PLANETS AND THE MOON—1863

♆	♂	♀	☿	☿	♄	☿
Ja 1♈	Ja 1♊	Ap 27♌	Ja 1♒	Ap 7♓	Jul 4♓	Oc 7♈
De 31♈	Fe 23♋	Ma 16♍	" 9♓	" 14♈	" 10♈	" 12♉
♅	Ap 28♌	Ju 3♋	" 14♈	" 20♉	" 16♉	" 17♊
Ja 1♊	Jul 6♍	" 22♏	" 21♉	" 25♊	" 21♊	" 22♋
De 31♊	Se 11♎	Jul 11♐	" 26♊	" 30♋	" 26♋	" 27♌
♄	No 16♏	" 30♑	" 31♋	Ma 5♌	" 31♌	No 2♍
Ja 1♍	♀	Au 17♒	Fe 5♌	" 10♍	" " "	" 9♎
" 18♎	Ja 1♑	Se 6♓	" 10♍	" 18♎	Au 6♍	" 17♏
De 31♎	" 6♒	" 25♈	" 18♎	" 25♏	" 13♎	" 28♐
" " "	" 24♓	Oc 14♉	" 27♏	" " "	" 21♏	" " "
♃	Fe 12♈	No 4♊	" " "	" " "	" " "	" 31♐ De 9♑
Ja 1♎	Mh 3♉	" 20♋	Mh 9♐	Ju 6♐	Se 11♑	" 19♒
Jul 21♏	" 22♊	De 8♌	" 19♑	" 16♑	" 21♒	" 26♓
De 31♏	Ap 9♋	" 26♍	" 29♒	" 26♒	" 30♓	" 31♓

Day	Jan.	Feb.	Mch.	April	May	June	July	Aug.	Sept.	Oct.	Nov.	Dec.
1	♉	♋	♌	♍	♎	♐	♑	♓	♉	♊	♋	♌
2	♊	..	..	♎	♏	♑	♒	♈	..	♌	..	♍
3	..	♌	..	..	..	..	..	..	..	..	..	..
4	♋	..	♍	♏	♐	♒	♓	..	♊	♋	..	♎
5	..	♍	..	..	..	..	..	♉	..	..	♍	..
6	..	..	♎	♐	♑	♓	♈	..	♋	♌	..	♏
7	♌	♎	..	..	..	..	..	♊	..	..	♎	..
8	..	..	♏	♑	♒	..	♉	..	..	♍	..	♐
9	♍	♏	..	..	..	♈	..	..	♌	..	♏	..
10	..	..	♐	♒	♓	..	..	♋	..	♎	..	♑
11	♎	..	..	..	..	♉	♊	..	♍	..	♐	..
12	..	♐	♑	..	♈	..	..	♌	..	..	..	♒
13	♏	..	..	♓	..	..	♋	..	..	♏	♑	..
14	..	♑	♒	..	..	♊	♋	..	..	..	..	..
15	♐	..	..	♈	♉	..	..	♍	♏	♐	♒	♓
16	..	♒	..	..	..	♋	♌	..	..	..	..	..
17	♑	..	♓	..	♊	..	..	♎	♐	♑	♓	♈
18	..	♓	..	♉	..	..	♍	..	..	..	..	..
19	..	..	♈	..	♊	♌	..	♏	♑	♒	..	♉
20	♒	..	..	♊	♋	..	♎	..	..	..	♈	..
21	..	♈	♉	..	..	♍	♎	..	♒	♓	..	..
22	♓	..	..	..	♌	..	..	♐	..	..	♉	♊
23	..	♉	..	♋	..	♎	♏	..	♓	..	..	..
24	♈	..	♊	..	♍	♏	..	♑	..	♈	..	♋
25	..	..	..	♌	♍	♏	♐	♒	..	..	♊	..
26	..	♊	♋	..	..	..	..	♓	♈	..	♋	♌
27	♉	..	..	♍	♎	♐	♑	♓	..	..	..	♌
28	..	♋	..	..	..	..	..	..	♉	♊	..	..
29	♊		♌	..	♏	♑	♒	..	..	..	..	♍
30	..		..	♎	..	..	..	♈	..	..	♌	..
31	..		♍		♐		♓	..		♋		..

1864—EPHEMERIS OF THE PLANETS AND THE MOON—1864

♆	♂	♀	☿	☿	☿	☿
Ja 1 ♈	Mh 10 ♑	Ap 18 ♓	Ja 1 ♓	Ap 6 ♉	Jul 3 ♉	Oc 4 ♊
De 31 ♈	Ap 28 ♒	Ma 8 ♈	" 3 ♈	" 11 ♊	" 8 ♊	" 9 ♋
♅	Ju 16 ♓	" 26 ♉	" 9 ♉	" 16 ♋	" 13 ♋	" 14 ♌
Ja 1 ♊	Au 1 ♈	Ju 13 ♊	" 14 ♊	" 21 ♌	" 18 ♌	" 19 ♍
De 31 ♊	Se 20 ♉	Jul 2 ♋	" 19 ♋	" 27 ♍	" 23 ♍	" 26 ♎
♄	No 13 ♊	" 20 ♌	" 24 ♌	" " "	" 30 ♎	No 4 ♏
Ja 1 ♎	De 31 ♊	Au 8 ♍	" 30 ♍	Ma 14 ♎	Au 7 ♏	" 14 ♐
De 31 ♎	♀	" 26 ♎	Fe 6 ♎	" 12 ♏	" 17 ♐	" 25 ♑
♃	Ja 1 ♍	Se 15 ♏	" 14 ♏	" 22 ♐	" 28 ♑	" " "
Ja 1 ♏	" 15 ♎	Oc 4 ♐	" 24 ♐	" " "	" " "	De 5 ♒
Au 13 ♐	Fe 2 ♏	" 23 ♑	Mh 6 ♑	Ju 2 ♑	Se 8 ♒	" 13 ♓
♂	" 21 ♐	No 11 ♒	" 16 ♒	" 12 ♒	" 16 ♓	" 20 ♈
Ja 1 ♏	Mh 11 ♑	" 29 ♓	" 24 ♓	" 20 ♓	" 23 ♈	" 26 ♉
" 14 ♐	" 30 ♒	De 17 ♈	" 31 ♈	" 27 ♈	" 29 ♉	" 31 ♊

Day	Jan.	Feb.	Mch.	April	May	June	July	Aug.	Sept.	Oct.	Nov.	Dec.
1	♎	♐	♐	♒	♓	♉	♊	♋	♍	♎	♐	♑
2	..	..	..	..	..	..	..	♌	..	..	..	..
3	♏	♑	♑	♓	♈	..	♋	..	♎	♏	♑	♒
4	..	..	..	..	..	♊	..	..	..	..	..	..
5	♐	♒	♒	♈	♉	..	..	♍	..	♐	..	♓
6	..	..	..	..	..	♋	♌	..	♏	..	♒	..
7	♑	♓	♓	..	♊	..	..	♎	..	♑	..	♈
8	..	..	..	♉	..	..	♍	..	♐	..	♓	..
9	♒	..	♈	..	..	♌	..	♏	..	♒	..	♉
10	..	♈	..	♊	♋	..	..	..	♑	..	♈	..
11	♓	..	♉	..	..	♍	♎	..	..	♓	..	..
12	..	♉	..	..	♌	..	..	♐	♒	..	♉	♊
13	♈	..	..	♋	..	..	♏	..	..	..	..	..
14	..	♊	♊	..	..	♎	..	♑	♓	♈	..	♋
15	..	..	..	♌	♍	..	♐	..	..	..	♊	..
16	♉	..	♋	..	..	♏	..	♒	♈	♉	..	..
17	..	♋	..	..	♎	..	♑	..	..	..	♋	♌
18	♊	..	..	♍	..	♐	..	♓	♉	♊	..	..
19	..	♌	♌	..	♏	..	♒	..	..	..	♌	♍
20	..	..	..	♎	..	♑	..	♈	..	..	..	..
21	♋	..	♍	..	♐	..	♓	..	♊	♋	..	..
22	..	♍	..	♏	..	♒	..	♉	..	..	♍	♎
23	♌	..	♎	..	♑	..	♈	..	♋	♌	..	..
24	..	♎	..	♐	..	♓	..	♊	..	..	♎	♏
25	..	..	..	..	♒	..	..	..	..	..	..	..
26	♍	♏	♏	♑	..	♈	♉	..	♌	♍	..	♐
27	..	..	..	..	..	..	..	♋	..	..	♏	..
28	♎	♐	♐	♒	♓	♉	♊	..	♍	♎	..	♑
29	..	♑	..	..	..	..	..	♌	..	..	♐	..
30	♏		♑	♓	♈	..	..	..	..	♏	..	♒
31	..		..		..		♋	..		..		..

1865—EPHEMERIS OF THE PLANETS AND THE MOON—1865

♆	♂	♀	☿	☿	☿	☿
Ja 1 ♈	Mh 15 ♌	Ma 14 ♐	Ja 1 ♊	Ap 2 ♋	Jul 4 ♌	Oc 5 ♍
De 31 ♈	Ma 21 ♍	Ju 2 ♑	" 4 ♋	" 7 ♌	" 9 ♍	" 12 ♎
♅	Jul 29 ♎	" 21 ♒	" 9 ♌	" 12 ♍	" 16 ♎	" 21 ♏
Ja 1 ♓	Oc 2 ♏	Jul 10 ♓	" 14 ♍	" 19 ♎	" 24 ♏	" 31 ♐
Jul 15 ♋	De 2 ♐	" 29 ♈	" 21 ♎	" 28 ♏	Au 4 ♐	No 11 ♑
♄	♀	Au 17 ♉	" 30 ♏	Ma 8 ♐	" 15 ♑	" 21 ♒
Ja 1 ♎	Ja 1 ♈	Se 4 ♊	Fe 9 ♐	" 19 ♑	" 25 ♒	" 29 ♓
Jul 15 ♏	" 5 ♉	" 23 ♋	" 20 ♑	" 29 ♒	" " "	" " "
♃	" 23 ♊	Oc 12 ♌	" " "	" " "	" " "	De 6 ♈
Ja 1 ♐	Fe 10 ♋	" 30 ♍	Mh 2 ♒	Ju 6 ♓	Se 2 ♓	" 12 ♉
Au 25 ♑	Mh 1 ♌	No 18 ♎	" 10 ♓	" 13 ♈	" 15 ♈	" 17 ♊
♂	" 19 ♍	De 6 ♏	" 17 ♈	" 19 ♉	" 20 ♊	" 21 ♋
Ja 1 ♊	Ap 7 ♎	" 25 ♐	" 23 ♉	" 24 ♊	" 25 ♋	" 26 ♌
" 10 ♋	" 25 ♏	" 31 ♐	" 28 ♊	" 29 ♋	" 30 ♌	" 31 ♌

Day	Jan.	Feb.	Mch.	Apr.	May	June	July	Aug.	Sept.	Oct.	Nov.	Dec.
1	♒	♈	♉	♊	♌	♍	♎	♐	♑	♒	♈	♉
2	..	..	..	♋	..	♎	♏	..	♒	♓	..	♊
3	♓	♉	..	..	..	..	..	♑	..	..	♉	..
4	..	..	♊	♌	♍	..	..	..	♓	♈	..	♋
5	♈	♊	..	..	..	♏	♐	..	..	..	♊	..
6	..	..	♋	♍	♎	..	..	♒	..	♉	..	♌
7	♉	..	..	..	..	♐	♑	..	♈	..	♋	..
8	..	♋	♌	..	..	..	..	♓	..	♊	..	♍
9	♊	..	..	♎	♏	..	..	..	♉	..	♌	..
10	..	♌	♍	..	..	♑	♒	♈	..	♋	..	♎
11	♋	..	..	♏	♐	..	..	..	♊	..	♍	..
12	..	♍	♎	..	..	♒	♓	..	..	♌	..	..
13	♌	..	..	..	..	..	..	♉	♋	..	♎	♏
14	..	♎	..	♐	♑	..	♈	..	..	..	..	..
15	..	..	♏	..	..	♓	..	♊	♌	♍	..	♐
16	♍	..	..	♑	♒	..	♉	..	..	..	♏	..
17	..	♏	♐	..	..	♈	..	♋	♍	♎	..	..
18	♎	..	..	..	♓	..	♊	..	..	..	♐	♑
19	..	♐	♑	♒	..	♉	..	♌	..	♏	..	..
20	♏	..	..	..	..	..	♋	..	♎	..	..	♒
21	..	..	..	♓	♈	♊	..	♍	..	..	♑	..
22	..	♑	♒	..	..	..	..	..	♏	♐	..	..
23	♐	..	..	♈	♉	♋	♌	♎	..	..	♒	♓
24	..	♒	♓	..	..	..	..	..	..	♑	..	..
25	♑	..	..	♉	♊	♌	♍	..	♐	..	♓	♈
26	..	♓	..	..	..	..	..	♏	..	..	..	..
27	..	..	♈	♊	♋	♍	♎	..	♑	♒	..	♉
28	♒	..	..	..	..	..	..	♐	..	..	♈	..
29	..	♈	♉	♋	♌	..	♏	..	..	♓	..	..
30	♓	..	..	..	..	♎	..	..	♒	..	♉	♊
31	..		♊		♍		..	♑		♈		..

1866—EPHEMERIS OF THE PLANETS AND THE MOON—1866

♆	♂	♀	☿	☿	☿	☿
Ja 1 ♈	Mh16 ♒	Ma 6 ♋	Ja 1 ♌	Ap 6 ♎	Jul 3 ♎	Oc 7 ♏
De 31 ♈	Ma 2 ♓	" 24 ♌	" 2 ♍	" 14 ♏	" 11 ♏	" 17 ♐
♅	Ju 19 ♈	Ju 12 ♍	" 8 ♎	" 25 ♐	" 18 ♐	" 28 ♑
Ja 1 ♋	Au 7 ♉	" 30 ♎	" 16 ♏	Ma 5 ♑	Au 1 ♑	No 7 ♒
De 31 ♋	Se 30 ♊	Jul 19 ♏	" 27 ♐	" 16 ♒	" 11 ♒	" 16 ♓
♄	No 27 ♋	Au 7 ♐	Fe 6 ♑	" 24 ♓	" 20 ♓	" 23 ♈
Ja 1 ♏	♀	" 25 ♑	" 16 ♒	" 31 ♈	" 27 ♈	" 28 ♉
De 31 ♏	Ja 1 ♐	Se 13 ♒	" 22 ♓	" " "	" " "	" " "
♃	" 13 ♑	Oc 2 ♓	Mh 4 ♈	" " "	Se 2 ♉	De 4 ♊
Ja 1 ♑	Fe 1 ♒	" 21 ♈	" 10 ♉	Ju 6 ♉	" 7 ♊	" 8 ♋
Au 19 ♒	" 20 ♓	No 9 ♉	" 15 ♊	" 11 ♊	" 11 ♋	" 13 ♌
♂	Mh10 ♈	" 28 ♊	" 20 ♋	" 15 ♋	" 16 ♌	" 19 ♍
Ja 1 ♐	" 29 ♉	De 16 ♋	" 25 ♌	" 20 ♌	" 22 ♍	" 26 ♎
" 24 ♑	Ap 17 ♊	" 31 ♋	" 30 ♍	" 26 ♍	" 29 ♎	" 31 ♎

Day	Jan	Feb.	Mch.	April	May	June	July	Aug.	Sept.	Oct.	Nov.	Dec.
1	♋	♌	♍	♎	♏	♑	♒	♈	♊	♋	♌	♎
2	..	♍	..	♏	♐	..	♓	..	..	..	♍	..
3	♌	..	..	..	..	♒	..	♉	♋	♌	..	..
4	..	♎	♎	..	♑	..	♈	..	..	..	♎	♏
5	♍	..	..	♐	..	♓	..	♊	..	♍	..	..
6	..	..	♏	..	..	..	♉	..	♌	..	..	♐
7	..	♏	..	♑	♒	♈	..	♋	..	..	♏	..
8	♎	..	..	..	..	..	..	..	♍	♎	..	..
9	..	♐	♐	♒	♓	♉	♊	♌	..	..	♐	♑
10	♏	..	..	..	..	..	..	..	..	♏	..	..
11	..	♑	♑	♓	♈	♊	♋	..	♎	..	..	♒
12	♐	..	..	..	..	..	..	♍	..	..	♑	..
13	..	..	♒	♈	♉	♋	♌	..	♏	♐	..	♓
14	..	♒	..	..	..	..	..	♎	..	..	♒	..
15	♑	..	♓	♉	♊	..	..	..	..	♑	..	♈
16	..	♓	..	..	..	♌	♍	..	♐	..	♓	..
17	♒	..	♈	♊	♋	..	..	♏	..	..	..	..
18	..	♈	..	..	..	♍	♎	..	♑	♒	♈	♉
19	♓	..	♉	..	♌	..	..	♐	..	..	..	..
20	..	♉	..	♋	..	..	..	..	♒	♓	♉	♊
21	♈	..	♊	..	..	♎	♏	..	..	..	..	..
22	..	♊	..	♌	♍	..	..	♑	♓	♈	♊	♋
23	♉	..	♋	..	..	♏	♐	..	..	..	..	..
24	..	♋	..	..	♎	..	..	♒	♈	♉	♋	♌
25	♊	..	..	♍	..	..	♑	..	..	..	..	..
26	..	♌	♌	..	..	♐	..	♓	♉	♊	..	♍
27	..	..	..	♎	♏	..	♒	..	..	..	♌	..
28	♋	..	♍	.	..	♑	..	♈	♊	♋	..	..
29	..		..	..	♐	..	♓	..	..	..	♍	♎
30	♌		..	♏	..	♒	..	♉	..	♌	..	..
31	..		♎		..		..	..		..		♏

1867—EPHEMERIS OF THE PLANETS AND THE MOON—1867

♆	♂	♀	☿	☿	☿	☿
Ja 1♈	Ap 9♍	Ma 16♓	Ja 1♎	Ap 2♏	Jul 9♐	Oc 5♐
De 31♈	Ju 17♎	Ju 4♈	" 4♏	" 13♐	" 20♑	" 16♑
♅	Au 21♏	" 23♉	" 15♐	" 23♑	" 30♒	" 26♒
Ja 1♋	Oc 20♐	Jul 12♊	" 25♑	Ma 3♒	Au 8♓	No 4♓
" 8♋	De 13♑	" 30♋	Fe 4♒	" 12♓	" 15♈	" 11♈
♄	♀	Au 18♌	" 13♓	" 19♈	" 21♉	" 17♉
Ja 1♏	Ja 1♋	Se 5♍	" 20♈	" 25♉	" 26♊	" 21♊
De 31♏	" 5♌	" 24♎	" 26♉	" 30♊	" 30♋	" 26♋
♃	" 23♍	Oc 12♏	" " "	" " "	" " "	" " "
Ja 1♒	Fe 11♎	" 31♐	Mh 3♊	Ju 3♋	" " "	De 1♌
Jul 28♓	Mh 2♏	No 19♑	" 7♋	" 8♌	Se 4♌	" 7♍
☌	" 20♐	De 8♒	" 12♌	" 14♍	" 10♍	" 14♎
Ja 1♋	Ap 8♑	" 27♓	" 18♍	" 21♎	" 17♎	" 22♏
Fe 1♌	" 27♒	" 31♓	" 25♎	" 29♏	" 25♏	" 31♏

Day	Jan.	Feb.	Mch.	April	May	June	July	Aug.	Sept.	Oct.	Nov.	Dec.
1	♏	♐	♑	♓	♈	♊	♋	♍	♎	♏	♑	♒
2	..	♑	♒	..	♉	..	♌	..	♏	♐	..	..
3	♐	..	..	♈	..	♋	..	♎	..	..	♒	♓
4	..	♒	♓	..	♊	..	♍	..	..	♑	..	..
5	♑	..	..	♉	..	♌	..	..	♐	..	♓	♈
6	..	♓	♈	..	♋	..	..	♏	..	..	..	..
7	♒	..	..	♊	..	♍	♎	..	♑	♒	..	♉
8	..	♈	♉	..	♌	..	♐	..	♒	♈	..	
9	..	..	..	♋	..	♎	♏	..	♓	..	♉	♊
10	♓	♉	♊	..	♎	..	..	♐	..	♓	..	..
11	..	..	..	♌	♍	♏	..	♑	..	♈	..	♋
12	♈	♊	..	..	..	♏	♐	..	♓	..	♊	..
13	..	..	♋	♍	♎	..	♑	♒	..	♉	..	♌
14	♉	♋	..	..	..	♑	..	..	♈	..	♋	..
15	..	..	♌	..	..	♐	..	♓	..	♊	..	♍
16	♊	..	..	♎	♏	..	♒	..	♉	..	♌	..
17	..	♌	♍	..	..	♑	♒	♈	..	♋	..	..
18	♋	..	..	..	♐	..	..	..	♊	..	♍	♎
19	..	♍	..	♏	..	♒	♓	♉	..	♌	..	♏
20	♌	..	♎	..	..	..	..	..	♋	..	♎	
21	..	♎	..	♐	♑	..	♈	..	..	♍	..	..
22	..	..	♏	..	..	♓	..	♊	♌	..	♏	..
23	♍	..	..	..	♒	..	♉	..	♍	♎	♏	♐
24	..	♏	..	♑	..	♈	..	♋	♍	♎	..	♑
25	♎	..	♐	..	♓	..	♊	..	..	..	♐	
26	..	♐	..	♒	..	♉	♌	..	♎	♏	..	..
27	..	..	♑	..	♈	..	♋	♌	♎	..	♑	♒
28	♏	♑	..	♓	♈	♊	..	♍	..	..	♑	♒
29	..		..	..	..	..	..	..	♏	♐	..	..
30	♐		♒	♈	♉	♋	♌	..	..	♒	..	♓
31	..		..		..		♎	..		..		..

1868—EPHEMERIS OF THE PLANETS AND THE MOON—1868

♆	♂	♀	☿	☿	☿	☿
Ja 1 ♈	Mh 20 ♓	Ma 5 ♎	Ja 1 ♐	Ap 9 ♑	Jul 6 ♑	Oc 2 ♑
De 31 ♈	Ma 7 ♈	" 24 ♏	" 12 ♑	" 19 ♒	" 16 ♒	" 12 ♒
♅	Ju 25 ♉	Ju 12 ♐	" 22 ♒	" 28 ♓	" 25 ♓	" 21 ♓
Ja 1 ♋	Au 18 ♊	Jul 1 ♑	" 31 ♓	Ma 5 ♈	Au 1 ♈	" 28 ♈
De 31 ♋	Oc 15 ♋	" 20 ♒	Fe 7 ♈	" 10 ♉	" 6 ♉	No 2 ♉
♄	De 18 ♌	Au 8 ♓	" 12 ♉	" 15 ♊	" 11 ♊	" 7 ♊
Ja 1 ♐	♀	" 26 ♈	" 17 ♊	" 20 ♋	" 16 ♋	" 12 ♋
Mh 5 ♐	Ja 1 ♓	Se 14 ♉	" 22 ♋	" 25 ♌	" 21 ♌	" 17 ♌
♃	" 15 ♈	Oc 3 ♊	" 27 ♌	" 31 ♍	" 27 ♍	" 23 ♍
Ja 1 ♓	Fe 2 ♉	" 22 ♋	" " "	" " "	" " "	" 29 ♎
Ju 24 ♈	" 21 ♊	No 9 ♌	Mh 4 ♍	" " "	" " "	De 8 ♏
♂	Mh 11 ♋	" 28 ♍	" 11 ♎	Ju 7 ♎	Se 2 ♎	" 18 ♐
Ja 1 ♑	" 29 ♌	De 16 ♎	" 19 ♏	" 15 ♏	" 11 ♏	" 29 ♑
Fe 2 ♒	Ap 17 ♍	" 31 ♎	" 29 ♐	" 25 ♐	" 21 ♐	" 31 ♑

Day	Jan.	Feb.	Mch.	Apr.	May	June	July	Aug.	Sept.	Oct.	Nov.	Dec.
1	♈	♉	♊	♌	♍	♎	♏	♑	♒	♈	♉	♋
2	..	♊	..	..	..	♏	♐	..	♓	..	♊	..
3	♉	..	♋	..	♎	..	..	♒	..	..	..	♌
4	..	♋	..	♍	..	♐	♑	..	♈	♉	♋	..
5	♊	..	♌	..	..	..	..	♓	..	..	..	..
6	..	♌	..	♎	♏	..	..	..	♉	♊	♌	♍
7	♋	..	♍	..	..	♑	♒	..	..	..	..	..
8	..	♍	..	♏	♐	..	..	♈	♊	♋	♍	♎
9	..	..	..	..	..	..	♓	..	..	..	..	..
10	♌	♎	♎	..	..	♒	..	♉	..	♌	..	♏
11	..	..	..	♐	♑	..	..	..	♋	..	♎	..
12	♍	..	♏	..	..	♓	♈	♊	..	♍	..	..
13	..	♏	..	♑	♒	..	..	..	♌	..	♏	♐
14	♎	..	..	..	..	♈	♉	♋	..	♎	..	..
15	..	♐	♐	..	..	..	..	..	♍	..	♐	♑
16	♏	..	..	♒	♓	♉	♊	♌	..	..	..	..
17	..	..	♑	..	..	..	..	..	♎	♏	..	..
18	..	♑	..	♓	♈	♊	♋	♍	..	..	♑	♒
19	♐	..	..	..	..	..	..	..	♏	♐	..	..
20	..	♒	♒	..	♉	♋	♌	..	..	..	♒	♓
21	♑	..	..	♈	..	..	..	♎	..	♑	..	..
22	..	..	♓	..	♊	♌	♍	..	♐	..	..	..
23	..	♓	..	♉	..	..	..	♏	..	..	♓	♈
24	♒	..	♈	..	♋	..	♎	..	♑	♒	..	..
25	..	♈	..	♊	..	♍	..	♐	..	..	♈	♉
26	♓	..	♉	..	♌	..	..	..	..	♓	..	..
27	..	♉	..	♋	..	♎	♏	..	♒	..	♉	♊
28	♈	..	♊	..	♍	..	..	♑	..	..	..	..
29	..		..	♌	..	♏	♐	..	♓	♈	♊	..
30	..		♋	..	..	..	..	♒	..	..	..	♋
31	♉		..		♎		..	..		♉		..

1869—EPHEMERIS OF THE PLANETS AND THE MOON—1869

♆	♂	♀	☿	☿	☿	☿
Ja 1♈	Ma 4♎	Ma 16♊	Ja 1♑	Ap 6♒	Jul 3♒	Oc 8♓
De 31♈	Jul 8♏	Ju 3♋	" 8♒	" 15♓	" 12♓	" 14♈
♅	Se 6♐	" 22♌	" 17♓	" 22♈	" 19♈	" 20♉
Ja 1♋	Oc 30♑	Jul 10♍	" 24♈	" 27♉	" 24♉	" 25♊
De 31♋	De 20♒	" 29♎	" 29♉	Ma 2♊	" 29♊	" 30♋
♄	♀	Au 16♏	Fe 3♊	" 7♋	Au 3♋	No 4♌
Ja 1♐	Ja 1♎	Se 4♐	" 8♋	" 12♌	" 8♌	" 9♍
De 31♐	" 4♏	" 23♑	" 13♌	" 18♍	" 13♍	" 16♎
♃	" 23♐	Oc 12♒	" 19♍	" 24♎	" 20♎	" 25♏
Ja 1♈	Fe 10♑	" 31♓	" 25♎	" " "	" 29♏	" " "
Ma 17♉	Mh 1♒	No 19♈	" " "	" " "	" " "	De 5♐
☊	" 20♓	De 8♉	Mh 6♏	Ju 2♏	Se 8♐	" 16♑
Ja 1♌	Ap 8♈	" 26♊	" 16♐	" 12♐	" 19♑	" 26♒
Fe 24♍	" 27♉	" 31♊	" 27♑	" 23♑	" 29♒	" 31♒

Day	Jan.	Feb	Mch.	April	May	June	July	Aug.	Sept.	Oct.	Nov.	Dec.
1	♌	♍	♏	♏	♐	♑	♓	♈	♊	♋	♍	♎
2	..	♎	♎	..	..	♒	..	♉	..	♌	..	♏
3	..	..	..	♐	♑	..	..	..	♋	..	♎	..
4	♍	..	♏	..	..	♓	♈	♊	..	♍	..	..
5	..	♏	..	♑	♒	..	..	..	♌	..	♏	♐
6	♎	..	..	..	..	♈	♉	♋	..	♎	..	..
7	..	♐	♐	..	..	..	..	..	♍	..	♐	♑
8	♏	..	..	♒	♓	♉	♊	♌	..	..	..	..
9	..	..	♑	..	..	..	..	..	♎	♏	..	..
10	..	♑	..	♓	♈	..	♋	♍	..	..	♑	♒
11	♐	..	..	..	..	♊	..	..	♏	♐	..	..
12	..	♒	♒	..	♉	..	♌	..	..	..	♒	♓
13	..	..	..	♈	..	♋	..	♎	..	♑	..	..
14	♑	..	♓	..	♊	..	♍	..	♐	..	..	..
15	..	♓	..	♉	..	♌	..	♏	..	..	♓	♈
16	♒	..	♈	..	♋	..	♎	..	♑	♒	..	..
17	..	♈	..	♊	..	♍	..	♐	..	..	♈	♉
18	♓	..	♉	..	♌	..	..	..	..	♓	..	..
19	..	♉	..	♋	..	♎	♏	..	♈	..	♉	♊
20	..	..	..	..	..	..	..	♑	..	..	..	..
21	♈	♊	♊	♌	♍	♏	♐	..	♓	♈	♊	♋
22	..	..	..	..	..	..	..	♒	..	..	..	..
23	♉	♋	♋	♍	♎	..	..	..	..	♉	..	♌
24	..	..	..	..	..	♐	♑	..	♈	..	♋	..
25	♊	♌	♌	♎	♏	..	..	♓	..	♊	..	♍
26	..	..	..	..	..	♑	♒	..	♉	..	♌	..
27	♋	..	♍	..	..	..	..	♈	..	♋	..	♎
28	..	♍	..	♏	♐	..	..	..	♊	..	♍	..
29	♌		♎	..	..	♒	♓	..	..	♌	..	♏
30	..		..	♐	♑	..	..	♉	♋	..	♎	..
31	♍		♏		..		♈	..		..		♐

1870—EPHEMERIS OF THE PLANETS AND THE MOON—1870

♆	♂	♀	☿	☿	☿	☿
Ja 1♈	Mh25♈	Ma25♒	Ja 1♒	Ap 1♓	Jul 5♈	Oc 1♈
De 31♈	Ma13♉	Ju 12♓	" 4♓	" 8♈	" 11♉	" 7♉
♅	Jul 6♊	Jul 2♈	" 11♈	" 14♉	" 16♊	" 12♊
Ja 1♋	Se 2♋	" 20♉	" 16♉	" 19♊	" 21♋	" 17♋
De 31♋	No 5♌	Au 8♊	" 21♊	" 24♋	" 26♌	" 22♌
♄	♀	" 27♋	" 26♋	" 29♌	" 30♍	" 27♍
Ja 1♐	Ja 1♊	Se 14♌	" 31♌	Ma 4♍	Au 7♎	No 3♎
No 21♑	" 14♋	Oc 3♍	Fe 5♍	" 11♎	" 16♏	" 11♏
♃	Fe 1♌	" 21♎	" 12♎	" 20♏	" 26♐	" 22♐
Ja 1♉	" 20♍	No 9♏	" 21♏	" 30♐	" " "	De 3♑
Ap 13♊	Mh10♎	" 28♐	" " "	" " "	" " "	" 13♒
♂	" 29♏	" " "	Mh 3♐	Ju 10♑	Se 6♑	" 21♓
Ja 1♒	Ap 17♐	De 16♑	" 14♑	" 20♒	" 16♒	" 28♈
Fe 5♓	Ma 6♑	" 31♑	" 24♒	" 28♓	" 24♓	" 31♈

Day	Jan.	Feb.	Mch.	April	May	June	July	Aug.	Sept.	Oct.	Nov.	Dec.
1	♐	♒	♒	♈	♉	♋	♌	♎	♏	♑	♒	⅄
2	♑	..	♓	..	..	..	..	..	♐	..	..	..
3	..	♓	..	♉	♊	♌	♍	♏	..	♒	♓	♈
4	♒	..	..	..	..	..	..	..	♑	..	..	..
5	..	♈	♈	..	♋	♍	♎	..	..	♓	♈	♉
6	..	..	..	♊	..	..	..	♐	..	..	..	..
7	♓	..	♉	..	♌	♎	♏	..	♒	..	..	♊
8	..	♉	..	♋	..	..	..	♑	..	♈	♉	..
9	♈	..	♊	..	♍	♏	♐	..	♓	..	..	..
10	..	♊	..	♌	..	..	..	♒	..	♉	♊	♋
11	♉	..	..	..	..	♐	..	..	..	..	..	..
12	..	♋	♋	♍	♎	..	♑	..	♈	..	♋	♌
13	..	..	..	..	..	♑	..	♓	..	♊	..	..
14	♊	♌	♌	♎	♏	..	♒	..	♉	..	..	♍
15	..	..	..	..	..	..	..	♈	..	♋	♌	..
16	♋	♍	♍	♏	♐	♒	..	..	..	..	..	♎
17	..	..	..	..	..	..	♓	..	♊	♌	♍	..
18	♌	♎	♎	♐	♑	♓	..	♉	..	..	..	♏
19	..	..	..	..	..	..	♈	..	♋	..	♎	..
20	♍	♏	♏	..	♒	..	..	♊	..	♍	..	♐
21	..	..	..	♑	..	♈	..	..	♌	..	♏	..
22	♎	..	♐	..	..	..	♉	..	..	♎	..	..
23	..	♐	..	♒	♓	♉	..	♋	♍	..	♐	♑
24	♏	..	♑	..	..	..	♊	..	..	♏	..	..
25	..	♑	..	..	♈	..	..	♌	♎	..	♑	♒
26	♐	..	..	♓	..	♊	♋	..	..	♐	..	..
27	..	..	♒	..	..	..	..	♍	♏	..	..	♓
28	..	♒	..	♈	♉	♋	♌	..	..	♑	♒	..
29	♑		♓	..	..	..	..	♎	♐	..	..	..
30	..		..	..	♊	..	♍	..	..	..	♓	♈
31	♒		..		..		..	♏		♒		..

1871—EPHEMERIS OF THE PLANETS AND THE MOON—1871

♆	♂	♀	☿	☿	☿	☿
Ja 1 ♈	Mh22 ♎	Ap 27 ♌	Ja 1 ♈	Ap 1 ♉	Jul 3 ♊	Oc 4 ♋
De 31 ♈	Ma 26 ♏	Ma 15 ♍	" 3 ♉	" 7 ♊	" 8 ♋	" 9 ♌
♅	Jul 25 ♐	Ju 3 ♎	" 8 ♊	" 11 ♋	" 13 ♌	" 14 ♍
Ja 1 ♋	Se 18 ♑	" 22 ♏	" 13 ♋	" 16 ♌	" 18 ♍	" 21 ♎
De 31 ♋	No 7 ♒	Jul 10 ♐	" 18 ♌	" 21 ♍	" 25 ♎	" 30 ♏
♄	De 25 ♓	" 29 ♑	" 23 ♍	" 26 ♎	Au 3 ♏	No 9 ♐
Ja 1 ♑	♀	Au 17 ♒	" 30 ♎	Ma 7 ♏	" 13 ♐	" 20 ♑
De 31 ♑	Ja 1 ♑	Se 6 ♓	Fe 8 ♏	" 17 ♐	" 24 ♑	" 29 ♒
♃	" 4 ♒	" 24 ♈	" 18 ♐	" 28 ♑	" " "	" " "
Ja 1 ♊	" 22 ♓	Oc 13 ♉	" " "	" " "	Se 3 ♒	De 8 ♓
Mh23 ♋	Fe 11 ♈	No 1 ♊	Mh 1 ♑	Ju 7 ♒	" 11 ♓	" 15 ♈
♂	Mh 2 ♉	" 19 ♋	" 11 ♒	" 15 ♓	" 18 ♈	" 21 ♉
Ja 1 ♌	" 21 ♊	De 8 ♌	" 19 ♓	" 22 ♈	" 24 ♉	" 26 ♊
" 12 ♍	Ap 8 ♋	" 26 ♍	" 26 ♈	" 28 ♉	" 29 ♊	" 31 ♋

Day	Jan.	Feb.	Mch.	April	May	June	July	Aug.	Sept.	Oct.	Nov.	Dec.
1	♈	♊	♋	♍	♎	♐	♑	♓	♈	♉	♋	♌
2	♉	♋	♌	..	♏	..	♒	..	♉	♊	..	..
3	..	..	..	♎	..	♑	..	♈	..	..	♌	♍
4	♊	..	♍	..	♐	..	♓	..	..	♋	..	..
5	..	♌	..	♏	..	♒	..	..	♊	..	♍	♎
6	♋	..	♎	..	♑	..	..	♉	..	..	..	..
7	..	♍	..	♐	..	♓	♈	..	♋	♌	♎	♏
8	♌	..	♏	..	♒	..	..	♊	..	..	..	..
9	..	♎	..	♑	..	..	♉	..	♌	♍	♏	♐
10	♍	..	♐	..	..	♈	..	..	..	..	..	..
11	..	♏	..	♒	♓	..	..	♋	..	♎	♐	♑
12	♎	..	♑	..	..	♉	♊	..	♍	..	..	..
13	..	♐	..	♓	♈	..	..	♌	..	♏	♑	♒
14	♏	..	..	..	..	..	♋	..	♎	..	..	..
15	..	♑	♒	..	..	♊	..	♍	..	♐	..	♓
16	..	..	..	♈	♉	..	..	..	♏	..	♒	..
17	♐	..	♓	.	..	♋	♌	♎	..	♑	..	..
18	..	♒	..	..	♊	..	..	..	♐	..	♓	♈
19	♑	..	..	♉	..	♌	♍	♏	..	♒	..	..
20	..	♓	♈	..	..	..	..	..	♑	..	♈	♉
21	♒	..	..	♊	♋	♍	♎	♐	..	..	..	..
22	..	♈	♉	..	..	..	..	..	♒	♓	..	..
23	..	..	..	♋	♌	..	♏	♑	..	..	♉	♊
24	♓	♉	..	..	..	♎	..	..	♓	♈	..	..
25	..	..	♊	..	♍	..	♐	..	..	..	♊	♋
26	♈	♊	..	♌	..	♏	..	♒	..	..	..	..
27	..	..	♋	..	♎	..	♑	..	♈	♉	..	..
28	..	♋	..	♍	..	♐	..	♓	..	..	[illegible]	♌
29	♉	..	..	..	♏	..	♒	..	♉	♊	..	..
30	..		♌	♎	..	♑	..	..	..	..	♌	♍
31	♊		..		♐		..	♈		..		..

1872—EPHEMERIS OF THE PLANETS AND THE MOON—1872

♆	♂	♀	☿	☿	☿	☿
Ja 1 ♈	Fe 9 ♈	Ma 5 ♈	Ja 1 ♋	Ap 2 ♌	Jul 5 ♍	Oc 1 ♍
De 31 ♈	Mh31 ♉	“ 25 ♉	“ 4 ♌	“ 8 ♍	“ 12 ♎	“ 8 ♎
♅	Ma22 ♊	Ju 12 ♊	“ 11 ♍	“ 15 ♎	“ 19 ♏	“ 16 ♏
Ja 1 ♋	Jul 21 ♋	“ 30 ♋	“ 18 ♎	“ 23 ♏	“ 29 ♐	“ 25 ♐
Mh21 ♌	Se 13 ♌	Jul 20 ♌	“ 26 ♏	Ma 3 ♐	Au 9 ♑	No 5 ♑
De 31 ♌	No30 ♍	Au 6 ♍	Fe 4 ♐	“ 14 ♑	“ 19 ♒	“ 15 ♒
♄	♀	“ 26 ♎	“ 15 ♑	“ 23 ♒	“ 29 ♓	“ 25 ♓
Ja 1 ♑	Ja 1 ♍	Se 14 ♏	“ 25 ♒	“ “ “	“ “ “	De 2 ♈
De 31 ♑	“ 14 ♎	Oc 2 ♐	“ “ “	Ju 2 ♓	“ “ “	“ 7 ♉
♃	Fe 2 ♏	“ 21 ♑	Mh 5 ♓	“ 9 ♈	Se 5 ♈	“ 13 ♊
Ja 1 ♋	“ 21 ♐	No 9 ♒	“ 12 ♈	“ 15 ♉	“ 11 ♉	“ 17 ♋
Mh19 ♌	Mh 9 ♑	“ 28 ♓	“ 18 ♉	“ 20 ♊	“ 16 ♊	“ 22 ♌
♂	“ 28 ♒	De 17 ♈	“ 23 ♊	“ 25 ♋	“ 20 ♋	“ 28 ♍
Ja 1 ♓	Ap 16 ♓	“ 31 ♈	“ 28 ♋	“ 30 ♌	“ 25 ♌	“ 31 ♍

Day	Jan.	Feb.	Mch.	Apr.	May	June	July	Aug.	Sept.	Oct.	Nov.	Dec.
1	♎	♐	♐	♒	♒	♈	♉	♋	♌	♎	♏	♑
2	..	..	..	..	♓	♉	♊	.	♍	..	♐	..
3	♏	..	♑	..	..	..	..	♌	..	♏	..	♒
4	..	♑	..	♓	♈	♊	♋	..	♎	..	♑	..
5	♐	..	♒	..	..	..	..	♍	..	♐	..	♓
6	..	♒	..	♈	..	..	..	..	♏	..	♒	..
7	♑	..	♓	..	♉	♋	♌	..	..	♑	..	..
8	..	♓	..	♉	..	..	..	♎	♐	..	♓	♈
9	♒	..	..	..	♊	♌	♍	..	..	..	..	..
10	..	♈	♈	..	..	..	..	♏	..	♒	♈	♉
11	..	..	..	♊	..	..	♎	..	♑	..	..	..
12	♓	..	♉	..	♋	♍	..	♐	..	♓	..	..
13	..	♉	..	..	..	..	..	..	♒	..	♉	♊
14	♈	..	..	♋	♌	♎	♏	♑	..	♈	..	..
15	..	♊	♊	..	..	..	..	..	..	..	♊	♋
16	♉	..	..	♌	..	♏	♐	♒	♓	..	..	..
17	..	..	♋	..	♍	..	..	..	..	♉	..	..
18	..	♋	..	♍	..	♐	♑	♓	♈	..	♋	♌
19	♊	..	..	..	♎	..	..	..	..	♊	..	..
20	..	♌	♌	..	..	♑	♒	♈	♉	..	♌	..
21	♋	..	..	♎	♏	..	..	..	..	..	..	♍
22	..	♍	♍	..	..	♒	♓	..	..	♋	..	..
23	..	..	..	♏	♐	..	..	♉	♊	..	♍	♎
24	♌	..	♎	..	..	♓	♈	..	..	♌	..	..
25	..	♎	..	♐	♑	..	..	♊	♋	..	♎	..
26	♍	..	♏	..	..	..	..	..	..	♍	..	♏
27	..	♏	..	♑	♒	♈	♉	..	..	..	♏	..
28	♎	..	♐	..	..	..	..	♋	♌	..	..	♐
29	..	..	..	..	♓	♉	♊	..	..	♎	♐	..
30	♏		♑	♒	..	..	..	♌	♍	..	..	♑
31	..		..		♈	..	..	..	..	♏		..

1873—EPHEMERIS OF THE PLANETS AND THE MOON—1873

	♆	♂	♀	♀	☿	☿	☿
Ja	1♈	Fe 5♎	Ap 8♎	De 26♐	Mh26♍	Jul 7♏	Oc 3♏
De 31♈	Ap 12♏	" 26♏	♉	Ap 2♎	" 16♐	" 12♐
♅	Ju 11♐	Ma15♐	Ja 1♍	" 10♏	" 27♑	" 24♑
Ja 1♌	Au 4♑	Ju 3♑	" 3♎	" 19♐	Au 6♒	No 2♒
De 31♌	Se 23♒	" 21♒	" 11♏	" 30♑	" 16♓	" 12♓
♄	No 10♓	Jul 10♓	" 21♐	M 10♒	" 23♈	" 19♈
Ja 1♑	De 28♈	" 30♈	Fe 1♑	" 20♓	" 27♉	" 23♉
Au 10♒	♀	Au 18♉	" 11♒	" 27♈	" "	" 28♊
De 31♒	Ja 1♈	Se 5♊	" 21♓	" 31♉	" "	" "
♃	" 4♉	" 24♋	" 28♈	Ju 5♊	Se 1♊	De 4♋
Ja 1♌	" 23♊	Oc 11♌	Mh 4♉	" 10♋	" 7♋	" 9♌
Mh31♍	Fe 11♋	" 31♍	" 9♊	" 15♌	" 12♌	" 15♍
♂	Mh 1♌	No 17♎	" 14♋	" 22♍	" 18♍	" 22♎
Ja 1♍	" 20♍	De 7♏	" 19♌	" 29♎	" 25♎	" 30♏

Day	Jan.	Feb.	Mch.	April	May	June	July	Aug.	Sept.	Oct.	Nov.	Dec.
1	♒	♓	♈	♉	♊	♌	♍	♏	♐	♒	♓	♈
2	..	♈	..	♊	..	..	♎	..	♑	..	♈	♉
3	♓	..	..	..	♋	♍	..	♐	..	♓	..	..
4	..	♉	♉	..	..	..	..	..	♒	..	..	♊
5	♈	..	..	♋	♌	♎	♏	♑	..	..	♉	..
6	..	..	♊	..	..	..	..	..	♓	♈	..	..
7	..	♊	..	♌	♍	♏	♐	..	..	..	♊	♋
8	♉	..	..	..	..	..	..	♒	♈	♉	..	..
9	..	♋	♋	..	♎	♐	♑	..	..	..	♋	♌
10	♊	..	..	♍	..	..	..	♓	..	..	..	..
11	..	♌	♌	..	♏	♑	♒	..	♉	♊	..	♍
12	..	..	..	..	..	..	..	♈	..	..	♌	..
13	♋	..	♍	♎	♐	..	♓	..	♊	♋	..	..
14	..	♍	..	♏	..	♒	..	♉	..	..	♍	♎
15	♌	..	♎	..	♑	..	..	..	..	..	..	..
16	..	♎	..	♐	..	♓	♈	..	♋	♌	..	♏
17	♍	..	♏	..	♒	..	..	♊	..	♍	♎	♐
18	..	♏	..	♑	..	♈	♉	..	♌	♍	..	♐
19	♎	..	♐	..	♓	..	..	..	..	..	♏	♑
20	..	♐	..	♒	..	..	♊	♋	..	♎	..	♑
21	..	..	♑	..	..	♉	♊	..	♍	..	♐	..
22	♏	♑	..	♓	♈	..	..	♌	..	♏	..	♒
23	..	..	♒	..	..	♊	♋	..	♎	..	♑	..
24	♐	♒	♒	..	♉	..	..	♍	..	♐	..	♓
25	..	..	..	♈	..	..	..	..	♏	..	♒	..
26	♑	..	♓	..	♊	♋	♌	♎	..	♑	..	♈
27	..	♓	..	♉	..	..	..	..	♐	..	♓	..
28	♒	..	♈	..	..	♌	♍	♏	..	♒	..	..
29	..		..	..	♋	..	..	..	♑	..	♈	♉
30	♓		♉	♊	..	♍	♎	..	..	♓	..	..
31	..		..		..		♐			♓		♊

1874—EPHEMERIS OF THE PLANETS AND THE MOON—1874

♆	♂	♀	☿	☿	☿	☿
Ja 1 ♈	Ap 10 ♊	Ma 7 ♋	Ja 1 ♏	Ap 7 ♐	Jul 4 ♐	Oc 11 ♑
De 31 ♈	Ju 8 ♋	" 25 ♌	" 9 ♐	" 18 ♑	" 15 ♑	" 21 ♒
♅	Au 11 ♌	Ju 13 ♍	" 20 ♑	" 28 ♒	" 25 ♒	" 30 ♓
Ja 1 ♌	Oc 18 ♍	Jul 1 ♎	" 30 ♒	" " "	Au 3 ♓	No 6 ♈
De 31 ♌	De 25 ♎	" 20 ♏	Fe 8 ♓	Ma 7 ♓	" 10 ♈	" 11 ♉
♄	" " "	Au 16 ♐	" 15 ♈	" 14 ♈	" 15 ♉	" 16 ♊
Ja 1 ♒	♀	" 26 ♑	" 20 ♉	" 19 ♉	" 20 ♊	" 21 ♋
De 31 ♒	Ja 1 ♐	Se 14 ♒	" 25 ♊	" 24 ♊	" 25 ♋	" 26 ♌
♃	" 14 ♑	Oc 3 ♓	" " "	" 29 ♋	" 30 ♌	" " "
Ja 1 ♍	Fe 2 ♒	" 22 ♈	Mh 2 ♋	" " "	" " "	De 2 ♍
Ap 28 ♎	" 21 ♓	No 10 ♉	" 7 ♌	Ju 3 ♌	Se 5 ♍	" 7 ♎
♂	Mh 10 ♈	" 29 ♊	" 13 ♍	" 9 ♍	" 10 ♎	" 17 ♏
Ja 1 ♈	" 30 ♉	De 17 ♋	" 20 ♎	" 14 ♎	" 20 ♏	" 27 ♐
Fe 16 ♉	Ap 18 ♊	" 31 ♋	" 28 ♏	" 24 ♏	" 30 ♐	" 31 ♐

Day	Jan.	Feb.	Mch.	Apr.	May	June	July	Aug.	Sept.	Oct.	Nov.	Dec.
1	♊	♋	♌	♎	♏	♑	♒	♈	♊	♊	♌	♍
2	..	♌	♍	..	♐	..	♓	..	..	♋	..	♎
3	♋	..	..	♏	..	♒	..	♉	..	..	..	..
4	..	..	♎	..	♑	..	..	..	♋	♌	♍	..
5	♌	♍	..	♐	..	♓	♈	..	..	..	..	♏
6	..	..	..	..	♒	..	..	♊	..	..	♎	..
7	..	♎	♏	♑	..	♈	..	..	♌	♍	..	♐
8	♍	..	..	..	..	..	♉	♋	..	..	..	..
9	..	..	♐	♒	♓	..	..	..	♍	♎	♏	♑
10	♎	♏	..	..	..	♉	♊	..	..	..	..	..
11	..	..	♑	♓	♈	..	..	♌	..	♏	♐	♒
12	♏	♐	..	..	..	♊	..	..	♎	..	..	..
13	..	..	♒	..	♉	..	♋	♍	..	♐	♑	♓
14	♐	♑	..	♈	..	..	..	..	♏	..	..	..
15	..	..	♓	..	..	♋	♌	♎	..	..	♒	♈
16	♑	♒	..	♉	♊	..	..	..	♐	♑	..	..
17	..	..	♈	..	..	♌	..	..	..	..	♓	..
18	♒	♓	..	..	♋	..	♍	♏	♑	♒	..	♉
19	..	..	..	♊	..	..	..	..	..	..	♈	..
20	♓	♈	♉	..	..	♍	♎	♐	♒	♓	..	♊
21	..	..	..	♋	♌	..	..	..	..	..	♉	..
22	..	♉	♊	..	..	♎	♏	♑	♓	♈	..	..
23	♈	..	..	..	♍	..	..	..	..	..	♊	♋
24	..	..	..	♌	..	♏	..	♒	..	♉	..	..
25	♉	♊	♋	..	..	..	♐	..	♈	..	♋	♌
26	..	..	..	♍	♎	♐	..	♓	..	..	..	..
27	..	♋	♌	..	..	..	♑	..	♉	♊	..	..
28	♊	..	..	♎	♏	♑	..	♈	..	..	♌	♍
29	..		..	..	..	..	♒	..	♊	♋	..	..
30	♋		♍	♏	♐	♒	..	♉	..	..	♍	♎
31	..		..		..		♓	..		..		..

1875—EPHEMERIS OF THE PLANETS AND THE MOON—1875

♆	♂	♀	☿	☿	☿	☿
Ja 1 ♈	Ap 28 ♐	Ap 28 ♒	Ja 1 ♐	Ap 5 ♑	Jul 2 ♑	Oc 8 ♒
" 29 ♉	Ju 23 ♑	Ma 16 ♓	" 7 ♑	" 15 ♒	" 12 ♒	" 16 ♓
♅	Au 12 ♒	Ju 4 ♈	" 17 ♒	" 24 ♓	" 21 ♓	" 23 ♈
Ja 1 ♌	Se 29 ♓	" 23 ♉	" 26 ♓	" 29 ♈	" 26 ♈	" 28 ♉
De 31 ♌	No 14 ♈	Jul 10 ♊	" 31 ♈	" " "	Au 2 ♉	No 2 ♊
♄	De 31 ♈	" 30 ♋	Fe 7 ♉	Ma 6 ♉	" 7 ♊	" 7 ♋
Ja 1 ♒	♀	Au 16 ♌	" 12 ♊	" 11 ♊	" 12 ♋	" 12 ♌
De 31 ♒	Ja 1 ♋	Se 5 ♍	" 17 ♋	" 16 ♋	" 17 ♌	" 17 ♍
♃	" 5 ♌	" 22 ♎	" 22 ♌	" 21 ♌	" 21 ♍	" 24 ♎
Ja 1 ♎	" 23 ♍	Oc 12 ♏	" 28 ♍	" 27 ♍	" 28 ♎	" " "
Ma 30 ♏	Fe 10 ♎	" 31 ♐	" " "	" " "	" " "	De 4 ♏
♂	" 28 ♏	No 19 ♑	Mh 5 ♎	Ju 1 ♎	Se 7 ♏	" 14 ♐
Ja 1 ♎	Mh 20 ♐	De 8 ♒	" 15 ♏	" 11 ♏	" 17 ♐	" 25 ♑
Fe 28 ♏	Ap 8 ♑	" 27 ♓	" 25 ♐	" 21 ♐	" 28 ♑	" 31 ♑

Day	Jan.	Feb.	Mch.	April	May	June	July	Aug.	Sept.	Oct.	Nov.	Dec.
1	♎	♐	♐	♒	♓	♉	♊	♌	♎	♏	♐	♑
2	♏	♑	♑	♓	♈	♊	♋	..	..	..	♑	♒
3	..	..	..	..	..	..	..	♍	..	..	..	..
4	♐	♒	♒	♈	♉	..	♌	..	♏	♐	♒	♓
5	..	..	..	..	..	♋	..	..	..	..	..	..
6	♑	♓	♓	♉	♊	..	..	♎	..	♑	..	♈
7	..	..	..	..	..	♌	♍	..	♐	..	♓	..
8	♒	♈	♈	..	♋	..	..	♏	..	♒	..	♉
9	..	..	..	♊	..	..	♎	..	♑	..	♈	..
10	♓	..	♉	..	..	♍	...	♐	..	♓	..	♊
11	..	♉	..	♋	♌	..	..	..	♒	..	♉	..
12	♈	..	♊	..	..	♎	♏	♑	..	♈	..	..
13	..	♊	..	..	♍	..	..	..	♓	..	♊	♋
14	♉	..	..	♌	..	..	♐	♒	..	♉	..	..
15	..	♋	♋	..	..	♏	..	..	♈	..	♋	♌
16	..	..	..	♍	♎	..	♑	♓	..	..	..	..
17	♊	..	♌	..	..	♐	..	..	♉	♊	..	..
18	..	♌	..	..	♏	..	♒	♈	..	..	♌	♍
19	♋	..	..	♎	..	♑	..	..	♊	♋	..	..
20	..	♍	♍	..	♐	..	♓	..	..	..	♍	♎
21	..	..	..	♏	..	♒	..	♉	..	♌	..	..
22	♌	..	♎	..	♑	..	♈	..	♋	..	..	..
23	..	♎	..	♐	..	♓	..	♊	..	..	♎	♏
24	♍	..	..	..	..	..	..	..	♌	♍	..	..
25	..	♏	♏	♑	♒	♈	♉	♋	..	..	♏	♐
26	..	..	..	..	..	..	..	..	..	♎	..	..
27	♎	..	♐	♒	♓	♉	♊	..	♍	..	♐	♑
28	..	♐	..	..	..	..	..	♌	..	..	..	..
29	♏		♑	♓	♈	..	♋	..	♎	♏	..	♒
30	..		..	..	..	♊	..	♍	..	..	♑	..
31	♐		♒		♉	..	..	..		♐		♓

1876—EPHEMERIS OF THE PLANETS AND THE MOON—1876

♆	♂	♀	☿	☿	☿	☿
Ja 1 ♉	Fe 27 ♊	Ma 23 ♏	Ja 1 ♑	Ap 9 ♓	Jul 6 ♓	Oc 2 ♓
De 31 ♉	Ap 24 ♋	Ju 11 ♐	" 3 ♒	" 16 ♈	" 13 ♈	" 9 ♈
♅	Ju 27 ♌	" 30 ♑	" 12 ♓	" 22 ♉	" 18 ♉	" 14 ♉
Ja 1 ♌	Se 3 ♍	Jul 19 ♒	" 19 ♈	" 26 ♊	" 23 ♊	" 19 ♊
De 13 ♌	No 9 ♎	Au 7 ♓	" 24 ♉	Ma 1 ♋	" 28 ♋	" 24 ♋
♄	♀	" 25 ♈	" 29 ♊	" 6 ♌	Au 2 ♌	" 29 ♌
Ja 1 ♏	Ja 1 ♓	Se 13 ♉	Fe 3 ♋	" 12 ♍	" 8 ♍	No 4 ♍
Ap 2 ♓	" 14 ♈	Oc 2 ♊	" 8 ♌	" 18 ♎	" 14 ♎	" 11 ♎
♃	Fe 2 ♉	" 21 ♋	" 14 ♍	" 27 ♏	" 23 ♏	" 19 ♏
Ja 1 ♏	" 20 ♊	No 8 ♌	" 21 ♎	" " "	" " "	" 29 ♐
Ju 23 ♐	Mh 10 ♋	" 27 ♍	" 29 ♏	" " "	" " "	De 10 ♑
♂	" 28 ♌	De 15 ♎	Mh 10 ♐	Ju 6 ♐	Se 3 ♐	" 20 ♒
Ja 1 ♈	Ap 16 ♍	" " "	" 21 ♑	" 17 ♑	" 13 ♑	" 29 ♓
" 3 ♉	Ma 4 ♎	" 31 "	" 31 ♒	" 27 ♒	" 23 ♒	" 31 ♓

Day	Jan.	Feb.	Mch.	Apr.	May	June	July	Aug.	Sept.	Oct.	Nov.	Dec.
1	♓	♉	♉	♋	♌	♍	♏	♐	♒	♓	♉	♊
2	♈	..	♊	..	..	♎	..	♑	..	..	..	..
3	..	♊	..	♌	♍	..	..	..	♓	♈	♊	♋
4	♉	..	♋	..	..	♏	♐	..	..	..	..	..
5	..	♋	..	..	..	..	..	♒	♈	♉	♋	♌
6	..	..	..	♍	♎	..	♑	..	..	..	..	..
7	♊	..	♌	..	..	♐	..	♓	♉	♊	..	♍
8	..	♌	..	♎	♏	..	♒	..	..	..	♌	..
9	♋	..	♍	..	..	♑	..	♈	♊	♋	..	..
10	..	♍	..	..	♐	..	..	..	..	..	♍	♎
11	♌	..	..	♏	..	♒	♓	♉	..	♌	..	..
12	..	..	♎	..	..	..	..	..	♋	..	..	♏
13	..	♎	..	♐	♑	♓	♈	♊	..	..	♎	..
14	♍	..	♏	..	..	..	..	..	♌	♍	..	..
15	..	♏	..	♑	♒	♈	♉	♋	..	..	♏	♐
16	♎	..	..	..	..	..	..	..	..	♎	..	..
17	..	..	♐	..	♓	..	♊	..	♍	..	..	♑
18	..	♐	..	♒	..	♉	..	♌	..	..	♐	..
19	♏	..	♑	..	♈	..	♋	..	♎	♏	..	♒
20	..	♑	..	♓	..	♊	..	♍	..	..	♑	..
21	♐	..	♒	..	♉	..	..	..	..	♐	..	..
22	..	♒	..	♈	..	♋	♌	..	♏	..	♒	♓
23	♑	..	♓	..	♊	..	..	♎	..	..	..	..
24	..	♓	..	♉	..	♌	♍	..	♐	♑	♓	♈
25	♒	..	♈	..	..	..	..	♏	..	..	..	..
26	..	♈	..	♊	♋	..	..	..	♑	♒	..	♉
27	♓	..	♉	..	..	♍	♎	..	..	..	♈	..
28	..	♉	..	♋	♌	..	..	♐	..	♓	..	♊
29	♈	..	..	..	..	♎	♏	..	♒	..	♉	..
30	..		♊	..	♍	..	..	♑	..	..	..	♋
31	..		..		..		♐	..		♈		..

1877—EPHEMERIS OF THE PLANETS AND THE MOON—1877

	♆	♂	♀	☿	☿	☿	☿	☿
Ja	1 ♉	Mh16 ♐	Ap26 ♉	Ja 1 ♓	Ap 2 ♈	Jul 5 ♉	Oc 1 ♉	
De 31 ♉	Ma 9 ♑	Ma15 ♊	" 5 ♈	" 8 ♉	" 10 ♊	" 6 ♊		
♅	Ju 29 ♒	Ju 2 ♋	" 10 ♉	" 13 ♊	" 15 ♋	" 11 ♋		
Ja 1 ♌	Au 15 ♓	" 21 ♌	" 15 ♊	" 18 ♋	" 20 ♌	" 16 ♌		
De 31 ♌	Oc 2 ♈	Jul 9 ♍	" 20 ♋	" 23 ♌	" 26 ♍	" 21 ♍		
♄	No 20 ♉	" 28 ♎	" 25 ♌	" 28 ♍	Au 1 ♎	" 28 ♎		
Ja 1 ♓	♀	Au 15 ♏	" 31 ♍	Ma 6 ♎	" 10 ♏	No 6 ♏		
De 31 ♓	Ja 1 ♎	Se 3 ♐	Fe 7 ♎	" 14 ♏	" 20 ♐	" 16 ♐		
♃	" 3 ♏	" 22 ♑	" 15 ♏	" 24 ♐	" 31 ♑	" 27 ♑		
Ja 1 ♐	" 21 ♐	Oc 11 ♒	" 25 ♐	" " "	" " "	De 7 ♒		
Jul 5 ♑	Fe 9 ♑	" 30 ♓	" " "	Ju 4 ♑	" " "	" 14 ♓		
♂	" 28 ♒	No 18 ♈	Mh 8 ♑	" 14 ♒	Se 10 ♒	" 22 ♈		
Ja 1 ♎	Mh19 ♓	De 6 ♉	" 18 ♒	" 23 ♓	" 18 ♓	" 28 ♉		
" 15 ♏	Ap 7 ♈	" 25 ♊	" 27 ♓	" 29 ♈	" 25 ♈	" 31 ♉		

Day	Jan.	Feb.	Mch.	April	May	June	July	Aug.	Sept.	Oct.	Nov.	Dec.
1	♌	♍	♍	♏	♐	♒	♓	♈	♊	♌	♍	♎
2	..	♎	♎	..	..	..	..	♉	♋	..	..	♏
3	..	..	..	♐	♑	..	♈	..	..	..	♎	..
4	♍	..	♏	..	..	♓	..	♊	♌	♍	..	..
5	..	♏	..	♑	♒	..	♉	..	..	..	♏	♐
6	♎	..	..	..	..	♈	..	♋	..	♎	..	..
7	..	..	♐	..	..	..	♊	..	♍	..	..	♑
8	..	♐	..	♒	♓	♉	..	♌	..	..	♐	..
9	♏	..	♑	..	..	..	♋	..	♎	♏	..	..
10	..	♑	..	♓	♈	♊	..	♍	..	..	♑	♒
11	♐	..	..	..	..	..	♌	..	♏	♐	..	..
12	..	♒	♒	♈	♉	♋	..	..	..	..	♒	♓
13	..	..	..	..	..	..	♍	♎	..	..	..	..
14	♑	♓	♓	♉	♊	♌	..	♏	♑	..	♓	♈
15	..	..	..	..	..	..	♎	..	..	♓	..	..
16	♒	♈	♈	♊	♋	..	♏	..	♒	..	♈	♉
17	..	..	..	..	♍	..	..	♐	..	♈	..	..
18	♓	♉	♉	♋	♌	..	♐	..	♓	..	♉	♊
19	..	..	..	..	♎	♏	..	♒	..	♉	..	..
20	♈	..	♊	..	♍	..	♑	..	♈	..	♊	♋
21	..	♊	..	♌	..	♐	..	♓	♈	♊	..	..
22	♉	..	♋	..	..	♏	♒	..	..	..	..	♌
23	..	♋	..	♍	♎	..	..	♈	♉	♋	♌	
24	♊	..	♌	..	..	♐	♑	..	..	..	♎	♍
25	..	♌	..	♎	♏	..	♓	♉	♊	♌	♍	
26	♋	..	..	..	♐	♒	..	..	..	♎	♍	♎
27	..	♍	♍	..	..	..	♈	♊	♋	♍	♎	
28	..	..	..	♏	♐	..	♓	..	..	..	..	..
29	♌	..	♎	..	..	♒	..	♉	♋	♌	..	..
30	..	..	..	♐	♑	..	♈	..	..	..	♎	♏
31	♍	..	..	..	..	..	♊	..	♍	..		

1878—EPHEMERIS OF THE PLANETS AND THE MOON—1878

♆	♂	♀	☿	☿	☿	☿
Ja 1 ♉	Ja 12 ♑	Ma 5 ♑	Ja 1 ♉	Ap 5 ♋	Jul 2 ♋	Oc 3 ♌
De 31 ♉	Mh 12 ♋	" 24 ♒	" 2 ♊	" 10 ♌	" 7 ♌	" 8 ♍
⛢	Ma 15 ♌	Ju 11 ♓	" 7 ♋	" 15 ♍	" 12 ♍	" 15 ♎
Ja 1 ♌	Jul 22 ♍	Jul 1 ♈	" 12 ♌	" 22 ♎	" 19 ♎	" 24 ♏
Se 3 ♍	Se 28 ♎	" 19 ♉	" 17 ♍	Ma 1 ♏	" 28 ♏	No 3 ♐
De 31 ♍	De 3 ♏	Au 7 ♊	" 21 ♎	" 11 ♐	Au 7 ♐	" 14 ♑
♄	♀	" 26 ♋	Fe 2 ♏	" 22 ♑	" 18 ♑	" 24 ♒
Ja 1 ♓	Ja 1 ♊	Se 13 ♌	" 12 ♐	" " "	" 28 ♒	De 2 ♓
Oc 8 ♈	" 13 ♋	Oc 2 ♍	" 23 ♑	" " "	" " "	" 9 ♈
♃	" 31 ♌	" 20 ♎	Mh 5 ♒	Ju 1 ♒	Se 5 ♓	" 15 ♉
Ja 1 ♑	Fe 19 ♍	No 8 ♏	" 13 ♓	" 9 ♓	" 12 ♈	" 20 ♊
Ju 29 ♒	Mh 9 ♎	" 26 ♐	" 20 ♈	" 16 ♈	" 18 ♉	" 25 ♋
♐	" 28 ♏	De 15 ♑	" 26 ♉	" 22 ♉	" 23 ♊	" 30 ♌
Ja 1 ♉	Ap 16 ♐	" 31 ♑	" 31 ♊	" 27 ♊	" 28 ♋	" 31 ♌

Day	Jan.	Feb.	Mch.	April	May	June	July	Aug.	Sept.	Oct.	Nov.	Dec.
1	♐	♑	♒	♈	♉	♋	♌	♍	♏	♐	♑	♓
2	..	♒	..	..	..	..	..	♎	..	..	♒	..
3	..	..	♓	..	♊	♌	♍	..	♐	♑	..	♈
4	♑	..	..	♉	..	..	♏	..	..	♓	..
5	..	♓	♈	..	♋	..	♎	..	..	♒	..	..
6	♒	..	..	♊	..	♍	..	..	♑	..	♈	♉
7	..	♈	♉	..	♌	..	..	♐	..	..	..	..
8	♓	..	..	♋	..	♎	♏	..	♒	♓	♉	♊
9	..	♉	♊	..	♍	..	..	♑	..	..	..	..
10	..	..	..	♌	..	♏	♐	..	♓	♈	..	♋
11	♈	♊	♋	..	..	..	..	..	..	..	♊	..
12	..	..	..	♍	♎	♐	..	♒	..	♉	..	♌
13	♉	♋	..	..	..	..	♑	..	♈	..	♋	..
14	..	..	♌	♎	♏	♑	..	♓	..	♊	..	♍
15	♊	♌	..	..	..	..	♒	..	♉	..	♌	..
16	..	..	♍	..	..	..	..	♈	..	♋	..	♎
17	♋	..	..	♏	♐	♒	..	..	♊	..	♍	..
18	..	♍	♎	..	..	..	♓	..	..	♌	..	..
19	♌	..	..	♐	♑	♓	..	♉	♋	..	♎	♏
20	..	♎	..	..	..	..	♈	..	..	♍	..	..
21	♍	..	♏	..	♒	..	..	♊	♌	..	♏	♐
22	..	♏	..	♑	♒	♈	♉	..	..	..	..	..
23	♎	..	♐	..	..	..	..	♋	♍	..	♐	♑
24	..	..	..	♒	♓	♉	♊	..	♍	♎	♐	♑
25	..	♐	..	..	..	..	..	♌	..	♏	..	..
26	♏	..	♑	..	♈	♊	♋	..	♎	..	♑	♒
27	..	♑	..	♓	..	..	♍	..	..	..	..
28	♐	..	♒	..	♉	♋	♌	..	♏	♐	..	♓
29	..		..	♈	..	..	..	♎	..	..	♒	..
30	..		♓	..	♊	..	..	..	♐	♑	..	..
31	♑		..		..		♍	♏	..	..		♈

1879—EPHEMERIS OF THE PLANETS AND THE MOON—1879

	♆	♂	♀	☿	☿	☿	☿
Ja 1	♉	Mh27♑	Ap26♌ Ja 1♌	Ap 2♍	Jul 6♎	Oc 2♎
De 31 ♉		Ma16♒	Ma14♍ " 4♍	" 9♎	" 51♏	" 11♏
	♅	Jul 3♓	Ju 2♎ " 11♎	" 18♏	" 25♐	" 21♐
Ja 1♍		Au20♈	" 20♏ " 19♏	" 28♐	Au 5♑	No 1♑
De 31♍		Oc 9♉	Jul 9♐ " 30♐	Ma 9♑	" 15♒	" 11♒
	♄	No30♊	" 28♑ Fe 10♑	" 19♒	" 23♓	" 19♓
Ja 1♈		♀	Au16♒ " 20♒	" 27♓	" 30♈	" 26♈
De 31♈	Ja 1♑	Se 4♓ " 28♓	" " "	" " "	" " "
	♃	" 3♒	" 23♈ " " "	Ju 3♈	" " "	De 2♉
Ja 1♒		" 22♓	Oc12♉ Mh 7♈	" 8♉	Se 5♉	" 7♊
Ju 6♓		Fe 10♈	" 30♊ " 12♉	" 14♊	" 10♊	" 12♋
	♂	Mh 1♉	No18♋ " 18♊	" 19♋	" 15♋	" 17♌
Ja 1♏		" 20♊	De 6♌ " 23♋	" 24♌	" 20♌	" 22♍
Fe 1♐		Ap 7♋	" 25♍ " 28♌	" 29♍	" 25♍	" 29♎

Day	Jan.	Feb	Mch.	April	May	June	July	Aug.	Sept.	Oct.	Nov.	Dec.
1	♈	♊	♊	♌	♍	♏	♐	♒	♓	♈	♊	♋
2	♉	..	..	♋	..	♎	..	..	..	♉	..	♌
3	..	♋	..	♍	..	♐	♑	..	♈	..	♋	..
4	♊	..	♌	..	♏	..	..	♓	..	♊	..	♍
5	..	♌	..	♎	..	..	♒	..	♉	..	♌	..
6	♋	..	♍	..	..	♑	..	♈	..	..	..	..
7	..	♍	..	♏	♐	..	..	..	♊	♋	♍	♎
8	♌	..	..	..	..	♒	♓	..	..	..	..	..
9	..	♎	♎	♐	♑	..	..	♉	♋	♌	♎	♏
10	♍	..	..	..	..	..	♈	..	..	..	..	..
11	..	♏	♏	..	..	♓	..	♊	♌	♍	♏	♐
12	♎	..	..	♑	♒	..	♉	..	..	..	..	..
13	..	..	♐	..	..	♈	..	♋	..	♎	♐	♑
14	..	♐	..	♒	..	..	..	♍	..	..	..	..
15	♏	..	..	..	♓	♉	♊	♌	..	♏	..	..
16	..	♑	♑	..	..	..	..	..	♎	..	♑	♒
17	♐	..	..	♓	♈	♊	♋	♍	..	♐	..	..
18	..	..	♒	..	..	..	..	..	♏	..	♒	♓
19	..	♒	..	♈	♉	♋	♌	♎	..	..	..	..
20	♑	..	..	..	..	..	..	♐	♑	..	..	..
21	..	♓	♓	..	♊	♌	♍	♏	..	..	♓	♈
22	♒	..	..	♉	..	..	..	♑	♒	..	..	..
23	..	..	♈	..	♋	♍	♎	..	..	..	..	♉
24	..	♈	..	♊	..	..	♐	♒	♓	..	♈	..
25	♓	..	♉	..	♌	..	♏	..	..	♓	..	..
26	..	♉	..	♋	..	♎	..	♓	♈	..	♉	♊
27	♈	..	♊	..	♍	..	♐	..	♓	♈	..	..
28	..	♊	..	♌	..	♏	..	..	..	..	♊	♋
29	..	..	♋	..	♎	..	♒	..	..	..	..	..
30	♉	..	♍	..	..	♐	♑	..	♈	♉	♋	♌
31	..	..	..	..	..	..	♓	..	..	..	..	..

1880—EPHEMERIS OF THE PLANETS AND THE MOON—1880

♆	♂	♀	☿	☿	☿	☿
Ja 1 ♉	Ja 1 ⬜	Ap 16 ♓	Ja 1 ♎	Ap 3 ♏	Jul 11 ♐	Oc 6 ♐
De 31 ♉	" 27 ♋	Ma 5 ♈	" 8 ♏	" 13 ♐	" 21 ♑	" 18 ♑
	Ap 2 ♌	" 23 ♉	" 17 ♐	" 24 ♑	" 31 ♒	" 28 ♒
♅						
Ja 1 ♍	Ju 9 ♍	Ju 10 ⬜	" 27 ♑	Ma 4 ♒	Au 9 ♓	No 5 ♓
De 31 ♍	Au 16 ♎	" 30 ♋	Fe 7 ♒	" 13 ♓	" 16 ♈	" 12 ♈
" " "	Oc 19 ♏	Jul 18 ♌	" 15 ♓	" 20 ♈	" 24 ♉	" 18 ♉
♄	De 18 ♐	Au 5 ♍	" 22 ♈	" 26 ♉	" 26 ⬜	" 22 ⬜
Ja 1 ♈	♀	" 24 ♎	" 28 ♉	" 31 ⬜	" 31 ♋	" 27 ♋
De 31 ♈	Ja 1 ♍	Se 12 ♏	" " "	" " "	" " "	" " "
" " "	" 13 ♎	" 30 ♐	Mh 3 ⬜	Ju 5 ♋	" " "	De 3 ♌
♃	Fe 1 ♏	Oc 19 ♑	" 8 ♋	" 9 ♌	Se 5 ♌	" 8 ♍
Ja 1 ♓	" 19 ♐	No 7 ♒	" 13 ♌	" 16 ♍	" 11 ♍	" 15 ♎
Ap 25 ♈	Mh 8 ♑	" 28 ♓	" 19 ♍	" 22 ♎	" 17 ♎	" 23 ♏
De 31 ♈	" 27 ♒	De 15 ♈	" 26 ♎	" 31 ♏	" 26 ♏	" 31 ♏

Day	Jan.	Feb.	Mch.	Apr.	May	June	July	Aug.	Sept.	Oct.	Nov.	Dec.
1	♍	♎	♏	♐	♒	♓	♈	⬜	♋	♍	♎	♐
2	..	♏	..	♑	..	♈	♉	..	♌	..	♏	..
3	♎	..	♐	..	..	..	..	♋	..	♎	..	♑
4	..	♐	..	♒	♓	..	..	♌	♍	..	♐	..
5	♏	♑	♑	..	..	♉	⬜	♌	..	♏	..	..
6	..	♑	..	..	♈	..	..	..	♎	..	♑	♒
7	♐	..	..	♓	..	⬜	♋	♍	..	♐	..	..
8	..	♒	♒	..	..	..	..	..	♏	..	♒	♓
9	..	..	..	♈	♉	..	♌	♎	..	..	..	..
10	♑	..	♓	..	..	♋	..	..	..	♐	♑	..
11	..	♓	..	♉	⬜	..	♍	♏	..	..	♓	♈
12	♒	..	..	..	..	♌	..	♏	♑	♒	..	..
13	..	..	♈	..	♋	..	♎	..	..	..	♈	♉
14	..	♈	..	⬜	..	♍	..	♐	..	..	..	..
15	♓	..	♉	..	♌	..	♏	..	♒	♓	..	..
16	..	♉	..	♋	..	♎	..	♑	..	..	♉	⬜
17	♈	..	..	..	..	..	..	..	♓	♈	..	..
18	..	⬜	⬜	♌	♍	♏	♐	..	..	..	⬜	♋
19	..	..	..	..	..	..	♒	..	..	..	..	..
20	♉	..	♋	♍	♎	♐	♑	♈	♉	..	..	♌
21	..	♋	..	..	..	..	♓	..	..	♋	..	..
22	⬜	..	♌	♎	♏	..	♒	♉	⬜	..	♌	♍
23	..	♌	..	..	..	♑	..	..	..	♌	..	..
24	♋	..	♍	♏	♐	..	♈	..	♋	..	♍	♎
25	..	♍	..	..	..	♒	♓	⬜	..	♍	..	..
26	♌	..	♎	..	♑	..	♉	..	♌	..	♎	♏
27	..	♎	..	♐	..	..	♈	..	♋	♎	..	..
28	♍	..	♏	..	..	♓	..	..	..	..	..	..
29	..	..	..	♑	♒	..	⬜	♌	♍	♏	♐	
30	♎		♐	..	..	♈	♉	..	..	..		
31	..		..		♓	..		♋		♎		♑

235

1881—EPHEMERIS OF THE PLANETS AND THE MOON—1881

♆	♂	♀	♀	☿	☿	☿
Ja 1 ♉	Fe 12 ♑	" 7 ♎	De 24 ♐	Mh21 ♏	Jul 8 ♑	Oc 4 ♑
De 31 ♉	Ap 3 ♒	" 24 ♏	☿	Ap 1 ♐	" 18 ♒	" 14 ♒
♅	Ma 20 ♓	Ma 13 ♐	Ja 1 ♏	" 11 ♑	" 27 ♓	" 22 ♓
Ja 1 ♍	Jul 6 ♈	Ju 1 ♑	" 2 ♐	" 22 ♒	Au 2 ♈	" 28 ♈
De 31 ♍	Au 25 ♉	" 20 ♒	" 13 ♑	" 30 ♓	" 8 ♉	No 4 ♉
♄	Oc 18 ♊	Jul 9 ♓	" 23 ♒	Ma 4 ♈	" 13 ♊	" 9 ♊
Ja 1 ♈	De 15 ♋	" 28 ♈	Fe 1 ♓	" 12 ♉	" 18 ♋	" 14 ♋
Fe 26 ♉	♀	Au 16 ♉	" 8 ♈	" 17 ♊	" 23 ♌	" 19 ♌
♃	Ja 1 ♈	" 29 ♊	" 13 ♉	" 22 ♋	" 29 ♍	" 25 ♍
Ja 1 ♈	" 3 ♉	Se 22 ♋	" 18 ♊	" 27 ♌	" " "	" " "
Mh26 ♉	" 22 ♊	Oc 10 ♌	" 23 ♋	Ju 3 ♍	" " "	De 1 ♎
De 31 ♉	Fe 14 ♋	" 29 ♍	" 28 ♌	" 9 ♎	Se 4 ♎	" 10 ♏
♂	" 28 ♌	No 16 ♎	Mh 6 ♍	" 17 ♏	" 13 ♏	" 20 ♐
Ja 1 ♐	Mh18 ♍	De 4 ♏	" 13 ♎	" 27 ♐	" 23 ♐	" 31 ♑

Day	Jan.	Feb.	Mch.	April	May	June	July	Aug.	Sept.	Oct.	Nov.	Dec.
1	♑	♓	♓	♈	♊	♋	♌	♎	♐	♑	♓	♈
2	..	..	..	♉	..	♌	..	♏	..	♒	..	..
3	♒	♈	♈	..	..	..	♍	..	♑	..	..	♉
4	..	..	..	♊	♋	♍	..	♐	..	..	♈	..
5	♓	..	♉	..	..	..	♎	..	♒	♓	..	..
6	..	♉	..	♋	♌	..	..	♑	..	..	♉	♊
7	♈	..	..	..	..	♎	♏	..	♓	♈	..	..
8	..	♊	♊	..	♍	..	..	..	..	..	♊	♋
9	..	..	..	♌	..	♏	♐	♒	♈	..	..	..
10	♉	..	♋	..	♎	..	..	..	..	♉	..	♌
11	..	♋	..	♍	..	♐	♑	♓	..	..	♋	..
12	♊	..	♌	..	♏	..	..	..	♉	♊	..	..
13	..	♌	..	♎	..	♑	..	♈	..	..	♌	♍
14	♋	..	♍	..	♐	..	♒	..	..	♋	..	..
15	..	♍	..	♏	..	♒	..	..	♊	..	..	♎
16	♌	..	♎	..	♑	..	♓	♉	..	..	♍	..
17	..	♎	..	♑	..	♓	..	..	♋	♌	..	♏
18	..	..	♏	..	..	..	♈	♊	..	..	♎	..
19	♍	♏	..	♐	♒	..	..	..	♌	♍	..	♐
20	..	..	♐	..	..	♈	♉	..	..	..	♏	..
21	♎	♐	..	♒	♓	..	..	♋	..	♎	..	♑
22	..	..	..	..	..	♉	♊	..	♍	..	♐	..
23	♏	♑	♑	..	♈	..	..	♌	..	♏	..	♒
24	..	..	..	♓	..	..	♋	..	♎	..	♑	..
25	♐	..	♒	..	..	♊	..	♍	..	♐	..	..
26	..	♒	..	♈	♉	..	..	..	♍	..	♒	♓
27	♑	..	♓	..	..	♋	♌	♎	..	♑	..	..
28	..	♓	..	..	..	..	..	..	♐	..	♓	♈
29	♒		..	♉	♊	♌	♍	..	..	..	..	..
30	..		♈	..	..	..	..	♏	♑	♒	..	♉
31	..		..		♋		♎	..		..		..

1882—EPHEMERIS OF THE PLANETS AND THE MOON—1882

♆	♂	♀	☿	☿	☿	☿
Ja 1 ♉	Ja 1 ♋	Ap 16 ♊	Ja 1 ♑	Ap 8 ♒	Jul 5 ♒	Oc 1 ♒
De 31 ♉	Fe 17 ♌	Ma 5 ♋	" 10 ♒	" 17 ♓	" 14 ♓	" 10 ♓
♅	Ap 25 ♍	" 23 ♌	" 19 ♓	" 24 ♈	" 21 ♈	" 16 ♈
Ja 1 ♍	Jul 3 ♎	Ju 11 ♍	" 26 ♈	" 29 ♉	" 26 ♉	" 22 ♉
De 31 ♍	Se 6 ♏	" 29 ♎	" 31 ♉	Ma 4 ♊	" 31 ♊	" 27 ♊
" " "	No 5 ♐	Jul 18 ♏	Fe 5 ♊	" 9 ♋	Au 5 ♋	No 1 ♋
♄	De 30 ♑	Au 5 ♐	" 10 ♋	" 15 ♌	" 10 ♌	" 6 ♌
Ja 1 ♉	♀	" 24 ♑	" 15 ♌	" 20 ♍	" 16 ♍	" 12 ♍
De 31 ♉	Ja 1 ♐	Se 12 ♒	" 21 ♍	" 26 ♎	" 22 ♎	" 19 ♎
" " "	" 12 ♑	Oc 1 ♓	" 27 ♎	" " "	" 31 ♏	" 26 ♏
♃	" 31 ♒	" 20 ♈	" " "	" " "	" " "	De 7 ♐
Ja 1 ♉	Fe 18 ♓	No 8 ♉	Mh 8 ♏	Ju 4 ♏	" " "	" 18 ♑
Fe 19 ♊	Mh 9 ♈	" 27 ♊	" 18 ♐	" 14 ♐	Se 10 ♐	" 28 ♒
De 31 ♊	" 29 ♉	De 16 ♋	" 29 ♑	" 25 ♑	" 21 ♑	" 31 ♒

Day	Jan.	Feb.	Mch.	April	May	June	July	Aug.	Sept.	Oct.	Nov.	Dec.
1	♉	♋	♌	♍	♎	♐	♑	♓	♉	♊	♋	♌
2	♊	..	..	♎	♏	♑	♒	♈	..	..	♌	♍
3	..	♌	..	..	..	..	..	..	..	..	..	..
4	♋	..	♍	♏	♐	♒	♓	..	♊	♋	..	♎
5	..	♍	..	..	..	..	..	♉	..	..	♍	..
6	..	..	♎	♐	♑	♓	♈	..	♋	♌	..	♏
7	♌	♎	..	..	..	..	..	♊	..	..	♎	..
8	..	..	♏	♑	♒	..	♉	..	..	♍	..	♐
9	♍	♏	..	..	..	♈	..	..	♌	..	♏	..
10	..	..	♐	♒	♓	..	..	♋	..	♎	..	♑
11	♎	..	..	..	..	♉	♊	..	♍	..	♐	..
12	..	♐	♑	..	♈	..	..	♌	..	..	..	♒
13	♏	..	..	♓	..	..	..	..	♎	♏	♑	..
14	..	♑	♒	..	..	♊	♋	..	..	..	..	..
15	♐	..	..	♈	♉	..	..	♍	♏	♐	♒	♓
16	..	♒	..	..	..	♋	♌	..	..	..	..	..
17	♑	..	♓	..	♊	..	..	♎	♐	♑	♓	♈
18	..	♓	..	♉	..	..	♍	..	..	..	..	..
19	..	..	♈	..	..	♌	..	♏	♑	♒	..	♉
20	♒	..	..	♊	♋	..	..	..	..	..	♈	..
21	..	♈	♉	..	..	♍	♎	♐	..	♓	..	..
22	♓	..	..	..	♌	..	..	..	♒	..	♉	♊
23	..	♉	..	♋	..	♎	♏	♑	..	♈	..	..
24	♈	..	♊	..	..	..	..	..	♓	..	..	♋
25	..	..	..	♌	♍	♏	♐	♒	..	..	♊	..
26	..	♊	♋	..	..	..	..	..	♈	♉	..	..
27	♉	..	..	♍	♎	♐	♑	♓	..	..	♋	♌
28	..	♋	..	..	..	..	..	..	♉	♊	..	..
29	♊		♌	..	♏	♑	♍	..	..	..	..	♍
30	..		..	♎	..	..	..	♈	..	..	♌	..
31	..		♍		♐		♓	..		♋		..

1883—EPHEMERIS OF THE PLANETS AND THE MOON—1883

♆	♂	♀	♀	☿	☿	☿
Ja 1 ♉	Ja 1 ♑	Ap 6 ♑	De 25 ♓	Mh 28 ♒	Jul 1 ♓	Oc 3 ♈
De 31 ♉	Fe 18 ♒	" 25 ♒	☿	Ap 4 ♓	" 7 ♈	" 9 ♉
♅	Ap 7 ♓	Ma 14 ♓	Ja 1 ♒	" 10 ♈	" 13 ♉	" 14 ♊
Ja 1 ♍	Ma 24 ♈	Ju 2 ♈	" 6 ♓	" 16 ♉	" 18 ♊	" 19 ♋
De 31 ♍	Jul 12 ♉	" 21 ♉	" 12 ♈	" 21 ♊	" 23 ♋	" 24 ♌
♄	De 4 ♊	Jul 9 ♊	" 18 ♉	" 26 ♋	" 28 ♌	" 29 ♍
Ja 1 ♉	No 1 ♋	" 28 ♋	" 23 ♊	Ma 1 ♌	Au 2 ♍	No 5 ♎
Ju 2 ♊	♀	Au 15 ♌	" 28 ♋	" 6 ♍	" 9 ♎	" 14 ♏
De 31 ♊	Ja 1 ♋	Se 3 ♍	Fe 2 ♌	" 13 ♎	" 18 ♏	" 25 ♐
" " "	" 3 ♌	" 22 ♎	" 8 ♍	" 22 ♏	" 28 ♐	De 4 ♑
♃	" 21 ♍	Oc 10 ♏	" 14 ♎	" " "	" " "	" 15 ♒
Ja 1 ♊	Fe 9 ♎	" 29 ♐	" 23 ♏	Ju 1 ♐	Se 8 ♑	" 23 ♓
" 29 ♋	" 27 ♏	No 17 ♑	Mh 5 ♐	" 12 ♑	" 18 ♒	" 30 ♈
De 31 ♋	Mh 18 ♐	De 6 ♒	" 16 ♑	" 22 ♒	" 26 ♓	" 31 ♈

Day	Jan.	Feb	Mch.	April	May	June	July	Aug.	Sept.	Oct.	Nov.	Dec.
1	♎	♐	♐	♒	♓	♉	♊	♋	♍	♎	♐	♑
2	..	..	..	..	..	..	..	♌	..	..	..	..
3	♏	♑	♑	♓	♈	..	♋	..	♎	♏	♑	♒
4	..	..	..	..	..	♊	..	..	..	..	..	..
5	♐	♒	♒	♈	♉	..	..	♍	..	♐	..	♓
6	..	..	..	..	..	♋	♌	..	♏	..	♒	..
7	♑	♓	♓	..	♊	..	..	♎	..	♑	..	♈
8	..	..	..	♉	..	..	♍	..	♐	..	♓	..
9	♒	..	♈	..	..	♌	..	♏	..	♒	..	♉
10	..	♈	..	♊	♋	..	..	..	♑	..	♈	..
11	♓	..	♉	..	..	♍	♎	..	..	♓	..	..
12	..	♉	..	..	♌	..	..	♐	♒	..	♉	♊
13	♈	..	..	♋	..	..	♏	..	..	..	..	..
14	..	♊	♊	..	..	♎	..	♑	♓	♈	..	♋
15	..	..	..	♌	♍	..	♐	..	..	..	♊	..
16	♉	..	♋	..	..	♏	..	♒	♈	♉	..	..
17	..	♋	..	..	♎	..	♑	..	..	..	♋	♌
18	♊	..	..	♍	..	♐	..	♓	♉	♊	..	..
19	..	♌	♌	..	♏	..	♒	..	..	..	♌	♍
20	..	..	..	♎	..	♑	..	♈	..	..	..	..
21	♋	..	♍	..	♐	..	♓	..	♊	♋	..	..
22	..	♍	..	♏	..	♒	..	♉	..	..	♍	♎
23	♌	..	♎	..	♑	..	♈	..	♋	♌	..	..
24	..	♎	..	♐	..	♓	..	♊	..	..	♎	♏
25	..	..	..	..	♒	..	..	..	..	..	..	..
26	♍	♏	♏	♑	..	♈	♉	..	♌	♍	..	♐
27	..	..	..	..	..	..	..	♋	..	..	♏	..
28	♎	♐	♐	♒	♓	♉	♊	..	♍	♎	..	♑
29	..		..	..	..	..	..	♌	..	..	♐	..
30	♏		♑	♓	♈	..	..	..	..	♏	..	♒
31	..		..		..		♋	..		..		..

1884—EPHEMERIS OF THE PLANETS AND THE MOON—1884

	♆		♂		♀		☿		☿		☿		☿
Ja	18	Ja	1♋	Ap	15♍	Ja	1♈	Ap	28	Jul	4☐	Oc	5♋
De	318	"	4♌	Ma	3♎	"	58	"	7☐	"	9♋	"	10♌
	♅		Mh	12♍	"	23♏	"	10☐	"	12♋	"	14♌	"	15♍
Ja	1♍	Ma	20♎	Ju	10♐	"	15♋	"	17♌	"	19♍	"	27♎
De	31♍	Jul	24♏	"	28♑	"	20♌	"	22♍	"	26♎	"	31♏
"	"	"	Se	22♐	Jul	18♒	"	26♍	"	29♎	Au	4♏	No	10♐
	♄		No	17♑	Au	6♓	Fe	1♎	Ma	8♏	"	14♐	"	21♑
Ja	1☐	♀	"	24♈	"	9♏	"	18♐	"	25♑	"	" "
De	31☐	Ja	1♓	Se	12♉	"	20♐	"	29♑	"	" "	De	1♒
"	" "	"	12♈	Oc	2☐	"	" "	"	" "	Se	4♒	"	9♓
	♃	Fe	18	"	19♋	Mh	2♑	Ju	8♒	"	12♓	"	16♈
Ja	1♋	"	19☐	No	7♌	"	12♒	"	16♓	"	19♈	"	22♉
"	25♌	Mh	9♋	"	25♍	"	20♓	"	23♈	"	23♉	"	27☐
De	31♌	"	28♌	De	14♎	"	27♈	"	27♉	"	30☐	"	31☐

Day	Jan.	Feb.	Mch.	Apr.	May	June	July	Aug.	Sept.	Oct.	Nov.	Dec.
1	♒	♈	♉	☐	♌	♍	♎	♐	♑	♒	♈	♉
2	..	..	..	♋	..	♎	♏	..	..	♒	♓	☐
3	♓	♉	..	..	..	..	..	♑	..	..	♉	..
4	..	..	☐	♌	♍	..	..	..	♓	♈	..	♋
5	♈	☐	..	..	..	♏	♐	..	..	..	☐	..
6	..	..	♋	♍	♎	..	..	♒	..	♉	..	♌
7	♉	..	..	..	..	♐	♑	..	♈	..	♋	..
8	..	♋	♌	..	..	..	..	♓	..	☐	..	♍
9	☐	..	..	♎	♏	..	..	..	♉	..	♌	..
10	..	♌	♍	..	..	♑	♒	♈	..	♋	..	♎
11	♋	..	..	♏	♐	..	..	..	☐	..	♍	..
12	..	♍	♎	..	..	♒	♓	..	..	♌	..	..
13	♌	..	..	..	..	..	..	♉	♋	..	♎	♏
14	..	♎	..	♐	♑	..	♈	..	..	..	..	..
15	..	..	♏	..	..	♓	..	☐	♌	♍	..	♐
16	♍	..	..	♑	♒	..	♉	..	..	..	♏	..
17	..	♏	♐	..	..	♈	..	♋	♍	♎	..	..
18	♎	..	..	♒	♓	..	☐	..	..	..	♐	♑
19	..	♐	♑	♒	..	♉	..	♌	..	♏	..	..
20	♏	..	..	..	♈	..	♋	..	♎	..	..	♒
21	..	..	♒	♓	..	☐	..	♍	..	..	♑	..
22	..	♑	♒	..	♉	..	♌	..	♏	♐	..	♓
23	♐	..	..	♈	♉	♋	♌	♎	..	..	♒	..
24	..	♒	♓	..	..	..	..	..	♐	♑	..	..
25	♑	..	..	♉	☐	♌	♍	..	♐	..	♓	♈
26	..	♓	..	..	..	..	..	♏	..	..	..	..
27	..	..	♈	☐	♋	♍	♎	..	♑	♒	..	♉
28	♒	"	..	..	..	..	♐	..	..	♓	..
29	..	..	♉	♋	♌	..	♏	..	..	♓	..
30	♓	..	..	..	♎	..	..	♒	..	♉	☐
31	..	..	☐	..	♍	..	♑	..	♈	..

1885—EPHEMERIS OF THE PLANETS AND THE MOON—1885

♆	♂	♀	☿	☿	☿	☿
Ja 1 ♉	Fe 21 ♓	Ap 26 ♉	Ja 1 ♋	Ap 4 ♌	Jul 6 ♍	Oc 2 ♍
De 31 ♉	Ap 10 ♈	Ma 15 ♊	" 6 ♌	" 9 ♍	" 13 ♎	" 9 ♎
♅	Ma 30 ♉	Ju 1 ♋	" 12 ♍	" 16 ♎	" 22 ♏	" 18 ♏
Ja 1 ♍	Jul 22 ♊	" 20 ♌	" 18 ♎	" 25 ♏	Au 1 ♐	" 28 ♐
" 11 ♎	Se 18 ♋	Jul 9 ♍	" 27 ♏	Ma 5 ♐	" 12 ♑	No 8 ♑
♄	No 22 ♌	" 27 ♎	Fe 6 ♐	" 16 ♑	" 19 ♒	" 18 ♒
Ja 1 ♊	♀	Au 14 ♏	" 17 ♑	" 26 ♒	" 28 ♓	" 26 ♓
Au 16 ♋	Ja 1 ♎	Se 3 ♐	" 27 ♒	" " "	" " "	De 3 ♈
♃	" 3 ♏	" 21 ♑	" " "	Ju 3 ♓	" " "	" 9 ♉
Ja 1 ♌	" 21 ♐	Oc 10 ♒	Mh 8 ♓	" 10 ♈	Se 6 ♈	" 14 ♊
Fe 7 ♍	Fe 8 ♑	" 29 ♓	" 14 ♈	" 16 ♉	" 12 ♉	" 19 ♋
♂	" 27 ♒	No 18 ♈	" 20 ♉	" 21 ♊	" 17 ♊	" 24 ♌
Ja 1 ♑	Mh 19 ♓	De 6 ♉	" 25 ♊	" 26 ♋	" 22 ♋	" 29 ♍
" 5 ♒	Ap 6 ♈	" 24 ♊	" 30 ♋	" 31 ♌	" 27 ♌	" 31 ♍

Day	Jan	Feb.	Mch.	April	May	June	July	Aug.	Sept.	Oct.	Nov.	Dec.
1	♋	♌	♍	♎	♏	♑	♒	♈	♊	♋	♌	♎
2	..	♍	..	♏	♐	..	♓	..	..	..	♍	..
3	♌	..	..	..	..	♒	..	♉	♋	♌	..	..
4	..	♎	♎	..	♑	..	♈	..	..	..	♎	♏
5	♍	..	..	♐	..	♓	..	♊	..	♍	..	..
6	..	..	♏	..	..	..	♉	..	♌	..	..	♐
7	..	♏	..	♑	♒	♈	..	♋	..	..	♏	..
8	♎	..	..	..	..	..	..	..	♍	♎	..	..
9	..	♐	♐	♒	♓	♉	♊	♌	..	..	♐	♑
10	♏	..	..	..	..	..	..	..	..	♏	..	..
11	..	♑	♑	♓	♈	♊	♋	..	♎	..	..	♒
12	♐	..	..	..	..	..	..	♍	..	..	♑	..
13	..	..	♒	♈	♉	♋	♌	..	♏	♐	..	♓
14	..	♒	..	..	..	..	..	♎	..	..	♒	..
15	♑	..	♓	♉	♊	..	..	..	..	♑	..	♈
16	..	♓	..	..	..	♌	♍	..	♐	..	♓	..
17	♒	..	♈	♊	♋	..	..	♏	..	..	..	..
18	..	♈	..	..	..	♍	♎	..	♑	♒	♈	♉
19	♓	..	♉	..	♌	..	..	♐	..	..	..	..
20	..	♉	..	♋	..	..	..	..	♒	♓	♉	♊
21	♈	..	♊	..	..	♎	♏	..	..	..	..	..
22	..	♊	..	♌	♍	..	..	♑	♓	♈	♊	♋
23	♉	..	♋	..	..	♏	♐	..	..	..	..	..
24	..	♋	..	..	♎	..	..	♒	♈	♉	♋	♌
25	♊	..	..	♍	..	..	♑	..	..	..	..	..
26	..	♌	♌	..	..	♐	..	♓	♉	♊	..	♍
27	..	..	..	♎	♏	..	♒	..	..	..	♌	..
28	♋	..	♍	..	..	♑	..	♈	♊	♋	..	..
29	..		..	..	♐	..	♓	..	..	..	♍	♎
30	♌		..	♏	..	♒	..	♉	..	♌	..	..
31	..		♎		..		..	..		..		♏

1886—EPHEMERIS OF THE PLANETS AND THE MOON—1886

♆	♂	♀	☿	☿	☿	☿
Ja 1 ♉	Ja 29 ♍	Ma 4 ♑	Ja 1 ♍	Ap 3 ♎	Jul 9 ♏	Oc 4 ♏
De 31 ♉	Mh 7 ♎	" 22 ♒	" 5 ♎	" 11 ♏	" 19 ♐	" 15 ♐
♅	Ju 11 ♏	Ju 10 ♓	" 14 ♏	" 22 ♐	" 30 ♑	" 26 ♑
Ja 1 ♎	Au 10 ♐	" 29 ♈	" 24 ♐	Ma 3 ♑	Au 9 ♒	No 5 ♒
De 31 ♎	Oc 3 ♑	Jul 18 ♉	Fe 4 ♑	" 13 ♒	" 17 ♓	" 13 ♓
♄	No 23 ♒	Au 6 ♊	" 14 ♒	" 21 ♓	" 24 ♈	" 20 ♈
Ja 1 ♋	♀	" 25 ♋	" 22 ♓	" 28 ♈	" 30 ♉	" 26 ♉
De 31 ♋	Ja 1 ♊	Se 12 ♌	" " "	" " "	" " "	" " "
♃	" 13 ♋	" 30 ♍	Mh 1 ♈	Ju 3 ♉	" " "	De 1 ♊
Ja 1 ♍	" 30 ♌	Oc 20 ♎	" 7 ♉	" 8 ♊	Se 4 ♊	" 6 ♋
Mh 6 ♎	Fe 18 ♍	No 7 ♏	" 12 ♊	" 13 ♋	" 9 ♋	" 11 ♌
De 31 ♎	Mh 8 ♎	" 25 ♐	" 17 ♋	" 18 ♌	" 14 ♌	" 16 ♍
♂	" 27 ♏	De 15 ♑	" 22 ♌	" 23 ♍	" 19 ♍	" 23 ♎
Ja 1 ♌	Ap 21 ♐	" 31 ♑	" 27 ♍	" 30 ♎	" 26 ♎	" 31 ♏

Day	Jan.	Feb.	Mch.	April	May	June	July	Aug.	Sept.	Oct.	Nov.	Dec.
1	♏	♐	♑	♓	♈	♊	♋	♍	♎	♏	♑	♒
2	..	♑	♒	..	♉	..	♌	..	♏	♐	..	..
3	♐	..	..	♈	..	♋	..	♎	..	..	♒	♓
4	..	♒	♓	..	♊	..	♍	..	..	♑	..	..
5	♑	..	..	♉	..	♌	..	..	♐	..	♓	♈
6	..	♓	♈	..	♋	..	..	♏	..	..	..	..
7	♒	..	..	♊	..	♍	♎	..	♑	♒	..	♉
8	..	♈	♉	..	♌	..	..	♐	..	..	♈	..
9	..	..	..	♋	..	..	♏	..	♒	♓	..	♊
10	♓	♉	♊	..	..	♎	..	..	..	..	♉	..
11	..	..	..	♌	♍	..	..	♑	..	♈	..	♋
12	♈	♊	..	..	..	♏	♐	..	♓	..	♊	..
13	..	..	♋	♍	♎	..	..	♒	..	♉	..	♌
14	♉	♋	..	..	..	..	♑	..	♈	..	♋	..
15	..	..	♌	..	..	♐	..	♓	..	♊	..	♍
16	♊	..	..	♎	♏	..	..	..	♉	..	♌	..
17	..	♌	♍	..	..	♑	♒	♈	..	♋	..	..
18	♋	..	..	..	♐	..	..	..	♊	..	♍	♎
19	..	♍	..	♏	..	♒	♓	♉	..	♌	..	..
20	♌	..	♎	..	..	..	..	..	♋	..	♎	♏
21	..	♎	..	♐	♑	..	♈	..	..	..	..	..
22	..	..	♏	..	..	♓	..	♊	♌	♍	..	..
23	♍	..	..	..	♒	..	♉	..	..	..	♏	♐
24	..	♏	..	♑	..	♈	..	♋	♍	♎	..	..
25	♎	..	♐	..	♓	..	♊	..	..	..	♐	♑
26	..	♐	..	♒	..	♉	..	♌	..	..	..	..
27	..	..	♑	..	..	..	♋	..	♎	♏	..	..
28	♏	♑	..	♓	♈	♊	..	♍	..	..	♑	♒
29	..		..	..	..	..	..	..	♏	♐	..	..
30	♐		♒	♈	♉	♋	♌	..	..	..	♒	♓
31	..				..	..	..	♎		..		..

1887—EPHEMERIS OF THE PLANETS AND THE MOON—1887

♆	♂	♀	☿	☿	☿	☿
Ja 1 ♉	Fe 26 ♑	Ap 25 ♌	Ja 1 ♏	Ap 9 ♐	Jul 6 ♐	Oc 1 ♐
De 31 ♉	Ap 16 ♒	Ma 13 ♍	" 11 ♐	" 20 ♑	" 17 ♑	" 13 ♑
♅	Ju 9 ♓	Ju 1 ♎	" 21 ♑	" 30 ♒	" 27 ♒	" 23 ♒
Ja 1 ♎	Au 6 ♈	" 19 ♏	Fe 1 ♒	Ma 8 ♓	" " "	" 31 ♓
De 31 ♎	Oc 9 ♉	Jul 8 ♐	" 9 ♓	" 15 ♈	Au 4 ♓	No 7 ♈
♄	De 16 ♊	" 27 ♑	" 16 ♈	" 21 ♉	" 11 ♈	" 13 ♉
Ja 1 ♋	♀	Au 16 ♒	" 22 ♉	" 26 ♊	" 17 ♉	" 16 ♊
Oc 31 ♌	Ja 1 ♑	Se 3 ♓	" 27 ♊	" " "	" 22 ♊	" 23 ♋
♃	" 2 ♒	" 22 ♈	" " "	" " "	" 27 ♋	" 27 ♌
Ja 1 ♎	" 21 ♓	Oc 11 ♉	Mh 4 ♋	" 31 ♋	" 31 ♌	" " "
Ap 7 ♏	Fe 9 ♈	" 29 ♊	" 9 ♌	Ju 5 ♌	" " "	De 3 ♍
♂	" 28 ♉	No 17 ♋	" 14 ♍	" 10 ♍	Se 6 ♍	" 10 ♎
Ja 1 ♏	Mh 19 ♊	De 6 ♌	" 21 ♎	" 17 ♎	" 13 ♎	" 18 ♏
" 25 ♐	Ap 7 ♋	" 24 ♍	" 29 ♏	" 25 ♏	" 21 ♏	" 29 ♐

Day	Jan.	Feb.	Mch.	Apr.	May	June	July	Aug.	Sept.	Oct.	Nov.	Dec.
1	♈	♉	♊	♌	♍	♎	♏	♑	♒	♈	♉	♋
2	..	♊	..	..	..	♏	♐	..	♓	..	♊	..
3	♉	..	♋	..	♎	..	..	♒	..	..	..	♌
4	..	♋	..	♍	..	♐	♑	..	♈	♉	♋	..
5	♊	..	♌	..	..	..	..	♓	..	..	..	..
6	..	♌	..	♎	♏	..	..	..	♉	♊	♌	♍
7	♋	..	♍	..	..	♑	♒	..	..	..	..	..
8	..	♍	..	♏	♐	..	..	♈	♊	♋	♍	♎
9	..	..	..	..	..	..	♓	..	..	..	..	..
10	♌	♎	♎	..	..	♒	..	♉	..	♌	..	♏
11	..	..	..	♐	♑	..	..	..	♋	..	♎	..
12	♍	..	♏	..	..	♓	♈	♊	..	♍	..	..
13	..	♏	..	♑	♒	..	..	..	♌	..	♏	♐
14	♎	..	..	..	..	♈	♉	♋	..	♎	..	..
15	..	♐	♐	..	..	..	..	..	♍	..	♐	♑
16	♏	..	..	♒	♓	♉	♊	♌	..	..	..	..
17	..	..	♑	..	..	..	..	..	♎	♏	..	..
18	..	♑	..	♓	♈	♊	♋	♍	..	..	♑	♒
19	♐	..	..	..	..	..	..	..	♏	♐	..	..
20	..	♒	♒	..	♉	♋	♌	..	..	..	♒	♓
21	♑	..	..	♈	..	..	..	♎	..	♑	..	..
22	..	..	♓	..	♊	♌	♍	..	♐	..	..	..
23	..	♓	..	♉	..	..	..	♏	..	..	♓	♈
24	♒	..	♈	..	♋	..	♎	..	♑	♒	..	..
25	..	♈	..	♊	..	♍	..	♐	..	..	♈	♉
26	♓	..	♉	..	♌	..	..	..	..	♓	..	..
27	..	♉	..	♋	..	♎	♏	..	♒	..	♉	♊
28	♈	..	♊	..	♍	..	..	♑	..	..	..	..
29	.		..	♌	..	♏	♐	..	♓	♈	♊	..
30	..		♋	..	..	..	..	♒	..	..	..	♋
31	♉		..		♎		..	..		♉		..

1888—EPHEMERIS OF THE PLANETS AND THE MOON—1888

♆	♂	♀	☿	☿	☿	☿
Ja 1 ♉	Ja 1 ♍	Ap 15 ♓	Ja 1 ♐	Ap 6 ♑	Jul 3 ♑	Oc 9 ♒
" 27 ♊	Fe 23 ♎	Ma 4 ♈	" 9 ♑	" 16 ♒	" 13 ♒	" 17 ♓
De 31 ♊	Ap 28 ♏	" 22 ♉	" 19 ♒	" 24 ♓	" 21 ♓	" 24 ♈
♅	Ju 27 ♐	Ju 10 ♊	" 27 ♓	Ma 1 ♈	" 28 ♈	" 30 ♉
Ja 1 ♎	Au 22 ♑	" 29 ♋	Fe 1 ♈	" 7 ♉	Au 3 ♉	No 4 ♊
De 31 ♎	Oc 10 ♒	Jul 17 ♌	" 9 ♉	" 12 ♊	" 8 ♊	" 8 ♋
♄	No 27 ♓	Au 5 ♍	" 14 ♊	" 16 ♋	" 12 ♋	" 14 ♌
Ja 1 ♌	♀	" 23 ♎	" 19 ♋	" 22 ♌	" 17 ♌	" 19 ♍
De 31 ♌	Ja 1 ♍	Se 11 ♏	" 23 ♌	" 27 ♍	" 25 ♍	" 26 ♎
" " "	" 13 ♎	Oc 1 ♐	" " "	" " "	" 30 ♎	" " "
♃	" 30 ♏	" 18 ♑	Mh 2 ♍	" " "	" " "	De 4 ♏
Ja 1 ♏	Fe 18 ♐	No 7 ♒	" 7 ♎	Ju 3 ♎	Se 7 ♏	" 17 ♐
Ma 2 ♐	Mh 8 ♑	" 26 ♓	" 15 ♏	" 11 ♏	" 17 ♐	" 25 ♑
De 31 ♐	" 27 ♒	De 14 ♈	" 25 ♐	" 22 ♐	" 29 ♑	" 31 ♑

Day	Jan.	Feb.	Mch.	April	May	June	July	Aug.	Sept.	Oct.	Nov.	Dec.
1	♌	♍	♏	♏	♐	♑	♓	♈	♊	♋	♍	♎
2	..	♎	♎	..	..	♒	..	♉	..	♌	..	♏
3	..	..	..	♐	♑	..	..	..	♋	..	♎	..
4	♍	..	♏	..	..	♓	♈	♊	..	♍	..	..
5	..	♏	..	♑	♒	..	..	..	♌	..	♏	♐
6	♎	..	..	..	..	♈	♉	♋	..	♎	..	..
7	..	♐	♐	..	..	..	..	..	♍	..	♐	♑
8	♏	..	..	♒	♓	♉	♊	♌	..	..	..	..
9	..	..	♑	..	..	..	..	..	♎	♏	..	..
10	..	♑	..	♓	♈	..	♋	♍	..	..	♑	♒
11	♐	..	..	..	..	♊	..	..	♏	♐	..	..
12	..	♒	♒	..	♉	..	♌	..	..	..	♒	♓
13	..	..	..	♈	..	♋	..	♎	..	♑	..	..
14	♑	..	♓	..	♊	..	♍	..	♐	..	..	..
15	..	♓	..	♉	..	♌	..	♏	..	..	♓	♈
16	♒	..	♈	..	♋	..	♎	..	♑	♒	..	..
17	..	♈	..	♊	..	♍	..	♐	..	..	♈	♉
18	♓	..	♉	..	♌	..	..	..	..	♓	..	..
19	..	♉	..	♋	..	♎	♏	..	♈	..	♉	♊
20	..	..	..	..	..	..	..	♑	..	..	..	..
21	♈	♊	♊	♌	♍	♏	♐	..	♓	♈	♊	♋
22	..	..	..	..	..	..	..	♒	..	..	..	..
23	♉	♋	♋	♍	♎	..	..	..	..	♉	..	♌
24	..	..	..	..	..	♐	♑	..	♈	..	♋	..
25	♊	♌	♌	♎	♏	..	..	♓	..	♊	..	♍
26	..	..	..	..	..	♑	♒	..	♉	..	♌	..
27	♋	..	♍	..	..	..	..	♈	..	♋	..	♎
28	..	♍	..	♏	♐	..	..	..	♊	..	♍	..
29	♌		♎	..	..	♒	♓	..	..	♌	..	♏
30	..		..	♐	♑	..	..	♉	♋	..	♎	..
31	♍		♏		..		♈	..		..		♐

1889—EPHEMERIS OF THE PLANETS AND THE MOON—1889

♆	♂	♀	☿	☿	☿	☿
Ja 1 ♊	Ja 11 ♈	Ap 24 ♏	Ja 1 ♑	Ap 2 ♒	Jul 8 ♓	Oc 4 ♓
De 31 ♊	Mh 3 ♉	Ma 13 ♐	" 3 ♒	" 11 ♓	" 15 ♈	" 11 ♈
♅	Ap 25 ♊	" 31 ♑	" 13 ♓	" 17 ♐	" 20 ♉	" 16 ♉
Ja 1 ♎	Ju 23 ♋	Ju 19 ♒	" 20 ♈	" 23 ♉	" 25 ♊	" 21 ♊
De 31 ♎	Au 26 ♌	Jul 8 ♓	" 26 ♉	" 28 ♊	" 30 ♋	" 26 ♋
♄	No 2 ♍	" 28 ♈	" 30 ♊	Ma 3 ♋	" " "	" 31 ♌
Ja 1 ♌	♀	Au 15 ♉	Fe 4 ♋	" 8 ♌	Au 4 ♌	No 6 ♍
De 31 ♌	Ja 1 ♈	Se 2 ♊	" 9 ♌	" 14 ♍	" 10 ♍	" 12 ♎
♃	" 2 ♉	" 21 ♋	" 15 ♍	" 21 ♎	" 16 ♎	" 21 ♏
Ja 1 ♐	" 21 ♊	Oc 9 ♌	" 22 ♎	" 29 ♏	" 25 ♏	" " "
Ma 14 ♑	Fe 8 ♋	" 28 ♍	" " "	" " "	" " "	De 1 ♐
De 31 ♑	" 27 ♌	No 16 ♎	Mh 2 ♏	Ju 8 ♐	Se 4 ♐	" 12 ♑
♂	Mh 17 ♍	De 4 ♏	" 12 ♐	" 19 ♑	" 15 ♑	" 19 ♒
Ja 1 ♓	Ap 5 ♎	" 23 ♐	" 23 ♑	" 29 ♒	" 25 ♒	" 31 ♓

Day	Jan.	Feb.	Mch.	April	May	June	July	Aug.	Sept.	Oct.	Nov.	Dec.
1	♐	♒	♒	♈	♉	♋	♌	♎	♏	♑	♒	♓
2	♑	..	♓	..	..	..	..	..	♐	..	..	..
3	..	♓	..	♉	♊	♌	♍	♏	..	♒	♓	♈
4	♒	..	..	..	..	..	..	..	♑	..	..	..
5	..	♈	♈	..	♋	♍	♎	..	..	♓	♈	♉
6	..	..	..	♊	..	..	..	♐	..	..	..	..
7	♓	..	♉	..	♌	♎	♏	..	♒	..	..	♊
8	..	♉	..	♋	..	..	..	♑	..	♈	♉	..
9	♈	..	♊	..	♍	♏	♐	..	♓	..	..	..
10	..	♊	..	♌	..	..	..	♒	..	♉	♊	♋
11	♉	..	..	..	..	♐	..	..	..	..	..	..
12	..	♋	♋	♍	♎	..	♑	..	♈	..	♋	♌
13	..	..	..	..	..	♑	..	♓	..	♊	..	..
14	♊	♌	♌	♎	♏	..	♒	..	♉	..	..	♍
15	..	..	..	..	..	..	..	♈	..	♋	♌	..
16	♋	♍	♍	♏	♐	♒	..	..	..	..	..	♎
17	..	..	..	..	..	..	♓	..	♊	♌	♍	..
18	♌	♎	♎	♐	♑	♓	..	♉	..	..	..	♏
19	..	..	..	..	..	..	♈	..	♋	..	♎	..
20	♍	♏	♏	..	♒	..	..	♊	..	♍	..	♐
21	..	..	..	♑	..	♈	..	..	♌	..	♏	..
22	♎	..	♐	..	..	..	♉	..	..	♎	..	..
23	..	♐	..	♒	♓	♉	..	♋	♍	..	♐	♑
24	♏	..	♑	..	..	..	♊	..	..	♏	..	..
25	..	♑	..	..	♈	..	..	♌	♎	..	♑	♒
26	♐	..	..	♓	..	♊	♋	..	..	♐	..	..
27	..	..	♒	..	..	..	..	♍	♏	..	..	♓
28	..	♒	..	♈	♉	♋	♌	..	..	♑	♒	..
29	♑		♓	..	..	..	..	♎	♐	..	..	..
30	..		..	..	♊	..	♍	..	..	..	♓	♈
31	♒		..		..		..	♏		♒		..

1890—EPHEMERIS OF THE PLANETS AND THE MOON—1890

♆	♂	♀	☿	☿	☿	☿
Ja 1 ♊	Ja 9 ♎	Ap 15 ♊	Ja 1 ♓	Ap 5 ♈	Jul 2 ♈	Oc 3 ♉
De 31 ♊	Mh 16 ♏	Ma 3 ♋	" 7 ♈	" 10 ♉	" 7 ♉	" 8 ♊
♅	Ma 15 ♐	" 22 ♌	" 12 ♉	" 15 ♊	" 12 ♊	" 13 ♋
Ja 1 ♎	Jul 8 ♑	Ju 10 ♍	" 17 ♊	" 20 ♋	" 17 ♋	" 18 ♌
De 31 ♎	Au 28 ♒	" 28 ♎	" 22 ♋	" 25 ♌	" 22 ♌	" 23 ♍
♄	Oc 15 ♓	Jul 17 ♏	" 27 ♌	Ma 1 ♍	" 27 ♍	" 30 ♎
Ja 1 ♌	De 1 ♈	Au 4 ♐	Fe 2 ♍	" 7 ♎	Au 3 ♎	No 8 ♏
Fe 4 ♍	♀	" 23 ♑	" 8 ♎	" 16 ♏	" 12 ♏	" 18 ♐
De 31 ♍	Ja 1 ♐	Se 11 ♒	" 17 ♏	" 26 ♐	" 22 ♐	" 29 ♑
♃	" 11 ♑	" 30 ♓	" 27 ♐	" " "	" " "	" " "
Ja 1 ♑	" 30 ♒	Oc 19 ♈	" " "	" " "	Se 2 ♑	De 7 ♒
Ma 7 ♒	Fe 18 ♓	No 7 ♉	Mh 10 ♑	Ju 6 ♑	" 12 ♒	" 18 ♓
♂	Mh 8 ♈	" 26 ♊	" 20 ♒	" 16 ♒	" 21 ♓	" 24 ♈
Ja 1 ♍	" 27 ♉	De 14 ♋	Mh 29 ♓	" 25 ♓	" 27 ♈	" 30 ♉

Day	Jan.	Feb.	Mch.	April	May	June	July	Aug.	Sept.	Oct.	Nov.	Dec.
1	♈	♊	♋	♍	♎	♐	♑	♓	♈	♉	♋	♌
2	♉	♋	♌	..	♏	..	♒	..	♉	♊	..	..
3	..	..	..	♎	..	♑	..	♈	..	..	♌	♍
4	♊	..	♍	..	♐	..	♓	..	..	♋	..	..
5	..	♌	..	♏	..	♒	..	..	♊	..	♍	♎
6	♋	..	♎	..	♑	..	..	♉	..	..	..	..
7	..	♍	..	♐	..	♓	♈	..	♋	♌	♎	♏
8	♌	..	♏	..	♒	..	..	♊	..	..	..	..
9	..	♎	..	♑	..	..	♉	..	♌	♍	♏	♐
10	♍	..	♐	..	..	♈	..	..	..	..	..	..
11	..	♏	..	♒	♓	..	..	♋	..	♎	♐	♑
12	♎	..	♑	..	..	♉	♊	..	♍	..	..	..
13	..	♐	..	♓	♈	..	..	♌	..	♏	♑	♒
14	♏	..	..	..	..	..	♋	..	♎	..	..	..
15	..	♑	♒	..	..	♊	..	♍	..	♐	..	♓
16	..	..	..	♈	♉	..	..	..	♏	..	♒	..
17	♐	..	♓	.	..	♋	♌	♎	..	♑	..	..
18	..	♒	..	..	♊	..	..	..	♐	..	♓	♈
19	♑	..	..	♉	..	♌	♍	♏	..	♒	..	..
20	..	♓	♈	..	..	..	..	..	♑	..	♈	♉
21	♒	..	..	♊	♋	♍	♎	♐	..	..	..	..
22	..	♈	♉	..	..	..	..	..	♒	♓	..	..
23	..	..	..	♋	♌	..	♏	♑	..	..	♉	♊
24	♓	♉	..	..	..	♎	..	..	♓	♈	..	..
25	..	..	♊	..	♍	..	♐	..	..	..	♊	♋
26	♈	♊	..	♌	..	♏	..	♒	..	..	..	..
27	..	..	♋	..	♎	..	♑	..	♈	♉	..	..
28	..	♋	..	♍	..	♐	..	♓	..	..	♋	♌
29	♉	..	..	..	♏	..	♒	..	♉	♊	..	..
30	..		♌	♎	..	♑	..	..	..	..	♌	♍
31	♊		..		♐		..	♈		..		..

1891—EPHEMERIS OF THE PLANETS AND THE MOON—1891

♆	♂	♀	☿	☿	☿	☿
Ja 1 ♊	Ja 1 ♈	Ap 24 ♒	Ja 1 ♉	Ap 2 ♊	Jul 4 ♋	Oc 5 ♌
De 31 ♊	" 18 ♉	Ma 13 ♓	" 4 ♊	" 7 ♋	" 9 ♌	" 10 ♍
♅	Mh 14 ♊	Ju 1 ♈	" 9 ♋	" 12 ♌	" 14 ♍	" 17 ♎
Ja 1 ♎	Ma 11 ♋	" 20 ♉	" 14 ♌	" 17 ♍	" 21 ♎	" 26 ♏
Ju 8 ♏	Jul 14 ♌	Jul 9 ♊	" 19 ♍	" 24 ♎	" 30 ♏	" " "
De 31 ♏	Se 20 ♍	" 27 ♋	" 26 ♎	Ma 3 ♏	Au 9 ♐	No 5 ♐
♄	No 27 ♎	Au 15 ♌	Fe 4 ♏	" 13 ♐	" 20 ♑	" 16 ♑
Ja 1 ♍	♀	Se 2 ♍	" 14 ♐	" 24 ♑	" 30 ♒	" 25 ♒
De 31 ♍	Ja 1 ♌	" 20 ♎	" 25 ♑	" " "	" " "	De 4 ♓
" " "	" 20 ♍	Oc 9 ♏	" " "	Ju 3 ♒	Se 7 ♓	" 11 ♈
♃	Fe 8 ♎	" 28 ♐	Mh 7 ♒	" 12 ♓	" 15 ♈	" 17 ♉
Ja 1 ♒	" 26 ♏	No 16 ♑	" 15 ♓	" 18 ♈	" 20 ♉	" 22 ♊
Ap 13 ♓	Mh 17 ♐	De 5 ♒	" 23 ♈	" 24 ♉	" 25 ♊	" 27 ♋
De 31 ♓	Ap 5 ♑	" 24 ♓	" 28 ♉	" 29 ♊	" 30 ♋	" 31 ♋

Day	Jan.	Feb.	Mch.	Apr.	May	June	July	Aug.	Sept.	Oct.	Nov.	Dec.
1	♎	♐	♐	♒	♒	♈	♉	♋	♌	♎	♏	♑
2	..	..	..	..	♓	♉	♊	..	♍	..	♐	..
3	♏	..	♑	..	..	..	..	♌	..	♏	..	♒
4	..	♑	..	♓	♈	♊	♋	..	♎	..	♑	..
5	♐	..	♒	..	..	..	..	♍	..	♐	..	♓
6	..	♒	..	♈	..	..	..	..	♏	..	♒	..
7	♑	..	♓	..	♉	♋	♌	..	..	♑	..	..
8	..	♓	..	♉	..	..	..	♎	♐	..	♓	♈
9	♒	..	..	..	♊	♌	♍	..	..	..	..	..
10	..	♈	♈	..	..	..	..	♏	..	♒	♈	♉
11	..	..	..	♊	..	..	♎	..	♑	..	..	..
12	♓	..	♉	..	♋	♍	..	♐	..	♓	..	..
13	..	♉	..	..	..	..	..	..	♒	..	♉	♊
14	♈	..	..	♋	♌	♎	♏	♑	..	♈	..	..
15	..	♊	♊	..	..	..	..	..	..	..	♊	♋
16	♉	..	..	♌	..	♏	♐	♒	♓	..	..	..
17	..	..	♋	..	♍	..	..	..	..	♉	..	..
18	..	♋	..	♍	..	♐	♑	♓	♈	..	♋	♌
19	♊	..	..	..	♎	..	..	..	..	♊	..	..
20	..	♌	♌	..	..	♑	♒	♈	♉	..	♌	..
21	♋	..	..	♎	♏	..	..	..	..	..	..	♍
22	..	♍	♍	..	..	♒	♓	..	..	♋	..	..
23	..	..	..	♏	♐	..	..	♉	♊	..	♍	♎
24	♌	..	♎	..	..	♓	♈	..	..	♌	..	..
25	..	♎	..	♐	♑	..	..	♊	♋	..	♎	..
26	♍	..	♏	..	..	..	..	..	..	♍	..	♏
27	..	♏	..	♑	♒	♈	♉	..	..	..	♏	..
28	♎	..	♐	..	..	..	..	♋	♌	..	..	♐
29	..	..	..	..	♓	♉	♊	..	..	♎	♐	..
30	♏		♑	♒	..	..	..	♌	♍	..	..	♑
31	..		..		♈	..	..	..	..	♏		..

1892—EPHEMERIS OF THE PLANETS AND THE MOON—1892

♆	♂	♀	♀	☿	☿	☿
Ja 1 ♊	Ja 1 ♎	Mh 26 ♌	De 13 ♎	Mh 29 ♌	Jul 7 ♎	Oc 3 ♎
De 31 ♊	Fe 1 ♏	Ap 14 ♍	☿	Ap 3 ♍	" 16 ♏	" 12 ♏
♅	Ap 1 ♐	Ma 2 ♎	Ja 1 ♌	" 10 ♎	" 26 ♐	" 22 ♐
Ja 1 ♏	Ma 25 ♑	" 21 ♏	" 6 ♍	" 19 ♏	Au 6 ♑	" " "
De 31 ♏	Jul 15 ♒	Ju 9 ♐	" 13 ♎	" 29 ♐	" 16 ♒	No 2 ♑
♄	Au 31 ♓	" 27 ♑	" 22 ♏	Ma 10 ♑	" 24 ♓	" 12 ♒
Ja 1 ♍	Oc 18 ♈	Jul 16 ♒	Fe 1 ♐	" 20 ♒	" 31 ♈	" 20 ♓
Ju 19 ♎	De 6 ♉	Au 4 ♓	" 12 ♑	" 28 ♓	" " "	" 27 ♈
De 31 ♎	♀	" 23 ♈	" 22 ♒	Ju 4 ♈	" " "	De 3 ♉
♃	Ja 1 ♓	Se 11 ♉	Mh 1 ♓	" 10 ♉	Se 6 ♉	" 8 ♊
Ja 1 ♓	" 12 ♈	" 30 ♊	" 8 ♈	" 15 ♊	" 11 ♊	" 13 ♋
Mh 9 ♈	" 30 ♉	Oc 18 ♋	" 14 ♉	" 20 ♋	" 16 ♋	" 18 ♌
" " "	Fe 18 ♊	No 6 ♌	" 19 ♊	" 25 ♌	" 21 ♌	" 23 ♍
De 31 "	Mh 8 ♋	" 24 ♍	" 24 ♋	" 30 ♍	" 26 ♍	" 30 ♎

Day	Jan.	Feb.	Mch.	April	May	June	July	Aug.	Sept.	Oct.	Nov.	Dec.
1	♒	♓	♈	♉	♊	♌	♍	♏	♐	♒	♓	♈
2	..	♈	..	♊	..	..	♎	..	♑	..	♈	♉
3	♓	..	..	..	♋	♍	..	♐	..	♓	..	..
4	..	♉	♉	..	..	..	..	..	♒	..	..	♊
5	♈	..	..	♋	♌	♎	♏	♑	..	..	♉	..
6	..	..	♊	..	..	..	..	..	♓	♈	..	..
7	..	♊	..	♌	♍	♏	♐	..	..	..	♊	♋
8	♉	..	..	..	..	..	..	♒	♈	♉	..	..
9	..	♋	♋	..	♎	♐	♑	..	..	..	♋	♌
10	♊	..	..	♍	..	..	..	♓	..	..	..	..
11	..	♌	♌	..	♏	♑	♒	..	♉	♊	..	..
12	..	..	..	♎	..	..	..	♈	..	..	♌	♍
13	♋	..	♍	..	♐	..	♓	..	♊	♋	..	..
14	..	♍	..	♏	..	♒	..	♉	..	..	♍	♎
15	♌	..	♎	..	♑	..	..	..	..	..	..	..
16	..	♎	..	♐	..	♓	♈	..	♋	♌	..	♏
17	♍	..	♏	..	♒	..	..	♊	..	..	♎	..
18	..	♏	..	♑	..	♈	♉	..	♌	♍	..	♐
19	♎	..	♐	..	♓	..	..	..	..	..	♏	..
20	..	♐	..	♒	..	..	..	♋	..	♎	..	♑
21	..	..	♑	..	..	♉	♊	..	♍	..	♐	..
22	♏	♑	..	♓	♈	..	..	♌	..	♏	..	♒
23	..	..	..	..	..	♊	♋	..	♎	..	♑	..
24	♐	♒	♒	..	♉	..	..	♍	..	♐	..	♓
25	..	..	..	♈	..	..	..	..	♏	..	♒	..
26	♑	..	♓	..	..	♋	♌	♎	..	♑	..	♈
27	..	♓	..	♉	♊	..	..	..	♐	..	♓	..
28	♒	..	♈	..	..	♌	♏	♏	..	♒	..	..
29	..	..	..	..	♋	..	..	..	♑	..	♈	♉
30	♓		♉	♊	..	♍	♎	..	..	..	..	..
31	..		..		..		..	♐		♓		♊

1893—EPHEMERIS OF THE PLANETS AND THE MOON—1893

♆	♂	♀	☿	☿	☿	☿
Ja 1 ♊	Ja 29 ♊	Ma 13 ♊	Ja 1 ♎	Ap 6 ♏	Jul 2 ♏	Oc 9 ♐
De 31 ♊	Mh 29 ♋	Ju 1 ♋	" 8 ♏	" 16 ♐	" 13 ♐	" 21 ♑
♅	Ju 1 ♌	" 19 ♌	" 18 ♐	" 27 ♑	" 24 ♑	" 30 ♒
Ja 1 ♏	Au 8 ♍	Jul 7 ♍	" 29 ♑	Ma 10 ♒	Au 3 ♒	No 7 ♓
De 31 ♏	Se 22 ♎	" 25 ♎	Fe 8 ♒	" 15 ♓	" 11 ♓	" 14 ♈
♄	De 19 ♏	Au 13 ♏	" 16 ♓	" 22 ♈	" 18 ♈	" 20 ♉
Ja 1 ♎	♀	Se 1 ♐	" 23 ♈	" 28 ♉	" 24 ♉	" 25 ♊
De 31 ♎	Ja 1 ♏	" 20 ♑	Mh 1 ♉	Ju 2 ♊	" 29 ♊	" 30 ♋
♃	" 19 ♐	Oc 9 ♒	" 6 ♊	" 7 ♋	" " "	" " "
Ja 1 ♈	Fe 7 ♑	" 28 ♓	" 11 ♋	" 12 ♌	Se 3 ♋	De 5 ♌
" 30 ♉	" 26 ♒	No 17 ♈	" 16 ♌	" " "	" 8 ♌	" 10 ♍
De 29 ♊	Mh 17 ♓	De 5 ♉	" 21 ♍	" " "	" 13 ♍	" 16 ♎
♂	Ap 5 ♈	" 23 ♊	" " "	" 17 ♍	" 18 ♎	" 26 ♏
Ja 1 ♉	" 24 ♉	" 31 ♊	" 26 ♎	" 22 ♎	" 29 ♏	" 31 ♏

Day	Jan.	Feb.	Mch.	Apr.	May	June	July	Aug.	Sept.	Oct.	Nov.	Dec.
1	♊	♋	♌	♎	♏	♑	♒	♈	♊	♊	♌	♍
2	..	♌	♍	..	♐	..	♓	..	..	♋	..	♎
3	♋	..	..	♏	..	♒	..	♉	..	..	..	..
4	..	..	♎	..	♑	..	..	..	♋	♌	♍	..
5	♌	♍	..	♐	..	♓	♈	..	..	..	..	♏
6	..	..	..	..	♒	..	..	♊	..	..	♎	..
7	..	♎	♏	♑	..	♈	..	..	♌	♍	..	♐
8	♍	..	..	..	..	..	♉	♋	..	..	..	..
9	..	..	♐	♒	♓	..	..	..	♍	♎	♏	♑
10	♎	♏	..	..	..	♉	♊	..	..	..	..	..
11	..	..	♑	♓	♈	..	..	♌	..	♏	♐	♒
12	♏	♐	..	..	..	♊	..	..	♎	..	..	..
13	..	..	♒	..	♉	..	♋	♍	..	♐	♑	♓
14	♐	♑	..	♈	..	..	..	..	♏	..	..	..
15	..	..	♓	..	..	♋	♌	♎	..	..	♒	♈
16	♑	♒	..	♉	♊	..	..	..	♐	♑	..	..
17	..	..	♈	..	..	♌	..	..	..	..	♓	..
18	♒	♓	..	..	♋	..	♍	♏	♑	♒	..	♉
19	..	..	..	♊	..	..	..	..	..	..	♈	..
20	♓	♈	♉	..	..	♍	♎	♐	♒	♓	..	♊
21	..	..	..	♋	♌	..	..	..	..	..	♉	..
22	..	♉	♊	..	..	♎	♏	♑	♓	♈	..	..
23	♈	..	..	..	♍	..	..	..	..	..	♊	♋
24	..	..	..	♌	..	♏	..	♒	..	♉	..	..
25	♉	♊	♋	..	..	..	♐	..	♈	..	♋	♌
26	..	..	..	♍	♎	♐	..	♓	..	..	..	..
27	..	♋	♌	..	..	..	♑	..	♉	♊	..	..
28	♊	..	..	♎	♏	♑	..	♈	..	..	♌	♍
29	..		..	..	..	..	♒	..	♊	♋	..	..
30	♋		♍	♏	♐	♒	..	♉	..	..	♍	♎
31	..		..		..		♓	..		..		..

1894—EPHEMERIS OF THE PLANETS AND THE MOON—1894

♆	♂	♀	☿	☿	☿	☿
Ja 1 ♊	Ap 12 ♑	Ma 3 ♑	Ja 1 ♏	Ap 3 ♐	Jul 11 ♑	Oc 7 ♑
De 31 ♊	Ju 1 ♒	" 22 ♒	" 5 ♐	" 14 ♑	" 21 ♒	" 17 ♒
♅	Jul 19 ♓	Ju 10 ♓	" 16 ♑	" 24 ♒	" 29 ♓	" 25 ♓
Ja 1 ♏	Se 5 ♈	" 29 ♈	" 26 ♒	Ma 2 ♓	Au 5 ♈	No 1 ♈
De 31 ♏	Oc 21 ♉	Jul 17 ♉	Fe 3 ♓	" 9 ♈	" 11 ♉	" 7 ♉
♄	De 17 ♊	Au 5 ♊	" 10 ♈	" 15 ♉	" 16 ♊	" 12 ♊
Ja 1 ♎	♀	" 24 ♋	" 16 ♉	" 20 ♊	" 21 ♋	" 17 ♋
De 22 ♏	Ja 1 ♊	Se 11 ♌	" 21 ♊	" 25 ♋	" 26 ♌	" 22 ♌
♃	" 11 ♋	" 80 ♍	" 26 ♋	" 30 ♌	" 31 ♍	" 27 ♍
Ja 1 ♊	" 30 ♌	Oc 18 ♎	" " "	" " "	" " "	" " "
De 7 ♋	Fe 17 ♍	No 6 ♏	Mh 3 ♌	Ju 4 ♍	" " "	De 4 ♎
♂	Mh 8 ♎	" 25 ♐	" 8 ♍	" 11 ♎	Se 8 ♎	" 13 ♏
Ja 1 ♏	" 26 ♏	De 13 ♑	" 15 ♋	" 20 ♏	" 16 ♏	" 23 ♐
Fe 17 ♐	Ap 14 ♐	" 31 ♑	" 24 ♏	" 30 ♐	" 26 ♐	" 31 ♐

Day	Jan.	Feb	Mch.	April	May	June	July	Aug.	Sept.	Oct.	Nov.	Dec.
1	♎	♐	♐	♒	♓	♉	♊	♌	♎	♏	♐	♑
2	♏	♑	♑	♓	♈	♊	♋	..	..	..	♑	♒
3	..	..	..	..	..	..	..	♍	..	..	..	..
4	♐	♒	♒	♈	♉	..	♌	..	♏	♐	♒	♓
5	..	..	..	..	..	♋	..	..	..	..	..	..
6	♑	♓	♓	♉	♊	..	..	♎	..	♑	..	♈
7	..	..	..	..	..	♌	♍	..	♐	..	♓	..
8	♒	♈	♈	..	♋	..	..	♏	..	♒	..	♉
9	..	..	..	♊	..	..	♎	..	♑	..	♈	..
10	♓	..	♉	..	..	♍	..	♐	..	♓	..	♊
11	..	♉	..	♋	♌	..	..	..	♒	..	♉	..
12	♈	..	♊	..	..	♎	♏	♑	..	♈	..	..
13	..	♊	..	..	♍	..	..	..	♓	..	♊	♋
14	♉	..	..	♌	..	..	♐	♒	..	♉	..	..
15	..	♋	♋	..	..	♏	..	..	♈	..	♋	♌
16	..	..	..	♍	♎	..	♑	♓	..	..	..	..
17	♊	..	♌	..	..	♐	..	..	♉	♊	..	..
18	..	♌	..	♎	..	..	♒	♈	..	..	♌	♍
19	♋	..	..	..	..	♑	..	..	♊	♋	..	..
20	..	♍	♍	..	♐	..	♓	..	..	..	♍	♎
21	..	..	..	♏	..	♒	..	♉	♋	♌	..	..
22	♌	..	♎	..	♑	..	♈	..	♋	..	..	..
23	..	♎	..	♐	..	♓	..	♊	..	..	♎	♏
24	♍	..	..	..	♒	..	..	..	♌	♍	..	..
25	..	♏	♏	♑	..	♈	♉	♋	..	..	♏	♐
26	..	..	..	..	..	..	..	..	..	♎	..	..
27	♎	..	♐	♒	♓	♉	♊	♌	♍	..	♐	♑
28	..	♐	..	..	..	..	..	..	..	..	..	..
29	♏		♑	♓	♈	..	♋	♍	♎	♏	..	♒
30	..		..	..	..	♊	..	♏	..	..	♑	..
31	♐		♒		♉	..	..	..		♐		♓

249

1895—EPHEMERIS OF THE PLANETS AND THE MOON—1895

♆	♂	♀	☿	☿	☿	☿
Ja 1 ♊	Ap 19 ♌	Ap 24 ♌	Ja 1 ♐	Ap 1 ♑	Jul 8 ♒	Oc 4 ♒
De 31 ♊	Ju 25 ♍	Ma 12 ♍	" 3 ♑	" 11 ♒	" 16 ♓	" 12 ♓
♅	Se 1 ♎	" 31 ♎	" 13 ♒	" 19 ♓	" 23 ♈	" 19 ♈
Ja 1 ♏	No 6 ♏	Ju 18 ♏	" 21 ♓	" 26 ♈	" 29 ♉	" 25 ♉
De 31 ♏	De 31 ♏	Jul 7 ♐	" 28 ♈	Ma 2 ♉	Au 3 ♊	" 29 ♊
♄	♀	" 26 ♑	Fe 3 ♉	" 7 ♊	" 8 ♋	No 3 ♋
Ja 1 ♏	" " "	Au 14 ♒	" 8 ♊	" 12 ♋	" 13 ♌	" 8 ♌
De 31 ♏	" " "	Se 2 ♓	" 13 ♋	" 17 ♌	" 18 ♍	" 14 ♍
♃	Ja 1 ♒	" 21 ♈	" 18 ♌	" 22 ♍	" 25 ♎	" 21 ♎
Ja 1 ♋	" 20 ♓	Oc 10 ♉	" 23 ♍	" 29 ♎	" " "	" 29 ♏
De 3 ♌	Fe 8 ♈	" 29 ♊	" " "	" " "	" " "	" " "
♂	" 27 ♉	No 16 ♋	Mh 3 ♎	Ju 6 ♏	Se 3 ♏	De 10 ♐
Ja 1 ♊	Mh 18 ♊	De 5 ♌	" 11 ♏	" 17 ♐	" 13 ♐	" 20 ♑
Fe 15 ♋	Ap 4 ♋	" 23 ♍	" 21 ♐	" 28 ♑	" 24 ♑	" 31 ♒

Day	Jan.	Feb.	Mch.	Apr.	May	June	July	Aug.	Sept.	Oct.	Nov.	Dec.
1	♓	♉	♉	♋	♌	♍	♏	♐	♒	♓	♉	♊
2	♈	..	♊	..	..	♎	..	♑	..	..	..	..
3	..	♊	..	♌	♍	..	..	..	♓	♈	♊	♋
4	♉	..	♋	..	..	♏	♐	..	..	..	..	..
5	..	♋	..	..	..	..	..	♒	♈	♉	♋	♌
6	..	..	..	♍	♎	..	♑	..	..	..	..	..
7	♊	..	♌	..	..	♐	..	♓	♉	♊	..	♍
8	..	♌	..	♎	♏	..	♒	..	..	..	♌	..
9	♋	..	♍	..	..	♑	..	♈	♊	♋	..	..
10	..	♍	..	..	♐	..	..	..	..	..	♍	♎
11	♌	..	..	♏	..	♒	♓	♉	..	♌	..	..
12	..	..	♎	..	..	..	..	..	♋	..	..	♏
13	..	♎	..	♐	♑	♓	♈	♊	..	..	♎	..
14	♍	..	♏	..	..	..	..	..	♌	♍	..	..
15	..	♏	..	♑	♒	♈	♉	♋	..	..	♏	♐
16	♎	..	..	..	..	..	..	..	..	♎	..	..
17	..	..	♐	..	♓	..	♊	..	♍	..	..	♑
18	..	♐	..	♒	..	♉	..	♌	..	..	♐	..
19	♏	..	♑	..	♈	..	♋	..	♎	♏	..	♒
20	..	♑	..	♓	..	♊	..	♍	..	..	♑	..
21	♐	..	♒	..	♉	..	..	..	..	♐	..	..
22	..	♒	..	♈	..	♋	♌	..	♏	..	♒	♓
23	♑	..	♓	..	♊	..	..	♎	..	..	..	..
24	..	♓	..	♉	..	♌	♍	..	♐	♑	♓	♈
25	♒	..	♈	..	..	..	..	♏	..	..	..	..
26	..	♈	..	♊	♋	..	..	..	♑	♒	..	♉
27	♓	..	♉	..	..	♍	♎	..	..	..	♈	..
28	..	♉	..	♋	♌	..	..	♐	..	♓	..	♊
29	♈	..	..	..	..	♎	♏	..	♒	..	♉	..
30	..		♊	..	♍	..	..	♑	..	..	..	♋
31	..		..		..		♐	..		♈		..

1896—EPHEMERIS OF THE PLANETS AND THE MOON—1896

♆	♂	♀	☿	☿	☿	☿
Ja 1 ♊	Fe 28 ♑	Ap 14 ♓	Ja 1 ♒	Ap 5 ♓	Jul 2 ♓	Oc 5 ♈
De 31 ♊	Ap 18 ♒	Ma 2 ♈	" 8 ♓	" 12 ♈	" 9 ♈	" 10 ♉
♅	Ju 5 ♓	" 21 ♉	" 15 ♈	" 17 ♉	" 14 ♉	" 15 ♊
Ja 1 ♏	Jul 23 ♈	Ju 9 ♊	" 20 ♉	" 22 ♊	" 19 ♊	" 20 ♋
De 31 ♏	Se 10 ♉	" 28 ♋	" 26 ♊	" 27 ♋	" 23 ♋	" 25 ♌
♄	No 2 ♊	Jul 16 ♌	" 30 ♋	Ma 2 ♌	Au 29 ♌	" 31 ♍
Ja 1 ♏	De 31 ♋	Au 4 ♍	Fe 4 ♌	" 8 ♍	" 4 ♍	No 7 ♎
De 31 ♏	♀	" 22 ♎	" 10 ♍	" 15 ♎	" 11 ♎	" 15 ♏
♃	Ja 1 ♍	Se 10 ♏	" 17 ♎	" 23 ♏	" 20 ♏	" 25 ♐
Ja 1 ♌	" 10 ♎	" 29 ♐	" 25 ♏	" " "	" 30 ♐	" " "
De 17 ♍	" 29 ♏	Oc 17 ♑	" " "	" " "	" " "	De 6 ♑
♂	Fe 17 ♐	No 5 ♒	Mh 6 ♐	Ju 2 ♐	Se 9 ♑	" 16 ♒
Ja 1 ♏	Mh 7 ♑	" 21 ♓	" 17 ♑	" 13 ♑	" 19 ♒	" 25 ♓
" 5 ♐	" 26 ♒	De 13 ♈	" 27 ♒	" 23 ♒	" 28 ♓	" 31 ♓

Day	Jan.	Feb.	Mch.	April	May	June	July	Aug.	Sept.	Oct.	Nov.	Dec.
1	♌	♍	♍	♏	♐	♒	♓	♈	♊	♌	♍	♎
2	..	♎	♎	..	..	..	..	♉	♋	..	..	♏
3	..	..	..	♐	♑	..	♈	..	..	..	♎	..
4	♍	..	♏	..	..	♓	..	♊	♌	♍	..	..
5	..	♏	..	..	♒	..	♉	..	..	..	♏	♐
6	♎	..	..	♑	..	♈	..	♋	..	♎	..	..
7	..	..	♐	..	..	..	♊	..	♍	..	..	♑
8	..	♐	..	♒	♓	♉	..	♌	..	..	♐	..
9	♏	..	♑	..	..	..	♋	..	♎	♏	..	..
10	..	♑	..	♓	♈	♊	..	♍	..	..	♑	♒
11	♐	..	..	..	..	..	..	..	♏	♐	..	..
12	..	♒	♒	♈	♉	♋	♌	..	..	..	♒	♓
13	..	..	..	..	..	..	..	♎	..	..	..	..
14	♑	♓	♓	♉	♊	♌	♍	..	♐	♑	..	♈
15	..	..	..	..	..	..	..	♏	..	..	♓	..
16	♒	♈	♈	♊	♋	..	♎	..	♑	♒	..	♉
17	..	..	..	..	..	♍	..	..	..	..	♈	..
18	♓	♉	♉	♋	♌	..	..	♐	..	♓	..	♊
19	..	..	..	..	..	♎	♏	..	♒	..	♉	..
20	♈	..	♊	..	♍	..	..	♑	..	..	..	♋
21	..	♊	..	♌	..	..	♐	..	♓	♈	♊	..
22	♉	..	♋	..	..	♏	..	♒	..	..	..	..
23	..	♋	..	♍	♎	..	..	..	♈	♉	♋	♌
24	♊	..	♌	..	..	♐	♑	..	..	..	..	..
25	..	♌	..	♎	♏	..	..	♓	♉	♊	♌	♍
26	♋	..	..	..	..	♑	♒	..	..	..	..	..
27	..	♍	♍	..	..	..	..	♈	♊	♋	♍	♎
28	..	..	..	♏	♐	..	♓	..	..	..	..	..
29	♌		♎	..	..	♒	..	♉	♋	♌	..	..
30	..		..	♐	♑	..	♈	..	..	..	♎	♏
31	♍		..		..		..	♊		♍		..

1897—EPHEMERIS OF THE PLANETS AND THE MOON—1897

♆	♂	♀	☿	☿	☿	☿
Ja 1 ♋	Mh 6 ♌	Ma 30 ♑	Ja 1 ♈	Ap 4 ♉	Jul 1 ♉	Oc 2 ♊
De 31 ♋	Ap 19 ♍	Ju 18 ♒	" 6 ♉	" 9 ♊	" 6 ♊	" 7 ♋
♅	Ju 26 ♎	Jul 7 ♓	" 11 ♊	" 14 ♋	" 11 ♋	" 12 ♌
Ja 1 ♏	Se 22 ♏	" 26 ♈	" 16 ♋	" 19 ♌	" 16 ♌	" 18 ♍
De 31 ♏	No 21 ♐	Au 14 ♉	" 21 ♌	" 25 ♍	" 22 ♍	" 24 ♎
♄	♀	Se 1 ♊	" 27 ♍	" " "	" 28 ♎	No 2 ♏
Ja 1 ♏	Ja 1 ♉	" 20 ♋	Fe 3 ♎	Ma 1 ♎	Au 6 ♏	" 12 ♐
Au 8 ♐	" 20 ♊	Oc 8 ♌	" 11 ♏	" 10 ♏	" 16 ♐	" 23 ♑
De 31 ♐	Fe 7 ♋	" 27 ♍	" 21 ♐	" 20 ♐	" 27 ♑	" " "
♃	" 26 ♌	No 15 ♎	" " "	" 31 ♑	" " "	De 3 ♒
Ja 1 ♍	Mh 17 ♍	De 3 ♏	Mh 4 ♑	" " "	Se 6 ♒	" 12 ♓
De 31 ♍	Ap 4 ♎	" 22 ♐	" 14 ♒	Ju 10 ♒	" 15 ♓	" 19 ♈
♂	" 22 ♏	" " "	" 23 ♓	" 19 ♓	" 22 ♈	" 24 ♉
Ja 1 ♋	Ma 11 ♐	De 31 ♐	" 30 ♈	" 26 ♈	" 27 ♉	" 31 ♉

Day	Jan.	Feb.	Mch.	April	May	June	July	Aug.	Sept.	Oct.	Nov.	Dec.
1	♐	♑	♒	♈	♉	♋	♌	♍	♏	♐	♑	♓
2	..	♒	..	..	..	..	..	♎	..	..	♒	..
3	..	..	♓	..	♊	♌	♍	..	♐	♑	..	♈
4	♑	..	..	♉	..	..	..	♏	..	..	♓	..
5	..	♓	♈	..	♋	..	♎	..	..	♒	..	..
6	♒	..	..	♊	..	♍	..	..	♑	..	♈	♉
7	..	♈	♉	..	♌	..	..	♐	..	..	..	..
8	♓	..	..	♋	..	♎	♏	..	♒	♓	♉	♊
9	..	♉	♊	..	♍	..	..	♑	..	..	..	..
10	..	..	..	♌	..	♏	♐	..	♓	♈	..	♋
11	♈	♊	♋	..	..	..	..	..	..	..	♊	..
12	..	..	..	♍	♎	♐	..	♒	..	♉	..	♌
13	♉	♋	..	..	..	..	♑	..	♈	..	♋	..
14	..	..	♌	♎	♏	♑	..	♓	..	♊	..	♍
15	♊	♌	..	..	..	..	♒	..	♉	..	♌	..
16	..	..	♍	..	..	..	..	♈	..	♋	..	♎
17	♋	..	..	♏	♐	♒	..	..	♊	..	♍	..
18	..	♍	♎	..	..	..	♓	..	..	♌	..	..
19	♌	..	..	♐	♑	♓	..	♉	♋	..	♎	♏
20	..	♎	..	..	..	..	♈	..	..	♍	..	..
21	♍	..	♏	..	..	..	..	♊	♌	..	♏	♐
22	..	♏	..	♑	♒	♈	♉	..	..	..	..	..
23	♎	..	♐	..	..	..	..	♋	..	♎	..	..
24	..	..	..	♒	♓	♉	♊	..	♍	..	♐	♑
25	..	♐	..	..	..	..	..	♌	..	♏	..	..
26	♏	..	♑	..	♈	♊	♋	..	♎	..	♑	♒
27	..	♑	..	♓	..	..	..	♍	..	..	..	..
28	♐	..	♒	..	♉	♋	♌	..	♏	♐	..	♓
29	..		..	♈	..	..	..	♎	..	..	♒	..
30	..		♓	..	♊		..	..	♐	♑	..	..
31	♑		..		..		♍	♏	..	..		♈

1898—EPHEMERIS OF THE PLANETS AND THE MOON—1898

♆	♂	♀	☿	☿	☿	☿
Ja 1 ♊	Ja 15 ♑	Ap 15 ♊	Ja 1 ♊	Ap 1 ♋	Jul 3 ♌	Oc 5 ♍
De 31 ♊	Mh 7 ♒	Ma 4 ♋	“ 4 ♋	“ 5 ♌	“ 9 ♍	“ 12 ♎
♅	Ap 23 ♓	“ 22 ♌	“ 9 ♌	“ 12 ♍	“ 16 ♎	“ 20 ♏
Ja 1 ♏	Ju 10 ♈	Ju 10 ♍	“ 14 ♍	“ 19 ♎	“ 24 ♏	“ 30 ♐
“ 15 ♐	Jul 30 ♉	“ 28 ♎	“ 21 ♎	“ 27 ♏	Au 3 ♐	No 10 ♑
De 31 ♐	Se 20 ♊	Jul 17 ♏	“ 29 ♏	Ma 7 ♐	“ 14 ♉	“ 20 ♒
♄	No 19 ♋	Au 3 ♐	Fe 8 ♐	“ 18 ♑	“ 24 ♒	“ 29 ♓
Ja 1 ♐	♀	“ 23 ♑	“ 19 ♑	“ 28 ♒	“ “ “	“ “ “
De 31 ♐	Ja 1 ♐	Se 11 ♒	“ “ “	“ “ “	Se 2 ♓	De 6 ♈
♃	“ 10 ♑	“ 30 ♓	Mh 1 ♒	Ju 6 ♓	“ 9 ♈	“ 11 ♉
Ja 1 ♍	“ 29 ♒	Oc 19 ♈	“ 10 ♓	“ 13 ♈	“ 14 ♉	“ 16 ♊
“ 13 ♎	Fe 18 ♓	No 7 ♉	“ 17 ♈	“ 18 ♉	“ 19 ♊	“ 21 ♋
♂	Mh 9 ♈	“ 26 ♊	“ 23 ♉	“ 23 ♊	“ 24 ♋	“ 26 ♌
Ja 1 ♐	“ 27 ♉	De 13 ♋	“ 28 ♊	“ 30 ♋	“ 29 ♌	“ 31 ♌

Day	Jan.	Feb	Mch.	April	May	June	July	Aug.	Sept.	Oct.	Nov.	Dec.
1	♈	♊	♊	♌	♍	♏	♐	♒	♓	♈	♊	♋
2	♉	..	♋	..	♎	..	..	..	..	♉	..	♌
3	..	♋	..	♍	..	♐	♑	..	♈	..	♋	..
4	♊	..	♌	..	♏	..	..	♓	..	♊	..	♍
5	..	♌	..	♎	..	..	♒	..	♉	..	♌	..
6	♋	..	♍	..	..	♑	..	♈	..	..	..	..
7	..	♍	..	♏	♐	..	..	..	♊	♋	♍	♎
8	♌	..	..	..	..	♒	♓	..	..	..	..	..
9	..	♎	♎	♐	♑	..	..	♉	♋	♌	♎	♏
10	♍	..	..	..	..	..	♈	..	..	..	..	..
11	..	♏	♏	..	..	♓	..	♊	♌	♍	♏	♐
12	♎	..	..	♑	♒	..	♉	..	..	..	..	..
13	..	..	♐	..	..	♈	..	♋	..	♎	♐	♑
14	..	♐	..	♒	..	..	..	..	♍	..	..	..
15	♏	..	..	..	♓	♉	♊	♌	..	♏	..	..
16	..	♑	♑	..	..	..	..	..	♎	..	♑	♒
17	♐	..	..	♓	♈	♊	♋	♍	..	♐	..	..
18	..	..	♒	..	..	..	..	..	♏	..	♒	♓
19	..	♒	..	♈	♉	♋	♌	♎	..	..	..	..
20	♑	..	..	..	..	..	..	..	♐	♑	..	..
21	..	♓	♓	..	♊	♌	♍	♏	..	..	♓	♈
22	♒	..	..	♉	..	..	..	..	♑	♒	..	..
23	..	..	♈	..	♋	♍	♎	..	..	..	..	♉
24	.	♈	..	♊	..	..	..	♐	..	..	♈	..
25	♓	..	♉	..	♌	..	♏	..	♒	♓	..	..
26	..	♉	..	♋	..	♎	..	♑	..	..	♉	♊
27	♈	..	♊	..	♍	..	♐	..	♓	♈	..	..
28	..	♊	..	♌	..	♏	..	..	..	..	♊	♋
29	..	..	♋	..	♎	..	..	♒	..	..	..	..
30	♉		..	♍	..	♐	♑	..	♈	♉	♋	♌
31	..		..		..		..	♓		..		..

1899—EPHEMERIS OF THE PLANETS AND THE MOON—1899

♆	♂	♀	☿	☿	☿	☿
Ja 1 ♊	Mh30 ♍	Ma31 ♈	Ja 1 ♍	Ap 6 ♎	Jul 2 ♎	Oc 7 ♏
De 31 ♊	Ju 6 ♎	Ju 19 ♉	" 8 ♎	" 14 ♏	" 11 ♏	" 17 ♐
♅	Au 8 ♏	Jul 8 ♊	" 16 ♏	" 24 ♐	" 21 ♐	" 28 ♑
Ja 1 ♐	Oc 10 ♐	" 26 ♐	" 26 ♐	Ma 5 ♑	Au 1 ♑	No 7 ♒
De 31 ♐	De 3 ♑	Au 14 ♌	Fe 6 ♑	" 15 ♒	" 11 ♒	" 16 ♓
♄	♀	Se 1 ♍	" 16 ♒	" 24 ♓	" 20 ♓	" 23 ♈
Ja 1 ♐	Ja 1 ♌	" 20 ♎	" 25 ♓	" 31 ♈	" 27 ♈	" 28 ♉
De 31 ♐	" 20 ♍	Oc 8 ♏	" " "	" " "	" " "	" " "
♃	Fe 7 ♎	" 27 ♐	Mh 4 ♈	" " "	Se 1 ♉	De 3 ♊
Ja 1 ♎	" 26 ♏	No 15 ♑	" 9 ♉	Ju 5 ♉	" 6 ♊	" 8 ♋
Fe 14 ♏	Mh17 ♐	De 4 ♒	" 14 ♊	" 9 ♊	" 11 ♋	" 13 ♌
♂	Ap 4 ♑	" 23 ♓	" 19 ♋	" 15 ♋	" 16 ♌	" 19 ♍
Ja 1 ♋	" 23 ♒	" " "	" 24 ♌	" 26 ♌	" 22 ♍	" 25 ♎
" 21 ♌	Ma 12 ♓	" 31 ♓	" 30 ♍	" 30 ♍	" 28 ♎	" 31 ♎

Day	Jan.	Feb.	Mch.	Apr.	May	June	July	Aug.	Sept.	Oct.	Nov.	Dec.
1	♍	♎	♏	♐	♒	♓	♈	♊	♋	♍	♎	♐
2	..	♏	..	♑	..	♈	♉	..	♌	..	♏	..
3	♎	..	♐	..	..	..	..	♋	..	♎	..	♑
4	..	♐	..	♒	♓	..	..	..	♍	..	♐	..
5	♏	..	♑	..	..	♉	♊	♌	..	♏	..	..
6	..	♑	..	..	♈	..	..	..	♎	..	♑	♒
7	♐	..	..	♓	..	♊	♋	♍	..	♐	..	..
8	..	♒	♒	..	..	..	..	..	♏	..	♒	♓
9	..	..	..	♈	♉	..	♌	♎	..	..	..	..
10	♑	..	♓	..	..	♋	..	..	♐	♑	..	..
11	..	♓	..	♉	♊	..	♍	..	..	..	♓	♈
12	♒	..	..	..	..	♌	..	♏	♑	♒	..	..
13	..	..	♈	..	♋	..	♎	..	..	..	♈	♉
14	..	♈	..	♊	..	♍	..	♐	..	..	..	..
15	♓	..	♉	..	♌	..	♏	..	♒	♓	..	..
16	..	♉	..	♋	..	♎	..	♑	..	..	♉	♊
17	♈	..	..	..	..	..	..	..	♓	♈	..	..
18	..	♊	♊	♌	♍	♏	♐	..	..	..	♊	♋
19	..	..	..	..	..	..	..	♒	..	..	..	..
20	♉	..	♋	♍	♎	♐	♑	..	♈	♉	..	♌
21	..	♋	..	..	..	..	..	♓	..	..	♋	..
22	♊	..	♌	♎	♏	..	♒	..	♉	♊	..	♍
23	..	♌	..	..	..	♑	..	..	..	..	♌	..
24	♋	..	♍	♏	♐	..	..	♈	..	♋	..	♎
25	..	♍	..	..	..	♒	♓	..	♊	..	♍	..
26	♌	..	♎	..	♑	..	..	♉	..	..	..	♏
27	..	♎	..	♐	..	..	♈	..	♋	♌	♎	..
28	♍	..	♏	..	..	♓	..	..	..	..	..	..
29	..	..	..	♑	♒	..	..	♊	♌	♍	♏	♐
30	♎		♐	..	..	♈	♉	..	..	..	..	..
31	..		..		♓	..	..	♋		♎		♑

1900—EPHEMERIS OF THE PLANETS AND THE MOON—1900

♆	♂	♀	☿	☿	☿	☿
Ja 1♊	Mh 11♓	Ma 3♎	Ja 1♎	Ap 1♏	Jul 8♐	Oc 4♐
De 31♊	Ap 28♈	" 21♏	" 3♏	" 11♐	" 19♑	" 15♑
♅	Ju 16♉	Ju 9♐	" 13♐	" 22♑	" 29♒	" 25♒
Ja 1♐	Au 9♊	" 28♑	" 24♑	Ma 2♒	Au 7♓	No 2♓
De 31♐	Oc 6♋	Jul 17♒	Fe 3♒	" 11♓	" 13♈	" 9♈
♄	De 10♌	Au 5♓	" 12♓	" 17♈	" 19♉	" 15♉
Ja 1♐	♀	" 24♈	" 19♈	" 23♉	" 24♊	" 20♊
Ap 26♑	Ja 1♓	Se 11♉	" 24♉	" 28♊	" 29♋	" 25♋
♃	" 11♈	" 30♊	" " "	" " "	" " "	" 30♌
Ja 1♏	" 30♉	Oc 18♋	Mh 1♊	Ju 2♋	" " "	" " "
Mh 12♐	Fe 18♊	No 6♌	" 6♋	" 7♌	Se 3♌	De 6♍
♂	Mh 8♋	" 25♍	" 11♌	" 12♍	" 9♍	" 13♎
Ja 1♑	" 27♌	De 13♎	" 16♍	" 19♎	" 15♎	" 21♏
" 23♒	Ap 14♍	" 31♏	" 23♎	" 28♏	" 24♏	" 31♐

Day	Jan.	Feb.	Mch.	April	May	June	July	Aug.	Sept.	Oct.	Nov.	Dec.
1	♑	♓	♓	♈	♊	♋	♌	♎	♐	♑	♓	♈
2	..	..	..	♉	..	♌	..	♏	..	♒	..	..
3	♒	♈	♈	..	..	..	♍	..	♑	..	..	♉
4	..	..	..	♊	♋	♍	..	♐	..	..	♈	..
5	♓	..	♉	..	..	..	♎	..	♒	♓	..	..
6	..	♉	..	♋	♌	..	..	♑	..	..	♉	♊
7	♈	..	..	..	..	♎	♏	..	♓	♈	..	..
8	..	♊	♊	..	♍	..	..	..	..	..	♊	♋
9	..	..	..	♌	..	♏	♐	♒	♈	..	..	..
10	♉	..	♋	..	♎	..	..	..	..	♉	..	♌
11	..	♋	..	♍	.	♐	♑	♓	..	..	♋	..
12	♊	..	♌	..	♏	..	..	..	♉	♊	..	..
13	..	♌	..	♎	..	♑	..	♈	..	..	♌	♍
14	♋	..	♍	..	♐	..	♒	..	..	♋	..	..
15	..	♍	..	♏	..	♒	..	..	♊	..	..	♎
16	♌	..	♎	..	♑	..	♓	♉	..	..	♍	..
17	..	♎	..	♑	..	♓	..	..	♋	♌	..	♏
18	..	..	♏	..	..	..	♈	♊	..	..	♎	..
19	♍	♏	..	♐	♒	..	..	..	♌	♍	..	♐
20	..	..	♐	..	..	♈	♉	..	..	..	♏	..
21	♎	♐	..	♒	♓	..	..	♋	..	♎	..	♑
22	..	..	..	..	..	♉	♊	..	♍	..	♐	..
23	♏	♑	♑	..	♈	..	..	♌	..	♏	..	♒
24	..	..	..	♓	..	..	♋	..	♎	..	♑	..
25	♐	..	♒	..	..	♊	..	♍	..	♐	..	..
26	..	♒	..	♈	♉	..	..	..	♍	..	♒	♓
27	♑	..	♓	..	..	♋	♌	♎	..	♑	..	..
28	..	♓	..	..	..	..	..	..	♐	..	♓	♈
29	♒		..	♉	♊	♌	♍	..	..	..	..	..
30	..		♈	..	..	..	..	♏	♑	♒	..	♉
31	..		..		♋		♎	..		..		..

1901—EPHEMERIS OF THE PLANETS AND THE MOON—1901

♆	♂	♀	☿	☿	☿	☿
Ja 1 ♊	Fe 15 ♍	Ma 13 ♊	Ja 1 ♐	Ap 9 ♑	Jul 6 ♑	Oc 2 ♑
De 3 ♋	Ap 26 ♎	" 31 ♋	" 11 ♑	" 19 ♒	" 16 ♒	" 12 ♒
♅	Ju 29 ♏	Ju 19 ♌	" 21 ♒	" 28 ♓	" 24 ♓	" 21 ♓
Ja 1 ♐	Au 28 ♐	Jul 7 ♍	" 29 ♓	Ma 4 ♈	" 31 ♈	" 27 ♈
De 31 ♐	Oc 21 ♑	" 26 ♎	Fe 5 ♈	" 10 ♉	Au 6 ♉	No 2 ♉
♄	De 11 ♒	Au 13 ♏	" 11 ♉	" 16 ♊	" 11 ♊	" 7 ♊
Ja 1 ♑	♀	Se 1 ♐	" 16 ♊	" 20 ♋	" 16 ♋	" 12 ♋
De 31 ♑	Ja 1 ♏	" 20 ♑	" 21 ♋	" 26 ♌	" 21 ♌	" 17 ♌
♃	" 20 ♐	Oc 9 ♒	" 26 ♌	" 31 ♍	" 26 ♍	" 22 ♍
Ja 1 ♐	Fe 7 ♑	" 28 ♓	" " "	" " "	" " "	" 30 ♎
Mh 23 ♑	" 26 ♒	No 16 ♈	Mh 4 ♍	" " "	" " "	De 8 ♏
De 31 ♑	Mh 17 ♓	De 5 ♉	" 11 ♎	Ju 6 ♎	Se 2 ♎	" 18 ♐
♂	Ap 5 ♈	" 28 ♊	" 20 ♏	" 15 ♏	" 11 ♏	" 29 ♑
Ja 1 ♌	" 24 ♉	" 31 ♊	" 30 ♐	" 25 ♐	" 21 ♐	" 31 ♑

Day	Jan.	Feb.	Mch.	April	May	June	July	Aug.	Sept.	Oct.	Nov.	Dec.
1	♉	♋	♌	♍	♎	♐	♑	♓	♉	♊	♋	♌
2	♊	..	..	♎	♏	♑	♒	♈	..	..	♌	♍
3	..	♌	..	..	..	..	..	..	..	..	..	..
4	♋	..	♍	♏	♐	♒	♓	..	♊	♋	..	♎
5	..	♍	..	..	..	..	..	♉	..	..	♍	..
6	..	..	♎	♐	♑	♓	♈	..	♋	♌	..	♏
7	♌	♎	..	..	..	..	..	♊	..	..	♎	..
8	..	..	♏	♑	♒	..	♉	..	..	♍	..	♐
9	♍	♏	..	..	..	♈	..	..	♌	..	♏	..
10	..	..	♐	♒	♓	..	..	♋	..	♎	..	♑
11	♎	..	..	..	..	♉	♊	..	♍	..	♐	..
12	..	♐	♑	..	♈	..	..	♌	..	..	..	♒
13	♏	..	..	♓	..	..	..	..	♎	♏	♑	..
14	..	♑	♒	..	..	♊	♋	..	..	..	..	..
15	♐	..	..	♈	♉	..	..	♍	♏	♐	♒	♓
16	..	♒	..	..	..	♋	♌	..	..	..	..	..
17	♑	..	♓	..	♊	..	..	♎	♐	♑	♓	♈
18	..	♓	..	♉	..	..	♍	..	..	..	..	..
19	..	..	♈	..	..	♌	..	♏	♑	♒	..	♉
20	♒	..	..	♊	♋	..	..	..	..	..	♈	..
21	..	♈	♉	..	..	♍	♎	♐	..	♓	..	..
22	♓	..	..	..	♌	..	..	..	♒	..	♉	♊
23	..	♉	..	♋	..	♎	♏	♑	..	♈	..	..
24	♈	..	♊	..	..	..	..	..	♓	..	..	♋
25	..	..	..	♌	♍	♏	♐	♒	..	..	♊	..
26	..	♊	♋	..	..	..	..	..	♈	♉	..	..
27	♉	..	..	♍	♎	♐	♑	♓	..	..	♋	♌
28	..	♋	..	..	..	..	..	..	♉	♊	..	..
29	♊		♌	..	♏	♑	♍	..	..	..	..	♍
30	..		..	♎	..	..	..	♈	..	..	♌	..
31	..		♍		♐		♓	..		♋		..

1902—EPHEMERIS OF THE PLANETS AND THE MOON—1902

♆	♂	♀	☿	☿	☿	☿
Ja 1 ♋	Mh 15 ♈	Ap 28 ♑	Ja 1 ♑	Ap 8 ♒	Jul 5 ♒	Oc 1 ♒
De 31 ♋	Ma 3 ♉	Ma 17 ♒	" 9 ♒	" 16 ♓	" 13 ♓	" 9 ♓
♅	Ju 25 ♊	Ju 5 ♓	" 17 ♓	" 23 ♈	" 25 ♈	" 16 ♈
Ja 1 ♐	Au 24 ♋	" 24 ♈	" 24 ♈	" 29 ♉	" 26 ♉	" 22 ♉
De 31 ♐	Oc 27 ♌	Jul 12 ♉	" 30 ♉	Ma 4 ♊	" 31 ♊	" 27 ♊
♄	De 31 ♌	" 30 ♊	Fe 4 ♊	" 9 ♋	Au 5 ♋	No 1 ♋
Ja 1 ♑	♀	Au 17 ♋	" 9 ♋	" 14 ♌	" 10 ♌	" 6 ♌
De 16 ♒	Ja 1 ♊	Se 4 ♌	" 14 ♌	" 19 ♍	" 15 ♍	" 13 ♍
♃	" 7 ♋	" 22 ♍	" 20 ♍	" 26 ♎	" 22 ♎	" 20 ♎
Ja 1 ♑	" 25 ♌	Oc 10 ♎	" 27 ♎	" " "	" 31 ♏	" 28 ♏
Mh 17 ♒	Fe 12 ♍	" 29 ♏	" " "	" " "	" " "	De 8 ♐
☊	Mh 2 ♎	No 17 ♐	Mh 8 ♏	Ju 4 ♏	" " "	" 19 ♑
Ja 1 ♒	" 21 ♏	De 6 ♍	" 18 ♐	" 14 ♐	Se 10 ♐	" 27 ♒
" 27 ♓	Ap 9 ♐	" 25 ♒	" 29 ♑	" 25 ♑	" 21 ♑	" 31 ♒

Day	Jan.	Feb	Mch.	April	May	June	July	Aug.	Sept.	Oct.	Nov.	Dec.
1	♎	♐	♐	♒	♓	♉	♊	♋	♍	♎	♐	♑
2	..	..	..	..	..	..	..	♌	..	..	..	..
3	♏	♑	♑	♓	♈	..	♋	..	♎	♏	♑	♒
4	..	..	..	..	..	♊	..	..	..	..	..	..
5	♐	♒	♒	♈	♉	..	..	♍	..	♐	..	♓
6	..	..	..	..	..	♋	♌	..	♏	..	♒	..
7	♑	♓	♓	..	♊	..	..	♎	..	♑	..	♈
8	..	..	..	♉	..	..	♍	..	♐	..	♓	..
9	♒	..	♈	..	..	♌	..	♏	..	♒	..	♉
10	..	♈	..	♊	♋	..	..	..	♑	..	♈	..
11	♓	..	♉	..	..	♍	♎	..	..	♓	..	..
12	..	♉	..	..	♌	..	..	♐	♒	..	♉	♊
13	♈	..	..	♋	..	..	♏	..	..	..	..	..
14	..	♊	♊	..	..	♎	..	♑	♓	♈	..	♋
15	..	..	..	♌	♍	..	♐	..	..	..	♊	..
16	♉	..	♋	..	..	♏	..	♒	♈	♉	..	..
17	..	♋	..	..	♎	..	♑	..	..	..	♋	♌
18	♊	..	..	♍	..	♐	..	♓	♉	♊	..	..
19	..	♌	♌	..	♏	..	♒	..	..	..	♌	♍
20	..	..	..	♎	..	♑	..	♈	..	..	..	..
21	♋	..	♍	..	♐	..	♓	..	♊	♋	..	..
22	..	♍	..	♏	..	♒	..	♉	..	..	♍	♎
23	♌	..	♎	..	♑	..	♈	..	♋	♌	..	..
24	..	♎	..	♐	..	♓	..	♊	..	..	♎	♏
25	..	..	..	..	♒	..	..	..	..	..	..	..
26	♍	♏	♏	♑	..	♈	♉	..	♌	♍	..	♐
27	..	..	..	..	..	..	..	♋	..	..	♏	..
28	♎	♐	♐	♒	♓	♉	♊	..	♍	♎	..	♑
29	..		..	..	..	..	..	♌	..	..	♐	..
30	♏		♑	♓	♈	..	..	..	..	♏	..	♒
31	..		..		..		♋	..		..		..

1903—EPHEMERIS OF THE PLANETS AND THE MOON—1903

♆	♂	♀	☿	☿	☿	☿
Ja 1♋	Mh13♎	Ma 1♍	Ja 1♒	Ap 3♓	Jul 7♈	Oc 3♈
De 31♋	Ma16♏	" 19♎	" 4♓	" 10♈	" 13♉	" 9♉
♅	Jul 15♐	Ju 6♏	" 11♈	" 16♉	" 18♊	" 14♊
Ja 1♐	Se 7♑	" 25♐	" 17♉	" 21♊	" 23♋	" 19♋
De 31♐	Oc 21♒	Jul 14♑	" 22♊	" 26♋	" 28♌	" 24♌
♄	De 14♓	Au 2♒	" 27♋	Ma 1♌	Au 2♍	" 30♍
Ja 1♒	♀	" 21♓	Fe 1♌	" 6♍	" 9♎	No 6♎
De 31♒	Ja 1♒	Se 9♈	" 7♍	" 13♎	" 18♏	" 14♏
♃	" 13♓	" 27♉	" 14♎	" 22♏	" 28♐	" 24♐
Ja 1♒	Fe 1♈	Oc 15♊	" 23♏	" " "	" " "	" " "
Fe 21♓	" 19♉	No 2♋	" " "	Ju 1♐	" " "	De 5♑
♂	Mh 8♊	" 20♌	Mh 5♐	" 12♑	Se 8♑	" 15♒
Ja 1♌	" 26♋	De 8♍	" 16♑	" 22♒	" 18♒	" 23♓
" 4♍	Ap 13♌	" 26♎	" 26♒	" 30♓	" 26♓	" 30♈

Day	Jan.	Feb.	Mch.	Apr.	May	June	July	Aug.	Sept.	Oct.	Nov.	Dec.
1	♒	♈	♉	♊	♌	♍	♎	♐	♑	♒	♈	♉
2	..	..	..	♋	..	♎	♏	..	♒	♓	..	♊
3	♓	♉	..	..	..	..	..	♑	..	..	♉	..
4	..	..	♊	..	♍	..	..	..	♓	♈	..	♋
5	♈	♊	..	♌	..	♏	♐	..	..	..	♊	..
6	..	..	♋	♍	♎	..	..	♒	..	♉	..	♌
7	♉	..	..	..	..	♐	♑	..	♈	..	♋	..
8	..	♋	♌	..	..	..	..	♓	..	♊	..	♍
9	♊	..	..	♎	♏	..	..	♉	..	♌	..
10	..	♌	♍	..	..	♑	♒	♈	..	♋	..	♎
11	♋	..	..	♏	♐	..	..	..	♊	..	♍	..
12	..	♍	♎	..	..	♒	♓	..	..	♌	..	..
13	♌	..	..	..	..	..	♉	♋	..	♎	♏
14	..	♎	..	♐	♑	..	♈	..	..	..	..	..
15	..	..	♏	..	..	♓	..	♊	♌	♍	..	♐
16	♍	..	..	♑	♒	..	♉	..	♋	..	♏	..
17	..	♏	♐	..	..	♈	..	♋	♍	♎	..	..
18	♎	..	..	..	♓	..	♊	..	..	..	♐	♑
19	..	♐	♑	♒	..	♉	..	♌	..	♏	..	..
20	♏	..	..	..	..	..	♋	..	♎	..	..	♒
21	..	..	..	♓	♈	♊	..	♍	..	..	♑	..
22	..	♑	♒	..	..	..	♌	..	♏	♐	..	♓
23	♐	..	..	♈	♉	♋	..	♎	..	..	♒	..
24	..	♒	♓	..	..	..	♍	..	..	♑	..	♈
25	♑	..	..	♉	♊	♌	..	♏	♐	..	♓	..
26	..	♓	..	..	..	♍	♎	..	..	♒	..	..
27	..	..	♈	♊	♋	..	..	♐	♑	..	♈	♉
28	♒	♈	..	..	..	..	♏	..	..	♓	..	..
29	..		..	♉	♌	♎	..	♑	♒	..	♉	♊
30	♓		..	..	..	♎	♐	..	..	♈	..	..
31	..		♊		♍		♑	♒		♈		..

1904—EPHEMERIS OF THE PLANETS AND THE MOON—1904

♆	♂	♀	☿	☿	☿	☿
Ja 1 ♋	Ja 31 ♈	Ma 6 ♉	Ja 1 ♈	Ap 2 ♉	Jul 4 ♊	Oc 5 ♋
De 31 ♋	Mh 20 ♉	" 24 ♊	" 5 ♉	" 7 ♊	" 9 ♋	" 10 ♌
♅	Ma 12 ♊	Ju 11 ♋	" 9 ♊	" 12 ♋	" 14 ♌	" 16 ♍
Ja 1 ♐	Jul 11 ♋	" 29 ♌	" 14 ♋	" 17 ♌	" 19 ♍	" 23 ♎
No 13 ♑	Se 3 ♌	Jul 17 ♍	" 19 ♌	" 22 ♍	" 26 ♎	" 31 ♏
♄	No 11 ♍	Au 4 ♎	" 25 ♍	" 29 ♎	Au 4 ♏	No 10 ♐
Ja 1 ♒	♀	" 23 ♏	Fe 1 ♎	Ma 8 ♏	" 14 ♐	" 21 ♑
De 31 ♒	Ja 1 ♎	Se 11 ♐	" 10 ♏	" 18 ♐	" 25 ♑	" " "
♃	" 14 ♏	" 30 ♑	" 20 ♐	" 29 ♑	" " "	De 1 ♒
Ja 1 ♓	Fe 2 ♐	Oc 19 ♒	" " "	" " "	Se 4 ♒	" 9 ♓
" 12 ♈	" 21 ♑	No 7 ♓	Mh 2 ♑	Ju 8 ♒	" 12 ♓	" 16 ♈
De 5 ♉	Mh 11 ♒	" 26 ♈	" 12 ♒	" 16 ♓	" 19 ♈	" 22 ♉
♂	" 30 ♓	De 14 ♉	" 20 ♓	" 23 ♈	" 25 ♉	" 27 ♊
Ja 1 ♓	Ap 18 ♈	" 31 ♉	" 27 ♈	" 29 ♉	" 30 ♊	" 31 ♊

Day	Jan	Feb.	Mch.	April	May	June	July	Aug.	Sept.	Oct.	Nov.	Dec.
1	♋	♌	♍	♎	♏	♑	♒	♈	♊	♋	♌	♎
2	..	♍	..	♏	♐	..	♓	..	..	..	♍	..
3	♌	..	..	..	..	♒	..	♉	♋	♌	..	..
4	..	♎	♎	..	♑	..	♈	..	..	..	♎	♏
5	♍	..	..	♐	..	♓	..	♊	..	♍	..	..
6	..	..	♏	..	..	..	♉	..	♌	..	..	♐
7	..	♏	..	♑	♒	♈	..	♋	..	..	♏	..
8	♎	..	..	..	..	..	..	..	♍	♎	..	..
9	..	♐	♐	♒	♓	♉	♊	♌	..	..	♐	♑
10	♏	..	..	..	..	..	..	..	..	♏	..	..
11	..	♑	♑	♓	♈	♊	♋	..	♎	..	..	♒
12	♐	..	..	..	..	..	..	♍	..	..	♑	..
13	..	..	♒	♈	♉	♋	♌	..	♏	♐	..	♓
14	..	♒	..	..	..	..	..	♎	..	..	♒	..
15	♑	..	♓	♉	♊	..	..	..	..	♑	..	♈
16	..	♓	..	..	..	♌	♍	..	♐	..	♓	..
17	♒	..	♈	♊	♋	..	..	♏	..	..	..	..
18	..	♈	..	..	..	♍	♎	..	♑	♒	♈	♉
19	♓	..	♉	..	♌	..	..	♐	..	..	..	..
20	..	♉	..	♋	..	..	..	..	♒	♓	♉	♊
21	♈	..	♊	..	..	♎	♏	..	..	..	..	..
22	..	♊	..	♌	♍	..	..	♑	♓	♈	♊	♋
23	♉	..	♋	..	..	♏	♐	..	..	..	..	..
24	..	♋	..	..	♎	..	..	♒	♈	♉	♋	♌
25	♊	..	..	♍	..	..	♑	..	..	..	..	..
26	..	♌	♌	..	..	♐	..	♓	♉	♊	..	♍
27	..	..	..	♎	♏	..	♒	..	..	..	♌	..
28	♋	..	♍	..	..	♑	..	♈	♊	♋	..	..
29	..		..	..	♐	..	♓	..	..	..	♍	♎
30	♌		..	♏	..	♒	..	♉	..	♌	..	..
31	..		♎		..		..	..		..		♏

1905—EPHEMERIS OF THE PLANETS AND THE MOON—1905

♆	♂	♀	☊	♄	♃	☿
Ja 1♋	Ja 18♎	Ap 21♐	Ja 1♋	Ap 1♋	Jul 3♌	Oc 5♍
De 31♋	Mh23♏	Ma10♑	" 6♌	" 6♌	" 8♍	" 12♎
♅	Ma22♐	" 29♒	" 12♍	" 11♍	" 15♎	" 20♏
Ja 1♑	Jul 15♑	Ju 17♓	" 19♎	" 18♎	" 24♏	" 30♐
De 31♑	Se 3♒	Jul 6♈	" 29♏	" 27♏	Au 3♐	No 10♑
♄	Oc 21♓	" 24♉	Fe 8♐	Ma 7♐	" 14♑	" 20♒
Ja 1♒	De 8♈	Au 11♊	" 19♑	" 18♑	" 24♒	" 28♓
Se 12♓	♀	" 29♋	" " "	" " "	" 28♒	" " "	" " "
De 31♓	Ja 1♊	Se 16♌	" " "	" " "	" " "	Se 1♓	De 5♈
♃	" 19♋	Oc 4♍	Mh 1♒	Ju 5♓	" 8♈	" 11♉
Ja 1♉	Fe 6♌	" 22♉	" 9♓	" 12♈	" 14♉	" 16♊
No 4♊	" 24♍	No 10♏	" 16♈	" 18♉	" 19♊	" 21♋
♂	Mh14♎	" 29♐	" 22♉	" 23♊	" 24♋	" 26♌
Ja 1♍	Ap 2♏	De 18♑	" 27♊	" 28♋	" 29♌	" 31♍

Day	Jan.	Feb.	Mch.	April	May	June	July	Aug.	Sept.	Oct.	Nov.	Dec.
1	♏	♐	♑	♓	♈	♊	♋	♍	♎	♏	♑	♒
2	..	♑	♒	..	♉	..	♌	..	♏	♐	..	..
3	♐	..	..	♈	..	♋	..	♎	..	..	♒	♓
4	..	♒	♓	..	♊	..	♍	..	..	♑	..	..
5	♑	..	..	♉	..	♌	..	..	♐	..	♓	♈
6	..	♓	♈	..	♋	..	..	♏	..	..	..	..
7	♒	..	..	♊	..	♍	♎	..	♑	♒	..	♉
8	..	♈	♉	..	♌	..	♐	..	..	..	♈	..
9	..	..	..	♋	..	♏	..	..	♒	♓	..	♊
10	♓	♉	♊	..	♎	..	..	♑	..	..	♉	..
11	..	..	..	♌	♍	..	..	♑	..	♈	..	♋
12	♈	♊	..	..	..	♏	♐	..	♓	..	♊	..
13	..	..	♋	♍	♎	..	♒	..	♉	..	♌
14	♉	♋	..	..	..	♑	..	♈	..	♋	..
15	..	..	♌	..	..	♐	..	♓	..	♊	..	♍
16	♊	..	..	♎	♏	..	..	♉	..	♌	..
17	..	♌	♍	..	..	♑	♒	♈	..	♋	..	♎
18	♋	..	..	..	♐	..	..	..	♊	..	♍	..
19	..	♍	..	♏	..	♒	♓	♉	..	♌	..	..
20	♌	..	♎	..	..	..	..	..	♋	..	♎	♏
21	..	♎	..	♐	♑	..	♈	..	..	..	..	..
22	..	..	♏	..	..	♓	..	♊	♌	♍	..	..
23	♍	..	..	..	♒	..	♉	..	..	..	♏	♐
24	..	♏	..	♑	..	♈	..	♋	♎	..	..
25	♎	..	♐	..	♓	..	♊	..	..	..	♐	♑
26	..	♐	..	♒	..	♉	..	♌	..	♎	..	..
27	..	..	♑	..	♈	..	♋	..	♏	..	..	♒
28	♏	♑	..	♓	♈	♊	..	♍	..	..	♑	♒
29	..		♒	..	..	..	♌	..	♐	..	..
30	♐		♒	♈	♉	♋	♌	..	..	♒	♓
31	..				..		♎			..

1906—EPHEMERIS OF THE PLANETS AND THE MOON—1906

♆	♂	♀	☿	☿	☿	☿
Ja 1♋	Mh 23♊	Ma 3♋	Ja 1♍	Ap 3♎	Jul 9♏	Oc 4♏
De 31♋	Ma 20♋	" 21♌	" 5♎	" 11♏	" 19♐	" 15♐
♅	Jul 23♌	Ju 9♍	" 14♏	" 22♐	" 30♑	" 26♑
Ja 1♑	Se 29♍	" 26♎	" 24♐	Ma 3♑	Au 9♒	No 5♒
De 31♑	De 6♎	Jul 16♏	Fe 4♑	" 13♒	" 17♓	" 13♓
♄	" 31♎	Au 3♐	" 14♒	" 21♓	" 24♈	" 20♈
Ja 1♓	♀	" 22♑	" 22♓	" 28♈	" 30♉	" 26♉
De 31♓	Ja 1♐	Se 11♒	" " "	" " "	" " "	" " "
♃	" 10♑	" 30♓	Mh 1♈	Ju 3♉	" " "	De 1♊
Ja 1♊	" 30♒	Oc 18♈	" 7♉	" 8♊	Se 4♊	" 6♋
Oc 16♋	Fe 17♓	No 7♉	" 12♊	" 13♋	" 9♋	" 11♌
♂	Mh 7♈	" 25♊	" 17♋	" 18♌	" 14♌	" 16♍
Ja 1♈	" 26♉	De 13♋	" 22♌	" 23♍	" 19♍	" 23♎
" 27♉	Ap 15♊	" 31♋	" 27♍	" 30♎	" 26♎	" 31♏

Day	Jan.	Feb.	Mch.	Apr.	May	June	July	Aug.	Sept.	Oct.	Nov.	Dec.
1	♈	♉	♊	♌	♍	♎	♏	♑	♒	♈	♉	♋
2	..	♊	..	..	..	♏	♐	..	♓	..	♊	..
3	♉	..	♋	..	♎	..	..	♒	..	..	..	♌
4	..	♋	..	♍	..	♐	♑	..	♈	♉	♋	..
5	♊	..	♌	..	..	..	..	♓	..	..	..	..
6	..	♌	..	♎	♏	..	..	..	♉	♊	♌	♍
7	♋	..	♍	..	..	♑	♒	..	..	..	..	..
8	..	♍	..	♏	♐	..	..	♈	♊	♋	♍	♎
9	..	..	..	..	..	..	♓	..	..	..	..	..
10	♌	♎	♎	..	..	♒	..	♉	..	♌	..	♏
11	..	..	..	♐	♑	..	..	..	♋	..	♎	..
12	♍	..	♏	..	..	♓	♈	♊	..	♍	..	..
13	..	♏	..	♑	♒	..	..	..	♌	..	♏	♐
14	♎	..	..	..	..	♈	♉	♋	..	♎	..	..
15	..	♐	♐	..	..	..	..	..	♍	..	♐	♑
16	♏	..	..	♒	♓	♉	♊	♌	..	..	..	..
17	..	..	♑	..	..	..	..	..	♎	♏	..	..
18	..	♑	..	♓	♈	♊	♋	♍	..	..	♑	♒
19	♐	..	..	..	..	..	..	..	♏	♐	..	..
20	..	♒	♒	..	♉	♋	♌	..	..	..	♒	♓
21	♑	.	..	♈	..	..	..	♎	..	♑	..	..
22	..	..	♓	..	♊	♌	♍	..	♐	..	..	..
23	..	♓	..	♉	..	..	..	♏	..	..	♓	♈
24	♒	..	♈	..	♋	..	♎	..	♑	♒	..	..
25	..	♈	..	♊	..	♍	..	♐	..	..	♈	♉
26	♓	..	♉	..	♌	..	..	..	..	♓	..	..
27	..	♉	..	♋	..	♎	♏	..	♒	..	♉	♊
28	♈	..	♊	..	♍	..	..	♑	..	..	..	..
29	.		..	♌	..	♏	♐	..	♓	♈	♊	..
30	..		♋	..	..	..	..	♒	..	..	..	♋
31	♉		..		♎		..	..		♉		..

1907—EPHEMERIS OF THE PLANETS AND THE MOON—1907

♆	♂	♀	☿	☿	☿	☿
Ja 1♋	Ap 10♐	Ma 12♓	Ja 1♏	Ap 9♐	Jul 6♐	Oc 1♐
De 31♋	Ju 3♑	Ju 1♈	" 11♐	" 20♑	" 17♑	" 13♑
♅	Jul 24♒	" 19♉	" 21♑	" 30♒	" 27♒	" 23♒
Ja 1♑	Se 9♓	Jul 8♊	Fe 1♒	Ma 8♓	Au 4♓	" 31♓
De 31♑	Oc 27♈	" 26♋	" 9♓	" 15♈	" 11♈	No 7♈
♄	De 15♉	Au 14♌	" 16♈	" 21♉	" 17♉	" 13♉
Ja 1♓	♀	Se 1♍	" 22♉	" 26♊	" 22♊	" 16♊
De 31♓	Ja 1♌	" 20♎	" 27♊	" 31♋	" 27♋	• 23♋
♃	" 19♍	Oc 8♏	" " "	" " "	" 31♌	" 27♌
Ja 1♋	Fe 7♎	" 26♐	Mh 4♋	" " "	" " "	De 3♍
Oc 11♌	" 24♏	No 15♑	" 9♌	Ju 5♌	" " "	" 10♎
♂	Mh16♐	De 4♒	" 14♍	" 10♍	Se 6♍	" 18♏
Ja 1♎	Ap 4♑	" 23♓	" 21♎	" 17♎	" 13♎	" 29♐
Fe 10♏	" 23♒	" 31♓	" 29♏	" 25♏	" 21♏	" 31♐

Day	Jan.	Feb	Mch.	April	May	June	July	Aug.	Sept.	Oct.	Nov.	Dec.
1	♌	♍	♏	♏	♐	♑	♓	♈	♊	♋	♍	♎
2	..	♎	♎	..	..	♒	..	♉	..	♌	..	♏
3	..	..	..	♐	♑	..	..	..	♋	..	♎	..
4	♍	..	♏	..	..	♓	♈	♊	..	♍	..	..
5	..	♏	..	♑	♒	..	..	..	♌	..	♏	♐
6	♎	..	..	..	..	♈	♉	♋	..	♎	..	..
7	..	♐	♐	..	..	.	..	..	♍	..	♐	♑
8	♏	..	..	♒	♓	♉	♊	♌	..	..	..	..
9	..	..	♑	..	..	..	..	..	♎	♏	..	..
10	..	♑	..	♓	♈	..	♋	♍	..	..	♑	♒
11	♐	..	..	..	.	♊	..	..	♏	♐	..	..
12	..	♒	♒	..	♉	..	♌	..	..	..	♒	♓
13	..	..	..	♈	..	♋	..	♎	..	♑	..	..
14	♑	..	♓	..	♊	..	♍	..	♐	..	..	..
15		♓	..	♉	..	♌	..	♏	..	..	♓	♈
16	♒	..	♈	..	♋	..	♎	..	♑	♒	..	..
17	..	♈	..	♊	..	♍	..	♐	..	..	♈	♉
18	♓	.	♉	..	♌	..	..	...	..	♓	..	..
19	..	♉	..	♋	..	♎	♏	..	♈	..	♉	♊
20	..	..	..	..	..	..	..	♑	..	..	..	..
21	♈	♊	♊	♌	♍	♏	♐	..	♓	♈	♊	♋
22	..	..	..	..	..	..	..	♒	..	..	..	..
23	♉	♋	♋	♍	♎	..	..	..	..	♉	..	♌
24	..	..	..	..	..	♐	♑	..	♈	..	♋	..
25	♊	♌	♌	♎	♏	..	..	♓	..	♊	..	♍
26	..	..	..	..	..	♑	♒	..	♉	..	♌	..
27	♋	..	♍	..	..	..	..	♈	..	♋	..	♎
28	..	♍	..	♏	♐	..	..	..	♊	..	♍	..
29	♌		♎	..	..	♒	♓	..	..	♌	..	♏
30	..		..	♐	♑	..	..	♉	♋	..	♎	..
31	♍		♏		..		♈	..		..		♐

1908—EPHEMERIS OF THE PLANETS AND THE MOON—1908

♆	♂	♀	☿	☿	☿	☿
Ja 1 ♋	Ap 7 ♋	Ma 20 ♏	Ja 1 ♐	Ap 6 ♑	Jul 3 ♑	Oc 9 ♒
De 31 ♋	Ju 10 ♌	Ju 8 ♐	“ 9 ♑	“ 16 ♒	“ 13 ♒	“ 17 ♓
♅	Au 17 ♍	“ 26 ♑	“ 19 ♒	“ 24 ♓	“ 21 ♓	“ 24 ♈
Ja 1 ♑	Oc 1 ♎	Jul 16 ♒	“ 27 ♓	Ma 1 ♈	“ 28 ♈	“ 30 ♉
De 31 ♑	De 28 ♏	Au 3 ♓	Fe 1 ♈	“ 7 ♉	Au 3 ♉	No 4 ♊
♄	♀	“ 22 ♈	“ 9 ♉	“ 12 ♊	“ 8 ♊	“ 9 ♋
Ja 1 ♓	Ja 1 ♓	Se 10 ♉	“ 14 ♊	“ 16 ♋	“ 12 ♋	“ 14 ♌
Ju 7 ♈	“ 10 ♈	“ 29 ♊	“ 19 ♋	“ 22 ♌	“ 17 ♌	“ 19 ♍
♃	“ 30 ♉	Oc 17 ♋	“ 23 ♌	“ 27 ♍	“ 25 ♍	“ 26 ♎
Ja 1 ♌	Fe 17 ♊	No 5 ♌	“ “ “	“ “ “	“ 30 ♎	“ “ “
Oc 25 ♍	Mh 7 ♋	“ 23 ♍	Mh 2 ♍	“ “ “	“ “ “	De 4 ♏
♂	“ 26 ♌	“ “ “	“ 7 ♎	Ju 3 ♎	Se 7 ♏	“ 17 ♐
Ja 7 ♉	Ap 13 ♍	De 12 ♎	“ 15 ♏	“ 11 ♏	“ 17 ♐	“ 25 ♑
Fe 7 ♊	Ma 1 ♎	“ 31 ♎	“ 25 ♐	“ 22 ♐	“ 29 ♑	“ 31 ♑

Day	Jan.	Feb.	Mch.	April	May	June	July	Aug.	Sept.	Oct.	Nov.	Dec.
1	♐	♒	♒	♈	♉	♋	♌	♎	♏	♑	♒	♓
2	♑	..	♓	..	..	..	..	..	♐	..	..	..
3	..	♓	..	♉	♊	♌	♍	♏	..	♒	♓	♈
4	♒	..	..	..	..	..	..	..	♑	..	..	..
5	..	♈	♈	..	♋	♍	♎	..	..	♓	♈	♉
6	..	..	..	♊	..	..	..	♐	..	..	..	..
7	♓	..	♉	..	♌	♎	♏	..	♒	..	..	♊
8	..	♉	..	♋	..	..	..	♑	..	♈	♉	..
9	♈	..	♊	..	♍	♏	♐	..	♓	..	..	..
10	..	♊	..	♌	..	..	..	♒	..	♉	♊	♋
11	♉	..	..	..	..	♐	..	..	..	..	..	..
12	..	♋	♋	♍	♎	..	♑	..	♈	..	♋	♌
13	..	..	..	..	..	♑	..	♓	..	♊	..	..
14	♊	♌	♌	♎	♏	..	♒	..	♉	..	..	♍
15	..	..	..	..	..	..	..	♈	..	♋	♌	..
16	♋	♍	♍	♏	♐	♒	..	..	..	..	..	♎
17	..	..	..	..	..	..	♓	..	♊	♌	♍	..
18	♌	♎	♎	♐	♑	♓	..	♉	..	..	..	♏
19	..	..	..	..	..	..	♈	..	♋	..	♎	..
20	♍	♏	♏	..	♒	..	..	♊	..	♍	..	♐
21	..	..	..	♑	..	♈	..	..	♌	..	♏	..
22	♎	..	♐	..	..	..	♉	..	..	♎	..	..
23	..	♐	..	♒	♓	♉	..	♋	♍	..	♐	♑
24	♏	..	♑	..	..	..	♊	..	..	♏	..	..
25	..	♑	..	..	♈	..	..	♌	♎	..	♑	♒
26	♐	..	..	♓	..	♊	♋	..	..	♐	..	..
27	..	..	♒	..	..	..	..	♍	♏	..	..	♓
28	..	♒	..	♈	♉	♋	♌	..	..	♑	♒	..
29	♑		♓	..	..	..	..	♎	♐	..	..	..
30	..		..	..	♊	..	♍	..	..	..	♓	♈
31	♒		..		..		..	♏		♒		..

1909—EPHEMERIS OF THE PLANETS AND THE MOON—1909

♆	♂	♀	☿	☿	☿	☿
Ja 1 ♋	Ap 21 ♑	Ma 12 ♊	Ja 1 ♑	Ap 2 ♒	Jul 8 ♓	Oc 4 ♓
De 31 ♋	Ju 10 ♒	" 30 ♋	" 3 ♒	" 11 ♓	" 15 ♈	" 11 ♈
♅	Jul 28 ♓	Ju 18 ♌	" 13 ♓	" 17 ♈	" 20 ♉	" 16 ♉
Ja 1 ♑	Se 14 ♈	Jul 6 ♍	" 20 ♈	" 23 ♉	" 25 ♊	" 21 ♊
De 31 ♑	Oc 30 ♉	" 25 ♎	" 26 ♉	" 28 ♊	" 30 ♋	" 26 ♋
♄	De 26 ♊	Au 12 ♏	" 30 ♊	Ma 3 ♋	Au 4 ♌	" 31 ♌
Ja 1 ♈	♀	" 31 ♐	Fe 4 ♋	" 9 ♌	" 10 ♍	No 6 ♍
De 31 ♈	Ja 1 ♏	Se 19 ♑	" 9 ♌	" 14 ♍	" 16 ♎	" 12 ♎
♃	" 18 ♐	Oc 8 ♒	" 15 ♍	" 21 ♎	" 25 ♏	" 21 ♏
Ja 1 ♍	Fe 6 ♑	" 27 ♓	" 22 ♎	" 29 ♏	" " "	" " "
No 22 ♎	" 24 ♒	No 15 ♈	" " "	" " "	" " "	De 1 ♐
♂	Mh 16 ♓	De 4 ♉	Mh 2 ♏	Ju 8 ♐	Se 4 ♐	" 12 ♑
Ja 1 ♏	Ap 4 ♈	" 22 ♊	" 12 ♐	" 19 ♑	" 15 ♑	" 19 ♒
Fe 26 ♐	" 23 ♉	" 31 ♊	" 23 ♑	" 29 ♒	" 25 ♒	" 31 ♓

Day	Jan.	Feb	Mch.	April	May	June	July	Aug.	Sept.	Oct.	Nov.	Dec.
1	♈	♊	♋	♍	♎	♐	♑	♓	♈	♉	♋	♌
2	♉	♋	♌	..	♏	..	♒	..	♉	♊	..	..
3	..	..	..	♎	..	♑	..	♈	..	..	♌	♍
4	♊	..	♍	..	♐	..	♓	..	..	♋	..	..
5	..	♌	..	♏	..	♒	..	..	♊	..	♍	♎
6	♋	..	♎	..	♑	..	..	♉	..	..	..	..
7	..	♍	..	♐	..	♓	♈	..	♋	♌	♎	♏
8	♌	..	♏	..	♒	..	..	♊	..	..	..	..
9	..	♎	..	♑	..	..	♉	..	♌	♍	♏	♐
10	♍	..	♐	..	..	♈	..	..	..	..	..	..
11	..	♏	..	♒	♓	.	..	♋	..	♎	♐	♑
12	♎	..	♑	..	..	♉	♊	..	♍	..	..	..
13	..	♐	..	♓	♈	..	..	♌	..	♏	♑	♒
14	♏	..	..	..	..	..	♋	..	♎	..	..	..
15	..	♑	♒	..	.	♊	..	♍	..	♐	..	♓
16	..	..	..	♈	♉	..	..	..	♏	..	♒	..
17	♐	..	♓	..	..	♋	♌	♎	..	♑	..	..
18	..	♒	..	..	♊	..	..	..	♐	..	♓	♈
19	♑	..	..	♉	..	♌	♍	♏	..	♒	..	..
20	..	♓	♈	..	..	..	..	..	♑	..	♈	♉
21	♒	..	..	♊	♋	♍	♎	♐	..	..	..	..
22	..	♈	♉	..	..	..	..	..	♒	♓	..	..
23	..	.	..	♋	♌	..	♏	♑	..	..	♉	♊
24	♓	♉	..	..	..	♎	..	..	♓	♈	..	..
25	..	..	♊	..	♍	..	♐	..	..	..	♊	♋
26	♈	♊	..	♌	..	♏	..	♒	..	..	..	..
27	..	..	♋	..	♎	..	♑	..	♈	♉	..	..
28	..	♋	..	♍	..	♐	..	♓	..	..	♋	♌
29	♉	..	..	..	♏	..	♒	..	♉	♊	..	..
30	..		♌	♎	..	♑	..	..	..	..	♌	♍
31	♊		..		♐		..	♈		..		..

1910—EPHEMERIS OF THE PLANETS AND THE MOON—1910

♆	♂	♀	☿	☿	☿	☿
Ja 1♋	Ap 28♌	Ma 2♒	Ja 1♓	Ap 5♈	Jul 2♈	Oc 3♉
De 31♋	Jul 2♍	Ju 9♓	" 7♈	" 10♉	" 7♉	" 8♊
♅	Se 10♎	" 26♈	" 12♉	" 15♊	" 12♊	" 13♋
Ja 1♑	No 15♏	Jul 16♉	" 17♊	" 20♋	" 17♋	" 18♌
De 31♑	De 31♏	Au 4♊	" 22♋	" 25♌	" 22♌	" 23♍
♄	♀	" 23♋	" 27♌	Ma 1♍	" 27♍	" 30♎
Ja 1♈	Ja 1♊	Se 10♌	Fe 2♍	" 7♎	Au 3♎	No 8♏
De 31♈	" 10♋	" 30♍	" 8♎	" 16♏	" 12♏	" 18♐
♃	" 28♌	Oc 17♎	" 17♏	" 26♐	" 22♐	" 29♑
Ja 1♎	Fe 16♍	No 5♏	" 27♐	" " "	" " "	De 7♒
De 23♏	Mh 6♎	" 23♐	" " "	" " "	Se 2♑	" 18♓
♂	" 25♏	" " "	Mh 10♑	Ju 6♑	" 12♒	" 24♈
Ja 1♊	Ap 13♐	De 12♑	" 20♒	" 16♒	" 21♓	" 30♉
Fe 24♋	Ma 2♑	" 31♑	" 29♓	" 25♓	" 27♈	" 31♉

Day	Jan.	Feb.	Mch.	April	May	June	July	Aug.	Sept.	Oct.	Nov.	Dec.
1	♎	♐	♐	♒	♒	♈	♊	♋	♌	♎	♏	♑
2	..	..	..	..	♓	♉	..	..	♍	..	♐	..
3	♏	..	♑	..	..	..	..	♌	..	♏	..	♒
4	..	♑	..	♓	♈	♊	♋	..	♎	..	♑	..
5	♐	..	♒	..	..	..	..	♍	..	♐	..	♓
6	..	♒	..	♈	..	..	..	..	♏	..	♒	..
7	♑	..	♓	..	♉	♋	♌	..	..	♑	..	..
8	..	♓	..	♉	..	..	..	♎	♐	..	♓	♈
9	♒	..	..	..	♊	♌	♍	..	..	..	..	..
10	..	♈	♈	..	..	..	..	♏	..	♒	♈	♉
11	..	..	..	♊	..	..	♎	..	♑	..	..	..
12	♓	..	♉	..	♋	♍	..	♐	..	♓	..	..
13	..	♉	..	..	..	..	..	..	♒	..	♉	♊
14	♈	..	..	♋	♌	♎	♏	♑	..	♈	..	..
15	..	♊	♊	..	..	..	..	..	..	..	♊	♋
16	♉	..	..	♌	..	♏	♐	♒	♓	..	..	..
17	..	..	♋	..	♍	..	..	..	..	♉	..	..
18	..	♋	..	♍	..	♐	♑	♓	♈	..	♋	♌
19	♊	..	..	..	♎	..	..	..	..	♊	..	..
20	..	♌	♌	..	..	♑	♒	♈	♉	..	♌	..
21	♋	..	..	♎	♏	..	..	..	..	..	..	♍
22	..	♍	♍	..	..	♒	♓	..	..	♋	..	..
23	..	..	..	♏	♐	..	..	♉	♊	..	♍	♎
24	♌	..	♎	..	..	♓	♈	..	..	♌	..	..
25	..	♎	..	♐	♑	..	.	♊	♋	..	♎	..
26	♍	..	♏	..	..	..	..	..	..	♍	..	♏
27	..	♏	..	♑	♒	♈	♉	..	..	..	♏	..
28	♎	..	♐	..	..	..	..	♋	♌	..	..	♐
29	..		..	..	♓	♉	♊	..	..	♎	♐	..
30	♏		♑	♒	..	..	..	♌	♍	..	..	♑
31	..		..		♈	..	..	..	..	♏		..

1911 ☿ GREENWICH MEAN ☿ NOON. ☿

Date	Jan.	Febr.	Mch.	Apr.	May	June	July	Aug.	Sept.	Oct.	Nov.	Dec.
1...	23.23	27.51	18.11	□6.00	♏1.08	♒0.29	25.08	13.13	14.07	20.05	25.09	25.07
2...	29.34	♏1.03	21.12	12.18	4.18	3.53	♎1.26	16.28	17.40	26.01	27.38	28.57
3...	□5.49	4.12	24.10	18.34	7.23	7.11	5.08	19.20	21.17	♌1.15	♐0.46	♓2.53
4...	12.06	7.17	27.22	24.56	10.25	10.34	11.26	23.13	25.00	7.30	3.32	6.56
5...	18.25	10.19	♒0.33	♎1.14	13.24	14.01	17.40	25.03	28.50	13.01	6.18	11.06
6...	24.43	13.18	3.47	7.28	16.20	17.83	23.49	27.53	♓2.45	14.23	9.03	15.23
7...	♎1.02	16.15	7.05	13.38	19.15	21.10	29.53	♐0.40	6.48	23.35	11.48	19.49
8...	7.16	19.09	10.27	19.42	22.07	24.53	♋5.50	3.27	10.54	28.37	14.33	24.22
9...	13.26	22.02	13.54	25.39	24.58	29.42	11.39	6.13	15.15	♍3.30	17.18	29.05
10...	19.31	24.52	17.26	♌1.28	27.47	♓2.38	17.20	8.58	19.40	8.13	20.03	♈3.56
11...	25.28	27.42	21.03	7.09	♐0.35	6.40	22.51	11.43	24.14	12.20	22.48	8.56
12...	♌1.17	♐0.29	24.46	12.41	3.22	10.50	29.13	14.28	28.56	17.13	25.36	14.05
13...	6.58	3.16	28.35	18.03	6.08	15.07	♍3.25	17.12	♈3.47	21.30	28.20	19.23
14...	12.30	6.02	♓2.30	23.15	8.53	19.23	8.28	19.52	8.46	23.37	♑1.08	24.50
15...	17.53	8.24	6.32	28.18	11.38	24.05	12.39	22.43	13.55	29.40	3.57	♉0.27
16...	23.06	11.32	10.42	♍3.12	14.22	28.47	17.05	25.38	19.13	♎3.85	6.47	6.11
17...	28.03	14.17	14.58	7.56	17.08	♈3.87	21.22	28.15	24.40	7.22	9.43	12.04
18...	♍3.02	17.02	19.23	12.30	19.52	8.37	25.31	♑1.33	♉0.16	11.13	12.34	18.03
19...	7.47	19.47	23.56	16.56	22.37	13.45	29.33	2.52	6.10	14.28	15.13	24.09
20...	12.22	22.32	28.38	21.14	25.25	19.03	♎3.27	6.42	11.53	18.02	18.28	□0.21
21...	16.48	25.18	♈3.28	25.23	28.10	24.30	7.15	9.34	17.52	21.34	21.29	6.36
22...	21.06	28.04	8.27	29.25	♑0.57	♉0.05	10.57	12.28	23.58	24.54	24.33	12.54
23...	25.15	♑0.15	13.35	♎3.20	3.46	5.49	14.32	15.32	□0.09	28.10	27.41	19.13
24...	29.18	3.41	18.53	7.08	6.37	11.41	18.02	18.23	6.24	♏1.21	♒0.51	25.33
25...	♎3.13	6.31	24.18	10.50	9.29	17.41	21.27	21.24	12.42	4.30	4.06	♎1.49
26...	7.01	9.23	29.55	14.25	12.22	23.46	24.48	24.28	19.01	7.34	7.34	8.03
27...	10.43	12.17	♉5.38	17.56	15.18	29.54	28.04	27.35	25.20	10.36	10.47	14.12
28...	14.19	15.13	11.30	21.21	18.17	□6.12	♏1.15	♒0.45	♎1.38	13.35	14.14	20.16
29...	17.49	....	17.29	24.41	21.18	12.50	4.24	3.59	7.52	16.32	17.46	26.12
30...	21.14	....	23.35	27.57	24.22	18.49	7.29	7.18	14.01	19.26	21.24	♌2.01
31...	24.35	....	29.46	....	27.29	....	10.30	10.40	....	22.18	....	7.41
	♀					♀						♀
2...	♒1.57	21.02	5.40	25.30	14.10	♎4.28	22.40	11.52	♓0.54	18.35	8.15	26.37
4...	5.28	24.13	8.52	28.44	17.25	7.42	25.52	15.02	4.04	21.47	11.28	29.53
6...	8.15	27.23	12.05	♎1.58	20.40	10.56	29.03	18.11	7.14	24.58	14.42	♌3.09
8...	11.25	♈0.34	15.17	5.13	23.55	14.10	♐2.14	21.23	10.25	28.10	17.56	6.22
10...	14.35	3.45	18.29	8.27	27.11	17.23	5.15	24.31	13.35	♉1.22	21.09	9.37
12...	17.45	6.56	21.42	11.41	♍0.26	20.36	8.36	27.40	16.45	4.34	24.23	12.52
14...	20.55	10.07	24.54	14.56	3.41	23.50	11.46	♒0.50	19.56	7.46	27.37	16.07
16...	24.05	13.19	28.07	18.10	6.56	27.03	14.57	4.00	23.07	10.58	♎0.51	19.22
18...	27.15	16.30	□1.20	21.25	10.11	♍0.16	18.07	7.10	26.17	14.10	4.05	22.37
20...	♓0.25	19.41	4.33	24.40	13.26	3.28	21.17	10.20	29.28	17.22	7.19	25.52
22...	3.35	22.53	7.46	27.54	16.40	6.41	24.27	13.29	♈2.35	20.35	10.24	29.07
24...	6.45	26.05	10.50	♌1.09	19.55	9.53	27.38	16.39	5.30	23.47	13.39	♏2.22
26...	9.56	29.16	14.13	4.25	23.10	13.05	♑0.48	19.49	9.01	27.00	16.53	5.37
28...	13.06	♉2.28	17.26	7.40	26.24	16.17	3.57	22.59	12.12	□0.13	20.08	8.52
30...	16.16	....	20.40	10.55	29.49	19.29	7.07	26.09	15.24	3.26	23.28	12.07
	♃♏					♃-♏						♃♏
1...	♏0.34	2.50	5.03	7.20	9.42	11.55	14.22	16.45	19.09	21.27	23.51	26.06
10...	1.15	3.36	5.44	8.06	10.23	12.46	15.05	17.27	19.50	22.09	24.33	26.53
20...	2.00	4.22	6.30	8.52	11.09	13.32	15.50	18.15	20.36	22.55	25.20	27.40

Date	Jan.	Febr.	Mch.	Apr.	May	June	July	Aug.	Sept.	Oct.	Nov.	Dec.
2...	♏19.28	5.33	20.50	8.37	26.38	15.55	4.55	24.46	13.45	1.42	19.25	5.41
4...	20.29	6.37	21.57	9.43	27.51	17.11	6.11	25.47	14.58	2.52	20.32	6.44
6...	21.29	7.41	23.05	10.59	29.06	18.26	7.27	27.01	16.11	4.02	21.39	7.47
8...	22.30	8.46	24.12	12.10	♒0.20	19.42	8.43	28.06	17.24	5.12	22.45	8.50
10...	23.32	9.51	25.20	13.22	1.35	20.56	9.58	29.20	18.36	6.21	23.51	9.53
12...	24.33	10.56	26.29	14.33	2.48	22.14	11.15	♈0.46	19.49	7.32	24.57	10.56
14...	25.35	12.01	27.37	15.45	4.04	23.29	12.31	2.01	21.01	8.40	26.02	11.59
16...	26.37	13.06	28.45	16.57	5.14	24.45	13.47	3.16	12.13	9.49	27.07	13.01
18...	27.39	14.12	29.54	18.09	6.31	26.02	15.03	4.30	23.25	10.57	28.12	14.03
20...	28.41	15.18	♑1.03	19.21	7.06	27.18	16.19	5.45	24.36	12.06	29.17	15.05
22...	29.44	16.24	2.13	20.34	9.00	28.34	17.35	6.59	25.48	13.14	♊0.11	16.07
24...	♐0.46	17.13	3.22	21.46	10.17	29.50	18.51	8.13	26.59	14.22	1.15	17.08
26...	1.49	18.36	4.31	22.59	11.30	♓1.06	20.07	9.27	28.10	15.30	2.19	18.09
28...	2.52	19.43	5.42	24.11	12.46	2.22	21.22	10.41	29.21	16.37	3.33	19.10
30...	3.56	....	6.52	25.25	14.01	3.38	22.38	11.55	♉0.32	17.44	4.38	20.11
	♄ ♉						♄					♄
2...	♉5.29	6.36	7.36	8.43	9.48	10.54	12.00	13.07	14.14	15.17	16.27	17.28
16...	15.59	7.06	8.06	9.13	10.18	11.25	12.30	13.37	14.44	15.50	16.57	18.03
	♅ ♑ ♆ ♋						♅ ♑ ♆ ♋					♅ ♑ ♆ ♋
2...	♅25.07	♑25.27	25.48	26.08	26.28	26.49	27.09	27.29	27.50	28.10	28.30	28.50
2...	♆20.06	♋20.17	20.28	20.39	20.50	21.01	21.12	21.23	21.34	21.45	21.56	22.07
)	Jan.	Febr.	Mch.	Apr.	May	June	☽	Aug.	Sept.	Oct.	Nov.	☽
1...	19.08	♓6.37	15.48	♉7.06	15.45	♌8.58	15.41	♏2.42	16.51	18.36	♓3.02	♈6.48
2...	♒1.32	19.55	29.31	21.38	♋0.32	23.00	28.15	14.32	28.42	♒0.32	15.49	20.18
3...	14.06	♈3.24	♈13.25	♊6.08	15.05	♍6.36	♎11.43	26.51	♑10.35	12.45	28.58	♉4.17
4...	26.51	17.01	27.26	20.32	29.19	19.46	24.09	♐8.42	22.36	25.14	♈12.22	18.48
5...	♓9.49	♉0.49	♉11.32	♋4.48	♌13.13	♎2.34	♏6.19	20.23	♒4.48	♓8.01	26.36	♊3.32
6...	23.00	14.43	25.39	18.52	26.45	15.03	18.18	♑2.23	17.12	21.07	♉10.49	18.38
7...	♈6.26	28.47	♊9.46	♌2.43	♍9.58	27.17	♐0.10	14.20	29.50	♈4.32	25.24	♋3.57
8...	20.07	♊13.00	23.53	16.22	22.53	♏9.21	11.59	26.25	♓12.43	18.35	♊10.10	18.59
9...	♉4.05	27.19	♋7.58	29.47	♎5.32	21.17	23.48	♒8.40	25.50	♉2.13	24.58	♌3.55
10...	18.21	♋11.42	22.00	♍12.58	17.57	♐3.08	♑5.41	21.15	♈9.10	16.22	♋9.41	18.29
11...	♊2.52	26.05	♌5.56	25.56	♏6.12	14.58	17.38	♓3.41	22.42	♊0.38	24.13	♍2.39
12...	17.36	♌10.21	19.43	♎8.40	12.17	26.48	29.42	16.28	♉6.23	14.57	♌8.30	16.22
13...	♋2.26	24.25	♍3.20	21.11	24.16	♍8.40	♒11.54	29.26	20.14	29.17	22.29	29.40
14...	17.15	♍8.11	16.43	♏3.30	♐6.09	20.36	24.15	♈12.35	♊4.12	♋13.32	♍6.10	♎12.36
15...	♌1.35	21.36	29.49	15.58	18.00	♒2.38	♓6.45	25.57	18.18	27.42	19.33	25.15
16...	16.17	♎4.38	♎12.38	27.37	29.49	14.49	19.28	♉9.31	♋2.29	♌11.43	♎2.40	♏7.38
17...	♍0.16	17.19	25.11	♐9.30	♑11.40	27.10	♈2.23	23.21	16.44	25.35	15.32	19.51
18...	13.49	29.39	♏7.28	21.20	23.38	♓9.44	15.35	♊7.25	♑1.00	♍9.16	28.11	♐1.56
19...	26.54	♏11.44	19.31	♑3.10	♒5.43	22.36	29.06	21.43	15.14	22.44	♏10.29	13.55
20...	♎9.34	23.39	♐1.26	15.05	18.01	♈5.48	♉12.57	♋6.14	29.21	♎5.59	22.56	25.56
21...	21.53	♐5.27	13.16	27.10	♓0.35	19.23	27.10	20.53	♍13.17	19.00	♐5.05	♑7.42
22...	♏3.56	17.16	25.06	♒9.28	13.29	♉3.24	♊11.44	♌5.33	26.59	♏1.47	17.07	19.34
23...	15.48	29.11	♑7.01	22.06	26.47	17.49	26.34	20.08	♎10.22	14.20	29.02	♒1.26
24...	27.35	♑11.15	19.06	♓5.05	♈10.31	♊2.38	♋11.35	♍4.29	23.26	26.39	♑10.58	13.24
25...	♐9.22	23.24	♒1.26	18.28	24.41	17.43	26.06	18.52	♏6.11	♐8.47	22.45	25.19
26...	21.15	♒6.10	14.06	♈2.18	♉9.17	♋2.57	♌11.31	♎2.11	18.37	20.46	♒4.37	♓7.26
27...	♑3.16	19.05	27.06	16.31	24.12	18.09	26.08	15.25	♐0.49	♑2.39	16.35	19.44
28...	15.29	♓2.18	♓10.03	♉1.05	♊9.21	♌3.09	♍10.21	28.16	12.50	14.30	28.42	♈2.19
29...	27.55	....	24.15	15.54	24.33	17.48	24.06	♏10.46	24.40	26.23	♓11.03	15.14
30...	♒10.36	....	♈8.19	♊0.50	♋9.39	♍1.59	♎7.23	22.58	♑6.35	♒8.23	24.44	28.34
31...	23.30	....	22.38	....	24.29	....	20.14	♐4.58	....	20.35	....	♉12.22

1912 ☿ GREENWICH ☿ MEAN NOON. ☿

Date	Jan.	Febr.	Mch.	Apr.	May	June	July	Aug.	Sept.	Oct.	Nov.	Dec.
1...	♌13.11	6.48	7.19	29.09	12.23	24.52	13.23	23.29	14.42	♎1.27	4.44	♐1.14
2...	18.49	8.32	11.29	♍3.57	15.07	29.34	17.49	26.12	20.01	4.22	7.34	6.58
3...	23.44	12.28	15.45	8.43	12.52	♈4.24	22.06	28.59	25.38	8.09	10.27	12.57
4...	28.51	15.03	20.17	13.12	20.37	9.24	26.15	♑1.48	81.04	11.15	13.21	18.50
5...	♍3.45	17.48	24.43	17.28	23.22	14.32	♎1.17	4.37	6.08	15.26	16.00	24.56
6...	8.29	20.33	29.25	21.56	26.08	19.50	4.11	7.27	12.41	18.56	19.15	♒1.08
7...	13.04	23.18	♈4.15	26.05	28.55	25.17	7.59	10.29	18.40	22.21	22.16	7.27
8...	17.28	26.04	9.14	♉0.07	♑1.42	80.52	11.41	15.12	24.44	25.41	25.20	13.41
9...	21.52	29.00	14.17	4.02	4.31	6.36	15.16	16.08	♓1.57	28.57	28.28	20.00
10...	26.00	♑1.38	19.41	7.50	7.22	12.28	18.24	19.07	7.11	♏2.08	♒1.38	26.20
11...	♎0.03	4.27	25.05	11.32	10.14	18.28	22.11	22.08	13.26	5.17	4.53	♓2.36
12...	3.58	7.17	80.42	15.07	13.07	24.33	25.32	25.12	19.48	8.21	8.21	8.50
13...	7.46	10.08	6.24	18.38	16.03	♓0.44	28.48	28.19	26.07	11.23	11.34	14.59
14...	11.28	13.03	12.18	22.03	19.02	6.59	♏1.59	♒1.31	♎2.45	14.22	15.01	21.03
15...	15.04	15.59	18.17	25.23	22.03	13.17	5.09	4.45	8.39	17.19	18.33	27.09
16...	18.34	18.55	24.22	28.39	25.07	19.36	8.12	8.04	14.48	20.13	22.11	♌2.48
17...	21.59	21.56	♓0.34	♏1.51	28.14	26.56	11.15	11.26	20.52	23.05	25.54	8.33
18...	25.20	25.02	6.48	5.00	♒1.14	♎2.14	14.15	14.53	26.48	25.56	29.44	14.08
19...	28.36	28.08	13.06	8.05	4.39	5.58	17.11	18.46	♏2.52	28.25	♓3.40	19.36
20...	♍0.48	♒1.19	19.25	11.07	7.51	12.14	20.05	22.03	8.17	♐1.33	7.43	24.51
21...	4.57	4.33	25.44	14.06	11.19	18.28	23.58	25.46	13.48	4.29	11.53	29.48
22...	8.02	8.01	♎2.02	17.02	14.47	24.36	25.48	29.36	19.10	7.03	16.10	♍4.32
23...	11.04	11.18	8.18	19.57	18.19	♏1.55	28.38	♓3.39	24.22	9.50	20.36	9.16
24...	13.03	14.40	14.28	22.49	21.56	6.38	♐1.25	7.34	29.24	12.35	25.09	13.51
25...	17.00	18.32	19.33	25.40	25.39	12.29	4.12	11.44	♍4.27	15.20	29.52	18.15
26...	19.56	21.49	26.30	28.29	29.28	18.08	6.58	16.01	9.00	18.05	♈4.43	22.44
27...	22.47	25.32	♎2.19	♐1.07	♓3.24	23.42	9.43	20.26	13.14	20.50	9.43	26.47
28...	25.38	29.22	7.59	4.04	7.26	29.04	12.28	25.06	18.00	23.15	14.52	♎6.50
29...	27.28	♓3.17	13.32	6.50	♈11.36	♍4.09	15.15	29.42	22.07	26.23	20.40	4.45
30...	♐1.15	....	18.54	9.38	15.53	9.12	17.57	♈4.34	24.24	29.07	25.37	8.33
31...	4.02	....	24.06	....	20.09	....	20.42	9.33	....	♑2.55	....	12.15
	♀						♀					♀
2...	♍17.08	7.09	23.29	11.54	29.28	18.58	7.19	27.38	17.52	5.53	25.00	12.29
4...	20.33	10.29	26.38	15.04	♈2.39	21.11	10.33	♍0.53	21.04	8.04	28.09	15.39
6...	23.38	13.41	29.48	18.14	5.50	24.23	13.47	4.08	24.18	12.15	♒1.19	18.50
8...	26.53	16.53	♎2.57	21.24	9.01	28.36	17.02	7.23	27.31	15.25	4.29	22.00
10...	♎0.06	20.05	6.07	24.36	12.12	♏1.49	20.16	10.38	♍0.47	18.36	7.39	25.11
12...	3.20	23.16	9.17	27.24	15.24	5.02	23.31	13.53	3.56	21.46	10.48	28.22
14...	6.36	26.28	12.27	♓0.54	18.35	8.15	26.46	17.08	7.09	24.56	13.58	♈1.33
16...	9.48	29.39	15.37	4.04	21.47	11.28	♎0.01	20.22	10.21	28.06	17.08	4.46
18...	13.02	♐2.50	18.46	7.14	24.58	14.41	3.15	23.37	13.33	♑1.16	20.18	7.55
20...	16.15	6.01	21.56	10.25	28.10	17.55	6.30	26.51	16.45	4.26	23.28	11.06
22...	19.28	9.12	25.06	13.35	81.22	21.08	9.44	♎0.06	19.57	7.36	26.38	14.18
24...	22.42	12.22	28.15	16.45	4.34	24.22	13.00	3.20	23.09	10.46	29.48	17.29
26...	25.57	15.33	♒1.25	19.56	7.46	27.36	16.15	6.36	26.20	13.56	♓2.58	20.40
28...	29.08	18.43	4.35	23.07	10.58	♎0.50	19.31	9.48	29.31	17.06	6.08	23.52
30...	♏2.20	....	7.45	26.17	14.10	4.04	23.45	13.02	♐2.42	20.15	9.18	27.03
	♃ ♏—♐					♃ ♐						♃ ♐
1...	♏28.36	0.58	3.18	5.41	8.02	10.24	12.46	15.09	17.33	19.57	22.21	24.45
10...	29.23	1.45	4.06	6.28	8.49	11.11	13.33	15.57	18.21	20.45	23.09	25.33
20...	♐0.10	2.32	4.53	7.15	9.37	11.59	14.21	16.45	19.09	21.33	23.57	26.21

268

Date	Jan.	Febr.	Mch.	Apr.	May	June	July	Aug.	Sept.	Oct.	Nov.	Dec.
2...	♊21.40	6.54	20.31	4.36	17.55	1.29	14.35	28.14	12.09	26.03	11.30	26.37
4...	22.41	7.51	21.24	5.29	18.48	2.20	15.27	29.07	13.04	27.00	12.29	27.39
6...	23.41	8.48	22.21	6.23	19.41	3.13	16.20	♎0.01	13.58	27.56	13.28	28.41
8...	24.40	9.45	23.17	7.17	20.33	4.07	17.12	0.54	14.53	28.53	14.28	29.44
10...	25.40	10.41	24.12	8.10	21.26	4.58	18.05	1.47	15.48	29.51	15.27	♐0.46
12...	26.40	11.39	25.07	9.04	22.19	5.50	18.58	2.41	16.44	♏0.48	16.27	1.49
14...	27.39	12.35	26.02	9.57	23.11	6.42	19.50	3.35	17.39	1.45	17.27	2.52
16...	28.38	13.31	26.56	10.51	24.04	7.35	20.43	4.29	18.39	2.43	18.27	3.56
18...	29.37	14.28	27.51	11.44	24.57	8.27	21.36	5.22	19.30	3.41	19.28	4.59
20...	♋0.36	15.25	28.46	12.37	25.49	9.20	22.29	6.16	20.26	4.39	20.29	0.63
22...	1.34	16.22	29.40	13.30	26.42	10.12	23.22	7.10	21.22	5.37	21.29	7.07
24...	2.33	17.17	♌0.34	14.23	27.33	11.05	24.15	8.05	22.18	6.35	22.30	8.11
26...	3.31	18.12	1.29	15.16	28.27	11.57	25.08	9.00	23.14	8.33	23.32	9.16
28...	4.29	19.08	2.23	16.09	29.19	12.50	26.01	9.53	24.10	9.32	24.33	10.21
30...	5.27	....	3.17	17.02	♍0.12	13.43	26.54	10.48	25.06	10.31	25.34	11.26
	♄-♉						♄ ♉.					♄-♊
2...	18.36	19.53	21.00	22.07	23.14	24.21	25.28	26.35	27.42	28.59	♊0.06	1.03
16...	19.19	20.26	21.33	22.40	23.47	24.54	26.01	27.08	28.15	29.32	0.39	1.37
	♅ ♑	♆ ♋				♅ ♒	♆ ♋				♅ ♒	♆ ♋
2...	♅29.10	♑29.30	29.50	♒0.11	0.32	0.43	1.05	1.26	1.47	2.08	2.40	3.01
2...	♆22.18	♋22.29	22.40	22.51	23.02	23.13	23.24	23.35	23.46	23.57	24.08	24.19

☽	Jan.	Febr.	Mch.	Apr.	May	June	☽	Aug.	Sept.	Oct.	Nov.	Dec.
1...	27.01	19.49	29.40	19.04	22.59	♐7.36	♑10.23	26.48	16.20	24.37	♋18.14	26.24
2...	♊11.46	♌4.07	♌13.19	♎1.40	♏5.00	19.25	22.29	♓9.41	♉0.09	♊8.59	♌2.24	♍9.53
3...	26.34	18.00	26.47	14.04	16.54	♑1.20	♒4.57	22.47	14.05	23.19	16.15	23.00
4...	♋11.17	♍1.35	♍9.59	26.16	28.45	13.19	17.14	♈6.05	28.11	♋7.34	29.46	♎5.47
5...	25.48	14.48	22.56	♏8.19	♐10.35	25.36	29.52	19.34	♊12.18	21.38	♍13.00	18.17
6...	♌10.06	27.39	♎5.36	20.14	22.25	♒7.41	♓12.42	♉3.18	26.30	♌5.36	25.58	♏0.33
7...	23.43	♎10.08	17.59	♐2.04	♑4.19	20.09	25.46	17.14	♋10.45	19.19	♎8.42	12.40
8...	♍7.02	22.21	♏0.09	13.53	16.20	♓2.52	♈9.07	♊1.24	24.58	♍2.52	21.13	24.41
9...	19.55	♏4.20	12.07	25.45	28.31	15.43	22.47	15.46	♌9.06	16.11	♏3.34	♐6.38
10...	♎2.24	16.11	23.58	♑7.44	♒10.56	29.15	♉6.48	♋0.08	23.05	29.17	15.45	18.30
11...	14.35	27.49	♐5.47	19.54	23.38	♈13.01	21.08	14.56	♍6.42	♎12.09	27.49	♑0.21
12...	26.32	♐9.49	17.39	♒2.21	♓6.43	27.12	♊5.48	29.31	20.22	24.47	♐9.48	12.13
13...	♏8.21	21.48	29.38	15.08	20.12	♉11.48	20.41	♌13.58	♎3.36	♏7.11	21.40	24.06
14...	20.08	♑4.00	♑11.50	28.18	♈4.08	26.43	♋5.41	28.08	16.28	19.23	♑3.30	♒6.03
15...	♐1.58	16.28	24.19	♓11.54	18.30	♊11.53	20.39	♍11.59	29.02	♐1.26	15.21	18.06
16...	13.42	29.16	♒7.08	25.56	♉3.16	27.06	♌5.24	25.25	♏11.21	13.21	27.16	♓0.19
17...	26.00	♒12.19	20.21	♈10.21	18.19	♋12.13	19.50	♎8.28	23.27	25.13	♒9.18	12.55
18...	♑8.21	25.43	♓3.56	25.04	♊3.31	27.04	♍3.50	21.08	♐5.23	♑7.04	21.32	25.29
19...	20.56	♓9.22	17.53	♉10.00	18.42	♌11.31	17.22	♏3.29	17.15	19.00	♓4.10	♈8.36
20...	♒3.35	23.15	♈2.08	24.53	♋3.43	25.30	♎0.27	15.34	29.07	♒1.05	16.53	22.09
21...	16.49	♈7.16	16.37	♊9.53	18.26	♍9.00	13.06	27.30	♑11.05	13.23	♈0.10	♉6.10
22...	♓0.04	21.22	♉1.08	24.36	♌2.44	22.01	25.26	♐9.24	23.12	26.00	13.43	20.41
23...	13.30	♉5.31	15.43	♋9.02	16.34	♎4.39	♏7.30	21.13	♒5.33	♓8.57	28.06	♊5.37
24...	27.08	19.39	♊0.13	23.07	29.58	16.57	19.25	♑3.10	18.11	22.19	♉12.46	20.51
25...	♈10.50	♊3.47	14.35	♌6.51	♍12.58	♏29.01	♐1.15	15.16	♓1.08	♈6.06	27.43	♒6.16
26...	24.41	17.52	28.45	20.13	25.36	16.55	13.04	27.34	14.24	20.15	♊12.54	21.33
27...	♉8.41	♋1.56	♋12.43	♍3.16	♎7.56	22.45	24.58	♒10.06	28.00	♉4.45	28.07	♌6.37
28...	22.46	15.50	26.27	16.01	20.04	♐4.33	♑6.59	22.53	♈11.53	19.28	♋13.13	21.17
29...	♊7.02	....	♌9.57	28.32	♏2.03	16.24	19.10	♓5.55	26.00	♊4.18	28.00	♍5.28
30...	21.21	....	23.13	♎10.50	13.55	28.19	♒1.31	19.11	♉10.16	19.07	♌12.24	19.08
31...	♋5.42	....	♍6.15	....	25.45	....	14.03	♈2.40	....	♋3.47	....	♎2.20

1913 ☿ GREENWICH ☿ MEAN NOON. ☿

Date	Jan.	Febr.	Mch.	Apr.	May	June	July	Aug.	Sept.	Oct.	Nov.	Dec.
1...	15.51	16.46	13.05	22.50	19.48	7.46	♏2.46	♎2.18	♎3.32	15.09	15.48	21.50
2...	19.21	19.42	19.04	26.10	22.50	14.04	5.56	5.32	9.26	18.06	19.21	27.56
3...	22.46	22.43	25.09	29.26	25.54	20.23	8.59	8.51	15.35	21.00	22.58	♌3.35
4...	26.07	25.49	♊1.21	♏2.38	29.01	27.43	12.02	12.13	21.39	23.52	26.41	9.25
5...	29.23	28.55	7.35	5.47	♎2.01	♎3.01	15.02	15.40	27.35	26.43	♓0.37	14.55
6...	♏2.35	♎2.06	13.53	8.52	5.26	8.43	18.58	19.33	♌3.39	29.12	4.27	20.23
7...	5.44	5.20	26.12	11.54	8.44	13.01	21.52	22.50	9.04	♐2.20	9.30	25.18
8...	8.49	8.48	26.31	14.53	12.06	19.15	24.45	26.33	14.35	5.16	12.40	♍0.35
9...	11.51	12.00	♎2.49	17.48	15.34	25.23	26.35	♓0.23	19.57	7.52	16.51	5.18
10...	13.50	15.27	9.05	20.44	19.06	♌2.40	29.25	4.26	25.11	10.37	21.23	10.03
11...	17.47	19.29	15.15	23.36	22.43	7.25	♐2.12	8.21	♍0.11	13.22	25.56	14.48
12...	20.43	22.36	20.20	26.27	26.26	13.16	4.59	12.31	5.14	16.07	♈0.39	19.02
13...	23.34	26.29	27.27	29.26	♓0.15	18.55	7.45	16.48	10.47	18.52	5.30	23.36
14...	26.25	♓1.09	♌3.06	♐1.54	4.11	24.29	10.30	21.13	14.01	21.37	10.30	27.34
15...	28.15	4.04	8.46	4.51	8.13	29.51	13.15	25.53	18.47	24.22	15.29	♎1.37
16...	♐2.02	8.06	14.29	7.37	12.23	♍4.56	16.02	♈0.29	22.54	27.10	21.07	5.32
17...	4.49	12.16	19.41	10.25	16.40	9.57	18.44	5.21	25.11	29.54	26.24	9.20
18...	7.35	16.32	24.53	13.10	20.56	14.10	21.29	10.20	♎2.11	♑3.42	♑2.01	13.02
19...	9.29	21.04	29.53	15.54	25.49	18.26	24.15	15.30	5.09	5.31	7.45	16.38
20...	13.15	25.30	♍4.44	18.39	♈0.21	22.53	26.59	24.48	8.55	8.21	13.48	20.08
21...	15.51	♈1.02	9.27	21.24	5.11	27.02	29.46	26.25	12.37	11.14	19.47	23.33
22...	18.35	5.02	14.09	24.07	10.11	♎1.04	♑2.35	♑1.51	16.13	14.08	25.43	26.54
23...	21.21	10.01	18.25	26.55	15.19	4.58	5.24	7.35	19.43	16.47	♊2.35	♏0.10
24...	24.05	15.04	22.43	29.42	20.37	8.46	8.14	13.28	23.09	20.02	8.10	3.22
25...	27.02	20.28	26.52	♑2.29	26.04	12.28	11.16	19.27	26.28	23.03	14.28	6.31
26...	29.47	25.52	♎0.54	5.28	♑1.39	16.03	13.59	25.31	29.44	26.07	20.47	9.36
27...	♑2.25	♑1.29	4.49	8.09	7.23	19.33	16.55	♊2.44	♏2.55	29.15	27.07	12.48
28...	5.14	7.11	8.37	11.01	13.15	22.58	19.54	7.57	6.04	♎2.25	♎3.23	14.37
29...	8.04	....	12.19	13.54	19.15	26.19	22.55	14.13	9.08	5.40	9.37	18.34
30...	10.55	....	15.54	16.50	25.20	29.35	25.59	20.35	12.10	9.08	15.46	21.30
31...	13.50	....	19.25	....	♊1.31	....	29.06	26.54	....	12.21	....	24.21

		♀				♀						♀
2...	♑1.50	21.39	6.59	26.19	14.38	♑3.56	20.27	9.38	29.13	17.56	8.14	26.50
4...	5.03	24.41	10.14	29.33	17.49	6.10	23.37	12.49	♊2.26	21.10	11.29	♍0.03
6...	8.14	28.05	13.29	♎2.47	21.01	9.20	26.47	16.00	5.39	24.24	14.44	3.17
8...	11.26	♎1.19	16.44	6.02	24.13	11.30	29.57	19.11	8.52	27.39	17.59	6.30
10...	14.38	4.33	19.59	9.15	27.24	14.40	♓3.07	22.23	12.05	♌0.53	21.15	9.42
12...	17.51	7.47	23.14	12.29	♐0.35	17.49	6.17	25.35	15.19	4.08	24.25	12.59
14...	21.03	11.01	26.29	15.44	3.46	20.59	9.27	28.46	18.32	7.23	27.43	16.08
16...	24.16	14.16	29.44	18.56	6.57	24.09	12.38	♑1.58	21.46	10.37	♎0.58	19.20
18...	27.28	17.30	♍2.59	22.10	10.08	27.18	15.48	5.10	24.59	13.52	4.12	22.32
20...	♊0.51	20.45	6.14	25.23	13.18	♎1.28	18.58	8.22	27.13	17.07	7.27	26.45
22...	3.54	24.00	9.29	28.36	16.29	4.38	22.09	11.35	♎1.27	20.22	10.41	29.00
24...	7.07	27.14	12.44	♏1.48	19.39	7.48	25.20	14.47	4.41	23.37	13.51	♐2.07
26...	10.20	♌0.29	15.59	5.01	22.49	9.58	28.30	17.59	7.56	26.52	17.09	5.19
28...	13.34	3.44	19.14	8.13	25.59	14.07	♈1.41	21.12	11.10	♍0.07	20.23	8.30
30...	16.47	....	22.28	11.26	29.10	17.17	4.52	24.24	14.24	3.22	23.37	11.41

	♃-♐—♑					♃ ♑						♃ ♑
1...	♐27.00	29.33	1.58	4.25	6.52	9.19	11.46	14.13	16.40	19.08	21.35	24.03
10...	27.57	♑0.23	2.47	5.14	7.41	10.08	12.35	15.02	17.29	19.51	22.25	24.52
20...	28.45	1.11	3.36	6.03	8.30	10.57	13.24	15.51	18.18	20.46	23.14	25.42

Date	Jan.	Febr.	Mch.	Apr.	May	June	July	Aug.	Sept.	Oct.	Nov.	Dec.
2...	13.03	♑0.59	17.24	6.21	25.15	14.55	3.45	22.40	10.50	27.32	13.55	29.01
4...	14.09	2.07	18.37	7.39	26.32	16.11	5.00	23.53	11.59	28.37	14.57	♋0.06
6...	15.15	3.17	19.49	8.54	27.48	17.27	6.14	25.03	13.07	29.42	15.59	0.58
8...	16.21	4.27	21.00	10.09	29.04	18.43	7.28	26.15	14.15	♊0.47	17.00	1.57
10...	17.27	5.36	22.14	11.26	♓0.20	19.59	8.42	27.26	15.23	1.51	18.01	2.54
12...	18.33	6.46	23.27	12.39	1.36	21.14	9.36	28.37	16.30	2.55	19.02	3.53
14...	19.40	7.56	24.39	13.54	2.52	22.30	11.10	29.48	17.37	3.59	20.03	4.51
16...	20.47	9.06	25.53	15.09	4.08	23.46	12.23	♉0.59	18.44	5.03	21.04	5.49
18...	21.54	10.17	27.06	16.25	5.25	25.01	13.37	2.09	19.51	6.06	22.04	6.46
20...	23.02	11.28	28.19	17.41	6.41	26.16	14.50	3.19	20.58	7.09	23.05	7.44
22...	24.09	12.39	29.33	18.56	7.57	27.31	16.03	4.29	22.04	8.12	24.04	8.41
24...	25.17	13.50	♒0.47	20.12	9.13	28.46	17.16	5.39	23.10	9.15	25.04	9.38
26...	26.26	15.01	2.01	21.28	10.29	♈0.01	18.28	6.48	24.16	10.17	26.04	10.35
28...	27.34	16.13	3.15	22.44	11.45	1.16	19.41	7.58	25.22	11.20	27.03	11.32
30...	28.45	....	4.29	23.59	13.01	2.31	20.53	9.07	26.27	12.22	28.02	12.28
	♄ ♊						♄ ♊					♄ ♊
2...	2.11	3.29	4.38	5.46	6.55	8.03	9.12	10.20	11.29	12.37	13.46	14.54
16...	2.55	4.03	5.12	6.20	7.29	8.38	9.46	10.55	12.03	13.11	14.20	15.29
	♅ ♒ ♆ ♋					♅ ♒ ♆ ♋						♅ ♒ ♆ ♋
2...	♑3.22	♒3.43	4.04	4.25	4.46	5.07	5.28	5.49	6.10	6.31	6.52	7.12
2...	♆24.39	♋24.41	24.52	25.03	25.14	25.25	25.36	25.47	25.58	26.09	26.20	26.31

☽	Jan.	Febr.	Mch.	Apr.	May	June	☽	Aug.	Sept.	Oct.	Nov.	☽
1...	♎15.07	♐0.25	♐8.33	22.08	24.05	♈10.03	15.40	♋8.21	♍2.16	♎9.36	28.12	♑1.33
2...	27.43	12.18	20.29	♒4.06	♓6.25	23.26	♊0.01	23.32	17.00	23.29	♐10.58	13.43
3...	♏9.46	24.08	♑2.21	16.13	19.03	♉7.18	14.42	♌8.47	♎1.26	♏7.02	23.27	25.42
4...	21.47	♑5.39	14.13	28.33	♈2.01	21.38	29.48	23.56	15.28	20.13	♑5.41	♒7.34
5...	♐3.39	17.56	26.10	♓11.09	15.24	♊6.20	♋15.05	♍8.47	29.05	♐3.04	17.43	19.23
6...	15.30	29.56	♒8.15	24.02	29.10	21.19	♌0.28	23.15	♏12.17	15.35	29.38	♓1.12
7...	27.21	♒12.01	20.31	♈7.14	♉13.18	♋6.25	15.27	♎7.16	25.06	27.50	♒11.28	13.08
8...	♑9.13	24.17	♓2.58	20.46	27.44	21.28	♍0.12	20.49	♐7.34	♑9.52	23.20	25.15
9...	21.08	♓6.42	15.39	♉4.30	♊12.22	♌6.19	14.33	♏3.56	19.47	22.47	♓5.19	♈7.39
10...	♒3.07	19.17	28.33	18.30	22.05	20.50	28.25	16.40	♑1.49	♒3.39	17.29	20.25
11...	15.12	♈2.02	♈11.41	♊2.40	♋11.45	♍4.59	♎11.52	29.05	13.43	15.33	29.56	♑3.38
12...	27.23	15.00	25.01	16.56	26.17	18.45	24.54	♐11.17	25.35	27.32	♈12.42	17.18
13...	♓9.42	28.11	♉8.33	♋1.13	♌10.35	♎2.09	♏7.36	23.18	♒7.28	♓9.42	25.51	♊1.25
14...	22.13	♉11.38	22.16	15.30	24.37	15.12	20.02	♑5.13	19.26	22.04	♉9.23	15.56
15...	♈4.58	25.22	♊6.10	29.42	♍8.23	28.00	♐2.16	17.06	♓1.30	♈4.43	23.15	♋0.43
16...	18.00	♊9.25	20.14	♌13.47	21.53	♏10.33	14.21	28.58	13.43	17.37	♊7.25	15.39
17...	♉1.24	23.45	♋4.25	27.44	♎5.08	22.56	26.20	♒10.52	26.08	♉0.49	21.47	♌0.34
18...	15.13	♋8.20	18.43	♍11.32	18.19	♐5.10	♑8.15	22.50	♈8.44	14.17	♋6.15	15.20
19...	29.27	23.06	♌3.04	25.08	♏0.58	17.16	20.08	♓4.53	21.32	27.58	20.43	29.50
20...	♊14.06	♌7.55	17.24	♎8.32	13.37	29.18	♒2.00	17.03	♉4.34	♊11.51	♌5.06	♍14.01
21...	29.05	22.39	♍1.38	21.44	26.04	♑11.14	13.53	29.22	17.50	25.50	19.20	27.52
22...	♋14.06	♍7.11	15.43	♏4.41	♐8.22	23.07	25.49	♈11.52	♊1.20	♋9.59	♍3.23	♎11.25
23...	29.28	21.23	29.34	17.24	20.31	♒4.58	♓7.49	24.36	15.03	24.08	17.15	24.41
24...	♌14.32	♎5.12	♎13.08	29.56	♑2.33	16.50	19.57	♉7.35	29.01	♌8.19	♎0.56	♏7.42
25...	29.17	18.35	26.23	♐12.11	14.29	28.46	♈2.16	20.52	♋13.11	22.29	14.36	20.32
26...	♍13.36	♏1.34	♏9.18	24.17	26.21	♓10.50	14.50	♊4.30	27.32	♍6.36	27.45	♐3.10
27...	27.26	14.10	21.55	♑6.15	♒8.13	23.05	27.42	18.30	♌12.01	20.38	♏10.44	15.38
28...	♎10.46	26.29	♐4.16	18.09	20.09	♈5.37	♉10.48	♋2.51	26.33	♎4.33	23.52	27.57
29...	23.40	....	16.23	♒0.02	♓2.13	18.31	24.40	17.31	♍11.03	18.18	♐6.38	♑10.06
30...	♏6.11	....	28.21	11.59	14.30	♉1.51	♊8.49	♌2.23	25.26	♏1.51	19.12	22.08
31...	18.24	....	♑10.15	....	27.05	....	23.24	17.21	....	15.10	....	♒4.03

THE GEO-CENTRIC RISING SIGN.

1	Jan.	Febr.	Mch.	Apr.	May	June	July	Aug.	Sept.	Oct.	Nov.	Dec.
2...	18°.44'	20°.46'	22.37	0°.30'	2°.37'	4°.39'	5°.38'	8°.40'	10°.42'	12°.04'	14°.43'	16°.41'
3...	♑	♒	♓	♈	♉	♊	♋	♌	♍	♎	♏	♐
4...	15.26	16.50	18.00	19.00	20.18	22.14	0.45	3.30	6.00	8.33	11.08	13.28
5...	♄♄	⊕♅	☽♆	♆♂	♂♀	☿♀	♀☽	☉☉	♅☿	♃♀	♂	♂♃

The Astrologer Hazelrigg worked out an ingenius table, given above, to find the geocentric Rising Sign; under the Helio-centric system, with its twelve laws of Chords, Responses and Polarities the Rising Sign is not as important as in the Geo-centric, or older system. In line 5 the Helio-centric governing plants are given first, the Geocentric second, in several instances we have found the older locations less specific than the new ones, and often very negative.

The *Ruling Sign* is the sign of nativity. Following this sign, the *Rising Sign* is often very influential. To discover the *Rising Sign* by this method, multiply the birthday by four. To this sum add the degrees and minutes given in the second row, found under the nativity on birth months; from this sum *subtract* the hours and minutes of birth, if before noon, or *add* them, if after noon. This will give, approximately, the sidereal time of birth, to be found in the fourth row, by taking the lesser most nearly equal amount. This *sidereal time* will give also the approximate degrees of the houses found under the hours and minutes of the Table of Houses for New York.

Thus: May 16th, at 3 P. M. Multiply 16 x 4, is 64 minutes, that is, 1 hour and 4 minutes; add this to 2.37, found under May, equals 3.43, *add* the hour of birth, 3 P. M., making 6.43. This directs us to the sign ♍ in the third row, as the Rising Sign, and the Helio-centric Usranus and the Geo-centric Mercury as the ruling planet.

For an A. M. nativity, take October 18, at 3.30 A. M., 18 x 4 is 72, or 1 hour and 12 minutes; add this to the 12° 4' under October, making 13.16, subtract the time before noon, 8.30, from the 13.16, leaves 4.46, and the Rising Sign is seen to be ♌, with the sun as the ruling planet.

In the above table the nature of the sign begins about 9 days of the preceding month, but its power is at its maximum the first third of the month named. It is the Vernal Equinox, and not the Constellations that determine the periods of power.

TABLES OF HOUSES FOR NEW YORK.

Latitude 40° 43′ North.

S. T. H.M.	10 ♈ °	11 ♉ °	12 ♊ °	1 ♋ ° ′	2 ♌ °	3 ♍ °	S. T. H.M.	10 ♊ °	11 ♋ °	12 ♌ °	1 ♍ ° ′	2 ♍ °	3 ♎ °
0.04	1	7	16	19 38	9	2	3.55	1	6	8	5 22	20	28
0.07	2	8	17	20 23	10	3	4.00	2	6	8	6 10	♎	29
0.11	3	9	18	21 12	11	4	4.04	3	7	9	7 0	1	♏
0.15	4	11	19	21 55	12	5	4.08	4	8	10	7 49	2	1
0.18	5	12	20	22 40	12	5	4.12	5	9	11	8 40	3	2
0.22	6	13	21	23 24	13	6	4.16	6	10	12	9 30	4	3
0.26	7	14	22	24 8	14	7	4.21	7	11	13	10 19	4	4
0.29	8	15	23	24 54	15	8	4.25	8	12	14	11 10	5	5
0.33	9	16	23	25 37	15	9	4.29	9	13	15	12 0	6	6
0.37	10	17	24	26 22	16	10	4.33	10	14	16	12 51	7	7
0.40	11	18	25	27 5	17	11	4.38	11	15	16	13 41	8	8
0.44	12	19	26	27 50	18	12	4.42	12	16	17	14 32	9	9
0.48	13	20	27	28 33	19	13	4.46	13	17	18	15 23	10	10
0.52	14	21	28	29 18	19	13	4.51	14	18	19	16 14	11	11
0.55	15	22	28	0♌ 3	20	14	4.55	15	19	20	17 5	12	12
0.59	16	23	29	0 46	21	15	5.59	16	20	21	17 56	13	13
1.03	17	24	♋	1 31	22	16	5.03	17	21	22	18 47	14	14
1.06	18	25	1	2 14	22	17	5.08	18	22	23	19 30	15	15
1.10	19	26	2	2 58	23	18	5.12	19	23	24	20 30	16	16
1.14	20	27	3	3 43	24	19	5.16	20	24	25	21 22	17	17
1.18	21	28	3	4 27	25	20	5.21	21	25	25	22 13	18	18
1.21	22	29	4	5 12	25	21	5.25	22	26	26	23 5	18	19
1.25	23	♊	5	5 56	26	22	5.29	23	27	27	23 57	19	20
1.29	24	1	6	6 40	27	22	4.34	24	28	28	24 49	20	21
1.33	25	2	7	7 25	28	23	5.38	25	20	20	25 40	21	22
1.36	26	2	8	8 9	29	24	5.43	26	♌	♍	26 32	22	23
1.40	27	3	9	8 53	♍	25	5.46	27	1	1	27 25	23	24
1.44	28	4	10	9 38	1	26	5.51	28	2	2	28 16	24	25
1.48	29	5	10	10 24	1	27	5.55	29	3	3	29 8	25	26
1.52	30	6	11	11 8	2	28	6.00	30	4	4	30 0	26	26
1.55	8 1	7	12	11 53	3	29	6.04	♋1	5	5	0♎32	27	27
1.59	2	8	13	12 38	4	♎	6.09	2	6	6	1 44	28	28
2.03	3	9	14	13 22	5	1	6.13	3	6	7	2 35	29	29
2.07	4	10	15	14 8	5	2	6.17	4	7	8	3 28	♏	♐
2.11	5	11	15	14 53	6	3	6.22	5	8	9	4 20	1	1
2.15	6	12	16	15 39	7	4	6.26	6	9	10	5 11	2	2
2.19	7	13	17	16 24	8	4	6.30	7	10	11	6 3	3	3
2.23	8	14	18	17 10	9	5	6.35	8	11	12	6 55	3	4
2.26	9	15	19	17 56	10	6	6.39	9	12	13	7 47	4	5
2.30	10	16	20	18 41	10	7	6.44	10	13	14	8 38	5	6
2.34	11	17	20	19 27	11	8	6.48	11	14	15	9 30	6	7
2.38	12	18	21	20 14	12	9	6.52	12	15	15	10 21	7	8
2.42	13	19	22	21 0	13	10	6.57	13	16	16	11 13	8	9
2.46	14	19	23	21 47	14	11	7.00	14	17	17	12 4	9	10
2.50	15	20	24	22 33	15	12	7.05	15	18	18	12 55	10	11
2.54	16	21	25	23 20	16	13	7.09	16	19	19	13 46	11	12
2.58	17	22	25	24 7	17	14	7.13	17	20	20	14 37	12	13
3.02	18	23	26	24 54	18	15	7.18	18	21	21	15 28	13	14
3.06	19	24	27	25 42	18	16	7.22	19	22	22	16 19	14	15
3.10	20	25	28	26 29	19	17	7.26	20	23	23	17 9	14	16
3.14	21	26	29	27 17	20	18	7.31	21	24	24	18 0	15	17
3.18	22	27	♌	28 4	21	19	7.35	22	25	24	18 50	16	18
3.22	23	28	1	28 52	22	20	7.39	23	26	25	19 41	17	19
3.26	24	29	1	29 40	23	21	7.44	24	27	26	20 30	18	20
3.31	25	♋	2	0♍29	24	22	7.48	25	28	27	21 20	19	21
3.35	26	1	3	1 17	24	23	7.52	26	29	28	22 11	20	22
3.39	27	2	4	2 6	25	24	7.56	27	♍	29	23 0	21	23
3.43	28	3	5	2 56	26	25	8.00	28	1	♎	23 50	21	24
3.47	29	4	6	3 43	27	26	8.04	29	2	1	24 38	22	24
3.51	30	5	6	4 32	28	27	8.09	30	3	2	25 28	23	25

TABLES OF HOUSES FOR NEW YORK.

Latitude 40° 43′ North.

	10	11	12	1	2	3		10	11	12	1	2	3
S. T.	♌	♍	♎	♎	♏	♐	S. T.	♎	♏	♏	♐	♑	♒
H.M.	°	°	°	° ′	°	°	H.M.	°	°	°	° ′	°	°
8.13	1	4	3	26 17	24	26	12.04	1	♏	22	11 52	16	25
8.17	2	5	4	27 5	25	27	12.08	2	1	23	12 37	17	26
8.21	3	6	5	27 54	26	28	12.11	3	1	24	13 19	17	27
8.25	4	7	6	28 43	27	29	12.15	4	2	25	14 7	18	28
8.29	5	8	7	29 31	28	♑	12.18	5	3	25	14 52	19	29
8.34	6	9	7	0♏20	28	1	12.22	6	4	26	15 38	20	♓
8.38	7	10	8	1 8	29	2	12.26	7	5	27	16 23	21	1
8.42	8	11	9	1 56	♐	3	12.29	8	6	28	17 11	22	2
8.46	9	12	10	2 43	1	4	12.33	9	6	28	17 58	23	3
8.50	10	13	11	3 31	2	5	12.36	10	7	29	18 45	24	4
8.54	11	14	12	4 18	3	6	12.40	11	8	♐	19 32	25	5
8.58	12	15	12	5 6	4	7	12.44	12	9	1	20 20	26	7
9.02	13	16	13	5 53	5	8	12.48	13	10	2	21 8	27	8
6.06	14	17	14	6 40	5	9	12.52	14	11	2	21 57	28	9
9.10	15	18	15	7 27	6	10	12.55	15	12	3	22 43	29	10
9.14	16	19	16	8 13	7	10	12.59	16	13	4	23 33	♒	11
9.18	17	20	17	9 0	8	11	13.03	17	13	5	24 22	1	12
9.22	18	21	18	9 46	9	12	13.06	18	14	6	·25 11	2	13
9.26	19	22	19	10 33	10	13	13.10	19	15	7	26 1	3	15
9.29	20	23	19	11 19	10	14	13.14	20	16	7	26 51	5	16
9.34	21	24	20	12 4	11	15	13.18	21	17	8	27 40	6	17
9.37	22	24	21	12 50	12	16	13.21	22	18	9	28 32	7	18
9.41	23	25	22	13 36	13	17	13.25	23	19	10	29 23	8	19
9.45	24	26	23	14 21	14	18	13.29	24	19	10	♑04	9	20
9.49	25	27	24	15 7	15	19	13.33	25	20	11	1 7	10	21
9.53	26	28	24	15 52	15	20	13.36	26	21	12	2 0	11	23
9.57	27	29	25	16 38	16	21	13.40	27	22	13	2 52	12	24
10.01	28	♎	26	17 22	17	22	13.44	28	23	13	3 46	13	25
10 05	29	1	27	18 7	18	23	13.48	29	24	14	4 41	15	26
10.08	30	2	28	18 52	19	24	13.52	30	25	15	5 35	16	27
10.12	♍1	3	29	19 36	20	25	13.55	♏1	25	16	6 30	17	29
10.16	2	4	29	20 22	20	26	13.59	2	26	17	7 27	18	♈
10.19	3	5	♏	21 7	21	27	14.03	3	27	18	8 23	20	1
10.24	4	6	1	21 51	22	28	14.07	4	28	18	9 20	21	2
10.27	5	7	1	22 35	23	28	14.11	5	29	19	10 18	22	3
10.31	6	7	2	23 20	24	29	14.15	6	♐	20	11 15	23	5
10.34	7	8	3	24 4	25	♒	14.19	7	1	21	12 15	24	6
10.38	8	9	4	24 48	25	1	14.23	8	2	22	13 16	26	7
10.42	9	10	5	25 33	26	2	14.26	9	2	23	14 16	27	8
10.46	10	11	6	26 17	27	3	14.30	10	3	24	15 17	28	9
10.50	11	12	7	27 2	28	4	14.34	11	4	24	16 19	♓	11
10.54	12	13	7	27 46	29	5	14.38	12	5	25	17 23	1	12
10.57	13	14	8	28 29	♑	6	14.42	13	6	26	18 27	2	13
11.01	14	15	9	29 14	1	7	14.46	14	7	27	19 32	4	14
11.05	15	16	10	29 57	1	8	14.50	15	8	28	20 37	5	16
11.08	16	17	11	0♐42	2	9	14.54	16	9	29	21 44	6	17
11.12	17	17	11	1 27	3	10	14.58	17	10	♑	22 51	8	18
11.15	18	18	12	2 10	4	11	15.02	18	10	1	23 59	9	19
11.19	19	19	13	2 55	5	12	15.06	19	11	2	25 9	11	20
11.23	20	20	14	3 38	6	13	15.10	20	12	3	26 19	12	22
11.27	21	21	14	4 23	7	14	15.14	21	13	4	27 31	14	23
11.31	22	22	15	5 6	7	15	15.18	22	14	5	28 43	15	24
11.34	23	23	16	5 52	8	16	15.22	23	15	6	29 57	16	25
11.28	24	23	17	6 36	9	17	15.26	24	16	6	1♒14	18	26
11.42	25	24	17	7 20	10	18	15.31	25	17	7	2 28	19	28
11.45	26	25	18	8 5	11	19	15.35	26	18	8	3 46	21	29
11.49	27	26	19	8 48	12	20	15.39	27	19	9	5 5	23	♉8
11.53	28	27	20	9 37	13	22	15.43	28	20	10	6 24	24	1
11.56	29	28	21	10 22	14	23	15.47	29	21	11	7 46	25	3
12.00	30	29	21	11 7	15	24	15.51	30	21	13	9 8	27	4

TABLES OF HOUSES FOR NEW YORK.
Latitude 40° 43′ North.

S. T. H.M.	10 ♐ °	11 ♐ °	12 ♑ °	1 ♒ ° ′	2 ♓ °	3 ♉ °	S. T. H.M.	10 ♒ °	11 ♒ °	12 ♈ °	1 ♉ ° ′	2 ♊ °	3 ♋ °
15.55	1	22	14	10 31	28	5	20.13	1	27	5	22 14	18	9
15.59	2	23	15	11 56	♈	6	20.17	2	29	6	23 35	19	10
16.04	3	24	16	13 23	1	7	20.21	3	♓	8	24 55	20	11
16.08	4	25	17	14 50	3	9	20.25	4	1	9	26 14	21	12
16.12	5	26	18	16 9	4	10	20.29	5	2	11	27 32	22	13
16.16	6	27	19	17 50	6	11	20.34	6	3	12	28 46	23	14
16.21	7	28	20	19 22	7	12	20.38	7	5	14	0♊ 3	24	15
16.25	8	29	21	20 56	9	13	20.42	8	6	15	1 17	25	16
16.29	9	♑	22	22 30	11	15	20.46	9	7	16	2 29	26	17
16.33	10	1	23	24 7	12	16	20.50	10	8	18	3 41	27	18
16.38	11	2	24	25 44	14	17	20.54	11	10	19	4 51	28	19
16.42	12	3	26	27 23	15	18	20.58	12	11	21	6 1	29	20
16.46	13	4	27	29 4	17	19	21.02	13	12	22	7 9	♋	20
16.51	14	5	28	0♒45	18	20	21.06	14	13	24	8 16	1	21
16.55	15	6	29	2 27	20	22	21.10	15	14	25	9 23	2	22
16.59	16	7	♒	4 11	21	23	21.14	16	16	26	10 30	3	23
17.03	17	8	2	5 56	23	24	21.18	17	17	28	11 33	4	24
17.08	18	9	3	7 43	24	25	21.22	18	19	29	12 37	5	25
17.12	19	10	4	9 30	26	26	21.26	19	20	♉	13 41	6	26
17.16	20	11	5	11 18	27	27	21.30	20	21	2	14 43	6	27
17.21	21	12	7	13 8	29	28	21.34	21	22	3	15 44	7	28
17.25	22	13	8	14 57	8	♊	21.37	22	23	4	16 45	8	28
17.29	23	14	9	16 48	2	1	21.41	23	24	6	17 45	9	29
17.34	24	15	10	18 41	3	2	21.45	24	25	7	18 44	10	♌
17.38	25	16	12	20 33	5	3	21.49	25	27	8	19 42	11	1
17.43	26	17	13	22 25	6	4	21.53	26	28	9	20 40	12	2
17.47	27	19	14	24 19	7	5	21.57	27	29	11	21 37	12	3
17.51	28	20	16	26 12	9	6	22.01	28	♈	12	22 33	13	4
17.56	29	21	17	28 7	10	7	22.05	29	1	13	23 30	14	5
18.00	30	22	18	30 0	12	9	22.08	30	3	14	24 25	15	5
18.04	♑1	23	20	1♈51	13	10	22.12	♓1	4	15	25 19	16	6
18.09	2	24	21	3 48	14	11	22.16	2	5	17	26 14	17	7
18.13	3	25	23	5 41	16	12	22.20	3	6	18	27 8	17	8
18.17	4	26	24	7 35	17	13	22.24	4	7	19	28 0	18	9
18.22	5	27	25	9 27	18	14	22.27	5	8	20	28 53	19	10
18.26	6	28	27	11 19	20	15	22.31	6	10	21	29 46	20	11
18.30	7	29	28	13 12	21	16	22.35	7	11	22	0♋37	21	11
18.35	8	♒	♓	15 3	22	17	22.39	8	12	23	1 28	21	12
18.39	9	2	1	16 52	23	18	22.42	9	13	24	2 20	22	13
18.44	10	3	3	18 42	25	19	22.46	10	14	25	3 9	23	14
18.48	11	4	4	20 30	26	20	22.50	11	15	27	3 59	24	15
18.52	12	5	5	22 17	27	21	22.54	12	17	28	4 49	24	16
18.57	13	6	7	24 4	29	22	22.57	13	18	29	5 38	25	17
19.00	14	7	9	25 50	♊	23	23.01	14	19	♊	6 27	26	17
19.05	15	9	10	27 33	1	24	23.05	15	20	1	7 17	27	18
19.09	16	10	12	29 15	2	25	23.08	16	21	2	8 2	28	19
19.14	17	11	13	0♉56	3	26	23.12	17	22	3	8 52	28	20
19.18	18	12	15	2 37	4	27	23.16	18	23	4	9 40	29	21
19.22	19	13	16	4 16	6	28	23.20	19	24	5	10 28	♌	22
19.27	20	14	18	5 52	7	29	23.23	20	26	6	11 15	1	23
19.31	21	16	19	7 30	8	♋	23.27	21	27	7	12 2	2	23
19.35	22	17	21	9 4	9	1	23.31	22	28	8	12 49	2	24
19.39	23	18	22	10 38	10	2	23.34	23	29	9	13 37	3	25
19.44	24	19	24	12 10	11	3	23.38	24	♉	10	14 22	4	26
19.48	25	20	25	13 51	12	4	23.42	25	1	11	15 8	5	27
19.52	26	21	27	15 10	13	5	23.45	26	2	12	15 53	5	28
19.56	27	23	29	16 37	14	6	23.49	27	3	12	16 41	6	29
20.00	28	24	♈	18 4	15	7	23.53	28	4	13	17 23	7	29
20.05	29	25	2	19 29	16	8	23.56	29	5	14	18 8	8	♍
20.09	30	26	3	20 52	17	9	24.00	30	6	15	18 53	9	1

275

www.ingramcontent.com/pod-product-compliance
Lightning Source LLC
Chambersburg PA
CBHW020224170426
43201CB00007B/312